THE LAST WARNINGS

THE YEAR 2017 AND THEREAFTER

JERALD JAMES

authorHOUSE®

AuthorHouse™
1663 Liberty Drive
Bloomington, IN 47403
www.authorhouse.com
Phone: 1 (800) 839-8640

Published by AuthorHouse 10/25/2017

ISBN: 978-1-5246-9338-1 (sc)
ISBN: 978-1-5246-9336-7 (hc)
ISBN: 978-1-5246-9337-4 (e)

Library of Congress Control Number: 2017908168

Print information available on the last page.

Table of Contents

JMJ
"You Are Now Receiving The Last Warnings"
Our Lady 1965 to Conchita
Compiled by Jerald James Slave of Our Lady of Sorrows Third Order

To my Dear Children and grandchildren,

I give you these pages only to prepare you for what is to happen **Between 2017 and 2029**. The world will end just before 2100. Finally, all that I have told my children for the past (40) years are coming to pass, read these pages seriously, **please**.

Pay close attention to page (29). And to Our Lady of La Salette page (2) and the true possible dates given by saints of this century. God reveals 'Satan's Plan' going into action and allowing his Vicar Pope Leo XIII to hear the conversation, but the total conversation was given **St.** Marie Julie Jahenny – French Mystic & Stigmatist; tells of the ending times and the great change that will take place creating a new church with new preachers (wolves in sheep's clothing) of new sacraments, new temples (churches). (Novus Ordo) Our Lord said the elect would be would be deceived in the latter times. And He wondered if He would fine anyone holding firm to the true Faith at the end of time. Learn who Luisa Piccarreta is and what she is trying to tell you about the "Divine Will" in the 6th period.

Both Pope Leo and Marie Julie received these warnings near the same time (as did St. Catherine Ann Emmerich) in the late1800's. I have listed some prophecies of many great saints please read: As Our Lord told St. Gertrude, "Read the Lives and mysteries of my saints and of My Church not the things of this world." How often I have told my children and teachers to read the science of saints and not the so called classics, which have done very little for anyone's good, compared to lifelong impression these books will leave on you as they have done me and many others. What we are missing from the old classic is the vocabulary and manner of speech. But there are similarities in these old spiritual classics, and true story's which make far deeper impressions of the truths of our Faith in good Catholic reading as suggested below. If you want to save your children from the WORLD, THE DEVIL, OR THE FLESH,

you must read to your CHILDREN daily of the beautiful stories of the saints and later of catholic doctrine. At night after the c hildren are tucked in, set in the hallway so all bedrooms can hear you and read a nice story that will take days to finish, each night they will beg you to read that story. This is the very best time to mold this young clay, because if you do not the world, the devil, or the flesh will do the molding and they will not be saved. A good story at night fills their mind for rest of the night. (10 books of St. Alphonsus Liguori or 40 Dreams of St. John Bosco, Imitation of Christ and many others.) There is so much that can and must be read daily to the children. "The majority of parents damn themselves because they daily neglect the teaching of the catholic faith." Morning, noon, and night prayers. Doctrines, Love of Mary, & the Catechism are most necessary. **(4) Last Things.** Know what they are and the Divine Will.

What you will find out about the 'Masonic (freemason) Jewish' takeover of the Catholic Church is that certain Holy Fathers (popes) have been manipulated (with a Masonic group, Codename "Gladio") as they sit in the seat of Peter since the time of Pope John XXIII. Are they still legitimate Popes, God knows. Just like your earthly father is still your father no matter if he is good or bad. No matter if you are so very upset with him and you say he is no longer my father because he does no good. Pray for him! ST. Cyetan, "One must resist the Pope who openly destroys the Church." But no person can be canonized without the traditional prescribed (3) miracles provided by Almighty God or any Holy Father (Pope) who has not obeyed the Queen's command to consecrate Russia to Her Immaculate Heart. A stigmatist has foretold that this **Pope Francis (or will it be Benedict XVI)** will make the Consecration of Russia during the invasion. The saints tell us that there will be two popes in Rome at the time Russia enters Rome. The young and ignorant will **not** understand and many too will try to discourage you from believing or read this. However both Our Lady and Our Lord ask everyone to help make this Knowledge of the Great Chastisement known to all people, so that they will think more prudently of 'prayer, penance and sacrifice'. Some will say that if you are praying your Rosary daily you don't need to pay any attention to this. Wrong! Pray for my brothers and sisters because they will not find the time read anything that may save their souls.

Some Protestants say we Catholics live in a cocoon. To avoid the world this is the best way to get home to the land of Heaven. Many have went to convents, monasteries, deserts, caves, islands, etc. to best save their souls. Our Lord said, 'He who love s the world is my enemy.' (**See YouTube: The Third Secret of Fatima and Malachi Martin & Communism Vatican??? Gladio**) most important. The Chastisement and Russia over running Europe marks the end of the 5th period of the Church. The 6th period of the Church is 35 to 40 yrs. long. And you children who will live to see this great and most prosperous time of the Catholic Church must remember not to let happen to you what will happen to the rest of us at the time of Vatican II.

The Antichrist will fool most all because they will allow themselves to become lukewarm, because of the good and prosperous times they will have. And they will lose the true Faith again, like the great Apostasy of the Rome through Vatican II. My Childre n I warn you to be on your guard. Remember the Rosary Daily and the words of Our Lady, 'You who watch at my gate will not be confounded.

I urge the reader to page (234) on stories of Hell. It will definitely bring you into a reality as to why you were created a nd what happens if you blow your one chance to obtain Heaven and see God. There are (22) pages of stories just for you. (Hot stuff.)

If this War is to happen, and the Chastisement (3 Days of Darkness), it will begin around the year 2017 to 2029. Our Lady said in 1917 July 13, she would asked for the Consecration of Russia to Her Immaculate Heart, she did June 13, 1929. Fr. Malach i Martin, who read the 3rd Secret, said, something will enter into our atmosphere and it will all be by 2020. The Rosary postponed this war, in the year 1995. In 1925 December Our Lady said, "I promise to assist at the hour of death with the graces necessary for salvation all those who, on the first Saturdays of five consecutive months, confess, receive Holy Communion, recite daily my Rosary, and keep me company for a quarter of an hour meditating on its mysteries of the Rosary with the intention of offering me reparation." The Key to Heaven is the Rosary and Scapular which is True Devotion to Mary's Immaculate Heart.

The Last Warnings

The vision of Pope Leo XIII

The prayer to St. Michael

"Saint Michael, the Archangel, defend us in battle; be our protection against the wickedness and snares of the devil. May God rebuke him, we humbly pray, and do thou, O prince of the heavenly host, by the power of God, thrust into Hell, Satan and all the other evil spirits, who prowl throughout the world, seeking the ruin of souls. Amen."

Exactly 33 years to the day prior to the great Miracle of the Sun in Fatima, that is, on October 13, 1884, Pope Leo XIII had a remarkable vision. When the aged Pontiff had finished celebrating Mass in his private Vatican Chapel, attended by a few Cardinals and members of the Vatican staff, he

suddenly stopped at the foot of the altar. He stood there for about 10 minutes, as if in a trance, his face ashen white. Then, going immediately from the Chapel to his office, he composed the above prayer to St. Michael, with instructions it be said after all Low Masses everywhere. Some priests think they don't have to say them. They are for the conversion of Russia.

When asked what had happened, he explained that, as he was about to leave the foot of the altar, he suddenly heard voices – two voices, one kind

1

and gentle, the other guttural and harsh. They seemed to come from near the tabernacle. *As he listened, he heard the following conversation:*

The guttural voice, the voice of Satan in his pride, boasted to Our Lord: "I can destroy your Church."

The gentle voice of Our Lord: "You can? Then go ahead and do so."

Satan: "To do so, I need more time and more power."

Our Lord: "How much time? How much power?

Satan: "75 to 100 years, and a greater power over those who will give themselves over to my service." (the masons and communists)

Our Lord: "You have the time, you will have the power. Do with them what you will."

In 1886, Pope Leo XIII decreed that this prayer to St. Michael be said at the end of "low" Mass (not "high", or sung Masses) throughout the universal Church, along with the Salve Regina (Hail, Holy Queen); and the practice of the congregation praying these prayers at the end of Mass *(10 years indulgence)* continued until about 1970, with the introduction of the '**New Mass**'. In Latin 'Novus Ordo Messa'.

This is where Satan started the ball rolling with the infiltration of both mason and communists into the Catholic Church. Infiltration of the Church became serious in the early 1900's.

September 19, 1846 Our Lady of La Salette appeared to two shepherd children Melanie and Maximin. Pope Leo XIII invited Melanie to Rome in 1879 to confer with her not only about the Secret, but about a rule for a religious order which our Lady wanted founded immediately against the coming crisis. Specifically the Order of the Mother of God, to be called "The Apostles of the Latter Times" predicted by St. Louis De Montfort, it was encouraged by the Pope, but never materialized. Now you can see how powerful Satan is.

He can stop and change things including dates.

Here is a portion of the Secret of La Salette: "Melanie, what I am about to tell you now will not always be a secret. You may make it public in 1858." "The priests, ministers of my Son, the priests, by their wicked lives, by their irreverence and their impiety in the celebration of the holy mysteries. (*many priests say their Mass very fast, so fast that the faithful cannot keep up and read all the prayers prescribed by church. The propers, collect, secret, offertory, the epistle,* *the gospel are read so fast that many do not bother to bring a missel to Mass any more, because it doesn't do any good to try to keep up with the priest. The most reverent of priests read or say the Mass slowly with great reverence.* **St. Padre Pio** *would take two hours to say his Mass. The* **Cura of Ares** *said he would say his Mass slowly especially at the cannon.* **St. Benedict** *says true reverence and devotion is shown in a devout person by their reverence in movement and in speech, not to move with rapidity. I have read where people have asked the priest to hold the each elevation on high for 30 seconds. In some places the bell is rang 3 times in honor of the 3 persons of the blessed Trinity. For where one is present, all 3 are present in Divinity. Our Lord is most pleased when you read the words of the Mass and when it comes from your heart and mind. When you set at Mass without a Missel and do not say the most beautiful prayers of adoration, thanksgiving and petitions which is said to be the most important prayer of the church, you make it very easy for your mind to wander. One saint had to spend (6) months in purgatory for not following Mass attentively.)* "By their love of money, their love of honors and pleasures, the priests have become cesspools of impurity. Yes, the priests are asking vengeance, and vengeance is hanging over their heads. Woe to the priests and to those dedicated to God who by their unfaithfulness and their wicked lives are crucifying my Son again! The sins of those dedicated to God cry out towards Heaven and call for vengeance, and now vengeance is at their door, for there is no one left to beg mercy and forgiveness for the people. There are no more generous souls; there is no one left worthy of offering a stainless sacrifice to the Eternal Father for the sake of the world. "And She continues:

"God will strike in an unprecedented way."
"Woe to the inhabitants of the earth! God will exhaust His wrath upon them and no one will be able to escape so many afflictions together." *(Each chastisement leads to greater chastisements because no one heeds them, people just think it nature, and do not know God is controlling these things.)*

"If my people do not obey, I shall be compelled to let loose my Son's arm. It is so heavy that I can no longer hold it. How long have I suffered for you! If my Son is not to abandon you, I am obliged to entreat him without ceasing. But you take no heed of that. No matter how well you pray in the future, no matter how well you act, you will never be able to make up what I have endured on your behalf."

"I have given you six days to work. The seventh I have reserved for myself, yet no one gives it to me. This is what causes the weight of my Son's arm to be so heavy. The cart drivers (today's labors) cannot swear without taking my Son's name in vain. These are the two things that make my Son's arm so heavy." *(Everyone uses God's name in vain today. After Sunday Mass, there must be spiritual reading at home alone and with family. Stay away from the stores, do your buying on Saturday.)*

"Ah, my children, your prayers, it is very important to do so, at night and in the morning. When you don't have time, at least say an **Our Father and a Hail Mary**, and whenever you can, say more."

"Only a few rather elderly women go to Mass in the summer. Everyone else works every Sunday all summer long. And in winter, when they don't know what else to do, they go to Mass only to scoff at religion. During Lent, they go to the butcher shop like dogs. Mélanie's secret, July 6, 1851: "Lastly, hell will reign on earth. It will be then that the Antichrist will be born ... That time is not far away, twice 50 years will not go by."

Maximin's secret, July 3, 1851: "A great country, now Protestant, in the north of Europe, will be converted; by the support of this country all the other nations of the world will be converted. But before all this arrives, great disorders will arrive, in the Church, and everywhere. *(1964)...* Then, after [that], our Holy Father the Pope will be persecuted. His successor will be a pontiff that nobody expects. (Masons implant a pope of their choosing.) Then, after [that], a great peace will come, but it will not last a long time. A monster will come to disturb it. All that I tell you here will arrive in the other (next) century, at the latest in the year two thousand…."

(Of course along with victim souls and the Rosary,
God will push back the severe of chastisements.)

Both Our Lady of La Salette and the messages to Sister Marie de Saint-Pierre foretold a great crisis in the Church. Our Lady of La Salette warned, "The Church will be in eclipse." Eclipse means darkness of something evil blocking out the true light of the Church. This means people will be fooled from seeing the truth or true Faith, because something bad will be forced on the people and something good taken away.

"The **chiefs**, the **leaders** of the people of God have neglected prayer and penance, and the devil has bedimmed their intelligence. They have become wandering **stars** which the old devil will drag along with his **tail** to make them **perish**. God will allow the old serpent to cause divisions among those who reign in every society and in every **family**. Physical and moral agonies will be suffered. <u>God will abandon</u> <u>mankind to itself and will send</u> <u>punishments</u> which will follow one after the other for more than thirty-five years." Book Of Jeremiah 6:16 "Walk in the Old Ways ....or God will abandon thee." *(Walk in the Tradition of the past 2000 years.)*

"The Society of men is on the eve of the most terrible scourges and of gravest events. Mankind must expect to be ruled with an iron rod and to drink from the chalice of the wrath of God. "(The invasion of Russian, and......)

"<u>In the year</u> **(1964), Lucifer** <u>together with a large number of demons</u> <u>will be unloosed from hell; they will</u> <u>put an end to the</u> **faith little by little,** <u>even in those dedicated to God.</u> They will blind them in such a way, that, unless they are blessed with a special grace, these people will take on the spirit of these angels of hell; several religious institutions will lose all faith and will lose many souls." *(Fruits of Vatican II long after 1964.)*

"The True Faith of the Lord having been forgotten, each individual will want to be on his own and be superior to people of same identity, they will abolish civil rights as well as ecclesiastical, all order and all justice would be trampled underfoot and only homicides, hate, jealousy, lies and dissension would be seen without love for country or family."

*(This is the **Definition of <u>Communism</u>** which leads to the hatred of God. As a result of this, God will be kicked out of all places, will not be allowed, His Name, His Commandments, or His Nativity Scenes. All will disappear. The 40 days of Christmas will be celebrated far in advance of when it actually comes. **And the three most important words of our Catholic Faith - Mary-Christ-Mass - will not be allowed to be spoken.)** Youtube: "Fatima and the forces of the antichrist" - John Vennari*

"The Holy Father will suffer a great deal. I will be with him until the end and receive his sacrifice." *(His death.)* All the civil governments will have one and the same plan, which will be to abolish and do away with every religious principle to **make way** for materialism, atheism, spiritualism and vice of all kinds." *(Socialistic Communism) (God will allow man to excel in sin as never before, than He will chastisement all mankind.)*

"In the year **(1965)**, there will be desecration of holy places. In convents, the flowers of the Church will decompose and the devil will make himself like the King of all hearts. May those in charge of religious communities be on their guard against the people they must receive, **for the devil will resort to all his evil tricks to introduce sinners into religious orders, for disorder, and the love of carnal pleasures will be spread all over the earth.**" *(Our passions will become unbearably stronger and uncontrollable. Obesity thanks to fructose corn syrup (aspartame) and sugars will have its effect on the brain and the body. All foods will be affected.) Carnal vise will in the clergy (masons) and people living together without marriage.)*

"**Rome** will lose the **Faith** and become the seat of the Antichrist. (anti-pope; anti-catholic)"

Meaning the Shepherds, bishops, will lose the Faith and will lead many of the faithful into perdition. Rome means the hierarchy. This thing called surrounded diabolical disorientation *will hypnotize you into thinking that the fashions you see around you are OK to wear, or the way people talk and act are OK, or the games and movies that everyone is doing to is OK, luxury and comfort and ease will dull the mind and cause you to be lazy in things to do with God. Believe me it's not hard to lose your soul, and it's the only thing God and the devil are fighting for. Be on your guard,* ***diabolical surrounded possession or disorientation*** *will cause you to develop habits and longings, and they will not be good. Especially in the self indulgence of dress and overeating, or any of the seven capital sins. Start Reading something spiritually good for You. Your catechism or Imitation of Christ. Spend more time in prayer talking and befriending God. Develop a bond with God.*

"The seasons will be altered, the earth will produce nothing but bad fruit, the stars will lose their regular motion, and the moon will only reflect a faint reddish glow. Water and fire will give the earth's global convulsions and terrible earthquakes which will swallow up mountains, cities, etc... (Some of this has been happening for many years.)

"Apostles of the Last Days, the faithful disciples of Jesus Christ who have lived in scorn for the world and for themselves, in poverty and in humility, in scorn and in silence, in prayer and in mortification, in chastity and in union with God, in suffering and unknown to the world. It is time they came out and filled the world with light. Go and reveal yourselves to be my cherished children. I am at your side and within you, provided that your faith is the light which shines upon you in these unhappy days. May your zeal make you famished for the glory and the honour of Jesus Christ. Fight, children of the light, you, the few who can see the Truth. For now is the time of all times, the end of all ends." *(Of course these type of people will be hated by the world and the false church most of them are already dead, but there are still many living.)*

"Woe to the inhabitants of the earth! There will be bloody wars and famines, plagues and infectious diseases. It will rain with a fearful hail of animals. There will be thunderstorms which will shake cities, earthquakes which will swallow up countries. Voices will be heard in the air. Men will beat their heads against walls, call for their death, and on another side death will be their torment. Blood will flow on all sides. Who will be the victor if God does not shorten the length of the test? All the blood, the tears and prayers of the righteous, God will relent. Enoch and Eli will be put to death. **Pagan Rome will disappear.** The fire of Heaven will fall and consume three cities. All the universe will be struck with terror and many will let themselves be lead astray because they have not worshipped the true Christ who lives among them. It is time; the sun is darkening; only faith will survive."

"Now is the time; the abyss is opening. Here is the king of kings of darkness; here is the Beast with his subjects, calling himself the Saviour of the world. He will rise proudly into the air to go to Heaven. He will be smothered by the breath of the Archangel Saint Michael. He will fall, and the earth, which will have been in a continuous series of convolutions for three days, will open up its fiery bowels; and he will have plunged for all eternity with all his followers into the everlasting chasms of hell. And then water and fire will purge the earth and consume all the works of men's pride and all will be renewed. God will be served and glorified." (These things are the very End.) (The devil tricked at Vatican II, we did not study our catechism enough.)

Book of St. Timothy 3:1-5 Tells the kind of people you will become and are living around you: "Know also this, that in the last days shall come on dangerous times. Men shall be <u>lovers of themselves</u>, covetous, haughty, proud, blasphemers, disobedient to parents, ungrateful, wicked, without affection, without peace, slanderers, incontinent, unmerciful, without kindness, traitors, stubborn, puffed up, and <u>lovers of pleasures</u> more than of God: having an appearance indeed of godliness but denying the power thereof." *"Surrounded diabolical disorientation".*

Our Lady of Garabandal: "Many Cardinals, many Bishops, and many priests are on the road to perdition and taking many souls with them." "Less and Less importance will be given to the Blessed Sacrament." "The Mass will become hard to say." (Hard to find it anywhere, only a Remnant are holding on to it.) John: Apoc.

So in your old Latin Missal where you begin with the sign of the cross, at the top of the page it is written "<u>The Unchangeable Parts of the Mass</u>". That is, until Vatican II when the **masons** stepped in and changed everything.

In 1962 Our Lady spoke to a seer and I don't have his name: "You can avoid all, by prayer. Through the Council (Vatican II), **the World will witness the completion of all these Events."** By events he means: evil books, a spirit of darkness will cause a universal relaxation in all that concerns the service of God. Churches will be openly serve and worship the Devil. **Technology** will advance so quickly as <u>to keep men from thinking</u> God and focused on worldly and carnal pleasures, and on entertainment and continuous music. Extraordinary prodigies will be wrought everywhere, because the True Faith will have been extinguished, and a false light will illuminate the world. Woe to the princes of the Church who will have occupied themselves in nothing more than in heaping up an accumulation of riches, in safeguarding their authority, and in ruling with pride. **All these things will work together for the loss of many souls.** Satan will penetrate into the Catholic Church through the new spirit of the priests (since Vatican II). He goes on to say that the New (spirit) church will believe it can co-exist with communism and freemasonryism and Heretics. By refusing to intensify her prayer- life and by her disrelish for the mystical life, she (Church) will fall into **heresy** such as one perceives. Everyday Modernism will grow in the modern churches and in the modern art, and in music, which will be horrid to listen to, unless you slowly allow yourself be brainwashed to it. She also mentions Russia be the scourge of God and China will have some part in it too.

Youtube: **("Freemason Converts to Catholicism and Exposes the Diabolic Cult of Freemasonry")** At the **Council of Trent** 1570 Pius V made the Mass from the time of Christ to the Council of Trent frozen. The Council of Trent declared; When a pope has made a declaration on faith and morals, no pope hereafter may not change any part of it without subjecting anathema. And no Vicar of Christ may change what has been made Dogmatic and morally sound for the good of the people. Not even an angel from heaven may change what the Vicar of Christ from the Chair of Peter has made bound on earth. This is the True Mass that Saints and Kings and Queens have attended for over 2000 years. What is right in the eyes of God can never be wrong. But the Devil will deceive nearly all the elect or faithful and according to St. John in the Apocalypse only a remnant of the faithful will stay true, so few that they will fit under the shade of two fig trees. (Apoc.) And elsewhere Our Lord said to John 'That He wondered if He would find any of the faithful left at the end of the world.' This according to saintly bishops and priests there is 60 to 70 yrs. before Our Lord will appear on the clouds with His Angels.

Bl. Ann Catherine Emmerich (1774) Augustinian nun of Germany was beatified on 3 October 2004, by Pope John Paul II. She had the wounds of Our Lord and was given by God to know all that happened to Jesus from birth until His death. And was told much about the ending times. We have learned very much from her. Let me quote one thing out of the (4) vols. Of Blessed Ann Catherine:

"I saw also the relationship between the **two** popes. . . I saw how baleful (sinister) would be the consequences of this false church. I saw it increase in size; heretics of every kind came into the city (Rome). The local clergy grew lukewarm, and I saw a great darkness. . . Then, the vision seemed to extend on every side. Whole Catholic communities were being oppressed, harassed, confined, and deprived of their freedom. I saw many churches close down, great miseries everywhere, wars and bloodshed. A wild and ignorant mob took to violent action. But it did not last long. "Once more I saw that the Church of Peter was undermined by a plan evolved by the secret sect, while storms were damaging it. But I saw also that help was coming when distress had reached its peak. . ."

(This 'undermined plan of the secret sect', go to Youtube and Listen: "Communist Vatican???Gladio:")

"I saw a strange big church that was being built there (Rome). There was nothing holy in it." (see Pg 27)

"I saw all sorts of people, things, doctrines, and opinions. There was something proud, presumptuous, and violent about it, and they seemed to be very successful."

"I had a vision of the holy Emperor Henry. I saw him at night kneeling alone at the foot of the main altar in a great and beautiful church . . . and I saw the Blessed Virgin coming down all alone. She laid on the Altar a red cloth (and) covered (it) with white linen. She placed a book inlaid with precious stones. She lit the candles and the perpetual lamp. Then came the Saviour Himself clad in priestly vestments. He was carrying the chalice and the veil. Two Angels were serving Him and two more were following . . .His chasuble was a full and heavy mantle in which red and white could be seen in transparency, gleaming with jewels. . .Although there was no altar bell, the cruets were there. The was short. The Gospel of St. John was not read at the end. When the Mass had ended, Mary came up to Henry (the Emperor), and she extended her right hand towards him, saying that it was in recognition of his purity. Then, she urged him not to falter. Thereupon I saw an angel, and he touched the sinew of his hip, like Jacob. He (Henry) was in great pain; and from that day on he walked with a limp. . ."

"The Church is in great danger. We must pray so that the Pope may not leave Rome; countless evils would result if he did. They are now demanding something from him. The Protestant doctrine and that of the schismatic Greeks are to spread everywhere. I now see that in this place (Rome) the (Catholic) Church is being so cleverly undermined, that there hardly remain a hundred or so priests even the clergy. A great devastation is now near at hand."

"Among the strangest things that I saw, were long processions of bishops. Their thoughts and utterances were made known to me through images issuing from their mouths. Their faults towards religion were shown by external deformities. A few had only a body, with a dark cloud of fog instead of a head *(errors in thinking)*. Others had only a head, *(high intellect)* their bodies and hearts *(no charity)* were like thick vapors. Some were lame *(half heartedly in duty)*; others were paralytics *(powerless)*; others were asleep or staggering *(unaware of the church problem)*.

"I saw what I believe to be nearly all the bishops of the world, but only a **small number** were perfectly sound. I saw that everything that pertained to Protestantism was gradually gaining the upper hand *(the Church* *would become protestant),* and the Catholic religion fell into complete decadence. Most priests were lured by the glittering but false knowledge of young school-teachers, and they all contributed to the work of destruction. *(**The True Mass has disappeared.** Unless you are faithful to Christ and the True Latin Mass you are bound to lose your soul. It is this Mass that Christ instituted on Holy Thursday night, the Last Supper, unto the time when Pope St. Pius V put it into perpetuity in his 'QUO PRIMUM' July 14, 1570 at the Council of Trent. So favorable was this to God, that He made Pope Pius V a saint. This is a signal grace and sign for us to adhere to IT, not abandon IT. The Council of Trent added that whosoever abandons all of Latin let him be anathema. Latin makes the church **Universal.** If any one of the four marks of the Catholic Church is missing the Church fails to be the True Church.*

*These are the **(4) marks of** the Church: **ONE, HOLY, CATHOLIC, AND APOSTOLIC**.) Latin is the language of the Church and the language of the angels. "Gloria in excelsis Deo, et in terra pax hominibus bonae voluntatis." Satan is clever and men are easily deceased. Not only Satan pull men away from the One True Church to start their own new churches, but now he has entered into the true church to make it protestant.*

Be Careful of priests eliminating parts of the Mass, which has already been done by Vatican II.

Even **traditional priests** due to laziness have **stopped** saying the **"leonine prayers"** which was commanded by Pope Leo XIII to be said after each Mass, (three Hail Marys, Hail Holy Queen, St. Michael, and Pope Pius XII added: "Most Sacred Heart of Jesus, Have mercy on us" and many priests have added Immaculate Heart of Mary, pray for us.) They were added for the **conversion of Russia** and stop Communism. And this is a bad time to stop saying them, unless you're with satan's group. Another problem is priests allowing altar boys to bow to the Sacramental King instead of genuflection. This should only be done when the tabernacle is empty. Our Lady would fall to her face on the ground when meeting her Son and He would always help her up. When Jesus was a baby in the crib, Our Lady would genuflect (3) times before approaching her Son. And would always ask permission to feed him or to kiss his face. (**St. Mary of Agreda**) Each time you genuflect there is an indulgence granted. As Fr. Brey said, "Even if the tabernacle is empty and there is a crucifix above it, a genuflection can still be made out of respect for the crucified Christ." Back to St. Catherine:

"I see many excommunicated ecclesiastics who do not seem to be concerned about it, nor even aware of it. Yet, they are **(ipso facto) excommunicated** whenever they cooperate to (changes install by the masonic sect) enterprises, enter into (secret) associations, and embrace opinions on which an anathema has been cast. It can be seen thereby that God ratifies the decrees, orders, and interdictions issued by the Head of the Church, and that He keeps them in force even though men show no concern for them, reject them, or laugh them to scorn."

> "I saw good pious Bishops; but they were weak and wavering, their cowardliness often got the upper hand... Then I saw darkness spreading around and people **no longer seeking the True Church**."

> "In those days, **Faith will fall very low**, and it will be preserved in some places only, in a **few cottages** and in a **few families** which God has protected from disasters and wars." (Family daily Rosary.)

> "I saw the Church of St. Peter: it has been destroyed but for the Sanctuary and the main altar. St. Michael came down into the Church, clad in his suit of armor, and he paused, threatening with his sword a number of unworthy pastors who wanted to enter." *(And we lay people trespass through the Sanctuary like it was a living room, not to mention all the talking in Church, which is not to God. In the New Order Church no more **cassock** to be worn in*

the Sanctuary. No more communion rail, and a table is used instead of the main altar. The priest no longer faces Christ in the tabernacle when he speaks to Him in his private prayer called the Canon of the Mass is to be said in silence. At this table he faces the people, and it becomes more a show than a devotion. See Pg. 93)

The Prophecy of Premol (5th Century) "Everywhere there is war! People and nations are pitted against each other. War, war, war! Civil and foreign wars! Mourning and death everywhere! Famine over the whole world. Will Lutetius (Paris) be destroyed? Why, O Lord, dost Thou not stop all of Thy wrath? Enough, O Lord, enough! The cities are destroyed, the natural elements are set loose, the earthquakes everywhere. But mercy, mercy for Rome! But Thou hearest not my entreaties, and Rome also collapses in tumult. And I see the King of Rome (Pope) with his Cross and his tiara, shaking the dust off his shoes and hastening in his flight to other shores. Thy Church, O Lord, is torn apart by her own children. One (small) camp is faithful to the fleeing Pontiff, the other is subject to the new order government of Rome which has **broken the Tiara**. But Almighty God will, in His mercy, put an end to this confusion and a new age will begin. Then, said the Holy Ghost, this is the beginning of the End of Time." *(Tiara is no longer worn. And the New Order Government of Rome began with Vatican II.)*

These Books you should read. She says the devil will change the Church completely and what was practiced before will be practiced only by a small numbers. Than will come the Chastisement, and the 6th period of the Church will begin. This will mark the end of the 5th period in the Church, and the over run of Europe by Russia. Also **Mary of Agreda (4) vol.** which you can hear on **youtube: The Life of the Blessed Virgin pt 1-8)**. (So very beautiful. You will definitely thank me for this. Listen to it.) **Ven. Bartholomew Holzhauser said,** "The Great Monarch will come when the Latin Church is desolated, humiliated, and afflicted with many heresies…..at that time the **muslims** will come again." He goes on, "When everyone believes that peace is assured, when everyone will least expect it, 'the great happenings will begin." Now the **muslims** come….. "a revolution (bloodshed) will spread to every French town. Wholesale slaughter will take place. This revolution will last a short time, but will be frightful; blood will flow everywhere, victims will be innumerable. Paris will look like a slaughter house. *(After being in the packing plant I know what that's like, blood everywhere.)* Priests will go into hiding. Many priests and bishops will be put to death. The Archbishop of Paris will be murdered and religious throats will be cut, because they did not have time to find a hiding place. The wicked will be masters for one year. (Blood shedding one month.) Read Holzhauser (17th Century)

"The Great Monarch… Will conquer the (Middle) East." Pareus, 17th Century

"He will restore the Church of Santa Sophia (in Constantinople)." St. Bridget, 14th Century

"The Empire of the Mohammedans will be broken up (by him)." Ven. Holzhauser, 17th Century

"He will assist the Pope in the reformation of the World." Caesar, 6th Century

"He will put out all heresies." Merlin the Bard, 7th Century

"The French King will restore the true Pope." Merlin 13th Century

".....by whom the decayed estate of the Church shall be reformed." Magdeburg Chronicle

"A Prince ... who shall reform the Church." Aystinger the German

"Having need of a powerful temporal assistance, the Holy Pontiff will ask for the co-operation of the generous

Monarch of France." Abbot J. Merlin, 13th Century

"By his means the nation's religion and laws shall have an admirable change." Bishop Ageda, 12 Century

"He shall restore the apostolic discipline." St. John of Capistrano 15th Century

"He will crush the enemies of the Pope." D. Pareus, 17the Century

"He will give back the Church her pristine preminence." Nostradamus

"This Prince shall help (the Holy Pontiff) in every way." Vatiguerro, 3th Century

"He shall reign over the entire ancient Roman Empire." Remy, 5th Century

"... whom God will choose to rule over Europe." J. von Bourg, 19th Century

"(He and the Holy Pontiff) shall obtain dominion over the whole world." St. Francis de Paola, 15th Century

"This Prince shall extend his dominion over the whole world." St. Caesar, 6th Century

"This peace among men will not last long: 25 years of abundant harvests will make them forget that the sins of men are the cause of all the woes which happen on earth." Our Lady of La Salette

St. Nilus was one of the many disciples and fervent defenders of St. John Chrysostom. He was an officer at the Court of Constantinople, married, with two sons. While St. John Chrysostom was patriarch, before his exile (398-403), he directed Nilus in the study of Scripture and in works of piety. St. Nilus left his wife and one son and took the other son, Theodulos, with him to Mount Sinai to be monks. The Bishop of Eleusa ordained both St. Nilus and his son to the priesthood. The mother and other son also embraced the religious life in Egypt.

From his monastery at Sinai, **St. Nilus** was a well-known person throughout the Eastern Church. Through his writings and correspondence, he played an important part in the history of his time. He was known as a theologian, Biblical scholar and ascetic writer, so people of all kinds, from the Emperor down wrote to consult him.

St. Nilus must be counted as one of the leading ascetic writers of the 5th century. His feast is kept on November 12th in the Byzantine Calendar; he is commemorated also in the Roman Martyrology on the same date. St. Nilus probably died around the year 430, as there is no evidence of his life after that.

The Prophecy of St. Nilus

"After the year 1900, toward the middle of the 20th century, the people of that time will become unrecognizable. When the time for the Advent of the Antichrist approaches, people's minds will grow cloudy from carnal passions, and dishonor and lawlessness will grow stronger. Then the world will become unrecognizable.

People's appearances will change, and it will be impossible to distinguish men from women due to their shamelessness in dress and style of hair. These people will be cruel and will be like wild animals because of the temptations of the Antichrist. There will be no respect for parents and elders, love will disappear, and Christian pastors, Bishops and priests will become vain men, completely failing to distinguish the right-hand way from the left.

At that time, the morals and **traditions** of Christians and of the Church will change. People will abandon decent dress, and modesty, and dissipation will reign. Falsehood and greed will attain great proportions, and woe to those who pile up treasures. Lust, adultery, homosexuality, secret deeds and murder will rule in society.

At that future time, due to the power of such great crimes and licentiousness, people will be deprived of the grace of the Holy Spirit, which they received in Holy Baptism and equally of remorse.

The Churches of God will be deprived of God-fearing and pious pastors, and woe to the Christians remaining in the world at that time; they will **completely lose their faith** because they will lack the opportunity of seeing the light of knowledge from anyone at all. Then they will separate themselves out of the world in holy refuges in search of lightening their spiritual sufferings, but everywhere they will meet obstacles and constraints. And all this will result from the fact that the Antichrist wants to be Lord over everything and become the ruler of the whole universe, and he will produce miracles and fantastic signs.

He will also give depraved wisdom to an unhappy man so that he will discover a way by which one man can carry on a conversation with another from one end of the earth to the other. At that time men will also fly through the air like birds and descend to the bottom of the sea like fish. And when they have achieved all this, these unhappy people will spend their lives in comfort without knowing, poor souls, that it is deceit of the Antichrist. And, the impious one! - he will so complete science with vanity that it will go off the right path and lead people to lose faith in the existence of God in three hypostases.

Then the All-good God will see the downfall of the human race and will shorten the days for the sake of those few who are being saved, because the enemy wants to lead even the chosen into temptation, if that is possible... then the sword of chastisement will suddenly appear and kill the Perverter and his servants.

Our Lady of Fatima 1917. Now this is a most interesting apparition because Our Lady said much to the three children about many things. That WWI and WWII were the punishments for sin, mainly the **tramping** and **miss use** of the first three **commandments**. (Our Lady of La Salette said the say thing of the potato famine.) Besides the breaking of these commandments which are directly against, God, Our Lady said, "wear the scapular and daily pray the Rosary **daily** and there would be peace in the world and you would save your soul. "And She said the following:

"Dangers threatening the faith (salvation) and life of all Christians... and therefore the world."

*P*lease read this astonishing report just released: **Sister Lucia's recently published Vision of the Chastisement (August 2014)** *(I hope you're sitting down for this.)* **"I saw the point of a lance like a flame that is detached, touches the axis of the earth and it trembles. Mountains, cities, town villages with their inhabitants are buried. The sea, the rivers, the clouds exceed their boundaries, inundating and dragging with them in a vortex houses**

and people in a number that cannot be counted. It is the purification of the world from the sin in which it is immersed." Sr. Lucia

Then will begin the 6ᵗʰ period of the Church. (Will Russia be consecrated in time to stop all this?) Make the (5) First Saturdays. Pray the Rosary every day, wear the scapular.

SISTER LUCIA FROM FATIMA INTERVIEW 1957: "Father, the Most Holy Virgin is very sad because no one has paid any attention to Her message of 1917. Neither the good nor the bad." "The good continue on their way but without concerning themselves about the Her message. They do not follow the directions that Heaven has given us. The bad, not seeing the punishment of God's chastisement actually falling upon them, continue their life of sin without even caring about the message and continue to walk the broad road of perdition!!"

"God is about to chastise the world and this will be in a terrible manner. The punishment from Heaven is imminent. Father, how much time before 1960 arrives?" "It will be sad for everyone. Not one person will rejoice at all if beforehand the world does not pray and do penance. I am not able to give any other details because it is still a secret. This is the part of the Message of Our Lady which will remain secret until 1960." "Tell them, Father, that many times the most Holy Virgin told my cousins Francisco and Jacinta, as well as myself, that **many nations will disappear** from the face of the earth. She said that Russia will be the instrument of chastisement chosen by Heaven to punish the whole world if we do not beforehand obtain the conversion of that poor nation."

"Father, that is why my mission is not to indicate to the world the material punishments which are certain to come if the world does not pray and do penance beforehand. No! My mission is to indicate to everyone the imminent danger of losing our souls for all eternity if we remain obstinate in sin."

"Father, the Most Holy Virgin did not tell me that we are in the end times of the world, but She made me understand this for three reasons."

"The **first reason** is because She told me that the devil is in the mood for engaging in a decisive battle against the Virgin. And a decisive battle is the final battle where one side will be victorious and the other side will suffer defeat. Also, from now on we must choose sides. Either we are for God or we are for the devil."

"The **second reason** is because She said to my cousins as well as to myself, that God is giving two last remedies to the world. These are the Holy Rosary, and Devotion to the Immaculate Heart of Mary (scapular). These are the last two remedies which signify that there will be no others." In another place I have read: "We have just enough time to ward off the chastisement of Heaven. We have two very efficacious means at our disposal: "Prayer and Sacrifice." "The devil is doing everything he can to distract us and to take away our taste for prayer." (How many of you are distracted when you have free time by listening to music or watching a video? This is when you should be in reading or in conversation with God.) "Either we will save our souls or we will not."

"The **third reason** is because in the plans of Divine Providence, God always, before He is about to chastise the world, exhausts all other remedies." "Now, when he sees that the world pays no attention whatsoever, then as we say in our imperfect manner of speaking, He offers us with 'certain fear' the last means of salvation, His Most Holy Mother." "It is with 'certain fear' because if you despise and repulse this ultimate means, we will not have and more forgiveness from Heaven, because we will have committed a sin which the Gospel calls the sin against the Holy Ghost. This sin consists of openly rejecting, with full knowledge and consent, the salvation which He offers." "Let us remember that Jesus Christ is a very good Son and that He does not permit that we offend and despise His Most Holy Mother."

"We have recorded through many centuries of Church history the obvious testimony which demonstrates by the terrible chastisements which have befallen those who have attacked the honor of His Most Holy Mother, how Our Lord Jesus Christ has always defended the honor of His Mother." "The devil knows what it is that most offends God and which in a short space of time will gain for him the greatest number of souls."

"The devil knows that religious and priests who fall away from their beautiful vocation drag numerous souls to Hell. The devil wishes to take possession of consecrated souls. He tries to corrupt them in order to lull to sleep the souls of lay people and thereby lead them to final impenitence."

"Tell them also, Father, what contributed to the sanctification of my cousins Francisco and Jacinta the sorrows of the Most Holy Virgin, and the vision of hell."

"She never smiled at us." "This sadness, this anguish which we noted in Her, penetrated our souls. This sadness is caused by the offenses against God and the punishments which menace sinners. And so, we children did not know what to think except to invent various means of praying and making sacrifices."

"Father, we should not wait for an appeal to the world to come from Rome on the part of the Holy Father, to do penance. Nor should we wait for the call to penance to come from our bishops in our diocese, nor from the religious congregations. No! Our Lord has already very often used these means, and the world has not paid attention!!"

"That is why now, it is necessary for each one of us to begin to reform himself spiritually. Each person must not only save his own soul but also help to save all the souls that God has placed in his care and on our path."

"The devil does all in his power to distract us and to take away from us the love for prayer; we shall be saved together or we shall be damned together."

"The Virgin finds Herself, so to speak, between two sword points: on the one hand, She ees the obstinacy of humanity and its indifference with regard to the threat of chastisement; on the other hand She sees us treading under foot the Sacraments and making light of the impending chastisement, by our continuing incredulity, sensuality and materialism."

"The Blessed Virgin said very explicitly: 'THE LAST DAYS ARE NEAR', and she repeated this (3) times. She said that the devil had begun the decisive battle, or the final battle. She repeated a second time that remedies offered to the world is: The Holy Rosary and (scapular) devotion to Her Immaculate Heart.

Go to Mass on Saturday's in honor of Mary and Her sorrows. Make the (5) first Saturdays. Bring flowers to Her.

Mother, Gate of Heaven; pray for us. Sr. Lucia

As Our Lady of Fatima waved goodbye to the three shepherd children, she said, "until San Sebastian Espana. (Spain)" 44 years later she appeared, again holding the baby Jesus 1961. Third Secret not revealed in 1960. She appears **at Church of St. Sebastian de Garabandal, Spain.** So Fatima continues at Garabandal. This 2nd half of Fatima.

Since 1960 when, after reading the Secret, Pope John XXIII decided **not** to reveal the contents publicly, there has been growing speculation concerning what it contains. While in the past, speculation often identified the 3rd Secret with all sorts of cataclysms and disasters, more recent scholars has indicated that it most likely concerns the widespread chaos, confusion and loss of the True Faith that has gripped the Roman Catholic Church over the last six decades. I wonder if She mentions all this because of a Council? No, wonder he didn't want to read it.

Free thinkers, Liberals, Communists, or Freemasons, they're all the same and carry the destructive poisonous orders of **Satan** to create chaos every where and to destroy the One True Church. In a group of modernist freethinkers, one we know very well is **Hans Kung** among others. He with others has distorted the trues of our Catholic Faith. Today we have many cardinals and bishops doing this same thing. One of the worst liberals today is **Cardinal Walter Kasper (mason)** ordained in 1957 and he assisted Hans Kung as a professor of theology. In 1987 bishop of the Diocese of Rottenburg, Stuttgart. (Many others to numerous to mention.)

In 1967, he (Kasper) wrote this new theology thesis: "The God who is enthroned over the world and history as a changeless being is an **offence to man.** One must **deny** him for man's sake, because he claims for himself the dignity and honor that belongs by **rights to man**.... We must **resist** this God, however, not only for man's sake, but also for God's sake (satan is their god). He is not the true God at all, but rather a wretched idol. For a God who is only alongside of and above history, who is not himself history, is a finite God. If we call such a being God, then for the sake of the Absolute we must become Absolute Atheists. Such a God springs from a rigid worldview; he is the guarantor of the status quo and the enemy of the **new**." (New what?!?) (New church & One World Gov.)

I have read the same in masonic writings. These priests **do not** have the gift of faith, but a drop of Hell's poison. Their objective is to distort any truth and normal traditional society communities.)

In the beginning ... the Lord God said to the serpent; I will put enmity between you and the woman ... She shall crush your head. (Gen 3:15-16) "in the end, my Immaculate Heart will triumph…"

> God told Adam and Eve and the Angels that He would send His only Son to redeem mankind. Born in a stable. And all power in Heaven and on Earth are given to Jesus Christ. He told his Apostles to go and teach all nations, baptizing them in the name of the Father, and of the Son, and of the Holy Ghost. Teaching them to observe all things whatsoever I have commanded you; and ……..((Matt. 28, 18-20.) I and the Father are One. (John 10,30)

Our Lady Of LaSalette (1846): "All the civil governments (90% are Freemason today) will have one and the same plan, which will be to abolish and do away with every religious principle, to make way for materialism, atheism, spiritualism and vice of all kinds… for disorder and the love of carnal pleasures will be spread all over the earth." And to establish a One World Government and One World Religion, headed in Rome.

Satan knew his time was right and this is when he **whispered into the ear** of Pope John XXIII to have a council. **Bishop Fulton J. Sheen** says he was shown by Pope John XXIII the exact spot in a vatican hallway where he said he heard someone whisper in his ear to have a council. Satan's masons took over the council to do Satan's bidding. Do they know they are on the road to **perdition**? (Oh, there I go judging again; Satan has intoxicated us not to judge others, and just let things go on as they are, but don't judge them, that's not nice. Kind of like parents who don't spank their children, but just say, no, no, and let them go, go on as they want, being loud and letting them get away with whatever.) **Bishop**

Fulton Sheen said, *"You must make a depression on the bottom side to make an impression on the inside." (Don't let the child test you, to see how far they can go to get away with something. A good parent disciplines the child, and a bad parent just yells at them.) Let me stay on this subject for a moment: We are speaking of the 4th* **Commandment; "Withhold not correction from a child, for if thou strike him with the rod, he will not die. Thou shalt beat (spank) him with the rod (stick), and save his soul from hell."** *(Prov. 23, 13. 14.) "The eye that mocketh at his father, and that despiseth the labor of his mother, let the ravens pick it (the child) out, and the young eagles eat it." (Prov.30, 17.) "If a man has a stubborn and unruly son, who will not hear the commandments of his father or mother, and being corrected, slightest obedience, the people shall stone him, and all Israel hearing it may be afraid."*

"Honor thy father and thy mother, which is the only commandment with a promise: **that it may be well with thee and thou mayest live long** *upon the earth." Eph. 6, 2. 3.)* (You children listen to this one.)

"With all thy soul fear the Lord, and reverence His priests." Ecclus. 7. 31.) "Let every soul be subject to higher powers; for there is no power which does not come from God: and those high powers, are ordained of God." (Rom. 13,1.) (His Divine Providence has sent all things in place.)

"Masters be to your servants that which is just and equal, knowing that thou also have a Master in Heaven."

(Col. 4, 1.) This is also to be said for the child. And it is a great virtue to pay your bills.

Many good people I have spoken with have told me that they are most grateful to their mother and father for having spanked them in their youth or they would not have turned out as well as they have. "A good name is better than great riches." (Prov. 22, 1.) Always a saints name. Not after some beverage or highway or town.

Practical Conclusion: Detest falsehood, for it belongs to the devil, the father of lies. Never speak unkindly of your parents, or neighbor, nor wound his feelings *by injurious language. For to hold a **grudge or anger** against any man, and not forgive before death is sure hellfire for you. (See story of Hell.)*

*Honor your parents, pastors, teachers, and all who by lawful authority, rank or age, are placed over you. Obey cheerfully and promptly after the example of our Divine Saviour. My youngest, you need to smile more, especially when you least want to, amongst your loved ones not just your friends. The **smile** will make things always go well for you throughout the day, throughout all your days, especially in those moments when you least want too. You bring blessings on yourself when you smile at a passing neighbor.*

*"**The devil has succeeded in bringing in evil (to the Church) under the guise of good, and the blind** (to the True Faith) **are beginning to lead others.**"* Good priests mislead and keep good souls in the false religion of the Novus Ordo, making all believe that they must be loyal to **Vatican II**. Pope Paul VI said, "The Smoke of Satan is in the Church." *"**Those who leave Tradition cease to be catholic." St. Anthaniaus***

Although Sister Lucy was not permitted to reveal the final 3rd Secret of Our Lady until the Holy Father himself deems the moment opportune, nothing has prevented her from giving her opinion on the crisis in the Church as an individual person. In a series of letters written between 1969 and 1972, Sister Lucy reacted vigorously against modernists and others in the Church, in particular those who seek to minimize the importance of the Rosary. "This **disorientation is diabolical**," she wrote, and "it is sad that so many people let themselves be dominated by the diabolical wave sweeping over the world! And they are blinded to the point where they are incapable of seeing error! Their principal fault is that they have abandoned prayer." The saddest part of all, according to Sister Lucy, is that so many priests, religious and bishops are swept away in the confusion." The devil has succeeded in bringing in evil (to the Church) under the guise of good and the blind are beginning to lead others, as the Lord tells us in His Gospel."

In the conclusion to his study of the Third Secret of Fatima, Frère Michel sums up his findings as follows:

"Having reached the end of our inquiry, we are able to discern, with near certainty, the essential elements of Our Lady's final secret: While 'in Portugal, the dogma of the Faith will always be preserved,' in many nations, perhaps in almost the entire world, the Faith will be lost. The pastors of the Church will fail gravely in the duties of their office. Through their fault, consecrated souls and the Faithful in great numbers will let themselves be seduced by **pernicious errors** spread everywhere. This will be the time of the decisive battle between the Blessed Virgin and the devil. A wave of **diabolical disorientation** will be hurled over the world. Satan will introduce himself even to the highest summit of the Church. He will blind the minds and harden the hearts of pastors. And God will deliver them to themselves as a **chastisement** for their refusal to obey the requests of the Immaculate Heart of Mary. This will be the great apostasy predicted for the **'last times'**; 'the False Lamb' and 'False Prophet' will **betray** the Church to the profit of 'the **Beast**,' according to the prophecy of the Apocalypse." *(The priest will set himself in the front of the tabernacle. And the Blessed Sacrament will be trampled under foot because of Communion in the Hand. Less and less importance will be given to the Blessed Sacrament. People will come dressed in everyday casual clothing. The new fashions will be tight to the body and low down below the base of the neck. People will talk in church. The cassock will not be worn by priest, sacristan or altar boy before or during Mass when entering into the sanctuary. Lay clothing will be the thing at the altar in church and out of church for both priests and nuns.)*

"Diabolical disorientation" will swept and seduce the people in the smallest of things, bad manners, to the worst sins. From the shower shoes to base ball caps, shorts, and 'T' shirts of the decadent sociality, wearing and eating with your hats on inside, bad language, to the homosexuality, to abortion, God's name in vain and don't forget working on Sundays and pre- marital sex. Man will constantly say bad things about each other and be held accountable before God on Judgement Day. What'd I forget? Oh freemasons and gang drugs and killings and ISIS and the CIA. There more?!?

St. Anthony saw in a vision the whole world entangled in a net of sin. "O Lord," he cried out, "who will escape these snares?" And a voice from Heaven answered: "ONLY THOSE WHO ARE HUMBLE OF HEART."

"If you accept adversities willingly from the hand of God, "says Thomas a Kempis, "you show Him great honor, rejoice the angels, edify your neighbor, shame the devil, and heap up treasures for yourself in Heaven. The trials of this life are brief, but your reward in Heaven will be exceedingly great and peace without end."

"After the year 1900, towards the middle of the 20th century, the people of that time will become UNRECOGNIZABLE. (Baseball caps, 'T' shirts, shorts, shower shoes. It will be the dressing of men and women in their underwear walking down the street.) When the time for the advent of the Antichrist approaches, people's minds will grow cloudy from carnal passions and dishonor and lawlessness will grow stronger. Then will the world become unrecognizable. People's appearances will change, (Immodest fashions: shoes, tight closes showing the form of the body.) It will be impossible to distinguish men from the women due to their shamelessness in dress and style of hair. These people will be cruel and will be like wild animals because of the temptations of the Antichrist. There will be no respect for parents and elders, love will disappear, and christian pastors, bishops, and priests will become vain men, completely failing to distinguish the right hand from the left. At that time the morals and traditions of christians and of the Church will change.

The Consecration of Russia

"I shall come to ask for the Consecration of Russia to My Immaculate Heart...If people attend to My requests, Russia will be converted and the world will have peace."

In the apparition of July 13, at Fatima, Our Lady warned the three seers, that if people did not stop offending God, He would punish the world "by means of war, hunger and persecution of the Church and of the Holy Father," using Russia as His chosen instrument of chastisement. She told the children that "to prevent this, I shall come to ask for the **Consecration of Russia to My Immaculate Heart**" and promised that, by this single public act, Russia would be converted and peace would be given to the world. (Breaking the first three Commandments are offend God the most.)

The Mother of God cautioned that if Her requests were *not* granted, **"Russia will spread its errors throughout the world, raising up wars and persecutions of the Church.** The good will be martyred, the Holy Father will have much to suffer and various nations will be annihilated."

I want to point out the meaning of Russia will spread her errors throughout the world. Russia is the mother of communism. All communistic countries answer to her and do her bidding. Besides the countries, there the cartel drug groups, all over the world. Isis takes their orders from Russia as do other so called independent groups. They kill the young as well as the old, and have promised to bring America to her knees. **Russia with her secret armies** will enter America from Alaska, Mexico, and Cuba, near the same time as they overran Europe. The Consecration of Russia could have been done at Vatican II, but Satan's people already had the 'Moscow - Rome Pax Agreement set up. Thanks to this set up, *(and Boy What a Setup)* Russia or should I say Satan, has had plenty of time to line up her ducks and demons. Russia has developed weapons of mass destruction, technology to kill thousands of square miles of people with magnetic electrical EMP bomb. It not only kills, but wipes out anything that uses electrical spark or energy. One World Gov. and Religion is closer now.

True to Her word, Our Lady appeared to Sister Lucy on **June 13, 1929** at Tuy, Spain, when in a **great and sublime vision** representing the Blessed Trinity, She announced that; "the moment has come for **God** to **command the Holy Father** to make, in union **with all the bishops** of the world, the Consecration of Russia to My Immaculate Heart. By this means, He promises to convert Russia and save the world."

When God sent Our Lady to convey His command that Russia be consecrated, it seems clear that He expected **swift obedience** from the Pope and bishops. The pastors of the Church, however, chose to delay and, two years later on **August 19, 1931 <u>Our Lord Himself appeared</u>** to Sister Lucy in Rianjo, Spain and expressed His displeasure, saying:

"Make it known to My ministers that, given, they follow the example of the King of France in delaying the execution My <u>command</u>, they will follow him also into <u>misfortune</u>."

Our Lord's warning is a grave one indeed, referring as it does to His command, through St. Margaret Mary Alacoque, said to the King of France Louis XIV June 17, 1689 that he consecrates his nation to the Sacred Heart of Jesus. The King chose to ignore the command and thus condemned his dynasty and throne to the horrors of <u>revolution, chaos and the guillotine</u>. This resulted in the 'French Revolution' exactly 100 years later June 17, 1789 which began as a result of this failure, grandson, King Louis XVI was decapitated on January 21, 1793 and the ruin of the type of government set up by Christ Catholic Kings and Queens loyal to the Holy Father under Christ.

In Heaven there is a King and Queen and God the Holy Father. In the Our Father we ask that be on earth as it is in Heaven. Satan replaced God's type of government (kings and queens) with democracy (demonic) government. Do what God says or heads will roll. Now I know where Dad got that saying. One note here to remember is that Our Lord asked for the Consecration of Russia were to on June 13, 1929, and if we were to wait 100 years for the punishment of Russia. This would be June 17, 2029. And the Miracle in April 15, 2032, because no numbers fall on the right dates in 2030. And the Chastisement, which will be the Great Comet will come a little later. But I don't think God will wait that long with all the corruption in the world today. (My guess 2017 Russia, 2018 The Warning.) We'll see. Our Lord never said 100 years, we are assuming, but before 2029.

At the Last Supper Our Lord instructed the Apostles _how to say the Mass and how to anoint Kings_, and He also instructed them as to how to fold their hands with the right thumb over the left thumb performing all ceremonies. The Good and Faithful who truly love God with sincere devotion show it in all they do, not just by folding their hands on the way up to Holy Communion, but in their genuflections, **well dressed no bare arms in the church**, and their charity. (_The manner in which you dress is the respect you show to that person you go to visit._) Read St. Catherine Emmerick The problem is that not just the ministers are going to get it, but the whole world is going suffer greatly. This Tesle electrical technology will wipe out entire nations. The basic idea of an e-bomb -- or more broadly, an **electromagnetic pulse (EMP) weapon** -- is pretty simple. These sorts of weapons are designed to overwhelm electrical circuitry with an intense **electromagnetic field**. Thus destroying or making it inoperable all communications and machinery. It is believed Russia will use this weapon before they invade America. (More than likely in 2017.)

Back to the Fatima point I am trying to make. What is generally called the "Third Secret" is, in actuality, the third and final part of the full prophetic Secret which the Blessed Virgin gave to three seers on July 13, 1917. The other two sections of the Secret (the vision of hell and the rise of Communist Russia) were publicly revealed with the publication of Sister Lucy's _Memoirs_ in the 1940s, the final part of the revelation remains in the possession of the Vatican and has not yet been disclosed to the world, even though they say they have.

"When you see a night illumined by an unknown light, know that this is the great sign given you by God that he is about to punish the world. To prevent this, I shall come to ask for the consecration of Russia to My Immaculate Heart, and the Communion of Reparation on the First Saturdays [of each month]. If My requests are heeded, Russia will be converted, and there will be peace; if not, she will spread her errors throughout the world, causing wars and persecutions of the Church. The good will be martyred, the Holy Father will have much to suffer, various nations will be annihilated." *Our Lady of Fatima's Second Prophecy*

November 2013, President Vladimir Putin of Russia came to Rome to visit with Pope Francis. During this meeting between these two men, Vladimir Putin asked Pope Francis about the consecration of Russia. And Pope Francis replied, "WE WILL NOT DISCUSS FATIMA." Mr. Putin took this as a snub. Later standing in front of a statue of Our Lady Fatima Cardinal Rovski said to Mr. Putin, "WE WILL DESTROY FATIMA." Cardinal Rovski is said to be a mason. *Obviously we can **not** do business with the enemy when they are holding the fort.* But if you want to walk into prison and become a prisoner, go head, negotiate, you will become swallowed by the snake and never be heard of again. These are Luciferians, Illuminati, Jewish Christ haters, freemasons, what a great bunch to join, if you want to lose your soul. These people control Rome and are not afraid to Kill You.

Ecclesiastical freemasons of Rome **objects** to the consecration of Russia to the Immaculate Heart of Mary, because the power a consecration in the name of Mary may put a stop to their One World Religion agenda. Russia wants the Consecration of their country to the Immaculate Heart of Mary, they want to be free of Communism. They want to be truly Catholic again. They want to see the One, True, Holy, Catholic, and Apostolic Traditional Faith come back into their country as it was so long ago when they had a King.

The consecration of Russia by the Pope in union with all the bishops of the world was to be made to the Immaculate Heart of Mary before 1960 and was never done. The point is believed that 100 years later the Russia will overrun Europe. And Rome will invade and the Holy Father will flee as was prophesied by many saints. From this comes the Warning, Great Miracle, and the Chastisement of Garabandal and Our Lady's **"Last Warning"**. As Our Lady requested the 3rd Secret of Fatima to be revealed in 1960. Our Lady appeared the very next year in San Sebastian de Garabandal, Spain 1961 – 1965. Local Bishop 2007 has approved the apparitions of Garabandal, Rome is waiting for the Warning, Miracle, and the Chastisement before giving final approval. By that time ¼ of the world will be left. Garabandal picks up where Fatima left off. The 6th period of the Church is where God will start all over again, for the last time.

> *Why do I say Garabandal is the 2nd half of Fatima? When Our Lady said goodbye to the three shepherd children at Fatima, she waved and said, "until San Sebastian Spain." Well, San Sebastian is the name of the Church in Garabandal, Spain.*

Let's touch on **Garabandal** a little, because it is most important and Our Lady said few would believe in it: It is the second half and the continuation of Fatima. At Garabandal Our Lady again tells of the **Warning**, which will **last (5) minutes** and every living soul will experience it no matter where in the world they are. They will see their sins on their soul the <u>wrong they are doing</u> and the <u>right they should be doing</u>. Many will die from shock of seeing their sins. For awhile people will become better. But due to their fallen nature (from the fall of Adam) they will go back to their old ways.

Then the **Miracle**, it will take place within a year after the Warning. (Actually the Warning will perhaps take place within (3) weeks or months of the Miracle.) The Miracle will last (15) minutes and will be seen by all who are in Garabandal at the time. The Holy Father will see it no matter where in the world he is. The Miracle will occur between the 8th -16th day of either March, April, or May. April is the month of the Eucharist.

Conchita was told by Our Lady to reveal the date (8) days before the miracle. It will happen on the feast of a Eucharist Martyr (child) on a Thursday at 8:30 pm. It will happen on a "Great Ecclesiastical event in the Church". (There is another prophecy that the **Holy Father will go to Moscow** in Russia and when he leaves, the Tribulation begins, which is the blood shedding of very many people of Europe by the muslims, and then over running of Europe by **Russia which is said will take them (3) days**. This Pope's trip to Moscow may be to bring back the Russian E. Orthodox into the Church, which would be a great ecclesiastical event in the Church that following **Spring**. (Russia will ruin Paris and Rome.) This will be the time of the Miracle. Our Lady of Garabandal also said, **"The Mass will become hard to say."** She's right, where can you find the Latin Mass?" Word has it that the Miracle will be on an even numbered year. Three months or weeks after the Warning.

St Edmund Campion is celebrated on 1ˢᵗ December. Campion moved between the houses of Catholics (the Recusants) who practised their religion in secret. At one such house, Lyford Grange in Oxfordshire, he was betrayed and arrested on 17ᵗʰ July 1581, barely a year after he had set foot in England. He was imprisoned and tortured in the Tower of London and tried at Westminster Hall in November.

With Fr. Alexander Briant SJ and Fr. Ralph Sherwin. He was hanged and then, before he was dead, his genitals cut off, his entrails ripped out and burned before him, his head hacked off and his body quartered.

St. Edmund had at least one vision of Our Lady, in which he was told of the Warning. Before he was arrested Campion spoke of a "great day!" "No other day was in my mind, I protest, than that wherein it should please God to make a restitution of faith and religion. Whereupon, as in every pulpit every Protestant doth, I pronounced a great day, not wherein any temporal potentate should minister, but wherein the terrible Judge should **REVEAL ALL MEN'S CONSCIENCES** and try every man of each kind of religion.

Mari Loli, one of the seers at Garabandal was asked the following questions on October 19, 1982:

Q. Do you remember what the Blessed Mother said about the communist tribulation that is to precede the Warning?

A. It would look like the communists would have taken over the whole world and it would be very hard to practice the religion, for priests to say Mass or for people to open the doors of the churches. (Communism is atheism both will spread and God will be forgotten.)

Q. Is that what you meant when you said that it would seem as though the Church had disappeared?

A. Yes.

Q. It would be because of the persecution and not because the people would stop practicing their religion?

A. Yes, but I guess a lot of people will stop. Whoever practices it will have to go into hiding. (The Old Church is under ground and today you have a new, new order Church unlike the old one, force upon the people.)

Q. Will this only be in Europe or do you think it will be here in the United States as well?

A. I don't know because for me at that time, Europe was the whole world. I just assumed it was that way. The Blessed Mother didn't specify in what place. To me it looked like it was everywhere.

Q. Approximately 67% of the earth s land is now dominated by communism. Do you think that's sufficient to fulfill Our Lady s prophecy?

A. I really don't know. It sounded to me like it would be more than that.

Q. In other words you think it will be worse than it is now?

A. That's what I thought from what she said but I really don't know exactly. To me it looked like it was every place out there, the places I saw in my mind. In a lot of countries in Europe you can still practice your religion.

Q. So, the situation in the world is not bad enough for the Warning to happen?

A. The Warning is not going to happen yet so it's probably going to get worse.

Q. You said that it would be very difficult for priests to say Mass. Was this something that the Blessed Mother told you or was it something that you thought yourself because of the communist tribulation?

A. From what I remember, it was something she said.

Q. And the Virgin said that it would seem as though the Church had disappeared?

A. Yes.

(Communism and freemasonry are twin sisters and have already infiltrated the Church and have destroyed the Mass Tridentine Mass of the Council of Trent St. Pius V and the Church has disappeared down to a remnant.) And Rome is not practicing the Faith of Our Fathers. Since Vatican II we have a very new religion AND a new church. How many will stay faithful to what made saints and can never be wrong.

St. Maximilian Kolbe was a Franciscan priest with a great love for God and His One True Church. In his fight with the **Freemasons** he foretells of the Great War when Russia invades Europe. In his writing of **1939**: "Before the **Great War, Rome**, the capital of Catholic life, (the seat of the Vicar of Christ) a **conspiracy**, *(to infiltrate and destroy the Catholic Church and the Mass)* condemned by the Roman Pontiffs, which grew larger from day to day. Nor did the Freemasons fear, on the day anniversary day of Giordano Bruno *(Dominican priest who apostatized and was burned at the stake for heresy)* to raise a flag with the image of **St. Michael the Archangel** being trodden underfoot by Lucifer, before the very windows of the Vatican to display the standards of the **Masons**. Some even raised on high with shouts: '**Satan will reign on Vatican Hill. The Supreme Pontiff will be his servant**,' and other opprobrious things similar. These wild movements of hatred against the Church of Christ and His Vicar on earth were not men mentally deranged but who acted according to a determined plan, way, and purpose, based on the **Masons' precepts: all divine doctrine, primarily Catholic, is to be destroyed."**

The **Freemasons** are particularly guided by this principle: **"The Catholic Church (and Her Sacred Tradition) cannot be vanquished by reasoning, but by the corruption of morals."** Hence, "the souls of men are tainted by the species of literature and art *(entertainment)* which most easily corrupts man's chastity and destroys a sense of morality, so that all parts of human society might be influenced by this sordid propaganda. Wise and strong men become weakened, families torn apart, hearts corrupted and an insane bitterness grows up (against God and Church). Such souls, when they are unable to throw off the infamous burden they carry, will avoid the Church or even rise up against Her."

When a man really doesn't want to pray and really doesn't want to go to church or except on occasion, really doesn't want to go to heaven. *(You boys all listening, pray the Rosary.)*

 St. Maximiian wrote in 1924: "Freemasonry is undoubtedly the head of the infernal serpent. …..there organization is aimed against God and the happiness of souls. Diverse heresies (and churches outside the ONE TRUE CHURCH OF JESUS CHRIST) are the limbs of the serpent…
 St. Maximilian Kolbe started a branch of Franciscans on October 16th, 1917. His weapons to fight the Freemasons were **Our Lady's Miraculous Medal** which he called **"the bullet that strikes down evil"** and **"the Holy Rosary which is the sword."**

To the prayer on the Miraculous Medal: **"O Mary conceived without sin, pray for us who have recourse to Thee,"** and he added this prayer, **"and for all who do not have recourse to Thee, especially the Freemasons."** He also recommended say the daily Rosary and preached on it.

These members take a fourth "Marian" vow, as all of us should, whereby they consecrated themselves to the Mother of God. Many of these priests offer the One True Mass the Latin Tridentine Mass. *(Which the Masons will try to destroy.)* They practice the "Traccia Mariana."

St. Maximilian wrote in October 1926, on the Masons:
"In the **'Protocols of the Elders of Zion'** a book by the Freemasons, they say of themselves: **"Who or what is capable of overthrowing an invisible (Satanic) power? And this is precisely what our power is. …. It will never be known by the people."**
(Maximilian now continuing): Gentleman, (speaking directly to the Masons), we are capable of overthrowing even an invisible power! I say, because you have no idea how sweet it is to be faithful and to serve God and His Immaculate Mother. I maintain that we are capable of overthrowing you and we shall overthrow you! *(With the above mentioned weapons.)*

Krakow, Poland, in 1919, Fr. Maximilian wrote on **"Catholic Action"** the need for prayer, especially the Rosary and meditation on the Passion of the Son of God, **secondly**, suffering and penance, do without the things you want, **thirdly**, "the action of the word" the press, keep the people informed on the truth between God and Satan, and what is happening around you in this world.

Maximilian wrote: **Napoleon said, a hundred years ago**, "The press is the fifth power of the world." The Jews understood that immediately; let me say it more clearly – the Masons, who with iron consistency are endeavoring to realize the motto adopted in 1717: **"to destroy all religion, especially Christianity (Catholism)."**

The French Jew, **Cremieux**, did not hesitate, over sixty ago, to say, **'hold everything as nothing, money as nothing, esteem as nothing, the press is everything.'**

"And at an international Congress of Rabbis in Krakow in 1848, the English rabbi Moses Montefiore proclaimed, 'As long as the newspapers of the world are not in our hands, all will be useless. Let us be mindful of the eleventh commandment: **thou shalt not suffer over yourself any foreign press, so that you rule long over the Gentiles. Let us control the press, and soon we will rule and direct the fate of all of Europe.'"**

Today as always ever never trust in the media, believe nothing you hear, and only half of what you see.

There was a monk who was caretaker of the 'House of Loreto" (where Jesus and Mary lived) and had a brick placed in the unsealed entry way wall of that year 1986, in the Vatican. The intentions were inscribed on that brick, which was, that a man named **Trump** would one day save America and help the world at the same time. He will be greatly hated by the media.

Pope Pius X speaking to the clergy, expressed: "Neither the people nor the clergy have understood the importance of the press. They say that in the past the press did not exist; they do not understand that times have changed. **It is good to build churches, preach sermons, establish missions and schools, but all these labors will be vain, if we neglect the most important weapon of our time, the press."**

Your life daily hangs on a thread between Heaven and Hell. God gives you a **free will** to choose your own direction up or down. If you're going with God you need to study how and what others used to get to God or Heaven. God has given us the treasures of His One True Church to obtain our final goal, **Heaven.** We have on the table of salvation the following: The Mass, the Rosary, the (7) sacraments, the sacramentals, metals, Holy water, and prayers to certain subjects: Blood of Christ, Sorrows of Mary, Stations of the Cross, St. Joseph or any of the saints, and much more.

If you choose to **avoid God** you choose the devil and the world and the Flesh. This automatically places you in Hell forever at the end of your life. By daily avoid bonding with God in thought, word, and deed. Not a smart move to go through the whole day and never speak to Him who is always there with you. Would you do that to your spouse?

God has created; Love, Peace, Order, and Light, all things are kept in order by Divine Providence.

Lucifer hates God so much, that he tries to put everything into chaos, what God has put into order and peace, Satan tries to turn upside down. To prove my point, go to youtube: "**Amazing! The Cure for Cancer and Disease Hidden in Plain Sight**" -- And: "**Fluoride on Tap**"

Satan will go so far as to rid us of the marriage state, the union that God made between man and woman. Create same sex marriage or just live together in mortal sin. Or completely rid us of the terms man and woman, no such thing as gender, this will be his new law, which those who serve Satan will help to achieve. People will not see clearly morality. The darkness of Satan has bedimmed their minds. This will

cause God to step in and again rid the world of mankind and start over one more time. First with a 3rd World War (Russia) and then the Comet as the saints of old have prophesied.

The Great Warning will occur when there is a revolution in Rome and the Pope will flee Rome in terror. At the same time a comet/asteroid or a piece of a comet/asteroid will hit the sun. The gigantic explosion will shake the earth. Not sure about that one. Pretty sure about the Comet coming according to prophecy and NASA. youtube: **NASA HIDDEN SECRET FOUND! THE END OF MANKIND - LEAKED DOCUMENT**

The Message of Our Lady at Garabandal: October 18, 1961

"We must make many sacrifices, perform much penance and visit the Blessed Sacrament frequently. But first we must be very good and lead good lives."

"And if we do not do this, a Chastisement will come upon us." "Already the cup is filling up, and if we do not change, a very great chastisement will come upon us."

The girls saw the vision of the chastisement and they begged the Blessed Virgin to take the children away. She told them they will be adults when this happens.

"June 18, 1965:" As my message of October 18th has not been made known to the world, I am advising you that this is the **'Last Warnings'.**"

"Before the cup was filling up, now it is overflowing. **Many Cardinals, many bishops, many priests** are on the road to **perdition** and taking many souls with them. **Less and less** importance being given to the **Eucharist**." (Communion in the Hand.)

"You should turn the wrath of God away from yourselves by your efforts. If you ask His forgiveness with sincere hearts, He will pardon you."

"I, your Mother, through the intercession of St. Michael the Archangel, ask you to amend your lives."

"You are now receiving the last warnings. I love you very much and do not want your condemnation. Pray to Us with sincerity and We will grant your requests. You should make more sacrifices."

"Think about the Passion of Jesus." (She said this through the intercession of St. Michael, because she did not come that day. She sent St. Michael because she said it pained her to give this message.) This is the message of Garabandal. And there were 1000's of miracles, and 2000 apparitions. Each time she asked all people to daily say the Rosary. (.... and wear the scapular.)

Another incident is the death of Mary Loli, one of the seers.

Mari Loli died a couple years ago on April 20, 2009. Asked when the "warning" would occur, she allegedly said, "When Russia will unexpectedly and suddenly overrun and overwhelm a great part of the free world. God does not want this to happen so quickly. In any case the Warning will come when you will see that Holy (Tridentine) Mass cannot be celebrated freely anymore; then it will be that the world will most need the intervention of God." *(Remember what both Our Lady and Our Lord said to **St. Marie Julie Jahenny**; that the New Mass was devised by our enemies and is an illicit Mass, not the true Mass put in perpetuity by St. Pius V)*

Both Our Lady and Our Lord tell of a tribulation, a 30 day blood shedding. This will be, no doubt, the Muslims killing throughout Europe just before Russia invades Europe.

Today June 18, 2014 - Joey Lomangino Died 53 years ago today, St. Michael the Archangel appeared in Garabandal.

Today unfortunately, this is not as happy an occasion. On December 6,

1962, Conchita had a 90 minute ecstasy around 5:30 in the afternoon after which, she provided two more pieces of information regarding the Miracle: Sometime, before the Miracle, something will happen that will cause many people to stop believing in the apparitions of Garabandal. The doubts and desertions will not be due to an excessive delay of the Miracle.

It will be due to the fact that Our Lady said that Joey would receive his eye site on the day of the miracle. Joey was blind.

Joey was told to go to Garabandal by St. Padre Pio.

St. Padre Pio told Joey, "yes, the Virgin is appearing in Garabandal." Padre Pio told other people that Our Lady was appearing in Garabandal. St. Padre Pio had communications with Conchita twice.

St. Padre Pio had the veil that covered his open casket sent to Conchita.

In 1961, Our Lady told the children that they would deny seeing Her. One of the (4) girls said, "How can that be since we are seeing you now?" And Our Lady replied, "You will go through a state of confusion, the same as the Church is entering into now."

Our Lady appears at Garabandal at a time when they lived a simple life without electricity. This is actually a signal of Our Lady the spirit of Poverty and what it will be like after the (3) Day Chastisement as to how we will have to live a simple good life. Garabandal is none the less true. Garabandal is the second half of Fatima and the high point of all Our Lady's visits and 'last warning' which has been repeated at La Salette, Quito, Guadalupe, Lourdes, Fatima, Akita, and Garabandal. "Pray the

Rosary and wear the Scapular." It seems that the greatest trauma of this Tribulation will be felt in Europe. St. Padre Pio is reported to have seen that the great Miracle to occur at Garabandal which will be paid for by the blood of the Europeans—oceans of blood. Our Lady told Conchita that **Communism** will "**come**" and that it will also come to Spain, but Spain would not suffer as intensely as the rest of Europe apparently because it had suffered Communism in the 1930's. Russians will come to Garabandal for (4) days and kill some people for the Faith.

Communism is the tearing down of God, the making of a decadent society which will become lacks in modest dress, behavior, and language. Communism is where everyone is always watching and spying on each other, because no one trusts each other. And where concentration camps are for non-believers. Satan will keep man so busy that he will have no time to think of God. And when man finds a little time, he will spend it trying to find a little pleasure in life. (Probably watching a football game or videos.)

St. Thomas puts it this way, Christians find it hard, often impossible, to get personal direction in the affairs of their souls. The main reason is the problem of time, here is where you must use your head, their only so many hours in a day to accomplish the things necessary for your survival and not enough time to do the things you would like to do, and little time to give to God for all the time He has given you. The tempo of modern existence puts upon us, with its new skills, new professions, and all the splendid fruits of its inventive genius. Thus the battle between Heaven and Hell is who will win your time? Thus who will win your soul? The growth of Christian virtue is largely the private relationship between God and the soul. With the benefit of counsel on occasion (Sunday sermon or a Retreat or confession and best of all is good spiritual reading) allows you the inspirations of the Paraclete to advance you in perfection. When you read, God speaks to you. When you pray you speak to God.

Someone once asked the saintly Irish workman, **Matt Talbot**, the name of his spiritual director he said, *"The Holy Ghost."* The Divine Comforter who shows us our end in life, and gives us the means of attaining it. He does this by creating in us certain dispositions to goodness; which gives us sanctifying grace and His sevenfold system of fixed qualities. Sanctifying grace reaches into the very substance or depth of the soul, the virtues and gifts have to do with its properties or powers. This is christianity which is the opposite of Communism.

Try this for an example, your fingers represent the virtues you're practicing, the hand represents sanctifying grace. The fingers work as long as they are attached to the hand, sanctifying grace, given by the Holy Ghost through the seven sacraments and actual graces by use of sacramentals. So how strong is your hand or spiritual muscles and working fingers, your virtues?

St. Augustine boldly says, "***God became man so that man might become God!***" Now this doesn't mean we are God, (like the modernist and liberals make themselves out to be) this means we will be like unto God in goodness to reign in Heaven with Him by use of the sacraments and our good works all being done in union with the Divine Will. Now St. Augustine defines this saying where he says: "*The Son of God became a son of man so that the sons of men might become sons of God.*" When you learn to unite, your will to the Will of God, to become, at every moment in every little thing your do, say, and think, for you my God, because now your will is so united with God's Will that you become so God like that you become a little god.

Because God wanted to share His beautiful creation and Himself with someone He created us. Like a painter want to share his creation with others. Selfishness is doing your own will. If you do this you lose God. This is why so few never see God, because they never learn to do God's Will. I have told you many times the definition of LOVE is to give up your will for the will of the other. Happiness in Marriage is based on this definition.

The **Great Miracle at Garabandal...**

The Great Miracle will occur on a great ecclesiastical event in the Church and the Feast of a Martyr of the Holy Eucharist.

- It will occur on a Thursday at 8:30 in the evening between the eighth and sixteenth of March, April or May. (We are thinking April.)
- It will coincide with a great ecclesiastical event in the Church.
- It will be on the feast day of a young martyr.
- It will last fifteen minutes.
- It will be seen in the sky.
- All those either in the village or on the surrounding mountains will see it.
- The sick who are present will be cured, sinners converted and the incredulous will believe.
- It will be the greatest miracle that Jesus has ever performed for the world.
- It will happen on an even number year, both Warning and Miracle. (I'm thinking 2018.) Warning to happen (3) mon. to (3) weeks before the Miracle. (April 12, 2018 if this is the year.)

Watch for the Holy Father to go to Moscow. On his return to Rome the tribulation of bloodshed. Which will be, I don't think Russia, but the existing Muslims in Europe will create bloodshed for 30 days. Then Russia will come. By this time most all priests and nuns will be killed. The churches will be closed. Revolution will break out in Italy. And the Red Flag will be seen over St. Peter's Dome. The Holy Father will flee over the dead bodies of Cardinals. And he will make the Consecration of Russia to Mary's Heart. Russia may even enter as far as Garabandal. And many will die for the Faith. I hope I can be there.

After the Great Miracle...

- A **permanent**, visible supernatural **sign** will remain over the Pines until the end of time. It will be possible to televise, film and photograph this wonder but not touch it. It has been likened to a column of smoke or a ray of sunlight but is not either one. (My guest is the crucifix, chalice, and the two hearts encircled by the Rosary. We'll see. Soon.)

- As a result of the Miracle, Russia and other countries will be converted.
- On the day after the Miracle, the body of Father Luis Andreu (who saw the Miracle) will be removed from his grave and found incorrupt. (St. Padre Pio also saw the Miracle before he died.)
- After the Great Miracle people will be good, but they will soon turn bad again, Chastisement.

Is the Miracle greater than the Warning?: When one considers that the Warning will touch the entire population of the world, it doesn't seem that anything could be more all-encompassing. But Conchita has said that the Warning would "correct the conscience of the world and *prepare it for the great Miracle.*" Something that is in preparation for something else is normally subordinate to it.

So how is the Miracle greater than the Warning? It is greater in its *purpose.* While the Warning is meant to illumine and correct all consciences, it is not designed to convert the world. That is reserved for the Miracle. The 'Great Miracle' will be the greatest miracle ever work by Jesus Christ. The will see, the crippled will be cured, sinner and non-believers and non-catholics will be converted. But best of all will all people present in Garabandal see the Glory of God, which will take a special grace from God not to be killed from seeing the Glory of God. This is why all will be converted. And a permanent sign will be left over the nine pines, until the end of times. (Not sure what that means actually, end of times.) This will be the end of the fifth period of the church. And begin with the sixth period, time of peace.)

In Conchita's locution with Our Lord dated: July 20, 1963, she asked Him: "Why is the Miracle going to take place, to convert many people?" And He answered: "TO CONVERT THE WHOLE WORLD." (But they will be good for only a short time, then will come the Chastisement.) While the Miracle will only take place in one geographical location, the graces that will radiate out from there will cover the entire world.

On October 20, 1961, two days after the Message was read at the Pines and caused so much disappointment, Jacinta was heard to say in ecstasy: "**No one believes us anymore**, do you know?... So you can perform a very great miracle in order that many will believe again." **The Virgin smiled and responded: "They will believe."**

From this point on, Conchita would have only four more apparitions: one more in 1963, none in 1964 and three in 1965 with the last one being on November 13, 1965. However, beginning in March, 1963, she began having locutions, and significantly enough, her first locution had to do with the Miracle.

When the other three visionaries stopped having visions, they immediately began to doubt their experiences, as Our Lady said they would, and **Conchita** also seems to have been smitten as she explains in **her diary:**

"I also doubted whether the miracle would take place. And one day when I was in my room doubting if the miracle would occur, I heard a voice that said: **"Conchita, do not doubt that my Son will perform a miracle!"**

I heard it interiorly, as clearly as if through my ears and even better than if it had been through words. It left me with a peace and a joy even greater than that experienced when I saw her.

On August 2, 1964, Conchita wrote a letter to Father Ramón Andreu which included this startling revelation: "On July 18, [1964] the feast day of San Sebastian de Garabandal, I had a locution, and in this locution, I was told that on the day after the Miracle your brother [Father Luis Andreu] will be taken out of his tomb and his body will be found incorrupt."

One thing Our Lady said about the people of our times, very very few will ever see God. When the Miracle comes people will be good for a short time, then will come the Chastisement, because they will go back to their immodesty and sins of wasting time with the pleasures of this earth. Read the message of Garabandal June 18, 1965 & October 18, 1961 below:

Garabandal Message

Between 1961-1965 Our Lady is said to have appeared as Our
Lady of Mount Carmel to four girls, Mary Loly, Conchita,
Jacinta and Mary Cruz, in the tiny village of San Sebastian
de Garabandal in northern Spain. The apparitions have been
approved by the local bishop, but Rome will wait for the Warning
and Miracle. The girls would receive (3) interiors, which can
signify the call of the (3) Persons in the Blessed Trinity and the
loving call they have for us to come running to Them. By the
3rd call they would be running to see their Heavenly Mother.
Four main messages were given, the first and the fourth being the
most important. The first message was given on October 18th 1961:
We must make many sacrifices, perform much penance,
and visit the Blessed Sacrament frequently. But first,
we must lead good lives. If we do not, a chastisement
will befall us. The cup is already filling up, if we do not
change, a very great chastisement will come upon us.

The fourth message was given on June 18th 1965. Since it pained
Our Lady so much it was given instead by St Michael the Archangel:
As my message of October 18th has not been complied with and has
not been made known to the world, I am advising you that this is
the last one. Before, the cup was filling up. Now it is flowing over.
Many cardinals, many bishops, and many priests are on the road
to perdition and are taking many souls with them. Less and less
importance is being given to the Eucharist. You should turn the
wrath of God away from yourselves by your efforts. If you ask His
forgiveness with sincere hearts, He will pardon you. I, your mother,
through the intercession of Saint Michael the archangel, ask you
to amend your lives. You are now receiving the last warnings. I
love you very much and do not want your condemnation. Pray
to us with sincerity and we will grant your requests. You should
make more sacrifices. Think about the passion of Jesus.

http://www.ourlady.ca/info/greatMiracle.htm

For more information on Our Lady's Apparitions at Garabandal go to: www.garabandal.org http://www.garabandal.us/home.html youtube: Thomas Fahy Garabandal)

One final reason why we should not doubt the Miracle is that *we need it*. In Conchita's diary is this entry:

"The Blessed Virgin advised me of a great miracle that God, Our Lord, will perform through Her intercession. Just as the chastisement will be very, very great, in keeping with what we deserve, so too, the miracle will be extremely great, in keeping with the needs of the world."

BEGINNING IN JUNE 18, 1961, the Blessed Mother appeared for over four years to four young girls in a small village of 300 people in the Cantabrian Mountains of Northwest Spain called Garabandal.

Below are some interesting facts known about the **Miracle**: It will take place on or between the eighth and sixteenth of March, **April** or May on a Thursday at 8:30 p.m.; it will be within a year of the **Warning**, and Conchita, one of the seers, will be able to announce the date eight days before it occurs; it will take place on the feast day of a martyr of the Eucharist (who is not a Spaniard, and bears a name that is rare to the Spanish; it will coincide with a great event of the Church; and the local Bishop will get a personal sign before the event and lift the ban on priests going up to the village.

Conchita speaks of the Miracle in Garabandal magazine: "It will be visible to all those who are in the village and surrounding mountains; that the sick who are present will be cured and the incredulous will believe. It will be the greatest miracle that Jesus will have performed for the world. There won't be the slightest doubt that it comes from God and that it is for the good of mankind. A sign of the Miracle, which it will be possible to film or televised, will remain forever."

No one knows what this permanent sign will be, but it will definitely be Catholic. I'll give you my best guess, it will be that which the girls carried from house to house, and that which we are to hold and have in front of us during the Three Days of Darkness. Yes, the crucifix and chalice encircled by the Rosary. Whosoever look upon the crucifix and prays the Rosary will not die. Just like the those Jews (Israelites) who looked upon the staff of Aaron did not die from the snake bits (the devil who goes around swallowing up souls.).

This Great Miracle will be the greatest miracle ever worked by Christ since the Resurrection of Christ. And there will be One God, One Baptism, and One Faith, outside of this Church there will be no salvation. Because man is so easily enticed by the flesh, Satan made Mohamed start a religion offering men (7) virgins in eternity. But most of what they adhere to is against the (10) commandments.

Jesus Christ was sent by His Father to establish One Holy Catholic Church, there is other church. At this point it seems good to speak about a few of the notable persons who have confirmed their belief in Garabandal.

1. **St. Padre Pio** saw the Great Miracle in advance, possibly in August of 1968. Joachim Bouflet, PH. D.(Univ.of Paris, 1972) tells a story about going to Confession to St. Padre Pio in July of 1968. Padre Pio told him: "Consecrate yourself to the Virgin of Carmel who appeared at Garabandal." When Mr. Bouflet responded, "So it's true?" P. Pio replied, "Certo e vero!" (Certainly it is true!)
2. **St. Maria Maravillas.** She warned Bishop Puchol Montis in advance about a sudden death, which did happen as a result of an automobile accident on May 8, 1967.
3. **Bishop Venancio of Leira**, Portugal. He is the Bishop who turned over the famous Secret of Fatima to the papal legate in 1960. Bishop Venancio said with good reason that Garabandal was the continuation of Fatima. When our Lady appeared for the last time at Fatima, She came with St. Joseph and the Baby Jesus, and She was dressed as Our Lady of Mt.

Carmel. *As She was giving her farewell to the three children of Fatima, Our Lady said, "Good-bye until San Sebastian, Spain."*

When Our Lady appeared for the first time at San Sebastian de Garabandal, Spain on July 2, 1962, She was dressed as Our Lady of Mt. Carmel and held the Baby Jesus in her arms. [That account of the last apparition of Fatima was published in a book by the Carmelites in 1937, but is no longer in print. I heard about it from a Priest in 1974 and again, from another source, in 2006.]

4. **Fr. Luis Andreu, S.J.,** who saw the Great Miracle in advance at 8:30 PM on August 8, 1961. He said that this was the happiest day of his life, that we should never fear the supernatural, that we should imitate the attitude of the little girls of Garabandal towards their Heavenly Mother, and then died in a state of quiet joy a little later, in the early hours of August 9, 1961.

5. **Blessed Mother Theresa of Calcutta.** She became a close friend of Conchita. Worked for spread of the message of Garabandal.

6. **The Servant of God Mother Esperanza,** nun, stigmatist founder of the Order of Merciful Love believed in the message of Garabandal. And spoke of it publicly.

7. Pope Paul VI. **Conchita** was invited to the Vatican in 1966 by **Cardinal Ottaviani**. Conchita was to have an appointment with Pope Paul VI after she got to Rome, but some Official kept interfering. But the Pope at an indoor General Audience, made a point of stopping when he passed Conchita and blessed her, saying: "I bless you and with me the whole Church blesses you." [Note: There are other versions of this encounter with Pope Paul VI, but it is certain that he blessed her and said what he said in his blessing just quoted."]

8. There are several signs of **Pope John Paul II's** belief in Garabandal, but one that is significant is that in the year 2000, after reading the German book on Garabandal mentioned above, the Holy Father, asked his secretary, Mons. Dziwisz (now Cardinal Dziwisz) to write to the author as follows: "May God reward you for everything, especially for the deep love with which you are making the events connected with Garabandal more widely known. May the Message of the Mother of God find an entrance

into hearts before it is too late. As an expression of joy and gratitude, the Holy Father gives you his apostolic blessing." Then, below Mons. Dziwisz signature, Pope John Paul II wrote a personal note in his own handwriting and signed it. [The author showed me and others a copy of that letter.]

9. **Pope Benedict XVI.** I can only say that I spoke to a Priest who lives in the Vatican. He told me that this Pope believes in Garabandal. I think, for some reason, all of them believed in Garabandal. Perhaps something to do with reading the 3rd secret.

10. **Fr. Malachi Martin** speaks of the Warning and Miracle of Garabandal.

11. **Fr. Adam Skwarczynski** a mystic whom Our Lord has been shown the future of these events. A Few More Interesting Points:

One day during the apparitions, Mary Loli asked Our Lady about how the human race was formed. Our Lady answered, that *man did not descend from a monkey, or by evolution, or by any animal but as perfect man, Adam was created by Almighty God.* Our Lady also said that man had been created on earth just as he is today. [Note: Our Lady obviously was referring here to our human nature and not to the state of our souls. In other words, we have **not** slowly evolved from so called "cave men or ape."] Only atheists and some scientists have, or so they think. Four candles in Advent signify the 4000 years from the time of Adam. Of course, if you want believe the world is billions and billions of years old, you're not catholic. The Bible proves it by looking at the generations from the time of Adam.

Our Lord told Luisa Piccarreta how He created man, by form a beautiful statue in clay of Adam and then breathed into him. So there was no monkey business involved.

Our Lady predicted the Confusion that would come after Vatican Council II. No doubt as result of the Council. Remember the Second Formal Message at Garabandal–June 18, 1965.

The Great Miracle that God will perform at Garabandal at 8:30 PM on a Thursday in the Spring of some future year will be the **greatest public miracle** since the creation of the world. During the Miracle we will see the Glory of God but won't die from seeing this due to a special preventative grace. The sick will be cured, and unbelievers will believe. There was a lady, now deceased, who worked with Fr. Laffineur investigating the events of Garabandal from the start. The two recorded thousands of testimonies and documentation, including a dialogue between Conchita and Our Lady, which was tape-recorded with Our Lady's voice audible on the tape. This same lady told me and others that during the Great Miracle, people will have a sensible experience of the Indwelling Trinity. [Apparently one would have to be in the state of grace.] She also said that Priests who are there would not only have that experience but would also have a sensible experience of the active presence of Our Lord as during the Consecration at Mass.

At the time of the Great Miracle the Spanish Military will generously support the sick coming to Garabandal and nothing negative will happen to them.

There will be a very happy event in the Church on the very same day of the Miracle but not associated directly with it. In the future the various religions will unite. Divisions will cease, etc. She even said that one day, everyone will be Catholic!

When Russia over runs Europe, the warning will take place soon after. Russian soldiers will come to Garabandal some will be killed for their faith. The Warning and Miracle will make it safe. Russian soldiers will be converted at this time. I know I've repeated myself several times, but I want you to remember. Maybe I shouldn't bring this up, but Our Lady was asked by one of the girls, "Is there other beings beyond the stars. And She said, yes, but that does not concern you."

"When men indulge in sensuous pleasures and voluptuousness, when no one wishes to obey any more, when there is widespread discontent among the people of the earth, then **Russia** will pour out her masses of **soldiers**, and they will reach the Rhine." *Prophecy of Jasper in the book 'Catholic Prophecy* "I also saw the various regions of the earth. My Guide (Jesus) named Europe, and pointing to a small and sandy region, He uttered these remarkable words:'Here is Prussia, the enemy.' Then He showed me another place, to the north, and He said: 'This is Moskva, the land of Moscow, bringing many evils." ***Bl. Anne Catherine Emmerich (1774-1824)*** Our Lady of Fatima said to Lucia: "The war (WW I) is going to end very soon, but if the people do not cease offending God, a worse war will break out during the Pontificate of Pius XI." Our Lady told Lucia the reason for these wars was because of sin mainly using **God's name in vain and working on Sunday.** 2nd & 3rd Command.

"I shall come to ask for the consecration of Russia to My Immaculate Heart if My requests are heeded, Russia will be converted, and there will be peace, if not she will spread her errors throughout the world **causing wars .....** various nations will be annihilated." *Warning and Miracle should change them, of course being atheistic means they don't believe in God. Therefore what is a Warning and Miracle to them. Some of them will not see the Miracle. After the Warning and Miracle the Holy Father should have Consecrated Russia to the Immaculate Heart of Mary. But it will be late and Rome will already be sacked. One thing about Garabandal is that some things have been missinturbeted, like the Our Lady never said the Vatican II council would be a success she did say that some things would be rotten and would fall and not continued. Still waiting for that.*

Venerable Marthe Robin (1902-1981) -French Mystic, Stigmatic, Victim Soul and Foundress of the Foyer de Charite

Source for this information is from the excellent book *"Marthe Robin-The Cross and the Joy"* by Rev Raymond Peyret, 1983, Alba House Publishers –Society of St Paul.

The sixth child of a family of simple farmers of the Drome (France), Marthe, Servant of God (1991), was twenty-three years old when she wrote, in her own handwriting, her complete Consecration as a "victim of Love" . . . Today, her name, like those of Blessed Padre Pio and Blessed Madre Maravillas, shine in the firmament of the Church of God.

Paralyzed since the age of twenty-seven, and also stigmatized, Marthe Robin would spend some fifty years of her life without sleep or food, nourishing herself uniquely with the Eucharistic Bread.

When Fr. Laffineur, O.P. died in November 1970, he had left behind him his plan for the diffusion of the Message of Garabandal in a difficult situation. His close collaborator Fr. Combe decided to ask Marthe, whom he knew well, for her advice. The famous woman mystic welcomed him in the first months of 1971, in her house of La Plaine . . . Here is the account of her meeting as reported by Fr. Combe himself:

Fr. Combe: "Dear Sister Marthe, as you know, I care about Garabandal . . ." Marthe: "Yes, Father . . ."

Fr. Combe: "I was helping Fr. Laffineur . . . He died last November. And all that has followed . . ." Marthe: "Yes, the critics . . ."

Fr. Combe: "I see that you know. So I come to ask for your advice. I have already enough work in this ministry, my parish of Chazay d'Azergues."

Marthe: (in a firm and almost cutting voice): "That's it, Father . . . You want to let everything go! . . ." Fr. Combe: (I received the blow right through the heart and waited for the rest . . .)

Marthe: "Aye! What must we do, Father, when we have received graces?"

Fr. Combe: "I understand, Sister Marthe . . . I must then take up again the spreading of the Message of Garabandal? But, by doing so, I will receive blows from all sides, from the 'critics,' from the priests, the vicar-generals, and even blows from the shepherd's crook of Bishops . . ."

Marthe: "Ah well! You will offer them to God. There, Father, give me some news of the "children" of Garabandal . . ."

This I did. Marthe listened, sometimes asking for details . . . Finally: Marthe: "Tell the four girls that I pray for them every day!"

The limited time allotted to me for our interview was drawing to an end. Then Marthe asked me: "Would you like us to say an Our Father and a Hail Mary together?" - "Yes, Marthe. For the girls of Garabandal and their Bishop, for yourself and for the Houses of Charity and also for the blows dealt to us with a stick! . . ."

After our prayer, I said: "Marthe, would you accept to have my Guardian Angel invite yours every day to take part in my Mass!" - "Oh! Yes, Father; they will pray together." And our conversation ended as usual with my blessing given with deep emotion.

Another of Marthe Robin's testimonies on Garabandal is the one she gave to Msgr. J. Bretault (Founder and first Bishop of the Diocese of Koudougou). One day, I took him to Chateauneuf-de-Galaure, which he liked so much. Before dropping him off, I asked him to remember me to Marthe and to ask her for a little word for me. The little word was a long report he wrote out immediately with tears of joy before the Blessed Sacrament . . . Msgr. J. Bretault had been overwhelmed by all the information Marthe knew about the difficulties in spreading the news about Garabandal in France after the death of Fr. Laffineur. She asked him to transmit a few details and some advice . . . that were very useful and effective for me."

[From 'Garabandal' Book, pages 228-229]

"There shall be great confusion of people against people, and nations against nations, with clashing of arms and beating of drums. The Russians and Prussians shall come to Italy. Many bishops shall fall from the Faith, but many will remain steadfast and suffer much for the Church. Priests and religious shall be butchered. The earth, especially in Italy, shall be soaked in their blood. **(Sister Rosa Asdenti Di Taggia 1847)** (Russians have been building up their military for the past many years. And they boast of it.)

"Terrible war will rage all over Europe. God has long been patient with the corruption of morals; over half of mankind He will destroy. Russia will witness many outrages. Great cities and small towns alike will be destroyed in a bloody revolution that will cause the death of half the population. In Istanbul (Constantinople) the Cross will replace the half-moon of Islam, and Jerusalem will be the seat of a King. The southern Slavs will form a great Catholic Empire and drive out of Europe the Turks (Muslims), who will withdraw to North Africa and subsequently embrace the Catholic Faith." **(Br. Louis Rocco 1800)**

"Russia will help Germany and France drive out the Turks from Europe and will take back Constantinople. Germany and France will suffer great loses. Than England will be visited by war." **(Brother Anthony of Aachen 1800's) Youtube: Fatima and the Sacrament of Confession - Father Isaac Relyea**

Prophecy of Sister Elena Aiello: The Madonna speaks: "The hour of the justice of God is close, and will be terrible!"

"Tremendous scourges are impending over the world, and various nations are struck by epidemics, famines, great earthquakes, terrific hurricanes, with overflowing rivers and seas, which bring ruin and death."

"If people do not recognize in these scourges (of nature) the warnings of Divine Mercy, and do not return to God with truly Christian living, ANOTHER TERRIBLE WAR WILL COME FROM THE EAST TO THE WEST. RUSSIA WITH HER SECRET ARMIES WILL BATTLE <u>AMERICA</u>; WILL OVERRUN EUROPE. The river Rhine will be overflowing with corpses and blood. Italy, also, will be harassed by a great revolution, and the Pope will suffer terribly." (see St. John Bosco below pg 37)

Russia controls all communistic countries. They will enter **America** through Alaska. China will enter from Mexico.

How many countries are under communist rule and are ready to take orders from Russia: Cuba, China, Venezuela, Bolivia, Ecuador, Argentina, North Korea, Vietnam, to name a few most of the flags use the freemason (5) pointed star.

"Spread the devotion to my Immaculate Heart, in order that many souls may be conquered by my love, and that many sinners may return to my

Maternal Heart. Do not fear, for I will accompany with my maternal protection for my faithful ones, and **all those who accept my urgent warnings**, and they - especially by the recitation of my **Rosary** - will be saved." *(Is this getting through to you kids? Well, keep reading.)*

"Flagstaffs (flying the Red flag over St. Peter's dome and elsewhere) These atheists are ever shouting: we want Satan to be our master!" Our Lady: "My daughter, Rome will not be saved, because the Italian rulers have forsaken the Divine Light and because only a few people really love the Church. The times are grievous. The whole world is in turmoil, because IT HAS BECOME WORSE THAN AT THE TIME OF THE DELUGE!"

"Satan goes furiously through this disordered world, and soon will show all his might. But, because of my Immaculate Heart, the triumph of Light will not delay in its triumph over the power of darkness, and the world, finally, will have tranquility and peace." Good Friday ---1961

The Sorrowful Madonna speaks:

"People pay no attention to my **Motherly Warnings**, and thus the world is falling headlong into an abyss of iniquity. Nations shall be convulsed by terrible disasters, causing destruction and death.

"**Russia**, spurred on by **Satan**, will seek to dominate over the **whole world** and, by **bloody revolutions**, will propagate her false teachings throughout all the nations, especially in Italy. The Church will be persecuted and the Pope and the priests shall suffer much."

Sister Elena Aiello (stigmatist) 1961 speaks:

"Oh, what a horrible vision I see! A great revolution is going on in Rome! They are entering the Vatican. The Pope is all alone; he is praying. They are holding the Pope. They take him by force. They knock him down on the floor. They are tying him. Oh God! Oh God! They are kicking him. What a horrible scene!"

"**Our Blessed Mother** is drawing near. Like corpses those evil men fall down to the floor. Our Lady helps the Pope to his feet and, taking him by the arm, she covers him with her mantle saying: "Fear not!"

"Flagstaffs (flying the Red Flag over St. Peter's dome and elsewhere) collapse, and power is gone out of the clubs of those evil brutes. These **atheists** are ever shouting: 'We don't want God to rule over us; we want Satan to be our master!" *(Sounds just like Freemasons shouts, when fighting the Cristaleros of Mexico 1925 to 1930.) Read it.*

Our Blessed Mother speaks again: "My daughter, **Rome will not be saved**, because the Italian rulers have forsaken the Divine Light and because only a **few people** really love the Church. But the day is not far off when all the wicked shall perish, under the tremendous blows of Divine Justice."

Blessed Elena was told by Our Lady that **America** would be spared the concentration camps because of its material generosity to less fortunate countries; however, only one area of the country would remain free from Military take over. Our Lady specified to her that it would be **the area that had the greatest devotion to the Most Holy Rosary.** *(I hope you're praying your nightly 7:30 family Rosary and afterwards night prayers.)*

Prophecy of Sister Elena Aiello

If you loose your Faith, you will not know you've lost it, God does not give it back. More precious than any gifts. Have you any idea what it is like to live in this wonderland where nothing grows old eternal bliss.

All other religions, Atheism, Protestantism, and Judaism will cease to be, Russia and the Jews, and the Muslims will be converted. Is Fr. Malichi Martin right about all this happening or start happening by 2020? Catholic prophecy says the end of the world will come before the year 2100.

Read the Books: AA-1025 by Marie Carre, the Communist Infiltration into the Church. Marie is a nurse and is assigned to the care of this catholic priest. He soon dies and she finds his briefcase with orders and information from the Kremlin (Stalin) to infiltration the Church and destroy it from within. (Results, we have another new protestant church, but this one is called catholic. Satan you have really outdone yourself this time. Before you just killed us, now we can live in error with a slow death and then go to Hell. Over 700 protestant churches are in the world today. Satan knows outside the Catholic Church there is no Salvation. He just tries to keep us from believing it.)

School of Darkness by Bella V. Dodd Communist Convert into the Catholic Church. She tells of the one thousand Communists she alone brought into the Church to undermine it. **(She tells Stalin's Kremlin Plan)**

The Rite of Sodomy by Randy Engel The infiltration of the Homosexuals to undermine the Church. According Fathers of the Church there is no worse sin than the sin against nature, than sodomy. This great sin against God and nature caused the great flood and Noah to build the ark. And the destruction of Sodom and Gomorrah. Today the whole world will be punished with a great comet bigger than the earth, which will cause the 3 days of darkness.

Pawns in the Game by William Guy Carr (1895-1959) on the evil conspiracy of masonic ultimate goal of total world domination through a dictatorial One World Government. (Albert Pike Luciferian Doctrine)

PAUL VI beatified? by Father Luigi Villa This is the priest assigned by Pope Pius XII to find out how many Masons were in the Vatican. He spoke with St. Padre Pio Twice about the masons.

Any of the (17) books by Fr. Malachi Martin. When I heard of Fr. Martin, he had (5) books of which I read (3).

Communism and Freemasonry are twin sisters and both hate the Church and will do whatever it takes to destroy it and society with its cultural background.

An absolute must read is the book Luisa Piccarreta a Servant of God. To her is given God's revelations as deeply and as precise as to St. Mary of Agreda or St. Catherine Emmerich or St. Bridget of Sweden, or St. Elizabeth of Shodan.

Our Lady has tried in these later times to prepare us for the Coming Chastisement. She appeared to many souls weeping. Most of them just common ordinary people. All the time saying the same thing: "Turn the wrath of God away from yourselves." It must be very very serious and frightful to make Our Lady come so many times to so many people and tell us look out, it coming. Are you not going to do anything to divert it? And to top it all off, She has gone as far as to ask God for a Warning, and Miracle to help us wake up. What a kind and Great Mother we have in Heaven. **The closer to the Chastisement we get the more often She appears to warn us.** But we are to worldly with our work, pleasures, and entertainment. We're too busy with our playing to be bothered with the end of our life and the world...? where are you going up or down? **Shucks**, I didn't see that coming, Somebody should've told me about, prayer, penance, sacrifice, Rosary, scapular ...etc. Nobody's ready. Mary came 1000 of times, bleeding statues, warning after WARNING, ... **Where were you? Picture yourself falling into Hell naked with all the others who have just died, did not take time for prayer or God. Forever to burn in the fires of Hell. Not to ever get out in a year or so.**

The Tears of Our Lady have been falling from all parts of the world and have seen this spectacular phonimum. Whenever a great catastrophe is about to happen in the world, tears would flow from statues as a warning from a statue of Mary or Jesus.

Such a noted time was the European invasion by the Moors, the French Revolution, the Blascovich Revolution in Russia, and the atheistic spread of Communism and the taking over of certain countries.

Since the 60's & the 70's these weeping of tears have come in tremendous numbers more than in any other time of the history of the church. Wake up call & no body is waking up. I have mentioned it to you my own good Catholic relatives and you don't want to believe it. Chastisements are for our sins. These tears of Our Lady are of deep emotion and speak to us as a warning for all humanity.

In Cochabamba, Bolivia a bust statue of Our Lord crowned with thorns is weeping tears. They are clear. A reporter and skeptic shows up early in the morning to watch the statue. Suddenly the left eye wels up with a tear and he takes a small piece of cloth to test it, but the tear on the cloth turns to blood when touch to the cloth. A scientist took some of this same tears and they changed to blood. He had them tested in two different parts of the world *(not telling them where he got them)* they came back postive blood of a male 32 or 33 years old. This same statue was catscan. Science can not explain where the tears are coming from.

So innumerable are the number of statues crying in all parts of the world for people to stop sinning and pray the Rosary *(slowly)* that the Chastisement will come with out notice and we will have no time to get into the state of sanctifying grace. (Confession)

"I have seen the Chastisement. I can assure you that it is worse than being enveloped in fire, worse than having fire above and beneath you." · "I do not know how much time will pass between the Miracle and the Chastisement." (words of Conchita) **People must spend more free time in prayer, to appease and satisfy God. I remember reading that Our Lady said there will be ample time between the Miracle and the Chastisement. I'm thinking two to eight years. We'll see. The time between the Warning and the Miracle has more recently been said three months or (3)weeks. Watch for the Holy Father to go to Moscow first.**

Akita, Japan 1975 (I am just released from the Army, active duty in Germany.) Bishop Shojiro Ito of the Convent of the Eucharistic Handmaids, actually sees the weeping statue of Our Lady weep (101 times) in 1973. This bishop was very concerned of what to do. He traveled to Rome (4) times to see Cardinal Ratzinger. Cardinal Ratzinger told him that everything he has been told by the apparition is the same as in the 3rd secret. Bishop Shojiro made a public approval of the apparitions.

Our Lady appeared to Sister Agnes Sasagawa. From these apparitions Sister Agnes who was deaf received her hearing back. She received many visits from her guardian Angel. On June 28, 1973, a mysterious and painful cross shaped wound appeared on her left hand, and began to bleed. The Bishop said the wound was very beautiful in a most perfect shape cross shape and if you held her hand up you could see right through her hand. It often bled and was very painful. It let off a beautiful fragrance. Her guardian angel told her that Mother of God is suffering much greater pain than you are in your hand. "If men do not repent and better themselves the Father of Heaven will inflict a terrible punishment on all Humanity. It will be a punishment greater than the Deluge, such as one has never seen before. Fire will fall from the sky. The survivors will find it so desolate that they will envy the dead. The only weapon left for you to use will be the Rosary and the Crucifix of Her Son. Recite the Rosary every day."

The reason this will be worse than the deluge is because you will have no time to think and say an "Act of Contrition". There will be no time to find a priest and receive the 2ⁿᵈ of the seven sacraments (confession). No more time for repentance or to turn your life towards God, as is the reason for your existence, to know. Love, and serve God, to practice virtue and do much spiritual reading. And by keeping God on your mind at every moment, like St. Joseph and all the saints. Your cold lukewarm life will be over before you have a chance to run for cover, or to spend it with Jesus in the Tabernacle. Since the earliest times in the Church, God has communicated with His saints on the ending times. That a **Chastisement** would be necessary if the people did not repent. In the 3ʳᵈ Secret that **Fr. Malachi Martin** read, he tells that something will enter our atmosphere and all will be finished by 2020. I think it will be long after that, because much prophecy still must come to pass. For instance the Warning, the Miracle, the invasion of Russia over Europe, the Great Monarch and the conversion of the Jews, turks, and Russia. Fr. Malachi Martin also said that in the great war, the men will look up and see something coming in the sky. They will lay down their arms in horror and go home. Saints have prophesied that a comet will cause the (3) days of Darkness.

Fort Knox where many countries have kept their gold, Germany for instance, 1500 ton of gold have asked for their gold. The masonic government has told them they can't give it back at this time, please try again around 2020. Where did the gold go or what was it used for? In all leading nations are have been completed this year under ground cities. In America along there are 103 small cities built.

NASA watches the far outer regions of our universe for an incoming object. Remember I think the late 1990's Vatican Bank was emptied overnight (Freemasons). The Vatican has built a telescope with infra Red lens in Arizona and named it "Lucifer". Of course only the masons will use the devil's name, the true Church would not dare anger God by using satan's name. *(youtube: Nibiru Confirmed 2016 Bob Fletcher Underground Cities, Declassified Docs Reveal, Global Government)* No more money is being spent on the infrastructure in major cities.

Predestination is what the Rosary, scapular, daily Mass, weekly confession, daily spiritual reading, catholic instructions, prayers, speaking often of God in all things so it becomes common place to the ears of our **children**. The earlier these are imposed on the children, the easier they take it as a custom habit of being this way or practicing the faith, because they are still in formation from the very first year he or she is born. The child from the first moment of speech, the child should learn of God, the Blessed Virgin, the Guardian Angel. The less God is mentioned and taught in work, play, studying, the easier it is for the growing formation to take in the World, the Devil, and the Flesh. To round out the child in good manners, respect for family members and neighbors, wear of proper clothing. When to remove their hat on entering a house or building as is stated in books of catholic edification. *"The manner in which you dress, is the respect you give to that person you go to visit."* Sunday wear your best before God. I've seen men dress in <u>everyday casual clothing</u> and tennis shoes when going to Sunday Mass. Even the altar boys wear tennis shoes on the altar instead of dress shoes. A true sign they have little respect for God. I've seen men eat with their hats on, like heathens or pigs. Mothers and grandmothers should have taught these men at an early age good manners, **pride** is stronger than good manners. It is a endless and tireless job to raise your children with respect for God and neighbor, but it will be one thing you will be thanked for and rewarded in this world and the next. Use your spanking stick. Obedience! One thing Our Lord talked to St. Bridget about was proper dress and modesty and decency.

To each person She appears to She says, "**Make my messages known**

to all the people. Tell my priests to makes these message known and to shout it continually from the pulpit." Maybe after the Warning, things might change. I doubt it. So far nobody is paying any attention. No body's changing. These things will happen when women put on men's clothing and men dress like women, with earrings, necklaces, and tattoos. (Like African voodoo doctors used tattoos of a evil worship of Satan of long ago. Satan is happy to see it coming back all over the world. Men and women defile their bodies with markings which simple bring interior sin to the skin's surface.)

The devil foretold he would strip man of his dignity. As I said elsewhere, man will be seen in public wearing nothing more than his **underwear:** 'T' shirt and boxer underwear shorts, his baseball cap (Phrygian liberty cap can't forget that) and his shower shoes, which were made for military man to wear from his room to the latrine for showering. People who dress like this, God should transferred them back into the early 1900's, so they can see just how immodest they are amongst the people of that time, and how ridiculous they look today walking down the street. Sheep follow sheep. They can't think. This goes to show how God gives grace where grace is deserved and where it's not deserved. Whatever happened to the button up shirts and blouses and dress pants and polished shoes on the smart dressed Catholic people? Now they just dress casual for their own comfort. Tennis shoes, and shirts hang out unbuttoned, arms uncovered. I never saw my father or grandfather with short sleeves. Women wear men's pants and short shorts and deep cut fronts, not up to the base of the neck. (*Wear your best for Christ when in Church. Don't be lazy and wear what you want just be comfortable. That show little respect for God.*)

Atheism or Evolution or Humanism: "The belief that there was nothing and nothing happened to nothing and then nothing magically exploded for no reason, creating everything and then a bunch of everything magically rearranged itself for no reason whatsoever into self-replicating bits which then turned into dinosaurs. And we get stupid scientist trying to tell us that the earth is a billions of years old." **Makes perfect Godless and mindless sense, doesn't it, if you're a mindless Godless atheist.**

Let us touch accouple of principle reason Darwin's Theory (Evolution) exists: In a book named "Masonic and Occult Symbols Illustrated" By Dr. Cathy Burns (a thick book) Pg 87 **IHEU** (International Humanist and Ethical Union) pamphlets says: "Creationism (meaning by God) is not scientific..." (when actually it is explained by science) and they continue "Evolution is the only presently known, strictly scientific, and not religiously explained…" when in fact **evolution** is not explained by science and never will be, there is no beginning to this one celled amoeba. It had to be created. Manly P. Hall 33rd degree mason boasts: "Man is a God in the making…."

Humanist Manifesto I written in 1933 plainly state that humanism is a religion. In 1973

Humanist Manifesto II was written and they put forth (13) reasons for in humanism being a religion. All lies from the father of lies. All these people are atheists. They do not believe in God at all, I think they made all this up so they could sleep in on Sundays. (The Sabbath for the Jews, is Saturday, but Jesus change the Sabbath for us to Sunday. The Sion Illuminati Jewish masons, which head all mansons from the time of Christ until to day and whom are in the Church today, have made many change to the Mass and even changed the holy day of Sunday to Saturday. In one piece of masonic literature I read, I remember the very mason who did this thing said that if he could, he would have put our Sunday on Friday, but that would be too obvious to these cattle. I can't remember his name.

About infiltrating the Roman Catholic Church: **Mrs./Dr. Bella V. Dodd told her friend, Mrs./Dr. Alice von Hildebrand,** theologian, says that:

"When she was an active party member, she had dealt with no fewer than four cardinals within the Vatican who were working for us, **[i.e. the Communist Party]**" **(Christian Order magazine, "The Church in Crisis", reprinted from The Latin Mass magazine).**

Mrs. /Dr. Bella V. Dodd made a public affidavit which was witnessed by a number of people, including Paul and Johnine Leininger.

In her public affidavit, among other things, Mrs. /Dr. Bella V. Dodd stated:

"In the late 1920's and 1930's, directives were sent from Moscow to all Communist Party organizations. In order to destroy the [Roman] Catholic Church from within, party members were to be planted in seminaries and within diocesan organizations... I, myself, put some 1,200 men in [Roman] Catholic seminaries".

In a lecture at Fordham University in 1950 Mrs./Dr. Bella V. Dodd stated:

"The idea was for these men to be Ordained and progress to positions of influence and authority as Monsignors and Bishops."

Mrs. /Dr. Alice von Hildebrand confirmed that Mrs./Dr. Bella V. Dodd had publicly stated the same things to which she attested in her public affidavit.

Mrs. Johnine Leininger confirmed that other people could also verify that Mrs. /Dr. Bella V. Dodd had made these statements regarding the infiltration of Communists into Roman Catholic seminaries.

Also in her lecture at Fordham University in 1950, a dozen years before Synod Vatican 2, Mrs. /Dr. **Bella V. Dodd, speaking as a former high ranking official of the American Communist Party said:**

"Right now they [the Communist infiltrators] are in the highest places in the Church

where they are working to bring about **CHANGE** in order to weaken the Church's effectiveness against Communism (not to mention what they did to the Mass). "

Mrs. /Dr. Bella V. Dodd also said that these CHANGES would be so drastic that:

"You will not recognize the Catholic Church."

Mrs. /Dr. Bella V. Dodd was no prophet. She merely told us what the anti-Catholic Infiltrators of the Church were planning to do. And guess what?! They have done it - ALL OF IT!

Mrs./Dr. Bella V. Dodd's Communist Infiltrators, along with all of the other tens of thousands of Communist Infiltrators, not to mention the other tens of thousands of other Infiltrators, e.g. Illuminati, Satanists, Freemasons, etc., whether they are those who either lost, or never actually had, the Catholic faith, would have been the teachers of this present generation of Communist, and other, Infiltrators - the tens of thousands today who say they are priests and bishops - but who are only Communist or other Infiltrators and not Catholics!

Instead, they are priests and bishops of an anti-Catholic church, which, using typical Communist deceptive practices, still call themselves Catholic, and who, in effect, are really conducting their very own **"School of Darkness"** by which to continue to victimize ignorant Catholics, turning these Catholics into nothing but pagans, or worse!! "School of Darkness" is a book written by Bella V. Dodd.

"The Venona Secrets - Exposing Soviet Espionage and America's Traitors", by Herbert Romerstein and Eric Breindel.

The subject matter concerns Soviet Communist espionage in the United States before, during, and after WWII. The source for this work was obtained from the official Communist Party archives in Moscow, Russia.

Among other things, these archives confirmed the existence of operation "Outstretched Hand" which included the infiltration of Communists into Roman Catholic Seminaries!

In addition, the official Communist Party archives in Moscow, Russia includes a document which divulges that members of the Communist Party had also infiltrated a number of important Roman Catholic organizations, including the Holy Name Society which used to be found in almost all Roman Catholic parishes in the U.S.!

Therefore, "**The Venona Secrets** - Exposing Soviet Espionage and America's Traitors", verifies the testimony Mrs./Dr. Bella V. Dodd gave to the U.S. Congress, as well as in her lectures, as well as her public affidavit, that:

"In the late 1920's and 1930's, directives were sent from Moscow to all Communist Party organizations. In order to destroy the [Roman] Catholic Church from within, party members were to be planted in seminaries and within diocesan organizations... I, myself, put some 1,200 men in [Roman] Catholic seminaries".

This is exactly what operation "Outstretched Hand" was about!

Other former Communists have also spoken of these directives from Moscow, although they may not have known that the actual name for this operation was called "Outstretched Hand"?

Former Communist, and celebrated Roman Catholic convert, **Douglas Arnold Hyde**, who revealed long ago that in the 1930's the Communist leadership issued a worldwide directive [i.e. Outstretched Hand] about infiltrating the Roman Catholic Church.

Outstretched Hand is found in this testimony of a former communist:

"This policy [i.e. Outstretched Hand] of infiltrating seminaries was successful beyond even our Communist expectations." (Manning R. Johnson's testimony in 1953 before the House Un-American Activities Committee regarding the Communist Agenda and the Catholic Church; emphasis added).

The testimony of these former Communists help to explain why:

Marie-Julie Jahenny speaks of a "horrible religion" which would replace the Roman Catholic Church.

Marie-Julie Jahenny saw "many, many bishops" embracing this "sacrilegious, infamous religion".

The "many, many bishops" she saw embracing this "sacrilegious, infamous religion" is the Satanic Vatican II church which was "birthed" by the Communist, Freemasonic, Modernist, Satanic Infiltrators at their Convention, called Synod Vatican II, including those "four cardinals within the Vatican who were working for" the Communist Party, not to mention those **"1,200 men"** that **Mrs./Dr. Bella V. Dodd** said she put in **"Roman Catholic seminaries"**.

The "many, many bishops" Marie-Julie Jahenny saw embracing this "sacrilegious, infamous religion" were the "three thousand good-for-nothings" who took part in the "sinister farce" known as Synod Vatican II (Bishop Antonio Romeo of the Sacred Congregation of Rites in Bob Considine's column On the Line in the NEW YORK JOURNAL AMERICAN of Friday, November 27, 1964).

In 2005, **Rev. Mieczyslaw Malinski**, (a close associate of John Paul II as being a Communist Infiltrator!]), was also discovered to have worked for Poland's Communist security police in the 1980's, along with several other Communist priests.

Just by looking at him in person, how many Catholics would know that this archbishop was a **Communist Infiltrator/Spy** who cooperated with the Communist secret services during the Communist era in Poland, or that even when he was a Seminarian, he spied on some classmates and gave this information to Communist authorities?

In January of 2007, it was announced by the Polish Roman Catholic Episcopate that it would disclose documents connecting priests and bishops with Poland's Communist regime.

One of those to be investigated was **archbishop Stanislaw Wielgus**, who admitted his connections with the Communist security police after twenty years of spying on fellow clerics and nonconformists, i.e. anti-Communists.

Members of the House Un-American Activities Committee - 1948

Rep. Richard B. Vail [R. Illinois]

Rep. John Parnell Thomas, a.k.a. John Parnell Feeney, Jr. [R. New Jersey]

Rep. John Ralph McDowell [R. Pennsylvania]

Robert E Stripling, Chief Counsel (Author of The Red Plot Against America)

Rep. Richard Nixon [R. California; future U.S. President]

Manning R. Johnson was the Communist candidate for U.S. Representative from New York 22nd District, 1935:

After leaving the Party, he testified in 1953 before the House un-American Activities Committee regarding the Communist Agenda and the Catholic Church:

"Once the tactic of infiltration of religious organizations was set by the **Kremlin** ... the Communists discovered that the destruction of religion could proceed much **faster** through **infiltration** of the (Catholic) Church by Communists operating within the Church itself. The Communist leadership in the United States realized that the infiltration tactic in this country would have to adapt itself to American conditions (Europe also had its cells) and the religious make-up peculiar to this country.

In the earliest stages it was determined that with only small forces available to them, it would be necessary to concentrate Communist agents in the seminaries. The practical conclusion drawn by the Red leaders was that these institutions would make it possible for a small Communist minority to influence the ideology of future clergymen in the paths conducive to Communist purposes This policy of infiltrating seminaries was successful beyond even our Communist expectations."

Ex-Communist and celebrated Roman Catholic convert, Douglas Hyde, revealed long ago that in the 1930's the Communist leadership issued a worldwide directive about infiltrating the Roman Catholic Church. He wrote a very good book: **"I Believe"** after he was converted.

Destruction of God's Church, homosexuality, Communism, Freemasonism, Atheism, using God's name in vain, working on Sundays, abortion, worldly pleasure, lack of morality, immodest fashions will all lead to the world destruction of ¾ the population in next few years. The War with Russia and the Comet will be God's correction as He did at Sodom and Gomorra, and at the time of Noah's Ark.

The great traditionalist theologians considered Pope Paul VI a heretic before he was even elected pope, because he wanted to change the Church before he was elected pope, and did so after he was elected. As a young priest he sided and helped the communist students in Roman and translated one of the worst books of the century entitled: "Integral Humanism" by Jocque Maricana. Which was to try to reconcile humanism with christianity, which is a folly, and can never happen, as we have read above.

A quick word on the Satanic Occult of the Masonic Order: They have hundreds of emblems, the upside down cross of Christ and the Circle meaning God and Eternity, is called the **'Peac e S ign '**. The hang loose hand sign which represents the goat or satan. The main sign is the five pointed star, signifying "The Cult of Humanity" is **1.)** Humanity without God: **2.)** Humanity that makes itself God: **3.)** Humanity against God. The "Dynamic" symbol of the Satanic aim of the "man-god". (All to do with God is to be turned upside down.

Chaos. Black is white and right is wrong, and wrong is right.) You get the picture? **Tabernacle moved to the side altar.**

It will take an act of God to rid the world of all masons, wrong doers, wrong thinkers, and all who are antichrist out of the Church. This will be the destruction Rome which so many saints have foretold.

I'll cover a couple **symbols:** the circle with an 'S' inside it starting at the top of the circle to the bottom of the circle. One side is white and one side is black. This is a religious symbol to the early Egyptians and Persian Creed. It is the worship of the phallus-kteis in Greece and Egypt, the lingam- yoni in India, the massebasher of Syria, the yoseki-inseki in Japan, **the yang-yin in China**, Lingam and yoni of the Hindus, the woden and friga of the Goths, and baal-peor of the Canaanites in the Bible. It represents night and day, good and evil, female (dark side) and male (light side). There is a lot more that I'm not going to go into. But let me tell you that 90% of all these symbols are of sexual, immoral, or satanic meaning all trying to take the beauty of the marriage act and turing it as far upside down as possible towards homosexuality. In the above symbol in the black side is a white dot, and on the white side is a black dot, this meaning according to the masons is for homosexuality which is most hateful to God, as is any sexual act outside the sacrament of Marriage.

These Jewish Masons have taken nearly all of the Jewish symbols of the Old Testament and given them their own meaning. Take for instance the two stars Hexagram (Greek) or also called sexagram (Latin) is a six pointed geometric star, was normally called Solomon's Star and Solomon's son David has also inherited the same star. This six pointed star has many meanings for the mansons, the witches, and the occult. This star has the compound of two <u>equilateral</u> <u>triangles</u>. This star is used by the hindus and by Eastern religions, by Jews, by Muslims, by Occultism, by Freemasonism, by Latter-day Saints, by Rastafarians, by Lutherans and is used in Heraldry and Theosophy. These two triangles according to Masonic arthur, R. H. MacKenzie represent OSIRIS (male), ISIS (female), producing the offspring HORUS also called son of Satan or Baal. It also represents Gays and Lesbians. It also represents the satanic number '666'.

How is this: first you count the outside and inside of one triangle = 6; now you count the outside and inside of the other triangle = 6; next you count the inside of the inter hexagram core of both triangles united = 6.

The other star is the five pointed star called the Pentagram. The use of this star is absolutely bad and satanic. In the Occult world the pentagram is considered a most potent means of conjuring spirits namely DEMONS and as an aid in the casting of spells. Laurie Cabot, a WITCH, explains: "It really isn't that difficult to distinguish the Craft from Satanism. Witches wear the pentacle with the point up. SATANISTS REVERSE IT WITH THE POINT DOWN….." The same is true with a single equilateral triangle.

Before Satan developed his two twin children: Communism and Freeasonism, his hatred for God and all who loved God, killed off eleven million Catholics in the first 300 years of Christ Church.

Then came the Protestant Revolution mid 1500's where Satan picked on men to separate catholics from the Catholic Church, and thus making them heretics. Now outside the Catholic Church you have over 700 different denominations all claiming to be the way to Heaven. But they are outside the One True Church Christ Himself started. And the dogma of the Church still to this day affirms that "OUTSIDE THE CATHOLIC CHURCH THERE IS NO SALVATION." This is Christ's Church.

Then came the French Revolution, many thousands were martyred for their fidelity to Christ's true Church. This Revolution came to full blossomed in 1962's Vatican II's Revolution within the Church. It has completely changed the Church of Tradition for 2000 years into a "new order ecumenicalism church" which combines all the heretical churches beliefs into one. Now you have covered up the One True Church so you can not find it. Just like Our Lady said.

We must bring up the most interesting stories of the Masonic-inspired Mexican Revolution. Fr. Fahey was writing *Secret Societies and the Kingship of Christ* in 1927, while the Calles government was striving to wipe out the Catholic Church and her influence from Mexico. He recorded the important role of Freemasonry in generating this Revolution, citing original documents from Masonic journals. (47) Popes have condemned Freemasonry with excommunication.

At the 1906 General Convention of Latin-American Lodges, held in **Buenos Aires**, (Pope Francis' home) it was resolved, among other things, that religious persecution should be initiated and carried out zealously by every possible means. The following Articles, taken from the minutes of the Convention in question, embody the program of action:

"Art. 5. Latin-American Masonry shall oppose by every possible means clerical propaganda as well as the establishment and development of religious communities. It shall, in addition, do all in its power to get these communities banished from the different countries under its jurisdiction. Accordingly, Masons shall not send their children to be educated in Catholic educational establishments, and shall use their influence over their wives and children to keep them from going to confession;

"Art. 6. Masons shall try to stir up the zeal of the members of the different political parties for Masonic ideals: the separation of Church and State, the expulsion of religious communities; civil marriage and divorce, purely secular education, the exclusion of religious from hospitals, the suppression of military chaplains."

"Art. 10. Masonry shall strive to get the representative at the Vatican withdrawn, thus showing that the Papacy is no longer considered an International power."

As the final stage in the attack on the Kingship of Christ in Mexico was accelerated by the Masonic Convention of Buenos Aires in 1906, it may be of interest to note that an International Convention of delegates of the Ancient and Accepted Scottish Rite was announced for the same city in 1927. Representatives from the Supreme Councils of the following countries would be in attendance: England and Wales, Ireland, Scotland, France, Belgium, Low Countries, Switzerland, Italy, Portugal, Slovakia, Poland, Serbia, Romania, Turkey, Greece, Egypt, United States, Canada, Mexico, Cuba, San Domingo, Panama, Brazil, Argentina, Peru, Chile, Ecuador, Colombia, Uruguay and Venezuela.

[Note: Ireland was the only country that broke diplomatic relations with Mexico in response to the atrocities committed by the Calles' government against Catholics.]

In the 1920s and 1930s, the infamous *Calles Persecution* occurred in Mexico. During this time, Freemasons tried to *bomb the image* of Our Lady of Guadalupe. The bomb did go off, but not even the glass was cracked, which was not bulletproof and very thin [supernatural protection]. A 5 foot brass cross on the altar was not as fortunate. The tremendous force of the blast caused the cross to be curved.

Testifying equally powerfully to the image's supernatural origins is its miraculous preservation in the face of numerous unfortunate circumstances and events throughout its centuries-old history. In 1791, while cleaning the image's silver frame, a worker accidentally spilled an entire bottle of nitric acid over the image. To his great surprise and enormous relief the acid did not leave the slightest trace. In the 1920s, during the bloody persecutions of the Church under President Plutarco Calles, thousands of priests were condemned to death merely for carrying out their priestly duties. The atheist Masonic regime closed down all the churches in Mexico except for the Basilica in Guadalupe. Nevertheless, the enemies of the Church devised a diabolic plan to destroy the image of Our Lady and kill most of the members of the hierarchy. On 14 November 1921 government agents hid a powerful time bomb in a flower vase under the miraculous image. The bomb exploded at 10:30 in the midst of a Pontifical Mass. The powerful explosion rocked the entire Basilica, destroying the floor, marble altar and stained glass windows. Miraculously no one was killed. A few people suffered minor wounds only. When the dust settled after the explosion, it turned out that the image had emerged untouched. A massive metal crucifix—bent out of shape—had shielded it from the force of the explosion.

Many Roman Catholic priests were martyred during the *Calles Persecution*, including Blessed Miguel

Pro. Over 30,000 Catholics were martyred. Masonic Mexican War was from 1925 to 1929.

In the book *Mexican Martyrs*, written by a Jesuit, there is the story that after one Mexican official executed a Catholic priest, he ate part of the Catholic priest for dinner. Such was the barbaric nature of the persecution of the Catholic Church by Freemasons in the 1920's and 1930's in Mexico.

From the <u>Marian Movement of Priests</u> that **Freemasonry** is the *black beast like a leopard* that is referenced in the book of Revelation:

Message from Our Lady to Father Stefan Gobbi:

"I am weeping because the Church is continuing along the road of division, of loss of the true faith, of apostasy and of errors which are being spread more and more without anyone offering opposition to them. Even now, that which I predicted at Fatima and that which I have revealed here in the third message confided to a little daughter of mine (i.e. Sister Lucia) is in the process of being accomplished. And so, even for the Church the moment of its great trial has come, because the man of iniquity will establish himself within it and the abomination of desolation will enter into the holy temple of God." (To the Priests, Our Lady's Beloved Sons, No. 362, September 15, 1987, p. 572.)

"The black beast like a leopard indicates <u>Freemasonry</u>; the beast with the two horns like a lamb indicates Freemasonry infiltrated into the interior of the Church, that is to say, ecclesiastical Masonry, which has spread especially among the members of the hierarchy. This Masonic infiltration, in the interior of the Church, was already foretold to you by me at Fatima, when I announced to you that Satan would enter in even to the summit of the Church. If the task of Masonry is to lead souls to perdition, bringing them to the worship of false divinities, the task of ecclesiastical Masonry on the other hand is that of destroying Christ and his Church, building a new idol, namely a false christ and a false church." (To the Priests, Our Lady's Beloved Sons, No. 406, June 13, 1989, p. 649)

A little old lady knowing the hungry of the Cristeros, who were fighting against the masonic government, brought a small basket of buns to feed the 50 soldiers. The Bishop Orozco y Jiménez showed up at that moment and asked the old lady why she was crying? She told them I brought just a few buns to eat, and look there is enough for everyone.

Bishop Orozco was walking at night down an ally to give Last Rites to a dying man, when a large black dog jumped in front of him and said, "He is mine." The Bishop tried to pass, but dog would let. The Bishop made the Sign of the Cross toward the dog. The dog howled to get away. And on passing the Bishop bit him in the back of the leg.

The Bishop after giving the Last Rites to the dying man was having something to eat. Noticing the pain in the back of his leg from the dog, he looked at it. It was not a dog bit but 3rd degree burns from the dog of Hell.

There are 100's of miracles by Our Lady during this Masonic Mexican War to help her faithful people, which had brought to the Church since appearing at Guadalupe to St. Juan Diego.

MEXICO CITY, Mexico, September 1 - Cardinal Juan Sandoval Iñiguez of Guadalajara, Mexico, announced the beatification of Anacleto Gonzalez Flores and eleven companions, all martyrs, who died defending the Cristeros uprising against the Masonic persecution of 1926-29.

He became a successful leader of the boycott launched by Catholics against the Masonic media and businesses. His example and teaching became a symbol for the Cristero uprising, which resulted in his imprisonment in April of 1927.

He was brutally tortured in an attempt to get him to disclose the location where Bishop Orozco y Jimenez were in hiding. His torturers hung him from the ceiling by his thumbs and used knives to slash his feet.

Unmoved by his heroic resistance, his captors began to slash his body with knives, subjecting him to innumerable and inexpressible tortures. As they began to torture the other companions with him, Anacleto shouted, "Do not mistreat these young men, if you want blood you can have mine!"

Anacleto was let down and struck on the shoulder, resulting in a complete fracture. Nevertheless, he continued to encourage his companions not to give up. He and his companions were sentenced to death for "supporting the rebels."

Upon hearing the sentence, Anacleto responded, "I will only say one thing, and that is that I have unselfishly worked to defend the cause of Jesus Christ and His Church. You shall kill me, but know that the cause will not die with me. Many will come after me willing to defend it unto martyrdom. I go, but with the confidence that from Heaven I will soon see the triumph of the faith of my country."

One of the young companions with him asked to make a confession before dying, but Anacleto told him, "No, brother. Now is not the time for confession but for asking for forgiveness and for forgiving! He who awaits you is Father and not judge. Your own blood will purify you."

Anacleto immediately began to recite the Act of Contrition and was joined by his companions. Upon concluding the prayer, his companions were executed by a firing squad. Still standing despite his pain, Anacleto said to the general in command at the execution, "General, I forgive you from the bottom of my heart. Very soon, we shall see one another before the divine court. The same judge who will judge me will judge you; at that time you find in me an intercessor before God."

As none of the soldiers had the courage to fire upon him, the general ordered a captain to stab Anacleto with a bayonet.

According to the testimonies of several soldiers who witnessed the martyrdom, after being stabbed Anacleto was able to utter, "For the second time may the Americas hear this cry: I die, but God does not. Long live Christ the King!"

The words "For the second time" were a reference to the same words uttered decades earlier by President Gabriel Garcia Moreno of Ecuador, who was murdered on the steps of the Cathedral of Quito by Masons who were furious that he had consecrated Ecuador to the Sacred Heart of Jesus.

Mexico's Tarcisius: José Sánchez del Río

In 1913, in the state of Michoacan, a boy was born to Macario and María Sánchez del Río. They called him José. Macario and Maria were cattle ranchers who loved Jesus Christ with all their hearts and who reared their four children, of whom José was the third, to do the same. José cultivated a strong devotion to the Blessed Virgin of Guadalupe and said his rosary each day with great care. He instructed the other young children of his town in the Catholic faith, and encouraged them to make holy hours before the Blessed Sacrament. José loved to play marbles with his companions, and he learned to ride and care for horses. When José was thirteen, his older brothers, Macario and Miguel, left home to join the Cristeros. José desired to join them, but his mother forbade it. For a year he begged her to let him go. "Mother," he said, "Will you deny me the chance to go to heaven, and so soon?"

At last his mother relented, and with tears in her eyes watched her youngest son ride off to join the crusade. The Cristero commander in José's town refused the boy's appeal to enlist, so he made his way some twenty or thirty miles to the next town, Cotija, where he presented himself to the Cristero commander, Prudencio Mendoza.

"What contribution can so small a boy make to our army?"

"I ride well. I know how to tend horses, clean weapons and spurs, and how to fry beans and tortillas." Mendoza was inspired by the boy's grit, so he made him the aide of the Cristero General Ruben Guizar Morfin. Impressed by José's service, Morfin promoted him to bugler. His job was to ride alongside the general in combat, carrying his battle standard and delivering the general's orders with his horn. The soldiers of José's regiment, inspired by his piety and fervor, nicknamed him Tarcisius after the Roman altar boy who died protecting the Blessed Sacrament from a pagan mob.

On February 6, 1928, the Cristero army was overwhelmed by the federal army in fierce and bloody combat outside of Cotija. General Morfin's horse was shot, and it looked as if he would soon be captured by the federal troops. José leapt off of his horse.

"General!" he shouted. "Take my mount and escape to safety. You are of far greater importance to the Cristero cause than I am."

Helping Morfin up into the saddle, José delivered a hard swat across the backside of the horse and sent it galloping away. He then took his rifle and bandolier and, taking cover behind a rock, began shooting the federal soldiers closing around him. At last the boy ran out of ammunition, and standing up shouted to the enemy, "I have not surrendered. I have only stopped shooting you because I am out of cartridges."

When the federal soldiers saw that they had been fired upon by a boy, they seized him in a fury. They put José in irons and dragged him off to the local church, which they had converted into a jail, a stable for their horses, and a coop for roosters they used in cockfights. These they had leashed to the church's monstrance. José scolded the soldiers for desecrating a holy place.

"Now we will see, *hombrecito,* how tough you are!" they sneered.

To test his resolve, they forced José to watch as they took another captured Cristero, tortured him, and hanged him from a telegraph pole. Instead of looking away, José encouraged the prisoner, telling him that they would soon meet up in heaven. For two days, José was locked in the sacristy of the church, during which time he wrote to his mother, telling her that he had no fear, that he had welcomed the will of God and looked forward to dying in the light of our Lord.

The captain of the guard offered José his freedom in exchange for information about the Cristeros, including the names of the people who were supplying them. José refused, so they pinned him down and cut the skin off the soles of his feet. At eleven at night, they marched José to the cemetery on the edge of town, all the while telling him that if he would deny Jesus Christ they would spare his life.

"Viva Cristo Rey!" shouted José, the rallying cry of the Cristeros. *"Viva Cristo Rey!"* over and over as he limped in his bloodied feet over the gravel and twigs. "Long Live Christ the King! Long Live the Virgin of Guadalupe!" At the graveyard, José was pushed into a shallow grave. Struggling to his feet he again shouted, *"Viva Cristo Rey!"* To avoid the sound of gunfire, the commander of the firing squad ordered his men to stab the boy with their bayonets. *"Viva Cristo Rey!"* Again the bayonet into his side. *"Viva Santa Maria de Guadalupe!"*

"Say 'Death to Christ the King' and save your life!" demanded the captain of the guard.

"*Viva Cristo Rey!*"

The captain lost all patience and drew his own pistol. The first bullet struck José in the head, knocking him to the ground. As blood pooled next to his face, José, in a final act of defiance against the enemies of Jesus Christ who had taken over his country, dipped his hand in his blood and with it drew a cross in the dirt, then touched his lips to the cross. Six more bullets at point-blank range sent the martyr into the arms of his Savior. Youtube: **"Freemason Converts to Catholicism and Exposes the Diabolic Cult of Freemasonry"**

See utube: <u>Bishop Williamson Conference St Paul MN Part 1</u> **and** <u>Archbishop Marcel Lefebvre: A</u> <u>Retrospective</u> **Talks of the seven periods of the Church and Chastisement at the end of the 5th period which we are at right now.**

Protestants say we Catholics live in a cocoon. Well, they're right. We Catholics who want to strive for perfection must hate the world, **for Our Lord said, "If you love the world you are my enemy."** So we Catholics have placed ourselves in caves, catacombs, islands, convents, and monasteries, and deserts to better contemplate God and Heaven avoid the world. And to keep the events of the world out of our minds. So what's wrong with that? He has saved his soul and gained Heaven. You do it your way. If there can be any other way.

But if you want to do it the right way, the catholic way, you better get rid of the TV.

> **Saint Catherine of Siena**, the great 14th century religious mystic, transmitted the words of Our Lord Jesus Christ about the **sin of homosexuality**, which contaminated some of the clergy in her time, the Renaissance. Referring to sacred ministers who committed this sin, He told her:
>
> They [**the homosexuals**] not only fail from resisting the weakness [of fallen human nature].... but they do even

worse when they commit the cursed sin against nature. Like the blind and stupid, having dimmed the light of their understanding, they do not recognize the disease and misery in which they find themselves. For this not only causes Me nausea, but is disgusting even to the devils themselves whom these depraved creatures have chosen as their lords.

For Me this sin against nature is so abominable that for it alone five cities were destroyed by virtue of the judgment of My Divine Justice, which could no longer bear their iniquity....

It is disgusting to the devils not because evil displeases them or because they find pleasure in good, but rather because their nature is angelic and flees upon seeing such a repulsive sin being committed. For while certainly it is the devil that first strikes the sinner with the poisoned arrow of concupiscence, nonetheless when a man actually carries out such a sinful act, **the devil goes away**. (St. Catherine of Siena, "El diálogo," en *Obras de Santa Catalina de Siena*, Madrid: BAC, 1991, p. 292).

Homosexuality is the reason God destroyed Sodom and Gomorrah and flooded the whole world. Now it is here again. God help us. This time ¾ of the world will be wiped out.

Now the Sixth and Ninth of those Commandments instruct human beings to make the proper use of the reproductive mechanism built into their bodies. This mechanism is not a toy, but a sacred instrument designed by God for the forming of human families here below to populate Heaven above, it is called the marriage act. Neither two men alone nor two women alone but only a man and a woman together can have children and form a family, and since the populating of Heaven is a sacred affair, then any breaking of those two Commandments rapidly becomes grave enough to deserve eternal damnation. "God is not mocked" – Galatians VI, 7. It is the lowest form of sin against nature.

Communism is where God is ignored and grace for true charity and understanding is lacking. There is chaos, fear, hatred, and war, and concentration camps. Lenin, Stalin, Hitler what more can one say.

Truth is everything. It divides the good from the bad. The God fearing from the godless. The faithful from the unfaithful and atheist and communist. Worse than forgetting the truth is forgetting that you have forgotten it. Never speak out against other men on any cause.

"Where there is no Love, there is no Truth." Truth is so well hidden today, and Lies so well established today, that unless one loves the truth with a Passion, one will never find it. Either you have men of truth and moral value whose have courage, or you have men of skepticism and moral decadency. Courage is lacking today. You do not realize that we are in the middle of surrounded evil presure. A pressure we impose upon ourselves by accepting all the fashionable evils around us. *(God gives us what we deserve.)* There is an inner spiritual struggle in most all people. Some want to know God better, some try to run away from Him, by not going near Him or not having anything to do with Him. And thus **never** creating a bond of friendship to establish salvation. God has created us to befriend Him, but our ill feelings are the same towards men and God. Examine your conscience. Neglecting God is neglecting your soul.

Word of Our Lord to the stigmatist Luisa Piccarreta: "My daughter, why do you look for Me outside of yourself, when you can find Me more easily within yourself? When you want to find Me, enter into yourself, go deep into your 'nothingness', there you will see the foundations that the Divine Being laid within you, as well as the factories I have raised in you. The very high walls are raised to heaven and keep out the things of this world, and to allow correspondence to heaven only."

Every soul is marked for Heaven or Hell by every choice in thought, word or deed he makes each day. Never speak out against another person. Always speak good of God and man. Imitation of Christ says: "Never speak good or bad of any person." Jeremy are you listening. Even to think it, and it is marked down.

"God will send two punishments: one will be in the form of wars, revolutions and other evils; it shall originate on earth. The other will be sent from Heaven. There shall come over the whole earth an intense darkness lasting three days and three nights. Nothing can be seen, and the air will be laden with pestilence which will claim mainly, but not only, the enemies of religion. It will be impossible to use any man-made lighting during this darkness, except blessed candles. He, who out of curiosity, opens his window to look out, or leaves his home, will fall dead on the spot. During these three days, people should remain in their homes, pray the Rosary and beg God for mercy."

"All the enemies of the Church, whether known or unknown, will perish over the whole earth during that universal darkness, with the exception of a few whom God will soon convert. The air shall be infected by demons who will appear under all sorts of hideous forms."

(Prophecy of Blessed Anna Maria Taigi (1769-1837 A.D.) who was Beatified by Pope Bendedict XV in 1920.)

"...Clouds with lightning flashes of fire in the sky and a tempest of fire shall fall upon the world. This terrible scourge, never before seen in the history of humanity, will last seventy hours. Godless persons will be crushed and wiped out. Many will be lost because they remain in their obstinacy of sin. Then shall be seen the power of light over the power of darkness." *Sister Elena Aiello, The Calabrian Holy Nun (1895-1961)*

St. Padre Pio said, "That if you could see the demons in the sky today, you would not be able to see the sun."

St. Padre Pio said, "Confession is the purification of the soul."

St. Padre Pio said, "Confession should be made no later than every eight days."

St. Padre Pio said, "Sleeves are to be covered the arms down to the wrist on both men and women." *(Padre Pio would not give Holy Communion to any person whose arms or legs were exposed. In church cover the arms and wear a dress jacket, dinner jacket, or suit jacket. Outside of church shirts can be worn to the elbow and no suit jacket is necessary. Your Sunday best before God on Holy days is a great sign of respect before God. A three piece suit is most traditional and respectful before God. On a summer hot offer it up, the priest does.)*

St. Padre Pio said, "The dress on women should be 8" below the knee." *(Hollywood, considered the headquarters of Satan, said they want the dress raised 8" above the knee.)* St. Padre Pio said, "Penance or Hell."

St. Padre Pio said, "The priest's mission is developed in (3) privileged places, the pulpit, the altar, and the confessional."

St. Padre Pio said, "Look for God in your books and in prayer you will find Him." *(When you pray you speak to God, when you read God speaks to you.) Imitation of Christ, and it should be read every day. When I read this beautiful book I feel that God made this book for me, and so will you. May it a part of your day.*

The Necessity of Prayer

It is by prayer that we are given grace to do the will of God and save our souls, Jesus says, "Ask, and you shall receive." No prayer, no grace. Remember Our Lady said prayer and mortification of the body is the way to obtain grace. ST. PAUL OF THE CROSS SAID: "WE ENTER ON THE BROAD WAY OF PERDITION WHEN WE NEGLECT TO PRAY." Prayer for the grace to do God's Will, and stay in His grace. St. Philip Neri used to say. "Lord, keep Thy hand over Philip this day, otherwise Philip will betray Thee."

We must say our prayers properly and respectfully and slowly. We are speaking to the Divine Majesty, the Father, Son and Holy Ghost, and in the Rosary, to the Most Holy Mary, Mother of the one true God. St. Louis de Montfort says: "It is really pathetic to see how most people say the Holy Rosary - they say it astonishingly fast and mumble so that the words are not properly pronounced at all. We could not possibly expect anyone, even the most compliment and yet we expect Jesus and Mary to be pleased with it." 44th Rose Chp. Secret of the Rosary.

In an exorcism the devil cry out, "If you christians knew the power of the Rosary, and that next to God, She has the Greatest Power in all Creation."

St. Peter Damian relates the story of St. Severinus, suffering in the purifying flames of purgatory, because, as he said, "….I sometimes said my prayers hurriedly and with distractions, I was so much taken up with my duties that I would sometimes put off my prayers or say them hurriedly …." From the book of Purgatory This book is a must Read, often, to resoak your soul in grace.

"He who does not know how to pray well, will not know how to live well," St. Augustine. "Never expect anything good from a soul that is <u>not</u> addicted to prayer." St. Francis of Assisi. *(I told you to pray or talk to God no matter what you're doing.)*

"Anyone who does not pray, and who does not wish to keep in continual communion with God, is dead, he has lost his reason, he must be insane, for he does not understand what a great honor it is to pray, and … not to pray is to bring death upon the soul." - St. Chrysostom

"Prayer is the most important means for our salvation." - St. Borromeo

"One of the greatest pains of the damned, they could have been saved by prayer and neglected to do so." "One can be certain salvation with prayer, as one can be certain of damnation without prayer." ST. ALPHONSUS de LIGUORI

If St. Francis De Sales was too busy to say his Rosary during the day, he would make sure he said it on his knees before he went to bed. One time it was midnight he had a very busy day, and as he was getting into bed he remembered he had not said his Rosary. His secretary told him go to bed you can say it tomorrow, your to tired. He got out of bed and said it.

"Let no man," says St. Bernard, "should think lightly of prayer, because God values it, and then gives us either what we ask, or what is still more useful to us: Let no one under value his prayers, for God does not undervalue it… He will give either what we ask, or what He knows to be better." St. Bernard

Proper Posture for praying is to knee. "Solomon…. Fixed both knees on the ground." 3 Kings 8:54 Stephen, falling on his knees, he prayed for his persecutors. Acts 7:59 Our Divine Saviour: "Kneeling down, He prayed." St. Lk. 22:47 repetitiously, He prayed three times.

"*Whosoever neglects Mary will perish in their sins.*"St. Alphonsus de Liguori
St. Thomas says, speaking of the validity of an indulgence: "It must be said that indulgences are simply worth what they are proclaimed to be, provided that on the part of the giver there be authority (Peter), on the part of the recipient there be charity, and on the part of the cause there be piety, which includes the honor of God, and the spiritual welfare of the members of the Church." (Supp.,q. 25, a. 2.)

On the Scapular and Purgatory: The Blessed Virgin promised Pope John XXII "that She would rescue from purgatory as speedily as possible, and especially on the first Saturday after their death, the member of the Confraternity of the Scapular," that is, those who have been properly enrolled in and who wear the scapular of Our Lady of Mt. Carmel. But to obtain the privilege of "The First Saturday," according to the "Bulla Sabbatina," it is requisite that you should practice the virtue of chastity according to your state, and recite every day the Little Office of the Blessed Virgin, if not bound to the Divine Office. Those who cannot read must abstain on from meat on Wednesdays and Saturdays, unless the rule be dispensed with, or commuted for other works of piety by a duly qualified superior.

What, then, are the more ordinary advantages to be derived from wearing the scapular? They enumerated in these words that Our Lady addressed to Blessed Simon Stock when She gave him the scapular, July 16, 1251: "Receive, my dear son, this scapular of your order, in token of the privilege which I have obtained for you and for the children of Carmel; he who at his death shall be found clothed in this gabit shall be preserved from eternal flames: it is a sign of salvation, a safeguard in time of danger (of death) and a pledge of special protection."

The learned and illustrious Pontiff, Benedict XIV, in his Treatise on the Feasts of the Blessed Virgin, declares that he fully believes in the vision of Blessed Simon as well as in the above mentioned revelation to Pope John XXII, made half a century later.

The Three Days of Darkness

St. Marie Julie Jahenny – French Mystic & Stigmatist; tells of the ending times and the many changes that will take place creating a **new church** with new preachers of new sacraments, new temple (churches).

Prophecy of Sister Mary of Jesus Crucified of Pau, (1878):
"During a darkness lasting Three Days the people given to evil will perish so that only one fourth of mankind will survive."

Prophecy of Blessed Rembordt (18ᵗʰ Century): "These things will come when they try to set up a new kingdom of Christ from which the true faith will be banished."

Old Oba Prophecy: "It (Warning, Miracle, and Chastisement) will come when the Catholic Church a new cult, when priests are forbidden to celebrate in any other than in the new cult, when the higher positions in the Church are given to perjurers and hypocrites, (gays) when only the renegades are admitted to occupy those positions."

Prophecy of Jasper: "When men indulge in sensuous pleasure and voluptuousness, when no one wishes to obey any more when there is widespread discontent among the people of the earth, then **Russia** will pour out masses of soldiers, and they will reach the Rhine."

Ven. Ann de La Foi: "There will be descoral within the Catholic Church. In those days men will wear women's, jewelry,(earrings, necklaces, you name it, some go as far as to become women and some marry another man) and women will put on men clothing. (They assume to be as good as men in strength, in all men's positions and they forget what God created them for.)

Prophecy of Mother Shipton (16ᵗʰ Century): "The Great Chastisement will come when carriages go without horses and many accidents fill the world with woe. It will come when thoughts are flying around the earth in the twinkling of an eye, when long tunnels are made for horseless machines, when men can fly in the air and ride under the sea, when ships are wholly made of metal, when fire and water great marvels do, when even the poor can read books, when many taxes are levied for war."

St. Anthony of the Desert (4ᵗʰ Century): *"Men will surrender to the spirit of the age. They will say that if they had lived in our day, faith would be simple and easy. But in their day, they will say, things are complex; the Church must be brought up to date and made meaningful to the day's problems. When the Church and the world are one, then those days are at hand for the Chastisement. But God has put a barrier between His things and the things of the world."*

Saint Hildegard of Bingen (12ᵗʰ Century)

"The time is coming when princes and peoples will reject the authority of the Pope. Some countries will prefer their own Church rulers to the Pope. The German Empire will be divided.

Before the **comet** comes, many nations, the good excepted, will be scourged by want and famine. The great nation in the ocean that is inhabited by people of different tribes and descent will be devastated by earthquake, storm, and tidal wave. It will be divided and, in great part, submerged. That nation will also have many misfortunes at sea and lose its colonies. (America)

[After the] great **Comet**, the great nation will be devastated by earthquakes, storms, and great waves of water, causing much want and plagues. The ocean will also flood many other countries, so that all coastal cities will live in fear, with many destroyed.

All sea coast cities will be fearful, and many of them will be destroyed by tidal waves, and most living creatures will be killed, and even those who escape will die from a horrible disease. For in none of those cities does a person live according to the Laws of God.

A powerful wind will rise in the North, carrying heavy fog and the densest dust, and it will fill their throats and eyes so that they will cease their butchery and be stricken with a great fear."

St. Pius X

During an audience for the general chapter of the Franciscan order in 1909, the pontiff appeared to enter a trance. Those present remained motionless and silent. After a few moments, Pius opened his eyes, rose from his seat, and cried, "What I have seen is terrifying! Will I be the one, or will it be a successor? What is certain is that the Pope will leave Rome and, in leaving the Vatican, he will have to pass over the dead bodies of his priests!" He then cautioned the witnesses, "Do not tell anyone this while I am alive."

Just before his death, Pius had another vision. "I have seen one of my successors, of the same name, who was fleeing over the bodies of his brethren. He will take refuge in some hiding place; but after a brief respite, he will die a cruel death. Respect for God has disappeared from human hearts. They wish to efface even God's memory. This perversity is nothing less than the beginning of the last days of the world."

Pius XII

There were occasional rumors of visions and "angelic" phenomena associated with Pius XII during the entire duration of his papacy (1939-58). After one of these mystical visions he reportedly told one of his assistants, "Mankind must prepare itself for sufferings such as it has never before experienced." He expressed dismay at what he saw facing humanity in the not so distant future, describing those times as "the darkest since the deluge." "When the Church Loses its Latin, The Church will go under ground."

Blessed Anna Maria Taigi (19th Century)

"All the enemies of the Church, whether known or unknown, will perish over the whole earth during that universal darkness, with the exception of a few whom God will soon convert. The air shall be infected by demons who will appear under all sorts of hideous forms." "Religion shall be persecuted, and priests massacred Churches shall be closed, but only for a short time. The Holy Father shall be obliged to leave Rome."

Venerable Mary of Agreda (17th Century)

"It was revealed to me that through the intercession of the Mother of God, all heresies will disappear. This victory over heresies has been reserved by Christ for His Blessed Mother... Before the Second Coming of Christ, Mary must, more than ever, shine in mercy, might and grace in order to bring unbelievers into the Catholic Faith."

Venerable Bartholomew Holzhauser (17th Century)

"During this unhappy period, there will be laxity in divine and human precepts. Discipline will suffer. The Holy Canons will be completely disregarded, and the Clergy will not respect the laws of the Church. Everyone will be carried away and led to believe and to do what he fancies, according to the manner of the flesh. They will ridicule Christian simplicity; they will call it folly and nonsense, but they will have the highest regard for advanced knowledge, and for the skill by which the axioms of the law, the precepts of morality, the Holy Canons and religious dogmas are clouded by senseless questions and elaborate arguments. As a result, no principle at all, however holy, authentic, ancient, and certain it may be, will remain free of censure, criticism, false interpretations, modification and delimitation by man."

On November 27,1902 and May 10, 1904 Our Lord and Our Lady announced to her the conspiracy to in ven t th e "New Mass":

"I give you a WARNING. The disciples who are not of My Gospel are now working hard to remake according to their ideas and under the influence of the enemy of souls, a MASS, that contains words that are **ODIOUS (Hateful)** in My sight. When the fatal hour arrives the faith of my priests will be put to the test, it will be (these texts) that will be celebrated in in this SECOND period. The FIRST period is (the one) of my priesthood which exists since Me. The SECOND is (the one) of the persecution when the ENEMIES of the Faith and of Holy Religion (will impose their formulas) in the book of the second celebration …. These infamous spirits are those who crucified Me and are awaiting the kingdom of A NEW MESSIAH."

Our Lord has said to more than one saint in our times that this is the "Mass of Babel." God does not want to hear the Mass said in the tongue of every language. He wants it said in the language of the Church, the language of the angels. A great European/Roman Theologian of the Church, named Fr. Gregory Hesse, who flat out says, "It is a sin for you to go the New Messed-Up Mass. And he give over a dozen reasons. From this will come the Three Days of Darkness. And she also mentions the coming **Comet** which will cause the Three Days of Darkness.

Marie Julie Jahenny says it was the Jews since the time of Christ that are behind all this and they are the beginning of the masons to this day. They have never stopped their persecution of Christ and His Church, His Government (Kings and Queens) since the crucifixion.

Mayer Amschel Bauer is the head Rothschild

Jews having a hard time of it were kick out of city, state and (47) countries, because they were blasphemous of Christ and His Mother and His Church and for their lending practices.

It was realized in late 1800's by Theodor Herzl (started the Zionist Movement) that the Jews needed a state to live in, so that their religious beliefs of the Talbot which were blasphemous of Christ the True Son of God, could live without being thrown out.

So England through the Lord Balfour Declaration written to Rothschild gave the Jews a homeland to place to move to in Palestine. Declared in 1917, but never was implemented until 1947. This was unanimous with all countries except the Arab states. Jews rounded up Arab and sent them out of Palestine. Thus we have war ever since in the Mid-east.

Mayer Amschel Bauer was born in Frankfort in 1744-1812 was a money lender whose sign out front had hexagram on it. (Six Pointed Star) He was also a gold smith. Soon he changed his name to Rothschild which is German for 'Red Sign'.

Mayer Bauer (Mayer Rothschild) When he died he left a will of how the Banking Houses of Rothschild were to operate. Only members of the family were to hold key positions. The family was to intermarry with their own first and second cousins, thus preserving the vast fortune. Rothschild's heirs were strictly forbidden to ever disclose the amount of their wealth. They were driven by lust of wealth and power they became the richest family in the world.

He had (5) sons he school on how to lend money to governments, especially in time of needs like wars. The loans were bigger and secured by the people's taxes.

1.) Nathan Mayer Rothschild was told to go to London.
2.) Amschel Mayer Rothschild was told to go to Frankfurt.
3.) Jakob Mayer Rothschild was told to go to Paris.
4.) Salomon Mayer Rothschild was told to go to Vienna.
5.) Calmann Mayer Rothschild was told to go to Naples.

From the book "Prophecies of La Fraudais." and **the book (PAUL VI beatified?) compiled by Fr. Luigi Villa.** He was assigned by **Pope Pius XII** to see how many masons were in the Church. Fr. Villa had spoke with St. Padre Pio on two occasions, and was told by Padre Pio the following: "Be brave, now... for the church has already been invaded by Freemasonry! Freemasonry have already made it into the shoes of the Pope!" (At that time it was Pope Paul VI with his signature emblem the five-pointed star.)

The end of this 5ᵗʰ period will be a tidal wave dress rehearsal of what will come again at the end of the world tidal wave, which will be worse because that will be with the actual Antichrist.

Marie-Julie announced the Three Days of Darkness during which the infernal powers will be loosed and will execute all the enemies of God. "***The crisis will explode suddenly***; the punishments will be shared by all and will succeed one another without interruption..." January 4, 1884: "The three days of darkness will be on a THURSDAY, FRIDAY, AND SATURDAY. (*Days which represent the Most Blessed Sacrament, the day of Crucifixion and day of Our Lady ;three days less one night.)*" (*Somewhere I remember March and April.*)

St. Catherine Emmerich Said, "Satan will be loosed from Hell (50) Years before the 2000." (Vatican II)

"During these three days of terrifying darkness, no windows must be opened, because no one will be able to see the earth and the terrible color it will have in those days of punishment without dying at once..."

"The sky will be on fire, the earth will split... During these three days of darkness let the blessed candle be lighted everywhere, no other light will shine..." *Beeswax candles blessed by a priest, same candles as used at the Mass.*

"NO ONE OUTSIDE A SHELTER... will survive. The earth will shake as at the judgment and fear will be great. Yes, We will listen to the prayers of our friends; NOT ONE WILL PERISH. We will need them to publish (profess) the glory of the Cross...." (December 8, 1882)

"THE CANDLES OF BLESSED BEES WAX ALONE WILL GIVE LIGHT during this horrible darkness. ONE CANDLE alone will be enough for the duration of this night of hell....In the homes of the wicked and blasphemers, these candles will give NO LIGHT."

"During this darkness the devils and the wicked will take on **the most hideous shapes** ... red clouds like blood will move across the sky. The crash of the thunder will shake the earth and sinister lightning will streak the heavens out of season. The earth will be shaken to its foundations. The sea will rise, its roaring waves will spread over the continent ... **the earth will become like a vast cemetery.**'" The bodies of the wicked and the just will cover the ground."

"Three-quarters of the population of the globe will disappear. Half the population of France will be destroyed." (Marie-Julie Jahenny prophecy as reported by the Marquis de la Franquerie)

Ven. Elizabeth Canori-Mora (d. 1825)"... The sky was covered with clouds so dense and dismal that it was impossible to look at them without dismay... (St. Padre Pio told a person, that if he could the demons in the air at this time, the demons would blot out the light of the sun.) The avenging arm of God will strike the wicked, and in his mighty power he will punish their pride and presumption. God will employ the powers of hell for the extermination of these impious and heretical persons who desire to overthrow the Church and destroy its foundation. ....

"Innumerable legions of demons shall overrun the earth and shall execute the orders of Divine Justice... Nothing on the earth shall be spared.

After this frightful punishment, I saw the heavens opening, and St. Peter coming down again upon earth; he was vested in his pontifical robes, and surrounded by a great number of angels, who were chanting hymns in his honor, and they proclaimed him as sovereign of the earth. I saw also St. Paul descending upon the earth. By God's command, he traversed the earth and chained the demons, whom he brought before St. Peter, who commanded them to return into hell, whence they had come.

"Then a great light appeared upon the earth which was the sign of the reconciliation of God with man. The angels conducted before the throne of the prince of the Apostles the small flock that had remained faithful to Jesus Christ. These good and zealous Christians testified to him the most profound respect, praising God and thanking the Apostles for having delivered them from the common destruction, and for having protected the Church of Jesus Christ by not permitting her to be infected with the false maxims of the world. St. Peter then chose the new pope. The Church was again organized..."

(Prophecy of Ven. Elizabeth Canori-Mora (d. 1825) as recorded in Fr. Culleton's book *The Prophets and Our Times*, 1941 A.D. *Imprimatur*)

Blessed Anna Maria Taigi "After the three days of darkness, St. Peter and St. Paul, having come down from Heaven, will preach in the whole world and designate a new Pope. A great light will flash from their bodies and will settle upon the cardinal who is to become Pope. Christianity, then, will spread throughout the world.

"He is the Holy Pontiff, chosen by God to withstand the storm. At the end, he will have the gift of miracles, and his name shall be praised over the whole earth. Whole nations will come back to the Church and the face of the earth will be renewed. Russia, England, and China will come back into the Church." (Prophecy of Blessed Anna Maria Taigi -1769-1837 A.D.)

And Our Lady states: "Everything will shake except the piece of furniture on which the blessed candle is burning. This will not shake. You will all gather around with the crucifix and my blessed picture. This is what will keep away this terror."

THE IMMEDIATE SIGN

The wind will howl and roar. <u>Lightning and thunderbolts of an _unprecedented magnitude_ will strike the earth</u>. The whole earth will shake, heavenly bodies will be disturbed (this will be the beginning of the Three Days). Every Demon, every evil spirit will be released from hell and allowed to roam the earth. Terrifying apparitions will take place. Many will die from sheer fright. Fire will rain forth from the sky, all large cities will be destroyed, poisonous gases will fill the air, cries and lamentations everywhere. The unbelievers will burn in the open like withered grass. The entire earth will be afflicted; it will look like a huge graveyard.

As soon as you notice (these signs), go indoors, lock all doors and windows, pull down the blinds, stick adhesive paper on vents and around windows and doors. Do not answer calls from outside, <u>do not look out the windows, or you will die on the spot: keep your eyes down to make sure you do not see the out the windows</u>; the Wrath of God is mighty and no one should attempt to behold it. Light blessed wax candles; nothing else will burn, but the candles will not be extinguished once lit. Nothing will put them out in the houses of the faithful, but they will not burn in the houses of the godless. **Sprinkle holy water about the house** and especially in the vicinity of doors and windows: **the devils fear holy water**. (You should have St. Benedict medals over the doors. Before Mass the priest is to hit every person with holy water to force the devil out of the Church. Bless yourself with it and anoint your five senses with it: eyes, ears, nose, mouth, hands, feet, and forehead. Keep on hand a sufficient supply of drinking water and, if possible, food also (but you can live without food for three days.) Kneel down and pray incessantly with outstretched arms, or prostrate on the floor. Make acts of contrition, faith, hope, and charity. Above all say the Rosary and meditate on the Sorrowful mysteries.

Some people, especially children, will be taken up to Heaven beforehand to spare them the horror of these days. People caught outdoors will die instantly. Three-quarters of the human race will be exterminated, more men than women. No one will escape the terror of these days.

Blessed Anna-Maria Taigi stated in regards to this terrible Three Days of Darkness Chastisement:

"God will send two punishments: one will be in the form of wars, revolutions and other evils; it shall originate on earth. The other will be sent from Heaven. There shall come over the whole earth an intense darkness lasting three days and three nights. Nothing can be seen, and the air will be laden with pestilence which will claim mainly, but not only, the enemies of religion. It will be impossible to use any man-made lighting during this darkness, except **blessed wax candles**. He, who out of curiosity, opens his window to look out, or leaves his home, will fall dead on the spot. During these three days, people should remain in their homes, pray the Rosary and beg God for mercy."

"All the enemies of the Church, whether known or unknown, will perish over the whole earth during that universal darkness, with the exception of a few whom God will soon convert. The air shall be infected by demons who will appear under all sorts of hideous forms."

But, when all seems lost and hopeless, then, in the twinkling of an eye, the ordeal will be over: the sun will rise and shine again as in springtime over a purified earth.

Some nations will disappear entirely, and the face of the earth will be changed. There will be no more "Big Business" and huge factories which sap men's souls. Craftsmanship will revive, and assembly lines will give way to the working bench. (Remember Garabandal no electricity and a plain good way of life, leading to God.)

People will return to the land, but food will be scarce for about three years. Married women will bear many children again, for it will be regarded as a disgrace not to have many children, no more "career women" addicted to the "pill". Unmarried females, there will be many, will enter the religious orders and form large congregations of Nuns within the reborn Church. Disease will decrease dramatically, and mental illnesses will be rare, for man will have retrieved his natural environment. It will be an age of faith, true brotherhood between neighbors, civil harmony, peace, and prosperity.

The land will yield crops as never before. Foods will be produced without chemicals. (No more harmful sprays.) Police will have little work to do: crime will disappear almost entirely. Mutual trust and honesty will be universal. There will be little work for lawyers, either. All the manpower which is currently taken up by the wickedness of the modern world will be released and available for the production of useful commodities. Thus, prosperity will be very great. This wonderful period will probably last 30 to 35 years approximately. (The need for large families (relatives) to come together to live together or close to each other.) To divide up the farm work, and some to get wood for winter, will be necessary.

As soon as you see the sun rise again at the end of the Three Days, drop to your knees and give thanks to God. Be warned, SPREAD THE MESSAGE, but do not fear: it would be an offense to God to show lack of confidence in His protection. Those who spread the message will be protected, but the scoffers, the skeptics, and those who dismiss the message because they are frightened, will not escape the chastisement."

"After the three days of darkness, St. Peter and St. Paul, having come down from Heaven, will preach in the whole world and designate

a new Pope. A great light will flash from their bodies and will settle upon the cardinal who is to become Pope. Christianity, then, will spread throughout the world. He is the Holy Pontiff, chosen by God to withstand the storm. At the end, he will have the gift of miracles, and his name shall be praised over the whole earth. Whole nations will come back to the Church and the face of the earth will be renewed. Russia, England, and China will come into the Church." (Prophecy of Blessed Anna Maria Taigi [1769-1837 A.D.]

THE PROXIMATE SIGNS

Here are the proximate signs in their probable order of occurrence. This, to be sure, is only my own opinion, and I may be wrong for I am no prophet myself; but, after studying a large number of prophecies, this order appears to me to be the most likely:

1. Flouting of church laws, irreverence and immodesty in church, fall in attendance at church. (These trends were observed in the 1950's, before the true Church was **criminally usurped** at the conclave.- *ED*)

2. Lack of charity towards others, heartlessness, indifference, divisions, contentions, godlessness, pride in human knowledge.

3. Breakdown of family life *(remember St. Anna Maria Taigi saw the devil's black box (TV) in the livingroom of every family):* immorality, adultery, perversion of youth via the media (e.g. homosexuals giving lectures in schools), immodest fashions, people concerned only with eating, drinking, dancing and other worldly pleasures. *(In their baseball caps, 'T' shirts, shorts, and shower shoes. Go back to the turn of the century and dress correctly. Take your hat off when you enter the room or house. Be courteous and have good manners. Show what quality of man you are, and be not indecent in dress, manner, or speech. Do not use God's name in vain and ko not work on Sundays.)*

4. Civil commotions, contempt for authority, downfall of governments, confusion in high places, corruption, coups d'etat, civil war, revolution. (The first four proximate signs have already come to pass, at least partly; for we have yet to see civil war and revolution in the West. But the sequence of events is not strictly chronological; there is room for some overlapping. Thus, the 5ᵗʰ proximate sign seems to have begun also.)

5. Floods and droughts, crop failures, unusual weather, tornadoes, earthquakes, tidal waves, famines, epidemics, unknown diseases (e.g. new strains of viruses). Are presigns of the worst to come.

6. Customs in most countries will lost or no longer used. The way they dressed and lived. They will become westernized into wearing

blue jeans and tennis shoes and shower shoes, and 'T' shirts and shorts.

7. People will be troubled at the times and think God has abandoned them. I have heard the protestant fundamentalist afraid of the things going on in the world and ask why is God not doing something about all this. His Mother told you to pray the Rosary and all will go right, plus Consecration of Russia. Go to youtube type in:'

Life of the Virgin Mary pt 1-8' *I can hardly go through a day without listening to this.*

Brittany, France: Sanctuary During & After The 3 Days of Darkness

This map shows the part of France called Brittany (red circle). Although Brittany will experience the 3 Days of Darkness - as the whole world will - multiple prophecies say Brittany will be the safest place on earth *during and after* the 3 Days Chastisement. It is also prophesied that a shrine will be erected there after "the 3 Days", where survivors (true Catholics) will flock. Similar to Garabandal and a permit sign left over the nine pines.

*THE WARNING

This will take place between the proximate and the immediate signs. It will be a supernatural occurrence.

During the Warning, many will be scared to their wits end, and many will wish to die, but the Warning itself will be completely harmless. However the shock of seeing your own sins will kill many.

The Warning must be viewed as the last act of mercy from God, a final appeal to mankind to do penance before the three days of darkness and the destruction of three-quarters of the human race. At a time when the murder of unborn babies and the sin of Sodom and Lesbos have become acceptable and "legal", we should not wonder why God is going to punish mankind.

By that time, war and revolution will have already caused a high death toll, and Communism will be victorious, but all this will be as nothing compared with the death toll caused by the Three Days.

***The Exact Date of *A Warning* Immediately to Proceed the 3 Days of Darkness Has Been Revealed: This **Warning is not the same warning of Garabandal, this warning is signaling the 3 Days of Darkness.

The prophetess <u>Sister Mary of St. Peter</u> is mentioned in the revelations of Marie-Julie Jahenny of La Fraudais, in a **most important of matters.** It was revealed to her by Heaven the **exact date of A Warning** which will come immediately before the 3 Days of Darkness Chastisement. (Only God knows the exact date.)

Revelations of Marie-Julie Jahenny (June 15, 1882)

<u>Jesus</u>: ". . . I forewarn you that **a day** will be found *and it is already appointed* when there will be little sun, few stars, and no light to take a step outside of your homes, the refuges of My people.

The days will be beginning to increase (days get longer on Dec 22). It will not be at the height of summer nor during the longer days of the year (summer time), but when the days are still short (winter time). It will not be at the end of the year, but during the first months (of the year) that I shall **give My clear warnings**. That day of darkness and lightning will be the first that I shall send to convert the impious, and to see if a great number will return to Me, *before* the Great Storm (Chastisement) which will closely follow. (The darkness and lightning of) that day will not cover all of France, (and all the world) but a part of Brittany will be tried by it. (However) on the side on which is found the land of the mother of My Immaculate Mother (the land of St. Anne) will not be covered by darkness to come, up to your place (home of Marie-Julie) . . . All the rest will be in the most terrible fright. From one night to the next — one complete day —, the thunder will not cease to rumble. The fire from the lightnings will do a lot of damage, even in the closed homes where someone will be living in sin. My children, that first day (of chastisement) will not take away anything from the three others (the 3-Day Chastisement) already pointed out and described.

That particular day was revealed to My servant, Catherine (Laboure), in the apparitions of My Blessed Mother under the name (title), 'Mary Conceived Without Sin'. **That day is (also) recorded in five well-sealed rolls of Sister St. Peter of Tours.** That roll will remain a secret until the day when a person of God will lay her predestined hand on that which the world will have ignored, including even the inhabitants of that cloister." **("Prophecies of La Fraudais of Marie-Julie Jahenny", pp. 50-51)**

Marie-Julie Jahenny is similar to Luisa Piccarreta whom God showed Heaven. Luisa wrote Book of Heaven in 36 vols. It's mainly about the Divine Will and how it works. St. Padre Pio said that after the Virgin Mary this Saint (Luisa) will soon be considered the greatest saint after Mary or so close to Her. Adam was immaculately conceived and committed one sin and never did commit another sin. He was the greatest in Heaven because all he did he did in the in <u>union </u>with the <u>Divine Will</u>. He lived 930 years on earth. As long as he was on earth, there was order. Mary from Her Immaculate Conception did all in union with the Divine Will, now She is the greatest in Heaven. From the time of Adam to the time of Christ Has been 4000 years. The Bible points out all the generations from Adam to Christ. <u>Evolution is a LIE, thanks to Satan.</u> And it never was real you can blame darn old Darwin for Darwinism his evolution theory (1809 - 1882).

Note: The writings of Sister St. Peter of Carmel of Tours were hidden on August 5th, 1850, by the order of Mgr. Morlot. **It is clear that the day** of which Our Blessed Lord is speaking is *A Warning*. That day is the "day" (Warning) which He is going to send to convert sinners before the "Great Storm" (the Great Chastisement) which will closely follow." Jesus said that, on that day, He would give His "Clear Warnings." **(See Garabandal.)**

"**Put a blessed Crucifix on the outside doors of your home,** just as the Israelites put lambs blood on the doorposts. This will be a sign for the Angels to protect you and your home. You may hear voices outside, but do not open your doors to anyone. Demons will imitate the voices of people you know.

"Demons will appear outside in terrifying and hideous forms. All Godless and wicked people will die during these three days of darkness. Prepare your soul now by confession and Communion and prayer.

"The Angels of God are standing by, ready with pointed swords. They will destroy all those who mock God and refuse to believe his words. They are simply waiting God's command."

The only Church that will survive the **Three Days of Darkness** will be the ONE, TRUE, HOLY, CATHOLIC, AND APOSTOLIC CHURCH, which Our Lord founded upon the Rock, when He said, "Thou are Peter and upon this Rock I shall build my Church." The true Church which stands on two legs: **Sacred Scripture** and **Sacred Tradition** where you will find the true Mass of Christ and held in perpetuity by the Council of Trent which is the Latin Tridentine Mass of the Roman Rite founded by Jesus Christ. There will be ONE FAITH, ONE GOD, ONE BAPTISM, and UNDER ONE POPE THE VICAR OF CHRIST. Again the Kings and Queens will reign and be close to God united under the Holy Father. ("... **Thy Kingdom Come Thy Will be Done on Earth as it is in Heaven."**
God brought about Kings and Queens, and at the Last Supper Jesus showed His Apostles how Kings should be anointed. Satan brought about Democracy, which is the demonic reign over the people without God and morality. There is another meaning of the above part of the 'Our Father' and that is the teachings of Jesus to Luisa Piccareta which I have already told you about and the Divine Will. The truths that Jesus taught to Luisa, He tells her are the truths that are saved for these later times. These truths are for those who will survive to live in the 6th period of the Church where there will be no sin, no evil, no need of policemen, no bad people. Only those who will practice this "God Kept Secret" Of the Divine Will, and how to practice it. Those who will survive to live in the 6th period of the Church and will practice the Divine Will as did St. Adam and Our Lady. This life is to be similar to time as in the Garden of Eden.

Our Lord said when He taught the "Our Father" to the Apostles, it was with great restraint that He did not reveal at the ending times the

true meaning of the "Our Father" would be revealed of the Divine Will.

On the last page of Vol. II Our Lord speaks to Lucia of the Rome: **"Poor Rome, how you will be destroyed!"**

The emblem of the double headed eagle with the cross in one claw (signifying the Church, God, and Spirituality) and in the other claw will be the orb (signifying the government of man under God). The double headed eagle will also signify the close union of Church and State, God and Man, the Body and Soul, which cannot be separated, (as Satan's Democracy does). This could be one of the future emblem for true believers of the One True Church of Christ outside of which there is no salvation. (We'll see.) The Divine Will Kingdom will reign for a time after the Chastisement in the 6th Period of the Church. Kings and Queens and The Tradition Church will return. Like the Saintly Kings of old, they will up hold true morality and punish immorality by laws such as St. Stephen of Hungary who punished severely crimes as blasphemy of the Holy Name of God, working on Sunday, murder, adultery and missing Mass on Sunday.

The armies of Heaven led by St. Michael will cast the devils into the abyss (after they (devils) have taken their harvest of ¾ of the world) and will bind them with chains. Then there will be peace for forty years. (this will be 6th period of the Church). It's possible that some of the 6th period could lap over into the time before the Chastisement, but I'm not sure. In the reign of the Pope that consecrates Russia (which is supposed to be Francis) the 6th period begins. He does so because the Moscow/Vatican Agreement is broken.

Then will come the Antichrist and the end of the world. (7th period of the Church) Christ will come on the clouds with His Angels. Judgment will take place and the angels will separate those who stayed in the true Faith and were loyal to Him and His Mother and stayed under Peter the Vicar of Christ. Which are those who will have looked upon the crucifix will be saved. Just as those who looked upon Aaron's staff with the serpent wrapped around it were safe at the time of Moses from the poisonous bit of the snake.

The Angels will herd those people to the left (goats) over a cliff opening in the earth ½ mile wide and 20 miles or so long, where they will fall miles into the abyss of Hell. St. Alphonsus Liguori says they will fall and be stack up on top of each and never to move again. These will be call the **living dead** in Hell forever. They are those who left the Church or belonged to false heretical churches outside the Catholic Church where there is no salvation, no sacraments to give <u>**sanctifying grace**</u> to save your soul by a Roman Catholic priest. You must be in the state of sanctifying grace to enter the land of Heaven.

Those to the right (sheep) will be raised up with Jesus Christ and lead into the beautiful land of Heaven. Where they shall see, feel, and taste the joys of good things in a land or country or Kingdom so bright and beautiful and endless and unimaginable of God, which is also called the land of the Divine Will, because all will be of the same will as God. On earth we had to work, plant, harvest, store, and eat the fruit of our hands, digest it, and expose of it to stay nourished and happy. In Heaven, to walk by the fruit and desire them in any way (smell or touch) will satisfy your five senses so that you <u>not</u> feel hunger or whatever you may long for etc…….

Satan for some unknown reason is bound to tell us before it happens all that is about to happen in the near future through Hollywood (his headquarters) by movies or on TV shows or series. Most of them are about battles or end of the world or destruction of the world all for told in the movies (The living dead or the Walking dead, I believe he is pointing at all the people who are so in love with the world today.

So the Consecration of Russia was not made by the Popes and all the bishops of the world, as was requested by Our Lady at Fatima 1917 and again in 1929. The possibility of 2017 the tribulation which is the over running of Europe by **Russia** and into Italy and the Vatican. Which will cause the flight of the Holy Father from Rome to flee over the dead bodies of his cardinals. Rome will be mostly destroyed. Remember that when the Holy Father goes to **Moscow**, this is considered an act of war to the Russians godless government, and this will be the excuse they have been waiting for. They will see their chance when the Muslims are all over Europe, causing the tribulation of blood shed for 30 days (Muslims). The massacre of many religious as well as lay people.

By the year 2029 the comet will come by. And possibly another one or the same one in 2036 which is to hid earth. However NASA say they will divert it. We'll see what God has in mind. He can tell an angel to stop it or move it. Or God can send one comet so huge that no one can stop it.

"I don't need you amateurs any more. Now I have my comrades,
The Communists, Marxists, Socialists, Liberals and Terrorists.
They are true professionals."

Rafael Brom: True Professionals (Ink) 1982

Russia will invade Europe. As well as most of the world. As far as France goes, I'm not sure, France may call upon Russia for help or they decide to invade on their own. At this point the **Warning of Garabandal** will take place within few weeks before April in the following year. The following Spring (April) the Great Miracle will happen. If the people do not repent and convert to Catholicism, by the year 2020 give or take a year. (So believes Fr. Malachi Martin an Irish priest now deceased. He was secretary to Cardinal Bea, who was secretary to John XIII, all having read the third secret of Fatima while driving across Rome one day.)

So, there you have it. Not a pretty picture for the next few years. Especially if Americans are locked up in concentration camps with mass arrests here in America.

Now God did not want to give the Church back the true Faith, when after the devil had robbed the True Faith from the Church at Vatican II.

But Our Lady begged Almighty God to raise up a Prelate (bishop) who would bring about an order of true and holy priests that would keep the true Faith alive. (Prophecy at Quito, Ecuador)

In the Bible it says God will give them a spirit of slumber, eyes that they should not see, and ears that they should not hear; they will be blinded. This is what happened after Vatican II, and the new catholic faith. In the book of Jeremiah chapter (6) God asked the people to walk in the **old ways** and they said we will not walk in the old ways. God said, "If you do not walk in the old ways then I should abandoned you and you will have confusion and …(and Vatican II)….. "A 90th Degree Mason - Whistle Blower" (Interesting?) youtube.

A Three Days of Darkness will happen, but when, is a good question. And Our Lady states: "Everything will shake except the piece of furniture on which the blessed candle is burning on. This will not shake. You will all gather around with the crucifix and my blessed picture. This is what will keep away this terror."

"During this darkness the devils and the wicked will take on THE MOST HIDEOUS SHAPES…red clouds like blood will move across the sky. The crash of the thunder will shake the earth and sinister lightning will streak the heavens out of season. The earth will be shaken to its foundations. The sea will rise, its roaring waves will spread over continents…"

"THE EARTH WILL BECOME LIKE A VAST CEMETERY. The bodies of the wicked and the just will cover the ground."

"Three-quarters of the population of the globe will disappear. Half the population of France will be destroyed. This "Three Days of Darkness" can happen at the beginning of the Sixth period or in the middle of the seventh period. Confusing isn't it. The Great Monarch comes after the invasion.

Pope John Paul on the 3rd Secret of Fatima said the contents (3rd Secret) are most serious: "….Christians know in this message… is written that oceans will flood whole areas of the earth and that from one moment to the next millions of people will perish…" (Is the Three Days of Darkness and the lose of the True Faith is the 3rd Secret of Fatima?) At this point the Holy Father grasped a Rosary and said: "Here is the remedy against this evil. Pray, pray, and ask for nothing more. Leave everything else to the Mother of God." John Paul II

Sister Lucia gave the actual date to John Paul II of the start of the war and blood shedding. He died with it.

St. Dominic said to the people: "prayed to Our Lady to force the devils who possessed this man to reveal the truth of devotion to Mary: "Now that we are forced to speak we must also tell you this: **Nobody who perseveres in praying the Rosary will be damned, because she obtains for her servants the grace of true contrition for their sins and by means of this they obtain God's forgiveness and mercy."**

Fr. Stefano Manelli in his weekly column Il Pensiero di Padre Pio, Pianeta Padre Pio, wrote that Padre Pio criticized those Christians who believe they can speak directly to God and receive instructions and do not have to submit to the authority of the pope.

This is also a dangerous road writes Fr. Manelli for Christians who believe they are in communion with God without his Vicar and the Catholic Church. They are mistaken and this is an illusion for them, as it is known, he writes, outside the church there is no salvation. Can not be called christians if they are heretics.

On this point, **Padre Pio**, with simple words, which were terrible, said that those who believe they can communicate with God directly, **are on the way to Hell.**

Luther's end was horrible and frightening, he writes, but this will also be the same history of many Christians and Catholics who believe in the teachings of **Luther**. They risk also going to Hell like **Luther**, for not listening to the **pope**.

'Thou art Peter,' said Jesus, 'and upon this rock I will build my Church, and the gates of Hell will not prevail against it.' (Mt.16,18).

Fr. Stefano Manelli, who personally knew the saint, said Padre Pio had kept a picture of the pope on his little working table. So always before him was the message, 'After Jesus comes the Pope'. (Dopo Gesù viene il papa).

In 1883, **Sister Maria Serafina Micheli** (1849-1911) **was beatified** in Faicchio in the province of Benevento in the diocese of Cerreto Sannita 28 May 2011, the foundress of the Sisters of the Angels, **was going to Eisleben, Saxony, the birthplace of Luther. The fourth centenary of the birth of the great heretic** (10 November 1483) **was celebrated on that day, and many people were there.** The streets were crowded, balconies included. Among the many personalities were expected at any time, with the arrival of **Emperor Wilhelm I, who presided over the solemn celebrations.**

The future Blessed, noting the great hoopla, was **not** interested in knowing the reason for this unusual animation, **wanted to find a church and pray** to be able to make a visit to the Blessed Sacrament. After walking for awhile, **she finally found one, but the doors were closed. She knelt on the steps** for serenity prayer. As it was in the evening, she had not noticed that **it was not a Catholic church, but Protestant. While praying, the angel appeared, who said to her. "Arise, because it is a Protestant church."** Then he added: **"But I want you to see where Martin Luther was condemned and the pain he suffered as a punishment for his pride."** *(Protestant is to protest against Christ and His Vicar, Peter and teachings.)*

After these words, **she saw a terrible abyss of fire, where they were cruelly tortured countless souls. In the bottom of this hole there was a man, Martin Luther, which differed from the others: he was surrounded by demons that forced him to kneel, and all armed with hammers, they tried in vain, to hammer a big nail into his head. The Religious thought, if some of the people had seen this dramatic scene, they would not have made honors and other commemorations and celebrations for such a character.**

Later, when the opportunity arose to remind her sisters live in humility and in silence. She was convinced that Martin Luther was punished in hell especially for the first deadly sin of pride. **Pride is a deadly sin, brought him open rebellion against the Roman Catholic Church.** His behavior, his attitude towards the Church, and his preaching were crucial to encourage and bring many souls to eternal ruin.

The following is a letter written by St. Padre Pio Stigmatist, was addressed to the Commission of Heroldsbach appointed by the Vatican that testifies to the truth and the reality of these relations on the **Three Days of Darkness; from Our Lord to St. Padre Pio:**

New Year's Eve 1949: Jesus to Padre Pio

"My son, My son, I have been longing for this hour in which I again shall reveal to you the great love of My heart . . . Pray and make reparation to Me. Admonish others to do the same because the time is near at hand in which I shall visit My unfaithful people because they have not heeded the time of My grace. Persevere in prayer, so that your adversary shall have no dominion over you. Tell My people to be prepared at all times, for My judgment shall come upon them suddenly and when least expected - and not one shall escape My hands, I shall find them all! I shall protect the just. Watch the sun and moon and the stars of the Heavens. When they appear to be unduly disturbed and restless, know that the day is not far away. Stay united in prayer and watching until the angel of destruction has passed your doors. Pray that these days will be shortened."

January 23, 1950: Jesus to Padre Pio

"Pray! Make reparation! Be fervent and practice mortification. Great things are at stake! Pray! Men are running toward the abyss of Hell in great rejoicing and merry-making, as though they were going to a masquerade ball or the wedding feast of the devil himself! Assist Me in the salvation of souls. The measure of sin is filled! The day of revenge, with its terrifying happenings is near - nearer then you can imagine! And the world is sleeping in false security! The Divine Judgment shall strike them like a thunderbolt! These Godless and wicked people shall be destroyed without mercy, as were the inhabitants of Sodom and Gomorrah of old. Yes, I tell you their wickedness was not as great as that of the human race today!"

JANUARY 28, 1950, "Keep your windows well covered. Do not look out. Light a blessed candle, which will suffice for many days. Pray the Rosary. Read spiritual books. Make acts of Spiritual Communion.

Also acts of love, which is so pleasing to God. Pray with outstretched arms, or prostrate on the ground, in order that many souls may be saved. Do not go outside the house. Provide yourself with sufficient food. The powers of nature shall be moved and a rain of fire shall make people tremble with fear. Have courage! I am in the midst of you.

February 7, 1950, "Take care of the animals during these days. I am the Creator and Preserver of all animals as well as man. I shall give you a Few Signs beforehand, at which time you should place more food before them. I will preserve the propriety of the elect, including the animals, for they shall be in need of sustenance after wards as well. Let no one go across the yard, even to feed the animals. He who steps outside will perish! **Cover your windows carefully.** My elect shall not see My wrath. Have confidence in Me, and I will be your protection. Your confidence obliges Me to come to your aid. The hour of My coming is near! But I will show mercy. A most dreadful punishment will bear witness to the times. My angels, who are the executioners of this work, are ready with their pointed swords! Storms, bad weather, thunderbolts and earthquakes will cover the earth for two days. An uninterrupted rain of fire will take place! It will begin during a very cold night. All this is to prove that God is the Master of Creation. Those who hope in Me, and believe in my words, have nothing to fear because I will not forsake them, nor those who spread My message. No harm will come to those who are in the state of grace and who seek My Mother's protection. That you may be prepared for these visitations, I will give you the following signs and instructions:

"The night will be very cold. The wind will roar. After a time, thunderbolts will be heard. **Lock** all the doors and windows. Talk to no one outside the house. Kneel down before a crucifix, be sorry for your sins, and beg Our Lady's protection. Do not look out during the earthquakes, because the anger of God is holy! Jesus does not want us to behold the anger of God, because God's anger must be contemplated with fear and trembling. Those who disregard this advice will be killed instantly."

"The wind will carry with it poisonous gases which will be diffused over the entire earth. Those who suffer and die innocently will be martyrs and they will be with Me in **My Kingdom**. Satan will triumph! But after three nights, the earthquakes and fire will cease. On the following day the sun will shine again. Angels will descend from Heaven and will spread the spirit of peace over the earth."

"A feeling of immeasurable gratitude will take possession of those who survive this terrible ordeal, the impending punishment, with which God has visited the earth since creation. God has chosen souls in other countries too, such as Belgium, Switzerland, and Spain, who have received these revelations so that other countries also may be prepared. Pray much during this Holy Year of 1950."

"**Pray the Rosary**, but pray it slowly and well and attentively, so that your prayers may reach Heaven. I am again warning the world through my instrument, as I have so often done here before. The sins of men have multiplied beyond measure: Irreverence in Church sinful pride committed in shameful religious activities, lack of true brotherly love, **indecency in dress**, especially at summer seasons... The world is filled with iniquity. This catastrophe shall come upon the earth like a flash of lightning at which moment the light of the morning sun shall be replaced by black darkness! There shall be great confusion because of this utter darkness in which the entire earth shall be enveloped, and many, many shall die from fear and despair. However, many shall burn in the open fields like withered grass! The godless shall be annihilated, so that afterwards the just shall be able to stand afresh. **On the day, as soon as complete darkness has set in, no one shall leave the house or look from out of the window.** The darkness shall last a day and a night, followed by another day and a night, and another day, but on the night following, the stars will shine again, and on the next morning the sun shall rise again, and it will be SPRING TIME!!"

"In the days of darkness, My elect shall not sleep, as did the disciples in the garden of olives. They shall pray incessantly, and they shall not be disappointed in Me. I shall gather My elect. Hell will believe itself to be in possession of the entire earth, but I shall reclaim it!"

"Do you, perhaps, think that I would permit My Father to have such terrible chastisements come upon the world, if the world would turn from iniquity to justice? But because of My great love, these afflictions shall be permitted to come upon man. Although many shall curse Me, yet thousands of souls shall be saved through them. No human understanding can fathom the depth of My love!

"Pray! Pray! I desire your prayers. My Dear Mother Mary, Saint Joseph, Saint Elizabeth, Saint Conrad,

Saint Michael. Saint Peter, the Little Therese, Your Holy Angels, shall be your intercessors. **Implore their aid!** Be courageous soldiers of Christ! At the return of light, let everyone give thanks to the Holy Trinity for their protection! The devastation shall be very great! But I, Your God, will have purified the earth. I am with you. Have confidence!"

"In the days of darkness, My elect shall not sleep, as did the disciples in the garden of olives. They shall pray incessantly, and they shall not be disappointed in Me. I shall gather My elect." **The End of St. Padre Pio's**

Three Days of Darkness: Paraphrasing Our Lady communicating through different apparitions since the early sixties: *Hurry to be converted. Do not wait for the great sign. (Warning) For the unbeliever, it will be too late to be converted.* **(I think because millions will die, from the sight of seeing their sinful soul in the Warning.)**

I have ordered and received the **French Book of "Prophecies of La Fraudais; Marie Julie Jahenny."** The first time it came to me it came in French, you're right, I can't read French. The company thought they were in English. They are now reordered it in English for here in America. I must be one of the first to get one. You have read above the short conversation God allowed Pope Leo XIII to hear, from this book I give a more complete version of the conversation which took place about the same time, as follows:

Our Lady and Our Lord told St. Marie Julie Jahenny the following:

"Desolation will be so great and a chastisement as terrible as many will die of fright and think the end of the world is coming."

Words of Our Lord to Satan: "You will be subject to Me, doing only what My eternal law will allows you to."

"Place no limits to my power", begs Satan, "leave me with the freedom to expand to the same extent as You are Yourself to spread out, **until the end of centuries**."

Our Lord: "Prostrate at My feet, and adore My will."

Satan: "I will bend my knee, but on one condition. Leave me free to make use, after Your example and according to my fancy, the **power over death**, to be master thereof."

Our Lord: "I leave you with the power of inducing temptations upon men, to cause them suffering up to a certain limit but I will be present."

Satan begs power of performing wonders. The Lord does not grant him entirely, but gives something of it, so that means, we may acquire greater merits.

Our Lord: "A time will come, in the not very far distant when you will be in possession of such a large crowd, as your portion will exceed Mine. You will become The Great Conqueror for a length which will last far too long, yet will nevertheless be quite short. While you will be receiving the conquest of multitudes, I will perform striking wonders and cause an earthquake to happen, at the moment when the world will be nearing its destruction, at that time you will have triumph and victory without measure. When almost all parts of the world, and the whole of Europe will arise, against one another. During the darkness a large number of conversations will take place; many stray individuals will come back to Me in repentance. "When they were about to depart, each one to return to his own kingdom, Satan begs for the power of assuming all shapes or appearances, in order to be able to pass through any place.

Our Lord: "I grant you permission to seduce My people, but I will never allow you to assume divine resemblance nor any likeness of My Faithful people. Be respectful to Me, in the Name of My Eternal Power."

Satan: At the beginning of this period, I will make use of every blasphemous word, and of everything unjust in view of the destruction of Your Kingdom.... **I will transform everything into a work tool, against You.** First of all, I will dig out that place where the larger number inhabit.....(Paris) I will dig out that place upon which you all make thunder lightning fall down.... You will destroy first, after I myself will get through with it; I will accomplish such devastation as never existed the like.

Our Lord: I will cover My own, with a protection of tenderness.

Satan: I will establish a rebellion between Your own and mine, I will upraise all kings; I will establish such a division leading to a civil war throughout the whole Universe.

Our Lord: On My part, I will send My Justice out: Punishment, miracles, deaths, scourges, pest, unknown diseases....

Satan: I will overthrow the temple of Your prayers, in which I will establish idols which they will adore. Everything which, in time of peace, is in residence in Your temples, will be broken down, dragged out of them and reduced to dust by my own.

Our Lord: I will show forth, that I am the Eternal King. I will crush down, under the lighting of Heaven, all those who will have given themselves over to Hell. I will restore My people. I will protect them against scourges, rebuild ruined buildings. I will cast you headlong into the abyss, but only after you will have made use of the powers I leave with you for the time being.

We have further prophecies of **Our Lord to Marie-Julie** mostly of France: "The time will come when I shall save my people, it will not be through any power of new. My Divine Heart is the one Who, alone, will bring salvation to this kingdom which will be left but a shameful disorder, where wickedness will be prevailing in full triumph." "I will come with My lightning and thunder. I will confound the wicked; I will reduce him to dust and ashes. The Chastisements will start in Paris. Chastisements in the south will be a slaughter." "In France, a greater amount of blood will be shed than in Rome. This will not last long." "**Brittany** and **Vendee** will be protected, number of Verdeans will shed their blood, but they will retain their Faith." "**Nantes** will have less to suffer. This diocese will be comparatively protected, but no mercy for the wicked or wrong doing families! How many misfortunes of sin (worldly pleasures and wasted time) there are within the families.

Pont chateau will be spared because of **Father Louis de Montfort**." "**Toulouse** will be spared because of **St. Germaine of Picric**, but Toulouse not through with her troubles. **Mende** and **Rodez** will be spared." Our Lord tells that His wrathful Justice will fall upon Valence, Marseille, Rome, Naples, England......"France, the one who has caused misfortune, is the one who caused My Heart to be rejected forever. Rest assured that never will the country of France be governed by anyone of his descendants. King Louis XIV June 16, 1689. Failure to consecrate France to the Sacred Heart. (see pg 16)

Our Lord continues to speak to Marie-Julie: "After those three days of hell, when daylight will be dark, My ministers will have greater freedom, they will **start over again** celebrating the **sacred mysteries, but secretly.**"

"Years ago a grave chastisement has taken place, during which My priests and My servants have been massacred. That chastisement lasted three years. This time it will be much shorter, but more terrible. I will call upon <u>**My Servant Henry**</u> *(The French Monarch)* to help France out. When all those things will **start** taking place, *(Vatican II)* the eyelids of your eyes will have been closed, you will see only the first spark of them."

"The Holy Father will call upon the youth to fight for the salvation of the Church. **Frenchmen and Spaniards will save him.**"

<u>**Our Lady tells Marie Julie that there will be a disease with a blazing fire.**</u> "This disease will attack first the heart, then the mind, and at the same time the tongue. The heat accompanying the disease will be a devouring fire, intolerable and so violent that the parts of the body touched within will be red from an intolerable redness. At the end of seven days, that disease, scattered a rounded like seeds in the field, it will rapidly grow on

every side, realizing immense progression (in other words very contagious, Ebola could become this disease, or)."

"My children, here is the only remedy with the power of saving you. You know the **leaves of the thorns (hawthorn tree)** may arrest the progression of this disease."

"You will pick up the **leaves**, not the branch (not sure if this means not to pick the leaves from the branches). Even dried up, they will retain their efficacy. (Which I think would mean that either dried or just off the branch they will work.) You place them in boiling water, leaving them for fourteen minutes, keeping the lid on (covered), so that the steam remains inside. From the very start of the attack of the disease, this **remedy** will have to be used **three** times a **day**."

"On the **Monday** after my **Assumption**, you will offer those leaves of the Hawthorn to me, **and pay close heed to my words**. The disease will produce a continuous sickness on the stomach, vomiting. If the remedy is taken too late (I believe this means noticed too late), the touched parts of the body will turn out black, and through the black part there will be traces turning to pale yellow." (From ecstasy of August 16, 1880 of the hawthorn leaf.)

"There will be two days of darkness, different from the three days already announced up til now. During these two days, the sky will be red and purple (clouds), as low as the tops of the trees.... The trees still wearing a few leaves will be turned as if by a blazing fire kindled throughout the whole earth. **Sap will stop, and the trees will bear no fruit on the following year.** From that low-soaring sky, a **rainfall** will come forth with with a **foul stench**..... with a frightening blackness but it will not damage the food of Christians. "During those two days, one should not place one's face in the opening of an outside door. Burning thunderbolts will take place, darkening the apple of the human eye. During the (three) days of darkness with the crucifix, say this prayer:

"I hail, adore, and embrace you, adorable Cross of my Savior. Protect us, guard us, save us. Jesus loved you so much. After this example, I

do love you. May your holy image appease my fears! Let me experience **nothing but calm and confidence!** you will experience so many graces, so much strength, that such a great deluge (of peace) will pass over you …....." "These times will be most frightful, and horrible....." pg 244

"When Rome is possessed by Satan, let the Faithful avoid Rome." Words of Our Lord to Marie Julie. The Church directs her Faithful to avoid contact of any kind with Satan or those who serve him whether they are possessed or not. This will be most necessary for the Remnant in the later times. Even the Remnant will be split before there is left the few to fit under the shade of two fig trees. (Apoc.) **(Will I find any part of the Faith alive when I return? Words of Our Lord.)** *I sincerely fear that nest of vipers (freemasons) in Rome will intoxicate the True Traditionalist Catholics into believing that Rome still believes in the Council of Trent and all others councils but will not follow them, will suck the true catholics into their snare and that will be the end of what Christ has worked for in the salvations of souls.*

So why are the True Traditionalist Priests giving in to Modernist Rome? Simple answer: Satan is using a new strategy of "let's talk or the Talking Game or Entrapment," but Satan tells his boys (masons); "don't outright go killing them, we've tried that before, all that did was put them on guard and make them stronger. And if we do it this way they don't know who the enemy is or where he is, this way I have a great chance of killing the whole church." From the month of the Father of Lies.

Now my children **do not** *compromise the True Faith handed down to you. We are only here a short time (pilgrims) to become saints, grow in sanctity, learn the Faith and spread it, convert souls, make a name for yourself in Heaven, your reward is in Heaven. If Christ had to suffer, so will you. Love poverty as Christ did, as Joseph did.*

Therefore, mind you, that you can not hold communion with the Modernist Rome. Satan is now controlling Rome and has made it his seat to rein. Our Lady of La Salatte has said in 1964 Rome will become the seat of the Antichrist. Many have foolishly tried to unite with Rome and have been deceived. If you unite with Rome you unite with the

following errors and heresies: *RIGHT TO RELIGIOUS LIBERTY *LIBERTY OF CONSCIENCE *SEPARATION OF CHURCH AND STATE (AMERICANISM HERESY) *FREEDOM OF PRESS/ FREEDOM OF SPEECH *HERESY OF INDIFFERENTISM/ UNIVERSALISM/FALSE ECUMENISM *COEXISTENCE/ TOLERANCE INTERFAITH GATHERINGS AND ALL THE MANY ERRORS OF VATICAN II MAKING MAN AUTONOMOUS.
Rome will be destroyed because of these errors. The masons are practicing communism too. The masons are hoodlums, first they threaten you to obey, and when you don't they simply kill you. They love using different poisonous techniques. (John Paul I= dead.) They want a "One World Religion" and the masons in the Vatican will make sure it happens their way, so don't get in their way. (Communist Vatican??? Gladio:) U-tube

The same above teachings are taught at your local Masonic Lodge.

We can unite with Rome when Rome returns to Tradition and the Councils of Trent and other traditionally minded councils this is the eternal Rome, the seat of Peter, before Vatican II. But I fear Our Lord will allow Rome to be destroyed because of the infiltrated masons and communists. The RATS and MICE have to be done away with. Wait for the Great Monarch Henry. Go to *Youtube* type in: **"Illuminati 2017: Predictions!! We must reach mass awareness!"**

Newrite of Consecration of New bishops introduced in 1969 provides remarkable confirmation of the second point of Freemasonry's three-point plan to destroy the Catholic Church, which the dying Cardinal Liénart (1884–1973) allegedly revealed on his deathbed. This Cardinal was a leading neo-modernist at Vatican II, and a Freemason himself. Let us remind readers that the validity of a Catholic sacrament requires, besides a valid Minister, a valid Form and Matter (words and actions at the heart of the ceremony) and the sacramental Intention to do what the Church does.

According to this Cardinal, Freemasonry's first objective at the Council was to break the Mass by so altering the Catholic Rite as to **undermine** in the long run the celebrant's Catholic Intention: "to do what the Church does." Gradually the Newrite was to induce priests and laity alike to take the Mass rather for a "memorial" or "sacred meal" than for a propitiatory sacrifice. Freemasonry's second objective was to break the Apostolic Succession by a Newrite of Consecration that would eventually undermine the bishop's power of Orders, both by a Newform not automatically invalidating but ambiguous enough to sow doubt, and above all by a Newrite which as a whole would eventually dissolve the consecrating bishops sacramental Intention. This would have the advantage of breaking the Apostolic Succession so gently that nobody would even notice.

Today's Newrites of Mass and Episcopal Consecration correspond exactly to the Masonic plan as unveiled by the Cardinal? Ever since these Newrites were introduced in the late 1960's and early 1970's, many serious Catholics have refused to believe that they could be used validly. Alas, they are not automatically invalid. How much simpler it would be, if they were. They are worse. Their sacramental Newform is Catholic enough to persuade many a celebrant that they can be validly used, but the Newrite and Newform are designed as a whole to be so ambiguous and so suggestive of a non-Catholic interpretation as to invalidate the sacrament over time by corrupting the Catholic Intention of any celebrant who is either too "obedient," or is not watching and praying enough to be enlightened. Newrites thus valid enough to get themselves accepted by nearly all Catholics in the short term, but ambiguous enough to invalidate the sacraments in the long term, constitute a trap satanically subtle.

"That which <u>does not</u> correspond to the truth or the moral law <u>has not any right</u>, objectively, to existence, or to propagation, nor to (have) action." **Pius XII**

Pope St. Pius X warned the Church of this in 1907: "They put into operation their designs for Her (the Church's) undoing, not from without but from within. Hence, the danger is present almost in the very veins and walls of the Church, whose injury is the more certain from the very fact that their knowledge of Her is more intimate. Moreover, they lay the ax not to the branches and shoots, but to the very root, that is, to the **faith** and its deepest fibers. **(the Mass and Tradition)**" **Pascendi Dominici Gregis Pius X**

Archbishop Lefebvre once said, "The Novus Ordo Mass will make you a protestant", and it is illisit. It will not give you the full graces you will become lukewarm in your devotions. "And ignorance will be dwelt with severely." Book of Ecclesiastes. Seek ye the Truth of the One, True, Holy, Catholic, and Apostolic Church. The Catholic Church stands on two legs: Sacred Tradition and Sacred Scripture. And unless you do penance and give up the pleasures of this world you will parish. "Learn to do without." Fr. Brey - God rest his soul.

One of the many great Cardinals was Ottaviani who pointed out to Pope Paul VI, in a Letter of September 25, 1969, that "the Novus Ordo Mass represents, both as a whole and in its details, a striking departure from the Catholic theology of the Mass as it was formulated in Sessions XXIII of the Council of Trent. Pope Paul knew he had done wrong, in not trying to stop this wild new religion. Near his death he wandered the halls of the vatican saying over and over the Apostles Creed. And to a Cardinal (can't think of his name) who complained to him the disorder in the new Mass. Pope Paul said, "I can do nothing they will not listen to me." I remember Holland was the first to start getting wild, and it just spread from there liked wildfire, clown masses, dancing girls in the church, women lectures, both men and women lay distributors. Statues thrown out, Communion rails thrown out, main altars tore down and table altar facing the people were installed.

Cardinal Ottaviani also wrote: "Because the New Mass, with its ambiguity and permissiveness, exposes us to the Wrath of God by facilitating the risk of invalid celebrations. Will priests of the near future who rely on the Novus Ordo with the intention of doing what the Church does, consecrate validly? One may be allowed to doubt it." Cardinal Ottaviani was good friends with Archbishop Lefebvre. Cardinal Ottaviani was asked by Archbishop Lefebvre to speak at the Council and to warn the Fathers of the Council of the **liberal ideas** that were creeping into the Council, and the Church. So as he began to speak to all the Council Fathers. The liberals pulled the plugs on the speakers so he would not be hear. He spoke nearly an hour, one heard him.

Archbishop of Birmingham Msgr. Dwyer, spokesman of Episcopal Synod wrote: "Along with the New Mass goes also a new catechism, a new morality, new prayers, new ideas, a new calendar, in a word, a New Church, a complete revolution from the old. The Liturgical reform, do not be deceived, this is where revolution begins."

Pope Paul VI assigned Cardinal Annibale Bugnini to reconstruct the Mass, he ruined the Mass with the help of (6) protestant ministers who help him dismantle the "old Latin Mass" the Mass of all time (Council of Trent). It became identical to the Lutheran Service. This plan was started before Vatican II. But they needed Vatican II to put their plan into action. You will find the Wednesday Night Service in the Lutheran church to be the same in the Novus Ordo Church too, no longer on Friday night 'Stations of the Cross.' Jewish Service is Saturday is the Sabbath and now the Novus Ordo Church is Saturday Mass also. In order to make the Novus Ordo Mass look good to everyone we need to have a Pope canonized to signify that is as good as the 'Old Ways' were before Vatican II. But as I have said before impossible in the eyes of God for any Pope to be canonized by the Church for three reasons 1.) He never obeyed the command of God to Consecrate Russia to the Immaculate Heart of Mary with the all the Bishops of the world. 2.) He never obeyed God when he was told to reveal the 'Third Secret' of Fatima. 3.) In any canonization of any person, out of the many miracles that are done by God for that person, three must be without question validly supernatural beyond a shadow of a doubt. They could not find one for Pope John Paul II, so they made one up. *(Personally I think highly of he man.)* Only two Popes have said and done something in the eyes of God to become canonized and they were St. Pius V and St. Pius X. WHY? Because of their "Bulls and Encyclicals".

In 1975 Cardinal **Bugnini** was found out to be a **mason**. He was exiled to Turkey by Pope Paul VI where he died in 1978. For (3) centuries Popes have written encyclicals on the secret societies mainly Freemasons are enemies of the Church. Any Catholic belonging to a secret sect, is automatically excommunicated.

Why you cannot attend the New Mass: Blessed Innocent XI, condemned the following sentence: "For pastoral reasons you may approach sacraments according to the probability as to its validity." NO you may not. This was condemned. It means if there is doubt you can not go to the New Mass. Because of it's doubtful validity. You can not and must not approach doubtful sacraments. Any church that denies any one or more dogma of past councils is in schism and heresy. Any church or person denying dogma ceases to be catholic. And the Novus Ordo denies nearly all the Council of Trent. This is why you can not go to the New Mass or have anything to do with the New Church, they are schismatic, heretical, and no longer catholic. Even if the sacraments were valid in the New Church they are still denying dogma of past councils and thus is a Schematic Rite, and of course it is not the Latin Rite. **"Whosoever denies one iota of Catholic Dogma, let him be anathema." Council of Trent**

All doctrines and all morality is enshrined in the Most Blessed Sacrament of the Altar. Destroy the Mass and you destroy the Catholic Church. Now do you see why true Mass is so hard to find. (As Our Lady of Garabandal said.) Only a remnant will hold fast to it. Many saints have said the True Faith would become oppressed and a new constitution would replace it. So I wonder when that is going to happen? Priest and nuns will dress in lay clothes. Less importance will be given to the Blessed Sacrament. Removal of the Communion rail. Now people talk, walk through the sanctuary in lay clothing like it's a living room. Even the **sacristans** do not wear a **cassock** any more the sanctuary since Vatican II, I find this very irreverent. Altar Boys used to have to put on a cassock before the entered the sanctuary. In the old testament no one was allowed to enter the sanctuary or the they would die instantly. Now God is actually present and people go through there instead of going around outside or through the basement. Everybody is in the sanctuary with lay clothes on since Vatican II.

Also many of the parishes are losing their catholic high schools. The people with children are moving where there is a high school. In most cases the high school could have kept going if the people were told they must support it or it will shut down. They were never giving the choice or notification. They just shut them down.

Father Constant Louis Marie PEL (1876–1966) (Our Lord speaks to this priest): is not a name well-known among the souls gifted by God with a knowledge of how God is going to set today's world straight, but for those who knew him he was a priest very close to God. Doctor in theology, seminary professor, founder of a convent for women and of a seminary for men, with a great devotion to the Sacred Heart of Jesus and to the Immaculate Heart of Mary, he was a personal friend of Padre Pio who said of him to some French pilgrims in San Giovanni Rotondo, "Why do you come to see me when you have so great a Saint in France?"

Fr. Pel would spend nights on his feet in church with his forehead leaning against the Tabernacle, conversing with God in a permanent ecstasy. He died in a car accident just after Vatican II, but not before a seminarian, one of his spiritual sons, had been able to note down a prophecy of his, dating from 1945, concerning the chastisement which will strike France in particular. **Here it is, quoted or abbreviated of the (3) Days of Darkness:**

"My son," said **Fr. Pel**, "knows that with the sins of the world increasing in horror as this age wears on, great punishments from God will come down on the world and no continent will be spared by the Wrath of God. France being guilty of apostasy and denying its vocation will be severely chastised. East of a line stretching from Bordeaux in the south-west to Lille in the north-east, everything will be laid waste and set on fire by people invading from the east, and also **by great flaming meteorites falling in a rain of fire** upon all the earth and upon these regions especially. Revolution, war, epidemics, plagues, chemical poison gases, violent earthquakes and the re-awakening of France's extinct volcanoes will destroy everything.

"**France** to the west of that line will be less affected . . . because of the faith rooted in the **Vendee** and in **Brittany** . . . but many of God's worst enemies seeking refuge there from the worldwide cataclysm will be found out, wherever they hide, and put to death by devil's, because the Wrath of the Lord is just and holy. **Thick darkness caused by the war, gigantic fires and fragments of burning stars falling for three days and nights** will cause the sun to disappear, and only candles blessed on Candlemas (February 2) will give light in the hands of believers, but the godless will not see this miraculous light because they have darkness in their souls.

"In this way, my son, **three quarters of mankind will be destroyed**, and in certain parts of France survivors will have to go 60 miles to find another live human being . . . . Several nations will disappear off the face of the map . . . . France thus purified will become the renewed "Eldest Daughter of the Church," because all the Cains and Judases will have disappeared in this 'Judgment upon the Nations'". This Judgment is not yet the end of times, but so great is the punishment due to the sins of the nations that **Our Lord told Fr. Pel** that the desolation at world's end will be lesser (Shortened).

My children, what do we conclude? Let each of us strive with all our might and every effort, and with the help of the Catholic sacraments given to us by God for that purpose, to live in God's grace and not in the state of sin, and let us make full use of the time He gives us between now and the Hour of his Justice to pray for the largest possible number of sinners to repent and save their souls for eternity when the Chastisement closes in. I'm not sure if it was Our Lady who said, "When asking of a grace or anything from God ask for large things with confidence, because it is no problem for God to give a large thing or small thing."

Vision of Sister Faustina: Our Lord said, "Before the day of justice arrives, there will be given to the people a sign in the heavens of this sort: 'All lights in the heavens will be extinguished, and there will be great darkness over the whole earth. Then the sign of the cross will be seen in the sky...'"

Our Lady of Good Success appeared in Quito, Ecuador

Because the faithful had not studied and held fast to the True Traditional Catholic Faith, God was going to allow it to disappear. Our Lady begged Almighty God to raise up a prelate (bishop) to bring about a group of priests that would keep a remnant of the True Faith alive. And here is that story.

During the fifteenth and sixteenth centuries, **Our Lady of Good Success appeared in Quito**, Ecuador to a Spanish nun whose little-known but extraordinary life has a direct connection with our days.

Early in the morning of January 21, 1610, the Archangels St. Michael, St. Gabriel and St. Raphael appeared to Mother Mariana. Then Our Lady appeared to her and predicted many things about our own times in the middle of the 1900's: this is part of what Mother Mariana afterwards related that Our Lady told her:

".... I make it known to you that from the end of the **19th century** and shortly after the middle of the **20th century (1964 La Sallette)....** the passions will erupt and there will be a total corruption of customs (dress and morals)....

The Pope's "infallibility will be declared a dogma of Faith by the same Pope chosen to proclaim the dogma of the mystery of my Immaculate Conception. He will be persecuted and imprisoned in the Vatican through the usurpation of the Pontifical States and through the malice, envy, and avarice of an earthly monarch."

"Unbridled strong passions will give way to a total corruption of customs because Satan will reign through the **Masonic sects**, targeting the children in particular to insure general corruption." *(Hollywood) Children's Disney movies, are why the children grow up and dress like they do today. Disney world is controlled by the Jewish Illuminati, and is made to excel and enhance sexual stimulation in the children's brain subversively. Whatever God tries to point upward for good, the devil points downward for evil. A constant struggle and fight.*

"Unhappy, the children of those times! <u>Seldom will they receive the sacraments of **Baptism** and **Confirmation**</u>. As for the <u>sacrament of **Penance**</u>, they will confess only while attending Catholic schools, which the devil will do his utmost to destroy by means of persons in authority. (No more St. Joseph Catholic School. The building was perfectly sound before they ripped it down in Woonsocket, S.D. and the nuns were sent away. Now that I'm older, I've noticed masonic symbols on the bass and top of nearly half the buildings in Woonsocket, S.D.) To belong to a secret society is automatic "anathema" for any catholic to belong to.

"Secular education (no more Catholic schools) will contribute to a <u>scarcity of priestly and religious</u> vocations." "The <u>holy sacrament of **Holy Orders**</u> will be ridiculed, oppressed, and despised, for in this both the Church and God Himself are oppressed and reviled, since He is represented by His priests. *(A priest can never be to religious or to Traditional when it comes to being a sound, pious sober priest. When a person thinks a priest is to pious, that person is farthest from God.)* Those who will thus scandalize the Christian flock will bring upon all priests the hatred of bad Christians and the enemies of the One, Holy, Roman Catholic, and Apostolic Church."

(Today the errors of Vatican II are being taught in the Novus Ordo seminarians.) "The same will occur with **Holy Communion**. Oh, how it hurts me to tell you that there will be many and enormous public and hidden sacrileges!" *(Communion in the Hand according to Mother Teresa is the worst sacrilege under the sun.)*

"In those times, the sacrament of **Unction Extreme** will be largely ignored.… Many will die without receiving it, being thereby deprived of innumerable graces, consolation, and strength in the great leap from time to eternity." "The sacrament of **Matrimony**, which symbolizes the union of Christ with the Church, will be thoroughly attacked and profaned. Masonry, then reigning, will implement iniquitous laws aimed at extinguishing this sacrament. They will make it easy for all to live in sin, thus multiplying the birth of illegitimate children without the Church's blessing…." (Yes, living together and same sex marriage.) "The **small number** of souls who will secretly safeguard the treasure of Faith and virtues will suffer a cruel, unspeakable, and long martyrdom. Many will descend to their graves through the violence of suffering and will be counted among the martyrs who sacrificed themselves for the country and the Church. "In those times the atmosphere will be saturated with the spirit of impurity which, like a filthy sea, will engulf the streets and public places with incredible license.… **Innocence will scarcely be found in children, or modesty in women.**" *(Sleeves must cover the arms on both men and women also cover legs half way between knee and ankle. Clothes clinging tightly to the body are forbidden. Shirts and blouses must come up to the base of the neck, not half way up your front. St. Padre Pio would not give Holy Communion to anyone who's arms were not covered and the leg must be covered (8") below the knee. Always a maxi dress is fine. Outside of church short sleeves are permitted. Inside of church wear a dress jacket, to cover your form. If it is hot, offer it up. There is a hotter place waiting for you. Men are to always dress with a suit jacket or dress jacket in Church. Your dress jacket is cover your fat or muscular body from women looking and paying attention to you, instead of paying attention to God. Remember the priest is clothed in his vestments which is more than you're wearing. The **Devil** will seduce many into the sins of the **flesh**, living together without **Matrimony**.)*

"Pray constantly, implore tirelessly, and weep bitter tears in the seclusion of your heart, beseeching the Eucharistic Heart of my most holy Son to take pity on His ministers and to end as soon as possible these unhappy times **by sending to His Church the Prelate** who shall restore the spirit of her priests." (*This Prelate was Archbishop Marcel Lefebvre 1905 – 1991. He started the Order of the Society of St. Pius X. Which is still going today. To find the true Mass go to: www.traditio.com)* **"When everything will seem lost and paralyzed, that will be the happy beginning of the complete restoration. This will mark the arrival of my hour, when I, in a marvelous way, will dethrone the proud and cursed Satan, trampling him under my feet and fettering him in the infernal abyss." Our Lady of Good Success**

Providence decided to throw a "nuclear" bomb on the enemies of the Church. The havoc wreaked in Hiroshima and Nagasaki is only a minor fever compared to this bomb. The "nuclear bomb" of Catholicism has been ready to explode for two centuries now. When it does, we will understand the full meaning of the expression from Scripture, "Non est qui se abscondat a calore ejus" ["no one can escape its heat."] The Love of Sacred Heart or The Chastisement of the Arm of God.

This bomb has a very sweet name: It is called the Treatise on True Devotion to the Blessed Virgin. In it, every word, every letter is a treasure. It is the book of the new times that are coming. To have any attachment or love for Mary is a sign is predestination, is to save your soul. (Scapular and Rosary.)

By uniting the world to Our Lady, Saint Louis Grignion de Montfort says, this devotion will unite it with God. The day when men know, appreciate and live this devotion, Our Lady will reign in all hearts and the face of the earth will be renewed. Somewhere **Our Lady said** that at time of the **Chastisement, those** who say my **Most Holy Rosary** and wear the **scapular** would be **saved**. Every time you hear of a person dying in an accident, you should think to wear your scapular and daily say your Rosary. After all it is the command of the Queen.

Saturday is the Queen's (Our Lady) day of the week. Our Lady visits Purgatory every Saturday to release souls Purgatory who have died during the week and who have worn the **brown scapular** of Our Lady of Mount Carmel. When Our Lady was assumed into Heaven on August 15, the undoubtedly took countless souls from Purgatory with her, perhaps all of them that were then there. Our Lady's promise to those who wear the brown scapular is this: "Whosoever dies wearing this scapular shall not suffer the eternal fires of Hell. On Saturday, as many as I shall find in Purgatory, i shall free." Saint Claude de la Colombiere says that, "Of all the forms of our love for the Blessed Virgin and its various modes of expression, the scapular is the most favored."

The prophecy of Ezekiel declares, "The gate of the inner court that looks toward the East shall be shut for six days, but on the sabbath day it shall be opened." This prophecy is read in the Saturday Mass in honor of Our Lady of Mount Carmel, that the "inner court" means Purgatory, and the sabbath day means" Saturday, the day when Our Lady abundantly releases souls from Purgatory and brings them to Heaven.

(Can a Pope be beatified who has not obeyed the Queen's command?) I don't think so. Read this book. PAUL VI beatified? --- 328 pages -The book that stopped the beatification process of Paul VI. Unfortunately Fr. Luigi Villa died before he could finish the book on Pope John Paul II.

Now made available in English. First published in 1998 by Editrice Civilta of Brescia, Italy and written by award winning author, Father Luigi Villa, Doctor of Dogmatic Theology. What is the significance of this book?

Father Luigi Villa was commissioned by **St. Padre Pio** and given a papal mandate from **Pope Pius XII** to dedicate his life to defend the Catholic Church from the work of Freemasonry – most especially Ecclesiastical Freemasonry.• **St. Padre Pio warned Father Villa**, in their second meeting in 1963, to be brave as Freemasonry had already invaded the Catholic Church and had even "made it into the shoes of the Pope!" The reigning pope of the time was Paul VI. This above book shows pictures in Rome, of monuments in honor of Paul VI by the masons.

When Pope John XXIII Read the opening address to the Council, he told them that this was not the time for the doomsday prophecies and this is part of the reason the 3rd Secret was not read. This opening address was written by none other than Cardinal Montini. Who became Pope Paul VI and continued the Second Vatican Council which he closed in 1965. Which Satan and his freemasons and communists have enjoyed. He also helped in setting up the Moscow/Rome Pax Agreement. Which is to this day keeping Rome from **Consecrating Russia** to Mary's Immaculate Heart. Which will stop the Russian Invasion and Communist take over.

- Playing the "Devil's Advocate" (as was once a requirement in the process for beatification), Father Villa answered the call of Cardinal Ruini, Vicar of the Pope for the city of Rome, who had issued an "Edict," appearing in the diocesan weekly "Roma Sette" on May 13, 1992, which, "invited every single faithful to communicate to us directly … any information" which, in any way, may argue against the reputation of sanctity of the said "Servant of God" by writing this book. • This book is based on the critical study of thousands of pages of encyclicals, speeches, Conciliar documents, historical journals, commentaries and magazines.

Pope John XXIII told a cardinal on his death bed, "that Cardinal Seri was right, that Council of Vatican II was a mistake." Funny the way people on their death bed admit the truth. Fr. Martin Luther the Augustinian monk on his death bed said the devil taught him reformation. And of course he was excommunicated and most all Lutherans follow him to hell, according to St. Teresa of Avila who had a vision of Hell.

- It was written in order "to transmit, … the "truth", in order to remain faithful to the Faith of Jesus Christ, Our Lord, which is transmitted by His Church, sole "custodian" of the "Depositum Fidei"! Anne McGinn Cillis, a spiritual daughter of Padre Pio, Franciscan tertiary and author of "Arrivederci, Padre Pio – A Spiritual Daughter Remembers" stated in regards to this book:

"In my opinion, it is one of the better books written in our time! … It reinforces that the **New Mass** is "**The Great Sacrilege**" as written by Father James Wathen." In this well written book **"The Great Sacrilege"** on pg. (41) points out that "Latin is the mystical liturgical language of the Roman Rite; the use of vernacular languages is forbidden."
Council of Trent (Sess.XXII Pg. 411 No. 1759, Canon 9: "If anyone says that the rite of the Roman Church by which a part of the Canon and the words of Consecration are said in a subdued voice (vernacular)

(they) should be condemned, or that the Mass should be said in the Vernacular only, or that water should not be added to the wine in the chalice, which is to be offered, since it is contrary to the institution of Christ, let him be anathema."

"Those therefore who after the manner of wicked heretics dare to set aside Ecclesiastical Traditions, and to invent any kind of novelty, or to reject any of those things entrusted to the Church, or who wrongfully and outrageously devise the destruction of any of those Traditions enshrined in the Catholic Church, are to be punished thus: IF THEY ARE BISHOPS, WE ORDER THEM TO BE DEPOSED; BUT IF THEY ARE MONKS OR LAY PERSONS, WE COMMAND THEM TO BE EXCLUDED FROM THE COMMUNITY."

--------- **Second Council of Nicaea 787 A.D.**

"The fort is betrayed even of them that should have defended it." --------- **St. John Fisher, Bishop and Martyr**

"Let us regard the **Tradition** of the Church also as worthy of belief. Is it a tradition? Seek no further!" ---------

---**St. John Chrysostom**

"To recoil before an enemy, or to keep silence when from all sides such clamors are raised against truth, is the part of a man either devoid of character or who entertains doubt as to the truth of what he professes to believe. In both cases such mode of behaving is base and is insulting to God, and both are incompatible with the salvation of mankind." **Pope Leo XIII, *Sapientiae Christianae***

"They knew only too well the intimate bond that unites faith with worship, the law of belief with the law of prayer, and so, under the pretext of restoring the order of the liturgy to its primitive form, they corrupted it in many respects to adapt it to the errors of the Innovators." **Pope Leo XIII, *Apostolicae Curae***

"It is better that the truth be known than that scandal be covered up." **St. Augustine**

"Not to oppose error is to approve it; and not to defend Truth is to suppress it; indeed to neglect to confound evil men when we can do it; is no less a sin than to encourage it!!!" **Pope St. Felix III**

"Not to oppose error is to approve it; and not to defend truth is to suppress it; and indeed to neglect to confound evil men, when we can do it, is no less a sin than to encourage them." **Pope St. Felix III**

"The greatest obstacle in the apostolate of the Church is the timidity or rather the cowardice of the faithful." **Pope St. Pius X**

James Duckett (1602) was a bookseller, in London, before and after the Protestant Reformation. But after the Reformation of King Henry VIII, Blessed James was martyred for selling Catholic books. As he was dying, he said to his fellow countryman: "It is as impossible for anyone to be saved outside the Catholic Church as it was for anyone to avoid the deluge who was outside Noah's Ark." *(No doubt he read some of those books.)*

St. Vincent of Lerins in the 5th century gave as a standard for the orthodoxy of doctrine that which has been believed everywhere (*ubique*), always (*semper*), and by all (*omnia*). **But**, as Cardinal Ratzinger points out, **the Council Fathers of Vatican II rejected** this hallowed definition: "Vatican II's refusal of the proposal to adopt the text of Lerins, familiar to, and, as it were, **sanctified by two Church Councils**, shows once more how **Trent** and **Vatican I** were <u>left behind</u>, how their texts were **continually reinterpreted**... Vatican II had a **new idea** of how historical identity and continuity were to be brought about." This new idea was nothing other than to create a **pseudo-tradition** from the "common consciousness" of the Council Fathers. This is **pure Modernism** and **totally contrary to the Deposit of Faith**. 'The Destruction of Catholic Worship is the Destruction of the Catholic Faith.' The Church has always set forth the firm and clear principle that: "*The way you worship or (**pray**), is the way we believe*." (Satan's Mansons destroyed this at their infiltration of Vatican II.)

The doctrinal truths of the Faith are embodied in the worship we offer to God. In other words, it is the Holy Sacrifice of the Mass that teaches us our theology and not the reverse. The **True Mass** comprises the Apostolic Traditions of faith and morals in its very essence. Every doctrine essential to the Faith is taught therein. Pope Leo XIII points out in *Apostolicae Curae* that the Church's enemies have always understood this principle as **"They knew only too well the intimate bond that unites faith with worship, the law of belief with the law of prayer, and so, under the pretext of restoring the order of the liturgy to its primitive form, they corrupted it in many respects to adapt it to the errors of the Innovators."** As the crisis of Faith and Liturgy continues decade after decade. The fundamental disorder of the New Mass (Novus Ordo) is best described not only British Historian Hugh Ross Williamson, who was an authority on Sixteenth and Seventeenth Centuries Protestantism says the New Mass is tailored after the (Anglican) Thomas Cranmer's principles to destroy the Mass. The **Novus Ordo** has been rightly nicknamed **"Cranmer's Mass."** (Calvinism and Lutheranism is what Cranmer's Mass is.)

Cardinals Ottaviani and Bacci (1969) along with Archbishop Lefebvre clearly and doctrinally warn: "It is obvious that the New Order of Mass has no intention of representing the Faith taught by the Council of Trent. But it is to this true Faith that Catholic conscience is bound to forever." (from 'Catholic Family News')

It is no wonder, then, that Luther coined the slogan: "Take away the Mass, you destroy the Church." St. Alphonsus Liguori (Bishop, Doctor of the Church and Patron of Theologians) explains that **"The devil has always attempted, by means of the heretics, to deprive the world of the True Mass**, making them precursors of the Antichrist, who, before anything else, will try to abolish and will actually abolish the Holy Sacrament of the altar, as a punishment for the sins of men, according to the prediction of Daniel: *'And strength was given him against the continual sacrifice' (Dan. 8:12)."* Jesus gave Satan time and power, for over 100 years, which will go on until the Chastisement.

The question then becomes: **Does the New Mass teach and preserve the deposit of the Catholic Faith?** "No," say both Cardinals Ottaviani and Bacci: "It is clear that the *Novus Ordo* no longer intends to present the Faith as taught by the Council of Trent." Pope St. Leo the Great (Father and Doctor of the Church) instructs us: "Teach nothing new, but implant in the hearts of everyone those things which the fathers of venerable memory taught with a uniform preaching... Whence, we preach nothing except what we have received from our forefathers. In all things, therefore, both in the rule of faith in the observance of discipline let the pattern of antiquity be observed." (*especially from the past Councils...*) How well founded, then, were the **concerns** expressed by Pope Pius XII shortly before the introduction of the **New Mass**: "I am worried by the Blessed Virgin's messages to Lucy at Fatima. This persistence of Our Lady about the dangers which menace the Church is a **Divine warning** against the **suicide** that would be represented **by the alteration of the Faith in Her liturgy.**" (*He must have understood this from the 3rd Secret of Fatima.*)

As Archbishop Lefebvre has more than once said, "Stay away from the New Mass, because it will make you a protestant little by little." In the later times the devil will work false miracles. And he has in the New Mass, which has caused good men to be fooled. Why would God do a miracle in the New Mass if He said He hates the New Mass, as He said to St. Marie Julie Jahenny. Stay in the Mass that you know is the Mass of the Saints.

Archbishop Marcel Lefebvre has said more than once: "Rome has left the Church, they have left the Church, they have left the Church! Enough said."

Here is a good question: "Why can I do **not** go to the Indult Mass?" The reason is because the "Indult Mass" is given under the condition that the priest saying this Mass accepts in theory or on paper, Vatican II. And as the best of Roman Theologians have recently stated: **you can not accept Vatican II and be a Catholic.** But if this same priest leaves Vatican II out of his sermons, and your salvation is not put in jeopardy, and you can not find the True Mass elsewhere, than go there and not to the New Mass. Besides the many reasons, one stands out is that Vatican II says: "The

Spirit of Christ does not deny to give salvation to the efforts of protestant churches." This is heresy directly against Pope Eugene IV (1442 Council of Florence) which says: **"Nobody who is not subject to the Roman Pontiff even if he thinks he can shed his blood for Our Lord can be saved." Now this is considered objective judgement, meaning we are to believe that 'Outside the Catholic Church there is no salvation.'** What happens to them, God knows, we do not.

The New Mass is said in the **vernacular** of the people which takes away one of the (4) marks of the Catholic Faith. Most priests in the Novus Ordo say the Mass only if there are people present. They do not understand that the Mass is a priest's daily (private) prayer, and is the sacrificial offering of the true Body and Blood of Christ to His Eternal Father for our sins, daily, because we are sinners daily. But those who assist at the Mass which is the priest's prayer, receive grace from reading their missal and following the Mass with meditation on the sorrowful passion of Christ. The priest was never meant to face the people, or to make a show of it as it is in most cases. It is to give us the Blessed Sacrament necessary for our salvation. And since our hands are not ordained to touch the Blessed Sacrament which is God, this is the Greatest sacrilege. These priest think that they are supposed to be talking to the people, but they should be talking to God in a low voice and we the people are to follow in the missal. Then there is the High Mass or Sung Mass, considered the public Mass, usually on Holy Days.

Without the Latin, the right form, and the intention, **you have nothing.** Just a prayer service. Totally Lutheran. There are deep theological differences and differences in the hierarchy of each Mass. The High Mass the Subdeacon has an important role. The subdiaconate is the lowest of the sacred or major orders in the Latin Church. It is defined as the power by which one ordained as a subdeacon may carry the chalice with wine to the altar, prepare the necessaries for the Eucharist, and read the Epistles before the people.

In the Novus Ordo the use of the Maniple has also been abolished. Tracing its origins to the 6th century handkerchiefs celebrants would use, the maniple became symbolic of the burden of sin and of the tears and sweat of sacrifice.

Tridentine	**Novus Ordo**
-Asperges Me (Ps. 50)	-Introductory Rites:
-Mass of the Catechumens:	-Confiteor (reduced)
-Foot of the altar prayers (Ps. 42)	-Kyrie Eleison (reduced)
-Confiteor	-Gloria in Excelsis Deo
-Introit	-Collect
-Kyrie Eleison (9 times)	**Liturgy of the Word:**
-Gloria in Excelsis Deo	-1st and 2nd Readings
-Collect	-Responsorial Psalms
-Epistle	-Creed
-Gradual or (Tract in Lent)	-Prayer of the Faithful
-Creed	
Mass of the Faithful:	**Liturgy of the Eucharist:**
-Offertory & Verse	-Preparation of Gifts
-Preface	-Prayer of Offerings
-Sanctus	-Preface
-Canon (complete mystical silence)	-Sanctus
-Consecration	-Canon (no longer silent)
-2nd Confiteor	-Consecration
-Domine non sum dignus (said 3x)	-Domine non sum dignus (said 1x)
-Communion & Post Communion Verse	-Ite Missa est
-Ita Missa Est	
-Last Gospel of St. John	
-Leonine Prayers of Pope Leo for the Conversation of Russia (10 yrs Ind.)	

The Last Gospel was meant to represent the summary of the Incarnation of Christ and the Christian Faith, this was requested by the people in earlier time to give them something to hear and take with them for the day.

The Altar Cards as well as the Last Gospel are abolished in the Novus Ordo Mass. Priest no longer faces Christ in the tabernacle, turn his back to Him or places Christ from His Main Place of Honor to the side altar.

Clearly this Extraordinary Form which can be traced back to the first centuries is a Living Tradition. Thanks to St. Pope Pius V and Summorum Pontificum, any priest can freely celebrate Latin Tridentine Mass.

Of course the main excuse of all Novus Ordo priests is: "I don't understand Latin." **That will come with time**, and should not be a concern. At any cost the Polka Masses, Balloon Masses, Lay Ministers, Communion in the Hand, Clown Masses, the new age protestant music, Dance Masses, Hindu pagan cultural Masses, Rock with electric concert Liturgies, Lounge about the sanctuary Masses, discussion panel Masses, buddhist style floor liturgy Masses, mime liturgy Masses, dinner table lawn Masses, halloween and costume with pumpkins and decorations with rainbow vestments Masses, dance and skit Masses, suitcase in the park with barefeet and shorts sit down picnic style Masses, the gather around the altar holding hands Masses with children colored hand prints all over the table altar cloth, culture manipulated Masses, burrito Masses (not sure if that is with or without Pepsi Cola), Lounge about the gym Masses, multiple glass cup Masses, skull Masses with a giant drop down picture of a skull or whatever other picture this Mass is to honor that day, a wanna be women's priest Masses with the young women standing around the altar and altar girls (which Rome said no to), barn Masses on bails, stuffed teddy bear's picnic Masses, show and tell throw it on floor in front of the altar Masses, new age hippy sit down with guitar coffee table style Masses, episcopal 'american idol' Masses, dining table guitar folk music Masses, ballerina dance Masses, classroom desk Masses, naked native Masses, the lay person of God (some young girls and boys holding up the Eucharist) Masses, a dress bizarre and celebrate ourselves Masses, the vestal virgins Masses, banner Masses, the childrens look at me dance Masses, a kooky backyard children's birthday Masses, beach Masses (some had shorts on and some didn't have much on at all), teen agers in shorts and barefoot lounge around the sanctuary Mass (not even wearing ridiculous shower shoes), biker Masses, pagan offering Mass, religious buddha Mass with large buddha on the table, in the park singlet table Mass in 'T' shirt and shorts and shower shoes, campfire woods Mass, goofy priest with cardboard box Mass (in the middle of a crowd), field blanket Mass, coffee pot and crockery and ceramic cups with the people completely surrounding the priest around a table, cookie Mass, dip Jesus yourself Masses, **cowboy show Mass** all in cowboy hats (didn't even take off their hat for Mass, I know guys like that, don't take off their hat inside or when they eat, disgusting and humiliating and certainly not catholic), **Lord have mercy on us!** Handshaking and hugging and crazy pictures and abstract wild art, liturgical brainwashing of children to become "women priests" talking in church and all the irreverence of the Novus Ordo Religion must come to a halt. Even when done reverently, it is not the Mass Christ is happy with, as you remember from pg 29. Our Lord told the Stigmatist Marie Julie Jahenny on two different occasions 1902 & 1907 He warned us that the enemies of the Church would invent a NEW MASS, totally ODIOUS to His Will. In the reign of the Great Monarch and the Holy Pontiff, Their will be one Mass. If you remember also Our Lady's word that what is rotten will fall and must be forgotten. The New Church teaches Christianity without the cross. The Crucifix is missing on the table altar. The cross or raising Christ is all you will find in the New Church. It seem that the New Mass was invalid up to the time Pope Benedict ordered the correct words for consecration namely: "for you and for many" changed form "for you and for all." Because the Mass may be valid doesn't mean you should go to it. **The Black Mass of Satan is valid, as is many sedevacantist, and Eastern Orthodox and many others.** *You are forbidden to go to them.* Things will straighten out after the over run of Europe by Russia and the Great Monarch come to help a Holy Pope and return things back as they were before Vatican II.

Cardinal Ratzinger did a writing on the the liturgy under the authority of the pope, where he says: "After the Vatican II the impression arose that the pope really could do anything (he wanted) in liturgical matters. Eventually,.....the fact that no one **cannot** do with it what one will, faded from the public consciousness...... In fact the First Vatican Council had not defined the pope as an absolute monarch (*over Tradition*). On the contrary, it presented him as the guarantor of obedience to the revealed Word. The pope's authority is bound to the Tradition of the Faith, and that also applies to the liturgy. It is not "manufactured" by the authorities. Even the pope can only be a humble servant of its lawful development and abiding integrity and identity... The authority of the pope is not unlimited;

it is at the service of Sacred Tradition *(that is to guard it)*. The Church stands or falls with the Liturgy."

He goes on to sight in the Council of Trent: "If anyone says that the received and approved rites of the Catholic Church customarily used in the solemn administration of the sacraments can be changed into other new rites by any Church pastor whosoever, let him be anathema." COUNCIL OF TRENT Session 7 Canon 13.

St. Catherine Emmerich: "Many priests and bishops would be, Ipso Facto, excommunicated and didn't even know it." (Poor Priests and Bishops.) This Crisis is not just due to the collapse of the liturgy, there are many other factors.

"...Lex orandi, lex credendi, lex vivende: the law of prayer, is the law of faith, is the law of life..." how we pray will affect what we believe which will affect how we live. How you live and well you pray at home kneeing all together devoutly and slowly, and are you attentive in your missal at Mass. The wording of the Liturgy is extremely important. That's why I tell you to use your missel when you assist at Mass. These prayers are most important to your salvation. And because the New Mass was written by Cardinal Bugnini (a mason) six protestants, I don't think you're going to get the same effect going to the New Mass, as going to the Old Latin Mass, which was written and formulated by the Old Councils and saintly Fathers of the Church. Christ gave His Life for it! Pray for the Restoration of the Sacred Liturgy. And for the Humane Dignity we have been striped of.

Why do we go to Mass, because it is we in the presence of God and if it is the One True Mass of the Church from the time of Christ you are a partaker in the True Sacrifice of offering the Body and Blood of Christ to His Father for your sins. Fourteen miracles take place at Mass. Truth and Doctrine can not change. The Modernist in the new church have changed it. There is only ONE CHURCH, ONE GOD, ONE FAITH, ONE BAPTISM. Stay away from the New Mass, it's illicit, because it's against Divine Law according to past popes and councils one can change Divine Liturgy. Divine Liturgy is the silent part of the Mass called the Canon. Silent because of the mysterious union between God and his priest. Not found in the New Mass.

The sacred vessels used to hold the Body and Blood of Christ must gilded in gold or silver, the inside must be a polished gold which holds the Body and Blood of God. This is a Rubric of the Church. The Mass vestments are equally important, they are the chasuble and the maniple (barrette is actually not a Mass vestment, but should be worn at all times except when offering the Mass, and put on at the sermon). The Chasuble and Maniple are taken off at the sermon, because the sermon is not part of the Mass. In the old days the sermon was given before Mass, before the chasuble and maniple were put on. The Church language is Latin, not the profane language called the vernacular. Cursing is called the using the profane Language. This is why the Council of Trent said only Latin can be used when is said under pain of sin. Vatican II documents are all ambiguous, they may say a good thing and turn around and say, but you can do it this way if it feels good to you. Vatican II documents are not written in a true legal doctrinal language. That is why we conclude that these people were liberals, modernists, masons, and crackpots.

Pope Pius VI (1775) in his document entitled **"Auctorem Fidei"** condemning that: "Catholics may not except any documents which are ambiguous and not clearly understood directly." This same pope said the purpose of an Ecumenical Council is to define and clarify things, not to make them ambiguous. Vatican II did not clarify anything.

The casual everyday dress and immodest dress must stop. The manner in which one dresses is the respect you give to God and Neighbor when you go to visit hjm. In Church at Mass, no bare arms, dress shirt and jacket. Dresses 8" below Knees. Clothes are not to be tight on the body, but loose. Blouse up to the base of the neck. Polished shoes and sockets. No shower shoes. No tennis shoes. No high heels on little girls. The fashion designer of this day and age are working for Satan, and we are at their mercy. The Global elite who serve Satan want to strip man of all human dignity. You will see migrants coming into a country which will destroy the dignity of all its modest cultures and traditions. Because of migrants coming into a country, this destroys the country's culture and causes it to lose its cultural heritage and the country becomes a melting pot of mud. This is like mixing Italians with Germans, or the Irish with Pygmies of Africa, the culture of each group of people belong to that group and must be preserved not destroyed as Satan is doing through his masons.

According to the great Saints, "Every Sunday is called "Little Easter." So dress your finest for love of God as if it is Easter, unless you love your comfort and self more than God. Imitation of Christ: "Always give up your will for the love of the other." (Polish your shoes and don't wear tennis shoes into church. We are losing our culture because of the fashions are causing this decadency in our catholic faith.)

You have the counterfeit Mass and you have the True Mass: Let's look at what you are sure to receive by going to the True Latin Tridentine Mass:

Tremendous value of the Holy Sacrifice of the True Mass:

- One Holy Mass heard during your life will be of more benefit to you than many heard after your death.
- At the hour of death the Holy Masses you have heard devoutly will be your greatest consolation.
- God forgives you all your venial sins which you sincerely determined to avoid.
- God forgives all unknown sins which you have never confessed.
- The power of the devil over you is diminished.
- Every Holy Mass will go with you to Judgment and will plead for pardon for you.
- By every Holy Mass you can diminish the temporal punishment due to your sins, more or less, according to your fervor.
- By every Holy Mass you assist at devoutly your time in Purgatory is **shortened**.
- By devoutly assisting at Holy Mass you render the greatest homage possible to the Sacred Humanity of Our Lord.
- Through the Holy Sacrifice, Our Lord Jesus Christ supplies for many of your negligences and omissions.
- By piously hearing Holy Mass you afford the Souls in Purgatory (the Church Suffering) the greatest possible relief.
- Through Holy Mass you are preserved from many dangers and misfortunes which would otherwise have befallen you.
- During Holy Mass you kneel amid a multitude of holy Angels, who are present at the Adorable Sacrifice with reverential awe.

- Through Holy Mass you are blessed in your temporal goods and affairs.
- When you hear Holy Mass devoutly, offering it to Almighty God in honor of any particular Saint or Angel, thanking God for the favors bestowed on him or her, you afford that Saint or Angel a new degree of honor, joy and happiness, and draw his special love and protection on yourself.
- Every time you assist at Holy Mass, besides other intentions, you should offer it in honor of the Saint of the Day in remembering the Church Triumphant.

This is why the Traditional Latin Mass is the most beautiful thing this side of Heaven.

To better understand the Holy of the Mass, go to **U-tube: "Explanation of the Traditional Latin Mass"** You will told there many things taught from the time of Christ and which the good Apostles handed down to, such as the reason the priest is asked to raise the host on high and hold it for 30 sec. The people would cry out raise it high and longer. It was so the people could gave some moments of adoration to Almighty God while looking at God raised on high in sacramental form. Today to priest seem to be in such a hurry. The host is not held up long at all, and the latin is sped through so fast that no one can read their missal prayers with any devotion. I hear this complaint from so many people. Priest need to say the Old Mass slowly, especially the Epistle and the Gospel. This will fall on deaf ears, surely. Actually the Mass is the priest's private prayer, so we can't tell him anything.

The Tridentine Mass = Translated from the Greek liturgy in 210 AD by Pope Victor I

Codified by St. Pius V in the papal bull "Quo Primum" stating: "This Missal is to be used by all Churches into perpetuity." (forever) Let me just quote the whole thing.

No priest can ever be prevented from offering exclusively the true mass, the Traditional Latin Tridentine Mass:

"Furthermore, by these presents (this Law), in virtue of Our Apostolic authority, We grant and concede in perpetuity that, for the chanting or reading of the Mass in any church whatsoever, this Missal is hereafter to be followed absolutely, without any scruple of conscience or fear of incurring any penalty, judgment, or censure, and may freely and lawfully be used."

Pope St. Pius V Quo Primum

"Let all everywhere adopt and observe what has been handed down by the Holy Roman Church, the Mother and Teacher of the other churches, and let Masses not be sung or read according to any other formula than that of this Missal published by Us."

Pope St. Pius V in Quo Primum (1570)

If a priest tries to explain the above away, do not be fooled by him, he is leading you to perdition.

The Church teaches us to go to Mass on Holy Days of Obligation, but she must provide you with the correct Mass. Also to keep this day holy by some further prayers and readings. You are **not** obligation to go to something in its place, your rite is Latin. Read the following.

Session 7, Canon 13 of the Council of Trent:

"If any one saith, that the received and approved rites of the Catholic Church, want to be used in the solemn administration of the sacraments, may be contemned, or without sin be omitted at pleasure by the ministers, or be CHANGED, by whomsoever pastor of the churches, into other NEW ones; LET HIM BE ANATHEMA."

Perhaps something worse than the Novus Ordo is the sight of seeing a **woman** putting on a chasuble and stole and maniple and assuming herself a priest. This can turn a man's stomach. This shows how far apart from the truth we have fallen.

Another touchy subject is **'Sedevacantism'**: my answer is, you are either catholic or not catholic, you either believe in Holy Father or not.

Where the pope is, there is the true Church, however if the pope doesn't hand down to us the Traditional Catholic Faith, at that point you can acknowledge the pope as pope but, you can not follow him into sin or heresy. So why should I acknowledge him as pope at all. Three good seasons: **first**, we assume he was legitimately elected, **secondly** how many of you children or your children are going to have enough common sense to come back to the Faith under a good pope when one shows up? **Thirdly**, no punishment falls upon you for holding true to the True Faith and when the pope does not. Our concern should be to hold firm to the Traditional True Faith, and not have to be a theologian. The Church stands on two legs **1.)** Sacred Tradition and **2.)** Sacred Scripture. (Outside the church Protestants don't have a pope.) Inside the Church we have Pope Francis, but because he does not hold to the full true Faith, denies most of it, he is called by many a heretic. Thus Pope Benedict VXI is still Pope and always was. Many will see this to be true both in this life and in the next.

Catholic Doctrine on Canon Law to Obey States:

Conscience is judgment by reason where by the human being recognizes the moral quality of a concrete act where he is going to perform or in the process of performing or has already completed. Is man obliged to follow faithfully what he knows to be just and right? It is by the judgement of his conscience that man perceives or recognizes the prescription of the Divine Law. A created human being must always obey the certain judgement of his conscience. If he were to deliberately act against it, he would condemn himself.

I think the best place for you to learn the truth on the Mass is to hear is the well known and loved Catholic **canon lawyer and theologian** of our modern time, in my opinion he is a modern day St. Thomas Aquinas. **He is Fr. Gregory Hesse, S.T.D., J.C.D., ST.L., J.C.L.,** He earned Doctorates and Sacred Licentiates in both Thomistic Theology and Canon Law from the pontifical University of St. Thomas Aquinas in Rome. He served as Personal Secretary to Cardinal Stickler at the Vatican from 1986 - 1988 and studied and worked among bishops and cardinals in Rome for 15 years. He has come to know about 45 cardinals.

He gives talks world wide. Go to U-tube: **"Fr. Hesse: The Messed - Up Mass (part 1)"**

Vatican II was not infallible by reason of the extraordinary Magisterium, for it refused to define anything. Pope Paul VI himself, in an audience on January 12, 1966 said, "that it had avoided proclaiming in an extraordinary manner any dogmas affected by the mark of infallibility." This was the first thing Pope John XXIII said at the opening is that we are not here to define anything.

Cardinal Brandmuller just recently said in 2012: "Strangely enough, the two most controversial documents of Vatican II do not have a binding doctrinal content, so one can dialogue about them." (CNS. May 21, 2012)

Recently, in 2011, fifty "non-traditional Catholic" leaders (Professors, Ph. D's, professionals, leaders of organizations) signed a petition to Pope Benedict XVI asking for a more in depth examination of the Second Vatican Council saying: "For the good of the Church - and more especially to bring about the salvation of souls, which is her first and highest law(cf. The 1983 CIC. canon 1752) - in the Second Ecumenical Vatican Council, it seems urgent that some clarity be made known by your answering authoritatively the **question about the continuity of this council with the other councils.** This question about its fidelity to the Tradition of the Church." (Petition of Msgr. Brunero Gherardini, 2009) *In other words too many ambiguous words. Or in other words what are we here for?*

Canon Lawyer Gregory Hesse, said he has tried for **fifteen years** to translate Vatican II in the light of tradition in a catholic way and says it is mostly a direct contradiction of the magisterium and of tradition and faith. *(See, I'm not the only one who thinks Vatican II is full of controversial hoooooy!?!)*

'Fruits of Vatican II and the New Mass' or Mass of Paul VI which by the way was never decreed by Paul VI nor did he sign anything that said use this New Mass, it was imposed upon the people by the bishops: =Since 1978 'The Council' is considered Vatican II, when in fact it was never a council. A council is to condemn error and define doctrine. Vatican II never did this. "By their fruits you shall know them. Do men gather grapes of thorns, or figs of thistles? Even so every good tree bringeth forth good fruit, and the evil tree bringeth forth evil fruit. **A good tree cannot bring forth evil fruit, neither can an evil tree bring forth good fruit**" (Matt. 7:15-17). Given the foregoing, it should be plain that the New Mass was conceived for an evil purpose and constructed by evil means. It only follows that such a tree would have disastrous effects on the Church. Let us look at its fruits as reported in *Index of Leading Catholic Indicators: The Church Since Vatican II* by Kenneth Jones:

Priests. While the number of priests in the United States more than doubled to 58,000, between 1930 and 1965, since then that number has fallen to 45,000. By 2020, there will be only 31,000 priests left, and more than half of these priests will be over 70.

Ordinations. In 1965, 1,575 new priests were ordained in the United States. In 2002, the number was 450. In 1965, only 1 percent of U.S. parishes were without a priest. Today, there are 3,000 priestless parishes, 15 percent of all U.S. parishes.

Seminarians. Between 1965 and 2002, the number of seminarians dropped from 49,000 to 4,700, a decline of over 90 percent. Two-thirds of the 600 seminaries that were operating in 1965 have now closed.

Sisters. In 1965, there were 180,000 Catholic nuns. By 2002, that had fallen to 75,000 and the average age of a Catholic nun is today 68. In 1965, there were 104,000 teaching nuns. Today, there are 8,200, a decline of 94 percent since the end of Vatican II.

Religious Orders. For religious orders in America, the end is in sight. In 1965, 3,559 young men were studying to become Jesuit priests. In 2000, the figure was 389. With the Christian Brothers, the situation is even more dire. Their number has shrunk by two-thirds, with the number of seminarians falling 99 percent. In 1965, there were 912 seminarians in the Christian Brothers. In 2000, there were only seven. The number of young men studying to become Franciscan and Redemptorist priests fell from 3,379 in 1965 to 84 in 2000.

Catholic schools. Almost half of all Catholic high schools in the United States have closed since 1965. The student population has fallen from 700,000 to 386,000. Parochial schools suffered an even greater decline. Some 4,000 have disappeared, and the number of pupils attending has fallen below 2 million – from 4.5 million.

Catholic Marriage. Catholic marriages have fallen in number by one-third since 1965, while the annual number of annulments has soared from 338 in 1968 to 50,000 in 2002.

Attendance at Mass. A 1958 Gallup Poll reported that three in four Catholics attended church on Sundays. A recent study by the University of Notre Dame found that only one in four now attend. Only 10 percent of lay religious teachers now accept church teaching on contraception. Fifty-three percent believe a Catholic can have an abortion and remain a good Catholic. Sixty-five percent believe that Catholics may divorce and remarry. Seventy-seven percent believe one can be a good Catholic without going to mass on Sundays. By one New York Times poll, 70 percent of all Catholics in the age group 18 to 44 believe the Eucharist is merely a "symbolic reminder" of Jesus.

Who could possibly claim that there is not a terrible crisis of faith in the Catholic Church!? It is no wonder that Cardinal Ratzinger affirmed: "I am convinced that the ecclesial crisis in which we find ourselves today depends in great part on the collapse of the liturgy." It is clear how the New Mass could create such a disaster. Liturgy dictates belief. A protestantized liturgy yields heretical belief, loss of the Faith, and devaluation of the priesthood. Satan has been able to accomplish more effective damage to the entire body of the Church in the past 35 years through the destruction of the Mass than ever before.

The New Mass is condemned by its own nature and by its fruits. The crisis in the Church will continue to worsen until we return to orthodoxy and discipline. What is a Catholic to do in such troublesome times? He must follow the advice of **St. Vincent of Lerins**: "What then shall the Catholic do if some portion of the Church detaches itself from communion of the universal Faith? (Tradition) If some new contagion attempts to poison, no longer a small part of the Church, but **the whole Church at once**, then his great concern will be to **attach himself to antiquity** (Tradition) which **can no longer be led astray** by any lying novelty." St. Athanasius, one of the four great Doctors of the Eastern Church, earned the title of "Father of Orthodoxy" for his strong and uncompromising defense of our Catholic Faith against the Arian Heresy which affected most of the hierarchy, including the pope. Athanasius was banned from his diocese at least five times, spending a total of seventeen years in exile. He sent the following letter to his flock which is a powerful lesson for our times: "What saddens you is the fact that others have occupied the churches by violence, while during this time you are on the outside. It is a fact that they have the premises (churches) – **but we have the Apostolic Faith**. They can occupy our churches, but they are outside the true Faith. You remain outside the places of worship, but the Faith dwells within us. Let us consider: *what is more important?* The place or the Faith? **The true Faith, obviously.** Who has lost and who has won in this struggle? The one who keeps the premises or the one who keeps the Faith?" *Remember that the Catholic Church stands on two feet 'Sacred Tradition and Holy Scripture'.*

They may be a minority but the masons are in charge and have taken over the Vatican, and the Government of every country. Fr. Brey tried to tell me what you will have already seen in the websites above. That Cardinal Siri was the legitimate Pope in the conclave of 1958. Where John XXIII was installed by force. According to three authors and two cardinals present, Cardinal Siri was elected and had taken a name, Pope Gregory XVII. White smoke came out the chimney for (5) min. Then all of a sudden it change to black. Cardinal Tiesurah (Dean of the College of Cardinals at the conclave of 1958) wrote in a letter: "The elected as John XXIII was illegitimate because it was willed and planned by forces alien to the Holy Spirit." Outside the masons were already speaking out loud of the new pope and that he would be Cardinal Roncalli (Patriarch of Venice) before he was even elected and became John XXIII.

The Irish and holy priest **Fr. Malachi Martin** was asked what he thought of Vatican II. He said it was a catastrophe, it was a bad idea, it performed badly, it was a bloody miss. Cardinal Ottaviani told Pope John XXIII that Vatican II was not necessary. Pope John XXIII on his death bed did admit that Cardinal Ottaviani and Cardinal Siri were right.

Fr. Malachi Martin tells of the devils take over in the Church. He sights that (3) or more cardinals with some prelates (bishops) had on June 29, 1963 had a satanic dedication to Lucifer. This was called the enthronement of the fallen angel Lucifer by the Luciferians. This confirmed by a Cardinal Malingo and an another bishop. These devil worshipers have no morality, and sex with creatures young or old is fine for them.

Cardinal Giuseppe Siri was elected at three conclaves of October 28th, 1958 taking the name Gregory XVII, again at the next two conclaves: Paul VI and John Paul I. Cardinal Siri was handed a note by a Masonic clergy which said, if you value your life and that of your family, you will reject the election. He did, but according to church law he was legitimately elect and had taken a name. Therefore he was pope until he died 1989. Thus making all the other pope's illegitimate popes." *(I really can't answer if he was pope for 5 or 10 min. or until he died. He knows and God knows. But this is what many believe.)*

In the magazine "The Apostolate of Our Lady of Good Success" also entitled: "Chiesa Viva" Oct. 2015

486. By Dr. Franco Adessa: **On December 29, 2004 Mel Gibson paid a visit to Fr. Luigi Villa**, at the Institute of Brescia, accompanied by a Canadian and an American journalist. The sole reason for the meeting was that of the election of Cardinal Siri to the Papacy in the Conclave of 1958. In your first encounter with Padre Pio, you were commissioned with the task of defending the Church of Christ from the work of the Ecclesiastical Masonry, when you were discouraged, **Padre Pio said: "But you know, and are a friend of Cardinal Giuseppe Siri."**

Fr. Villa spoke many times of the conclave of 1958 and 1963 and the threats that had been made to prevent him from sitting once again a second time on the Chair of Peter. In his book: "Paul VI beatified?" (pg. 147), is taken from a writing of Prince Scotersco, first cousin of Prince Borghese, who was the president of the Conclave that elected Montini (Paul VI) as Supreme Pontiff; one "writing that contains the following information about the Conclave of June 21, 1963: "During the Conclave, a Cardinal left the Sistine Chapel, he met with representatives of B'nai B'rith, announcing to them the election of Cardinal Sire. THEY RESPONDED BY SAYING

THAT THE PERSECUTION AGAINST THE CHURCH WOULD RESUME IMMEDIATELY. RETURNING TO THE CONCLAVE, THIS CARDINAL HAD MONTINI ELECTED POPE!" This is where Cardinal Siri was handed the note. And they elected their man.

We continue with Fr. Villa: In the installments 40-41 of the article **"The Secret of the Empty Tomb of Padre Pio"**, I reported some quotes from a book by **Guy Carr**, describing **Ugo Montagna** *(our leading bad man)*, the main architect of the "Montese Case" of 1953, as the **Agentur of the Order of Illuminati of Bavaria**, in Rome, who had to control Mussolini, but secretly had to steer the Italian politics to the left.

During this research, on the subject of the "Empty Tomb," I discovered that the doctor of Pius XII, Riccardo Galeazzi Lisi, was a very close friend of **Ugo Montagna**, whose whose method to subject certain persons to his evil will was corruption and by involving them in **Black Masses and Satanic orgies.**

Because the principal promoter *(stooch)* of the steering of the Italian politics to the left in the Vatican was Msgr. Giambattista Montini *(Paul VI to be)*, who was to be thrown out of the Secretary of State on November 1, 1954 for betraying Pius XII's Anti-Communist policy, I submitted to Fr. Villa the possibility of a possible murder of Pius XII. Father told me what was said and what was already known in the Holy Office: **"We think that Pius XII was killed for two reasons: If Pius XII had lived yet another year and a half, the Masonic world's plan to place their man, Roncalli and Montini, at the top of the Church would have fail."** (In other words there would have never had been a Vatican **II Council, and the Faith would still be stronger in the Church, than it is today.)**

In 1960, Pius XII would certainly have published the **Third Secret of Fatima** that contained the sentence: **"Satan will actually succeed in reaching the top of the Church"** furthermore, Freemasonry could not have impose Roncalli (John XXIII), as their **"masonic or substituted pope"** because at that time he was already ill with cancer and had been given only five years to live. If Pius XII had remained alive for another year and a half, Roncalli would never be elected pope, because the news of his disease would be widespread and would prevent him from having the necessary votes for his election to the papacy. **And Montini would**

never have become Cardinal, nor Pope. *(Don't tell me Satan don't know what he is doing. He plays this like a chess game and we ideos fall into place, I mean Hell. But Satan could not fool the few strong in Faith, like Archbishop Lefebvre.)*

The best knowledge of the 3rd Secret that I have ever heard or read is giving by Fr. Nicholas Gruner on Youtube: **God will Punish the World - 3rd Secret of Fatima - Apocalypse** *(Much is revealed. Listen to it.)*

Continuing speaking of Cardinal Siri, Fr. Villa introduced a topic by telling me of a personal meeting he had, in Genoa, with Siri who proposed to entrust a monastery to him in order to found a seminary that Fr. Villa would direct. Fr. Villa told me he had to refuse due to the incompatibility of this assignment with his Papal mandate.

Because of the Papal mandate to Fr. Villa by Pius XII, Cardinal Siri's obligation to secrecy, on what happened at the Conclaves, **was not binding in regards to Fr. Villa's papal mandate.** He had the right to know the secrets of the Church relation to the mission entrusted to him. In this meeting Cardinal Siri told Fr. Villa: **"THEY HAD THREATENED THAT IF HE HAD NOT RETREATED, THEY WOULD HAVE KILLED HIM AND EXTERMINATED HIS WHOLE FAMILY."**

In the Conclave of 1978, it was a duel that ended between Siri and Benelli, with the election of Cardinal Siri. But again, this time, Siri was forced to retreat, always under pressure of a terribly threat. Fr. Villa used these words: "If he had not retreated, THEY WOULD HAVE CREATED A SCHISM IN THE CHURCH."

On hearing these words, I was reminded of the threat made to Pope Pius XII when, having when, having thrown Montini out of the Secretary of State for treason to papal policy against communism, **he decided to lock him up permanently in a monastery.**

"The Pope was forced to make other arrangements," Fr. Villa said, **"only because his enemies had threatened him with CREATING A SCHISM IN THE CHURCH."** With expressions of pain on his face, and in a grave tone, Fr. Villa told me: **BUT.....I HAVE TO TAKE SOME SECRETS TO MY GRAVE!"**

A month before Father Villa died on Nov. 18, 2012. He wrote a last editorial entitled: **"THE HOLY ROSARY AND THE ATOMIC BOMB"** about the 1945 atomic bomb on Hiroshima 150,000 killed. The four Jesuit Priests who lived in a rectory only eight blocks from the center of the explosion. Why were they unharmed? They said, "WE ALWAYS PRAYED THE ROSARY DAILY, SO WE CONCLUDED THAT THE PRAYER OF THE ROSARY WAS MUCH STRONGER THAN THE ATOMIC BOMB."

A similar miracle also occurred in Nagasaki the Catholic city of Japan, where over 70% Japanese Catholics lived. The Franciscan monastery, **"Lugenzai no Somo," (The Garden of the Immaculate)** founded by St. Maximilian Kolbe. With the explosion of the atomic bomb, this monastery went unscathed as in Hiroshima. (Notice the masons always pick a catholic community, this is the same with South Vietnam and the Catholic President and his country.) Somehow I just don't think that excuse I like English, because I don't understand Latin is a good enough reason for staying away from the True Faith and losing your soul.

The Prophecies of St. Malachy (1148) of Ireland tells of the 112 popes. This last 112ᵗʰ pope is said to be the Last Pope of the 5ᵗʰ period of time when the Chastisement and the destruction of Rome is to come. This is Pope Francis I the 112 Pope, (or is it Benedict XVI?) Priests say 112 it is Pope Francis. But he a heretic and will leave the seat soon.

Malachy's final words, "Rome, the seat of the Vatican, will be destroyed and the dreadful Judge will judge the people."

St. Columcille/Columba (521-597)

"Seven years before the last day, the sea shall submerge Eirin [Ireland] in one inundation."

"Hold firm to that true Faith which identical with that of the Ancients. Deny this and you loose and dissolve the unity of the Church." **St. Thomas Aquinas**

"Beyond a doubt, they perish eternally who do not keep the Catholic Faith entire and unchanged.

Pope Gregory XVI

"God commands us to believe and unchangeable Faith. **(Catechism of Trent)**

"The true religion was always one from the beginning, and must always be the same." **St. Augustine**

"With the Almighty Father of Lights, there is no change nor shadow of alteration." **James I:I7**

Our Lord said, "My doctrine is not Mine, but His that sent Me." **John 7:16**

God does not change, nor does Truth, nor does the One True Faith, But Luther and Vatican II did.

The month of Peter or whosoever sits in the chair of Peter speaks with the month of Christ, but only when pronouncing matters of Faith and Morals, as St. Pius V did at the Council of Trent.

We know that the **conversion** of the **Jews** has to happen before Our Lord comes. This website tells of **"Orthodox Rabbi Reveals Name of Messiah is "JESUS"(Yehoshua)" his name is Rabbi Kaduri.** He was 108 years old when he died. He told his 80 yr. Old son that he had many dreams and had personally met the Messiah in a vision. When he died he gave a letter to his son not to be opened until one year after his death. This letter reveals the name of the Messiah as Jesus. This should make the conversion of the Jews happen after the Warning, and Miracle of Garabandal. Here are some interesting Prophecies:

Prophecy: "It (Warning, Miracle, and Chastisement) will come when the Catholic Church authorities issues directives to promote a new cult (Novus Order), when priests are forbidden to celebrate in any other than in the new cult, when the higher positions in the Church are given to perjurers and hypocrites, when only the renegades (gays, communists, and masons) are admitted to occupy those positions."

Prophecy of Blessed Rembordt (18ᵗʰ Century): "These things will come when they try to set up a new kingdom of Christ from which the true Faith will be banished."

Prophecy of Mother Shipton (16ᵗʰ Century): "The Great Chastisement will come when carriages go without horses and many accidents fill the world with woe. It will come when thoughts are flying round the earth in the twinkling of an eye, when long tunnels are made for horseless machines, when men can fly in the air and ride under the sea, when ships are wholly made of metal, when fire and water great marvels do, when even the poor can read books, when many taxes are levied for war."

Prophecy of Jasper: "When men indulge in sensuous pleasure and voluptuousness, when no one wishes to obey any more, when there is widespread discontentment among the people of the earth, then Russia will pour out masses of soldiers, and they will reach the Rhine."

Prophecy of Ven. Ann de la Foi: "There will be discoral within the Catholic Church. In those days men will wear women's clothes and jewelry, earrings and necklaces and women will put on men's clothes." (No full length dresses, or no more dresses. Satan will fill the woman to want to be equal to man in all things.)

Old English Prophecy (found on a tombstone on Kirby Cemetery in Essex): When pictures look alive, with movements free, When ships like fish swim beneath the sea, When men outstripping birds can soar the sky, Then half the world deep drenched in blood shall die. (Warning, Great Miracle, and Chastisement)

St. Pius X (20ᵗʰ Century): "I saw one of my successors taking to flight over the bodies of his brethren. He will take refuge in disguise somewhere, and after a short retirement he will die a cruel death. The present wickedness of the world is only the beginning of the sorrows which must take place before the place before the end of the world." (Some say he names his successor Joseph.) (So who is the true Pope, Francis or Benedict?)

St. Vincent of Lerins: "When a Foulness invades the whole Church we must return to the Church of the Past."

St. Cajetan: "One must resist the Pope who openly destroys the Church."

"If any person say he went to Heaven or Hell, that person is a heretic." Council of Trent

Third Secret of Fatima as Our Lady tells us in many apparitions: "A Great Chastisement will come over all mankind, not today or tomorrow, but at the turn of the century. What I have already announced at La Salette through the children Melanie and Maximin, I repeat to you now. Humanity has not developed as God desired. Mankind has been sacrilegious and has trampled underfoot the wondrous Blessings of God. No longer does order reign anywhere. EVEN IN THE HIGHEST PLACES SATAN REIGNS AND DIRECTS THE COURSE OF THINGS. SATAN WILL EVEN SUCCEED IN INFILTRATING INTO THE HIGHEST POSITIONS OF THE CHURCH. Cardinals will oppose Cardinals and bishops will oppose bishops, they will be obscured and all the world will be thrown into great confusion. A **great war** will break out."

The hierarchy is to be of one mind, one will when it comes to our Faith, just as there is one will in Heaven, not three wills in the Trinity, and not cardinals and bishops opposing each other.

This Chastisement which was to happen in the 1990's was postponed according to Our Lady, because of the Rosary. The following events will soon take place:1.) A Great War will break out. (Russia will overrun Europe.) 2.) The Holy Father will flee from Rome. 3.) The Great Warning. 4.) The Great Miracle. 5.) The Terrible Chastisement. Somewhere in all this, before the Chastisement, the Turks will invade Europe. The Great Monarch will come about. Russia will be converted and help to push the Turks (Muslims) out of Europe. China invades Europe and Russia. US and England are slow to join the war, after two years. St. John Bosco tells of the conversion heretics and schematics and the Jews. He says it will be a glorious time for the Church when there shall be one flock and one shepherd as One God as He intended it to be, with Kings and Queens loyal to the Pope. One must be under Peter the Vicar of Christ and hold firm to Sacred Tradition to be saved. President Obama is a bad president, but we still acknowledge him as president. It is the same with a bad pope or else you are a heretic, not to be under the pope, even if he's not holding firm to tradiction you have to.

The God of all Creation told **Adam and Eve** He would send His Son to Redeem mankind and open gates of paradise.

God told the Angels He was going to create man and that man would fall. He told the angels He would send His Son to become a man to redeem mankind and to begin His Church. No this is not why Lucifer refused to serve. No, it was because the Son of God would be born of a creature lesser than the angels and lesser than man. **God told the angels that this creature would be more perfect and more beautiful and would be the highest and most powerful of all creatures. This is where Lucifer said he would not serve.** One can not go to Heaven without going through Christ's Mother, and from there, one can not go to the Father without going through the Son. We were all created by God and we are the children of Adam and Eve. When God the Son started His, One, Holy, Catholic, and Apostolic Church, He intended all men were to join to obtain their salvation. Any other religion was started with the help of Satan. And of course man is easily taken in by false promises. Now let's say you belong to an organization and you abandon the organization. Do you still belong to the organization? No. And if you leave the Catholic Church as as given to us by Christ for the past 2000 years or more, you are outside the only organization that gave sanctifying grace to save your soul.

Than the **fight** began between Lucifer and "Michael", which means "who is like unto God" which means who is in the state of grace and who is imitating God in virtue and in his suffering, with patience and charity. Our Lord told Luisa Piccarreta that anyone could be as beautiful in Heaven as they want to be, by simply giving up their will (with world, the devil, and the flesh) and enduring all sufferings and crosses with a smile and patience. (When I was in grade school the sisters told me, "smile at all times, no matter what you are doing or who ever you see, and never let anyone see you without a smile." They told me a smile can change your day and everyone you meet for the better.) It's the grampy stone faces that make life miserable. (How ever he who enjoys this world will not enjoy the next world.)

"Hold firmly to that Faith which is identical with that of the Ancients. Deny this and you dissolve the unity of the Church." St. Thomas Aquinas

Mother Teresa of Calcutta was asked, of all the sacrileges today, which is the worst? She said, "the worst sacrilege today is **Communion in the hand.**"

The Anglican Prayer Book (Thomas Cranmer, England) was published in 1552, had the **"Black Rubric"** in it (people were **not** allowed to worship Our Lord in Eucharistic Form because they did **not** believe it was truly God.) They were made to receive Our Lord in the hand for two reasons: 1.) To stress that this was not truly Our Lord, and 2.) To stress that the consecrated hands of a priest are no different than the common layman's. (We have communion in the hand again. And a table instead of an Alter.) History repeats itself.

That consecrated Communion Host is truly God and He is truly present. In each Host is a heart beat, which you can not hear if you are not turned inwardly to contemplate His true presence. There are (14) miracles in the Canon of the Mass.

The Fact is that the hands of a priest touch God every day by his own pronouncing of the words of consecration which were set in perpetuity at the Council of Trent by Pope Pius V. This is why we believe Our Lord's words at the Last Supper, "This **is** My Body" and "This **is** My Blood." "Whoever eats My Body and Drinks My Blood and believes shall have life eternal."

Stay away from the New Mass and stay true to the the True Traditional Tridentine Mass. The difference between the two Mass; is **the same difference between Jesus Christ and Barabbas.**

Satan was a snake in the Garden of Eden. Satan is still a snake in the Garden of Rome, but now satan will swallow you up if you come close to Rome. We stay loyal to Eternal Rome, but not to Modernist Rome.

The Our Lord has worked hundreds of Miracles of the Holy Eucharist to prove His True Presents in the Tabernacles not only to show us believers, but also for those unbelievers.

This is why the obligation to stay away from the Novus Ordo Mass is proportional to one's knowledge of how wrong it is. It has enormously contributed to countless Catholics losing their faith, without realizing it. The Novus Ordo Mass is a combination of both the Anglican and Lutheran service. I went into a **Lutheran Church** *and bought one of their service books and compared it to the* **New Mass**. *Than I showed it to a priest who was horrified that they were* **identical**. *The Archbishop said it would make you a protestant, and you wouldn't even know it. Cardinal Bugnini and six protestant ministries designed it.*

St. John Bosco in the dream of January 5-6, 1870 referred to future shortcomings of the Holy Father, France and Italy. And St. John Bosco also tells: "**Four hundred days** after the month of flowers, which will have had two new moons, revolution will be proclaimed in Italy. **Two hundred days** later the pope will be forced to leave Rome and will be wandering for **one hundred days**, then will return to his capital city, to sing Te Deum in St. Peter's church." This is thought to have been for the end of the 20th century, but the Rosary has prolonged this.

This is confusing since the Apocalypse says the Holy Father will flee Rome to go to distant shores where he will live for three and a half years, only to die a cruel death. The question is, are we talking about the same times and pope. The one thing that points to our times is Russia and the invasion of Europe.

And Russia is now testing the One World Government to see the reaction before they invade Europe. Before we go to **Hell,** in the next Chapter, let us touch on why many are going to Hell due to the cunning work of Satan (with his Freemasons and Communists) in his finishing works which he started with the **French Revolution** and has blossomed into the **Errors of Vatican II** which is now the cause of the lose of the True Faith.

The Principal Errors of Vatican II

These errors and Vatican II are highly praised by all freemasons.

Many Masonic Magazines have praised themselves the accomplishments of Vatican II.

1. *Unitatis Reintegratio* - the Decree on Ecumenism
2. *Orientalium ecclesiarum* - the Decree on Eastern Catholic Churches
3. *Lumen Gentium* - Constitution on the Church
4. *Dignitatis Humanae* - Declaration on Religious Liberty
5. *Ad Gentes* - Decree on Missionary Activity
6. *Nostra Aetate* - Decree on Non-Christian Religions
7. *Sacrosanctum Concilium* - Constitution on the Sacred Liturgy
8. *Gaudium et Spes* - Constitution on the Church in the Modern World

"It is dangerous for men in power to have no one to tell them they are doing wrong." St. Thomas Becket

1. Unitatis Redintegratio - the Decree on Ecumenism. (bond)

Vatican II was therefore denying that the Catholic Church is the One Universal Church of Christ. Therefore you can find salvation outside the Catholic Faith. Vatican II in its decree on ecumenism was indeed **longing** for the one universal Church of Christ. Vatican II was therefore denying that the Catholic Church is the one universal Church of Christ. "Men can find the way of eternal salvation and reach eternal salvation in any form of religious worship." This is a Big error, listen to the following decrees:

Pope Boniface VIII, *Unam Sanctam*, Nov. 18, 1302:

"With Faith urging us we are forced to believe and to hold the one, holy, Catholic Church and that, apostolic, and we firmly believe and simply confess **this Church outside of which there is no salvation <u>nor</u> remission of sin**, the

Spouse in the Canticle proclaiming: 'One is my dove, my perfect one.'"

Pope Pius X, *Editae saepe* (# 29), May 26, 1910: **"The Church alone** possesses together with her magisterium the power of governing and sanctifying human society. Through her ministers and servants (each in his own station and office), **she confers on mankind suitable and necessary means of salvation."**

Pope Eugene IV, *Council of Florence*, "Cantate Domino," 1441, *ex cathedra*:

"The Holy Roman Church firmly believes, professes and preaches that all those who are outside the Catholic Church, not only pagans but also Jews or heretics and schismatics, **cannot share in eternal life** *and will go into the everlasting fire which was prepared for the devil and his angels, unless they are joined to the Church before the end of their lives ..."*

Pope Leo XIII wrote in his encyclical *Satis Cognitum* (1896):

"There is nothing more dangerous than those heretics who admit nearly the whole series of doctrines and yet, by one word as with a drop of poison, taint the real and simple faith taught by Our Lord and handed down by Apostolic Tradition."

Pope Pius XII *Ci Riesce* (December 6,1953):

"It must be clearly affirmed that no human authority, no State, no Community of States, of whatever religious character, can give a positive mandate or a positive authorization to teach or to do that which would be contrary to religious truth or moral good... Whatever does not respond to truth and the moral law has objectively no right to existence, nor to propaganda, nor to action."

2. *Orientalium ecclesiarum* - Decree on Eastern Catholic Churches

The Vatican II decree *Orientalium ecclesiarum* deals with eastern Catholic churches. It also deals with the Eastern Schismatic sects, the so-called "Orthodox" non-Catholic churches. In dealing with the so-called Orthodox in #27 of this decree, Vatican II provides us with one of its most significant heresies.

Orientalium Ecclesiarum # 27:

"Given the above-mentioned principles, the sacraments of Penance,

Holy Eucharist, and the anointing of sick may be conferred on eastern Christians who in good faith are separated from the Catholic Church, if they make the request of their own accord and are properly disposed.

For 20 centuries the Catholic Church has consistently taught that heretics cannot receive the sacraments of Penance, Holy Eucharist and Extreme Unction. This teaching is founded on the dogma that outside the Catholic Church there is no remission of sins, defined by Pope Boniface VIII.

Pope Boniface VIII, *Unam Sanctam*, Nov. 18, 1302: "With Faith urging us we are forced to believe and to hold the one, holy, Catholic Church and that, apostolic, and we firmly believe and simply confess **this Church outside of which there is no salvation nor remission of sin**, the Spouse in the Canticle proclaiming: 'One is my dove, my perfect one."

Pope Eugene IV, *Council of Florence*, "Cantate Domino," 1441, *ex cathedra*: "*The* Holy Roman Church firmly believes, professes and preaches that all those who are outside the Catholic Church, not only pagans but also Jews or heretics and schismatics, cannot share in eternal life and will go into the everlasting fire which was prepared for the devil and his angels, unless they are joined to the Church before the end of their lives; **that the unity of this ecclesiastical body is of such importance that only those who abide in it do the Church's sacraments contribute to salvation** and do fasts, almsgiving and other works of piety and practices of the Christian militia productive of eternal rewards; and that nobody can be saved, no matter how much he has given away in alms and even if he has shed blood in the name of Christ, unless he has persevered in the bosom and unity of the Catholic Church."

Pope Pius VIII, *Traditi Humilitati* (# 4), May 24, 1829:

"Jerome used to say it this way: **he who eats the Lamb outside this house will perish as did those during the flood who were not with Noah in the ark.**"

Pope Gregory XVI, *Commissum divinitus* (# 11), May 17, 1835:

"... whoever dares to depart from the unity of Peter might understand that he no longer shares in the divine mystery...'**Whoever eats the Lamb outside of this house is unholy.**'"

Pope Leo XII, *Ubi Primum* (# 14), May 5, 1824:

"It is impossible for the most true God, who is Truth itself, the best, the wisest Provider, and the Rewarder of good men, **to approve all sects who profess false teachings** which are often inconsistent with one another and contradictory, **and to confer eternal salvation on their members**... by divine faith we hold one Lord, one faith, one baptism... **This is why we profess that there is no salvation outside the Church.**"

Other Popes could be quoted to condemn Vatican II's indifferentism, but Pope Leo XII and Pope St. Celestine should suffice. Finally, operating on the principle that all heretical sects are as good as the Catholic Church - and that the Holy Ghost approves of all heretical sects - *Orientalium ecclesiarum* calls for Catholics to share their churches with heretics and schismatics.

3. *Lumen Gentium* - Constitution on the Church (The light)
Lumen Gentium, Vatican II's constitution on the Church, became famous (or rather, notorious) for its heretical teaching of collegiality. This is the idea that the bishops, taken as a whole, also are the supreme head of the Catholic Church.

We see that *Lumen Gentium* explicitly teaches that the College of Bishops possesses supreme and full power over the universal Church. If this were true it would mean that Christ did not institute single head in the Catholic Church in the person of St. Peter, but two supreme heads - the college of bishops and Peter - which would make the Church a monster with two heads.

Pope Boniface VIII, *Unam Sanctam,* Nov. 18, 1302:

"... Of the one and only Church there is one body, **one head**, not two heads as a monster..." The Pope alone possesses the supreme authority in the Church. The Bishops do not.

Pope Leo XIII, *Satis Cognitum* (# 14), June 29, 1896:

"For He who made Peter the foundation of the Church also 'chose, twelve, whom He called apostles' (Luke 6:13); and just as it is necessary that the authority of Peter should be perpetuated in the Roman Pontiff, by the fact that the **bishops succeed the Apostles**, they inherit their ordinary power, and thus the episcopal order necessarily belongs to the essential constitution of the Church. Although **they do not receive plenary, or universal, or supreme authority**, they are not to be looked as vicars of the Roman Pontiffs; because they exercise a power really their own, and are most truly called ordinary pastors of the peoples over whom they rule."

Pope Leo XIII, *Satis Cognitum* (# 15):

"But the power of the Roman Pontiff is supreme, universal, and definitely peculiar to itself; but that of the bishops is circumscribed by definite limits, and definitely peculiar to themselves."

Lumen Gentium # 16:

"But the plan of salvation also embraces those who acknowledge the Creator, and among these the MUSLIMS are first; the profess to hold the faith of **Abraham AND ALONG WITH US THEY WORSHIP THE ONE MERCIFUL GOD WHO WILL JUDGE MANKIND ON THE LAST DAY.**"

This is an amazing blasphemy! Catholics are worshippers of Jesus Christ and the Most Holy Trinity; the Muslims are not! A child can understand that **we don't have the same God.**

> Pope Gregory XVI, *Summo Iugiter Studio* (# 6), May 27, 1832:
>
> "Therefore, they must instruct them in **the true worship of God, which is unique to the Catholic religion.**"

> Pope St. Gregory the Great:
>
> **"The holy universal Church teaches that it is not possible to worship God truly except in Her ..."**

It is a clearly a denial of the Most Blessed Trinity to say that Muslims worship the true God without worshipping the Trinity. Secondly, and even worse when considered carefully, is the astounding statement that Muslims worship the One Merciful Who **will judge mankind on the last day!** This is an incredible heresy. As stated already, Muslims don't worship Jesus Christ - mankind's supreme Judge on the last day. Therefore, they do not worship God who will judge mankind on the last day! This is quite simple. To say that Muslims do worship God *who will judge mankind on the last day,* as Vatican II does in *Lumen Gentium 16,* is to totally deny that Jesus Christ will judge mankind on the last day.

> Pope St. Damasus I, *Council of Rome,* Can. 15:
>
> "If anyone does not say that HE **(JESUS CHRIST) ...WILL COME TO JUDGE THE LIVING AND THE DEAD, HE IS A HERETIC.**"

Lumen Gentium # 16:

"Nor does divine providence deny the helps that are necessary for salvation to <u>those who, through no fault of</u> their own, have not yet attained to the express recognition of God yet who strive, not without divine grace, to lead an upright life."

Vatican II is teaching here in *Lumen Gentium* that there are some people who, **THROUGH NO FAULT OF THEIR OWN**, **have not yet attained to the express recognition of God**. In other words, there are some atheists who are atheists through no fault of their own. This is pure heresy.

It is infallibly taught in Sacred Scripture that everyone above the age of reason can know with certainty that there is a God. They know this by the things that are made: the trees, the grass, the sun, the moon, the stars, etc. Therefore, anyone who is an atheist - who believes that there is no God - is without excuse. The natural law convicts him. Read the teaching of Sacred Scripture.

Romans 1:19-21:

"Because that which is known of God is manifest in them. For God hath manifested it unto them. For the invisible things of Him, from the creation of the world, are clearly seen, being understood by the things that are made; His eternal power also, and divinity: **SO THAT THEY ARE INEXCUSABLE**."

St. Paul teaches that atheists are inexcusable, because of the things that God has made. Vatican II, on the contrary, teaches that atheists can be excused. This causes us to ask, "What bible was Vatican II using?" It must have been the revised Satanic edition. Their statement about atheists is not only condemned by St. Paul, but it is also explicitly condemned by Vatican Council I, which dogmatically defined the principle set forth in Romans Chapter 1.

Pope Pius IX, *First Vatican Council*, Session 3, On Revelation, Can. 1:

"If anyone shall have said that the one true God, our Creator and Lord, **cannot be known with certitude by** those things which have been made, by the natural light of human reason: let him be anathema."

Lumen Gentium # 15:

"For several reasons the Church recognizes that it is joined to those who, though baptized and so honoured with the Christian name, do not profess the faith in its entirety or do not preserve communion under the successor of St. Peter."

It is a dogma that those who reject the Papacy are not joined to the Catholic Church.

Pope Pius IX, *Amantissimus* (# 3), April 8, 1862:

"There are other, almost countless, proofs drawn from the most trustworthy witnesses which clearly and openly testify with great faith, exactitude, respect and obedience that **all who want to belong to the true and only Church of Christ must honor and obey this Apostolic See and the Roman Pontiff."**

Pope Pius VI, *Charitas* (# 32), April 13, 1791:

"Finally, in one word, stay close to Us. **For no one can be in the Church of Christ without being in unity with its visible head and founded on the See of Peter."**[

Pope Leo XIII, *Satis Cognitum* (# 13), June 29, 1896:

"Therefore if a man does not want to be, or to be called, a heretic, let him not strive to please this or that man... but let him hasten before all things to be in communion with the Roman See."

Lumen Gentium # 15, speaking of non-Catholics:

"For there are many who hold the sacred scripture in honour as the norm for believing and living, displaying a sincere religious zeal... They are marked baptism... and indeed there are other sacraments that they recognize and accept in their own Churches or ecclesiastical communities."

The Catholic Church teaches that heretics repudiate the traditional Word of God.

> Pope Gregory XVI, *Inter Praecipuas* (# 2), May 8, 1844:
>
> "Indeed, you are aware that from the first ages called Christian, it has **been the peculiar artifice of heretics that, repudiating the traditional Word of God**, and rejecting the authority of the Catholic Church, they either falsify the Scriptures at hand, or alter the explanation of the meaning."

4. *Dignitatis Humanae* - Declaration on Religious liberty (Human dignity)

Vatican II's declaration on religious liberty was without question the most notorious of all the documents of Vatican II. This is because its teaching on religious liberty was so heretical, so contrary to the teaching of the Catholic Magisterium, that even the most liberal heretics had trouble rationalizing it.

Dignitatis humanae # 2:

"This Vatican synod declares that the human person has a right to religious freedom. Such freedom consists in this, that all should have such immunity from coercion by individuals, or by groups, or by any human power, that no one should be forced to act against his conscience in religious matters, nor prevented from acting according to his conscience, whether in private or in public, within due limits."

Dignitatis humanae # 2:

"Therefore <u>this right to non-interference persists even in those who do not carry out their obligations of seeking the truth and standing by it; and the exercise of this right should not be curtailed</u>, as long as due public order is preserved."[56]

It is a dogma of the Catholic Church that states have a right, and indeed a duty, to prevent false religions from publicly propagating and practicing their false faiths. States must do this to protect the common good - the good of souls, which is harmed by the public dissemination of evil. This is why the Catholic Church has always taught that Catholicism should be the only religion of the state; and that the State should exclude and forbid the *public* profession and propagation of any other.

> Pope Pius IX, *Syllabus of Errors*, Dec. 8, 1864, # 77:
>
> "In this age of ours **it is no longer expedient that the Catholic religion should be the only religion of the state, to the exclusion of all other cults whatsoever.**" - Condemned.

> Pope Pius IX, *Syllabus of Errors*, # 78:
>
> "Hence in certain regions of Catholic name, it has been laudably sanctioned by law that **men immigrating there be allowed to have public exercises of any form of worship of their own.**" - Condemned.

> Pope Pius IX, *Syllabus of Errors*, Dec. 8, 1864, # 55:
>
> **"The Church is to be separated from the state, and the state from the Church."** - Condemned. Thus, it is abundantly clear that the teaching of Vatican II is *direct* heresy against the infallible teaching of Pope Pius IX and a host of other Popes we could quote. The teaching of Vatican II on religious liberty could literally have been

added to the errors of the Syllabus condemned by Pope Pius IX.

Dignitatis humanae # 3:

"So the state, whose proper purpose it is to provide for the temporal common good, should certainly recognize and promote the religious life of its citizens. With equal certainty it exceeds the limits of its authority, if it takes upon itself to direct or to prevent religious activity."

Here Vatican II says that the State exceeds its authority if it dares to direct or prevent religious activity. In other words, the state exceeds its authority if it is not godless. This is why, after Vatican II, a number of formerly Catholic nations changed their Catholic Constitutions in favor of secular ones! They went from Catholic nations to godless nations all because of Vatican II. But justice, reason and Catholic dogma forbid the State to be godless.

Pope Leo XIII, *Libertas (# 21)*, June 20, 1888:

"Justice therefore forbids, and reason itself forbids, the State to be godless; or to adopt a line of action which would end in godlessness - namely, to treat the various religions (as they call them) alike, and to bestow upon them promiscuously equal rights and privileges. Since, then, the profession of one religion is necessary in the State, **that religion must be professed which alone is true**, and which can be recognized without difficulty, especially in the Catholic States, because the marks of truth are, as it were, engraven upon it."

Pope St. Pius X, *Vehementer Nos*, Feb. 11, 1906:

"We, in accord with the supreme authority which We hold from God, disprove and condemn the established law which separates the French state from the Church, for those reasons which We have set forth: **because it inflicts the greatest injury upon God whom it solemnly**

rejects, declaring in the beginning that the state is devoid of any religious worship..."

Pope Gregory XVI, *Inter Praecipuas* (# 14), May 8, 1844:

"Experience shows that there is no more direct way of alienating the populace from fidelity and obedience to their leaders than through **that indifference to religion propagated by the sect members under the name of religious liberty.**"

In line with its heretical teaching on religious liberty, Vatican II naturally teaches the heresy that all religions have liberty of speech and liberty of the press. These same creators that give us the errors in Vatican II are same creators that run the governments throughout the world under the demonic title democracy. These same creators are giving us the separation of church and state which is godlessness. These same creators (Freemasons and/or Communists) are the twin sisters who brought about all revolutions and civil wars in the world. To name a few The French Revolution, Spanish (Spain) Revolution, Mexican Revolution, Italy, Russia, Germany, United States, Vietnam, many more, but they are to stop Catholicism make no mistake about that.

Dignitatis Humanae # 4:

"In addition, religious communities are entitled to teach and give witness to their faith publicly **in speech and writing** without hindrance."

The idea that everyone has the right to liberty of speech and the press has been condemned by countless Popes. We will only quote Gregory XVI and Leo XIII.

Pope Gregory XVI, *Mirari Vos* (# 15), Aug. 15, 1832:

"Here We must include **that harmful and never sufficiently denounced freedom to publish any writings whatever** and disseminate them to the people, which some dare to demand and promote with so great a clamor. **We are horrified** to see what **monstrous** doctrines and prodigious errors are disseminated far and wide in countless books, pamphlets, and other writings which, though small in weight, are very great in malice."

Pope Leo XIII, *Libertas* (# 42), June 20, 1888:

"From what has been said it follows that **it is quite unlawful to demand, to defend, or to grant unconditional freedom of thought, of speech, or writing, or of worship, as if these were so many rights given by nature to man.**"

Pope Leo XIII, *Immortale Dei* (# 34), Nov. 1, 1885:

"**Thus, Gregory XVI in his encyclical letter *Mirari Vos*, dated August 15, 1832, inveighed with weighty words against the sophisms which even at his time were being publicly inculcated - namely, that no preference should be shown for any particular form of worship**; that it is right for individuals to form their own personal judgments about religion; that each man's conscience is his sole and all-sufficing guide; and **that it is lawful for every man to publish his own views, whatever they may be**, and even to conspire against the state."

5. *Ad Gentes* - *Decree on Missionary Activity (To Nations)*
Not surprisingly, we also find heresy in Vatican II's decree on missionary activity.

Ad Gentes # 6:

"For although the Church possesses totally and fully the means of salvation, it neither always nor at once puts or can put them all into operation, but is subject to beginnings and stages in the activity by which it strives to bring God's plan into effect. Indeed, at times, after a successful start and advance, it has to grieve at another reverse, <u>or at least it halts in</u> <u>a certain state of semi-fulfillment and insufficiency.</u>"

One will search in vain for a clearer denial of the necessity of the Catholic Church for salvation; for here Vatican II asserts that the Catholic Church is <u>insufficient</u> as a means of salvation. This is a blasphemy against the Church Christ has established, as if what Our Savior founded upon Peter the Rock so that all nations might receive the Gospel truth just wasn't sufficient for the grave needs of the world. According to Vatican II, the Church Christ established is not sufficient in itself for providing for the salvation of mankind. This is most easy to see that this is complete hersey.

I hope Satan and his masons are not feeling to low about being exposed for their erroneous deceptions, deceits, and lies. True, Satan has taken and will take the majority catholics which have given up the Faith and turned protestant and started numerous new religions since the time of Fr. Martin Luther the Augustinian monk. Most Catholics are **Lukewarm**, and don't even know it. And Our Lord said, "if you are **lukewarm** I will vomit you out of My Mouth."

As long as a person is alive he has time to save his soul (and family) by their nightly Rosary and spiritual reading. A good father should read something about the Faith or the saints each night after Rosary. But once he enters Hell he will only despair over the time wasted in frivolous entertainment, or a moment's pleasure, or chasing after the dollar bill and not spending enough time with the family to make sure they are on the small narrow **path** to Heaven. 'For many are called, but few are chosen.'

Time goes so fast and you will say, where has the time gone? Where are my little children who sat around me at the table? Grandmother told me time would pass quickly in the blink of an eye. Now you say, why are my children not saying their nightly Rosary or wearing the Scapular? One should treat this earthly life as if he is imprisoned and the only way out is to study the Catholic Faith and achieve that charity and virtuous perfection necessary to obtain Heaven the land of our fathers and many kind and gentle wonderful friends.

Pope Innocent III, *Eius exemplo*, Dec. 18, 1208:

"By the heart we believe and by the mouth we confess the one Church, not of heretics, but **the Holy Roman, Catholic, and Apostolic Church outside of which we believe that no one is saved.**"

Pope Clement VI, *Super quibusdam*, Sept. 20, 1351:

"In the second place, we ask whether you and the Armenians obedient to you believe that **no man of the wayfarers outside the faith of this Church**, and outside the obedience to the Pope of Rome, **can finally be saved.**"

Pope Leo X, *Fifth Lateran Council*, Session 8, Dec. 19, 1513:

"And since truth cannot contradict truth, we define that every statement contrary to the enlightened truth of the faith is totally false and we strictly forbid teaching otherwise to be permitted. **We decree that all those who cling to erroneous statements of this kind, thus sowing heresies which are wholly condemned, should be avoided in every way and punished as detestable and odious heretics and infidels who are undermining the Catholic faith.**"

2 Cor. 4:3:

"**And if our gospel be also hid, it is hid to them that are lost,** In whom the god of this world (that is, Satan) hath blinded the minds of unbelievers, that the light of the gospel of the glory of Christ, who is the image of God, should not shine unto them."

The Gospel is hidden from those that are lost, not those whose religion is great. Non-Christians are in darkness and are under the power of the devil. THE TITLE 'CHRISTIAN' belongs only to those who adhere to Peter the Vicar of Christ.

John 8:23-24

> "And Jesus said to them: You are from beneath, I am from above. You are of this world, I am not of this world. Therefore I said to you, that you shall die in your sins. **For if you do not believe that I am He, you shall die in your sin.**"

John 3:35-36:

> "The Father loveth the Son: and he hath given all things into His hand. He that believeth in the Son, hath life everlasting; but **he that believeth not the Son, shall not see life; but the wrath of God abideth on him.**"

Ad Gentes # 29:

"Together with the Secretariate for the promotion of Christian unity, it should search out ways and means for bringing about and organizing cooperation and harmonious relationships with other communities of Christians in their missionary projects, so that as far as possible the scandal of division may be removed."

Ad Gentes 29 teaches that Catholics should work with Protestant sects in their missionary projects. This means that Vatican II considers a conversion to Protestantism a true conversion. This again is heresy, since, as we have proven, there is no salvation outside the Catholic Church. A conversion to Protestantism is not a true conversion.

> Pope Leo X, *Fifth Lateran Council*, Session 8, Dec. 19, 1513:

> "And since truth cannot contradict truth, we define that every statement contrary to the enlightened truth of

the faith is totally false and we strictly forbid teaching otherwise to be permitted. **We decree that all those who cling to erroneous statements of this kind, thus sowing heresies which are wholly condemned, should be avoided in every way and punished as detestable and odious heretics and infidels who are undermining the Catholic faith."**

6. *Nostra Aetate* - *Decree on Non-Christian Religions (Our Ages) Nostra aetate # 3:*

"The Church also looks upon <u>Muslims</u> with respect. They worship the one God living and subsistent, merciful and mighty, creator of heaven and earth, who has spoken to humanity and to whose decrees, even the hidden ones, they <u>seek to submit themselves whole-heartedly</u>, just as Abraham, to whom the Islamic faith readily relates itself, submitted <u>to God... Hence they have regard for the moral life and worship God in prayer, almsgiving and fasting</u>."

Here we find Vatican II teaching that Muslims worship the one God, the Creator of Heaven and earth. This is similar to, but slightly different from, the heresy that we have already exposed in *Lumen Gentium*. Here Vatican II does not say that Muslims worship God who will judge mankind on the last day, but that Muslims worship the One God who ***created heaven and earth***. The false god of the Muslims did not create heaven and earth. The Most Holy Trinity created heaven and earth.

> Pope St. Leo IX, *Congratulamur vehementer*, April 13, 1053:
>
> **"For I firmly believe that the Holy Trinity, the Father and the Son and the Holy Spirit**, is one omnipotent God, and in the Trinity the whole Godhead is co-essential and consubstantial, co-eternal and co-omnipotent, and of one will, power, majesty; **the creator of all creation, from whom all things, through whom all things, in whom all things which are in heaven or on earth, visible or**

invisible. Likewise I believe that each person in the Holy Trinity is the one true God, complete and perfect."

Nostra Aetate 3 also says that the Catholic Church looks upon Muslims with respect, who seek to submit themselves to God wholeheartedly, just as Abraham did. But Vatican II's admiration for the infidel Muslims is not shared by the Catholic Church. The Church desires the conversion and eternal happiness of all the Muslims, but she recognizes that Islam is a horrible and false religion; and she does not pretend that they submit themselves to God. She knows that they belong to a false religion.

Pope Clement V, *Council of Vienne*, 1311-1312:

> "**It is an insult to the holy name and a disgrace to the Christian faith** that in certain parts of the world subject to Christian princes where Saracens (i.e., The followers of Islam, also called Muslims) live, sometimes apart, sometimes intermingled with Christians, the Saracen priests, commonly called Zabazala, in their temples or mosques, in which the Saracens meet to adore **the infidel Mahomet**, loudly invoke and extol his name each day at certain hours from a high place... **This brings disrepute on our faith and gives great scandal to the faithful. These practices cannot be tolerated without displeasing the divine majesty.** We therefore, with the sacred council's approval, strictly forbid such practices henceforth in Christian lands. We enjoin on Catholic princes, one and all. **They are to forbid expressly the public invocation of the sacrilegious name of Mahomet**... Those who presume to act otherwise are to be so chastised by the princes for their irreverence, that others may be deterred from such boldness."

Pope Benedict XIV, *Quod Provinciale*, Aug. 1, 1754:

> "The Provincial Council of your province of Albania... decreed most solemnly in its third canon, among other

matters, as you know, that **Turkish or Mohammedan names should not be given either to children or adults in baptism... This should not be hard for any one of you, venerable brothers, for none of the schismatics and heretics has been rash enough to take a Mohammedan name, and unless your justice abounds more than theirs, you shall not enter the kingdom of God."**

Vatican II's document *Nostra Aetate* likewise expresses its great esteem for Jews who reject Our Lord Jesus Christ. Pope Benedict strictly forbade Catholics to even give Muslim names to their children under pain of damnation. *Nostra aetate # 4*:

"Since, therefore, the spiritual heritage common to Christians and Jews is so great, this synod wishes to promote and recommend that mutual knowledge and esteem which is required especially from biblical and theological studies and from friendly dialogues."

Nostra aetate # 4:

"As holy scripture is witness, Jerusalem did not know the time of its visitation, and for the most part the Jews did not accept the Gospel, indeed many of them opposed its dissemination. Nevertheless, according to the apostle, because of their ancestors the Jews still remain very dear to God, whose gift and call are without regret."

The Catholic Church does not look upon the Jews with esteem, but with sadness, acknowledging that they exist in a state of rejection of the true God; and that they need to be recalled from their false religion in order to be saved.

Pope Benedict XIV, *A Quo Primum* (# 4), June 14, 1751:

"Surely it is not in vain that the Church has established the universal prayer which is offered up for the faithless Jews from the rising of the sun to its setting, that the Lord God may remove the veil from their hearts, that

they may be rescued from their darkness into the light of truth. For unless it hoped that those who do not believe would believe, it would obviously be futile and empty to pray for them."

Pope Benedict XIV is referring to the prayer in the Catholic liturgy which implored God to convert the perfidious Jews. The word perfidious means unfaithful.[81] Not surprisingly, in 1960, the phrase "perfidious Jews" was removed from the Good Friday liturgy by Pope John XXIII. Furthermore, Pope Eugene IV dogmatically defined that everyone who practices the Mosaic law - that is, the Jewish religion - cannot be saved.

Pope Eugene IV, Council of Florence, *Cantate Domino*, Feb. 4, 1441:

"**The Holy Roman Church firmly believes, professes and teaches that the matter pertaining to the law of the Old Testament, of the Mosaic Law**, which are divided into ceremonies, sacred rites, sacrifices, and sacraments, because they were established to signify something in the future, although they were suited to divine worship at that time, after our Lord's coming had been signified by them, **ceased**, and the sacraments of the New Testament began; **and that whoever, even after the passion, placed hope in these matters of the law and submitted himself to them** as necessary for salvation, as if faith in Christ could not save without them, **sinned mortally**. Yet it does not deny that after the passion of Christ up to the promulgation of the Gospel they could have been observed until they were believed to be in no way necessary for salvation; **but after the promulgation of the Gospel it asserts that they cannot be observed without the loss of eternal salvation. All, therefore, who after that time (the promulgation of the Gospel) observe circumcision and the Sabbath and the other requirements of the law, it declares alien to the Christian faith and not in**

the least fit to participate in eternal salvation, unless someday they recover from these errors."

Besides Jews and Muslims, *Nostra Aetate* made sure to remind the world how great Buddhism is and how this false religion leads to the highest illumination.

Nostra aetate # 2:

"In Buddhism, according to its various forms, the radical inadequacy of this changeable world is acknowledged and a way is taught whereby those with a devout and trustful spirit may be able to reach either a state of perfect freedom or, relying on their own efforts or on help from a higher source, the highest illumination."

And the false religion of Hinduism is praised for its inexhaustible wealth of penetrating philosophical investigations, as well as its ascetical life and deep meditation.

Nostra aetate # 2: "Thus in Hinduism the divine mystery is explored and propounded with an inexhaustible wealth of myths and penetrating philosophical investigations, and liberation is sought from the distresses of our state either through various forms of ascetical life or deep meditation or taking refuge in God with loving confidence."

Amid all of this blasphemy, no mention is made that these infidels must be converted to Christ; no prayer is offered that the faith may be granted to them; and no admonition that these idolaters must be delivered from their impiety. What we see is praise and esteem for these religions of the devil. What we see is an unequivocal syncretism, which treats all religions as if they are paths to God.

Pope Pius XI, *Mortalium Animos* (# 2), Jan. 6, 1928:

"... that false opinion which considers all religions to be more or less good and praiseworthy, ... Not only are those who hold this opinion in error and deceived, but

also in distorting the idea of true religion they reject it, and little by little, turn aside to naturalism and atheism, as it is called; **from which it clearly follows that one who supports those who hold these theories and attempt to realize them, is altogether abandoning the divinely revealed religion."**

Pope Pius IX, *Qui Pluribus* (# 15), Nov. 9, 1846:

"Also perverse is that shocking theory that it makes no difference to which religion one belongs, a theory greatly at variance even with reason. By means of this theory, those crafty men remove all distinction between virtue and vice, truth and error, honorable and vile action. **They pretend that men can gain eternal salvation by the practice of any religion, as if there could ever be any sharing between justice and iniquity, any collaboration between light and darkness, or any agreement between Christ and Belial."**

Pope Eugene IV, *Council of Florence*, Cantate Domino, Session 11, Feb. 4, 1442:

"The Holy Roman Church firmly believes, professes and preaches that all those who are outside the Catholic Church, not only pagans but also Jews or heretics and schismatics, cannot share in the eternal life and will go into the everlasting fire which was prepared for the devil and his angels, unless they are joined to the Catholic Church before the end of their lives..."

7. Sacrosanctum Concilium - **Constitution on the Sacred Liturgy** (Second Vatican Council)

Sacrosanctum Concilium was Vatican II's constitution on the sacred liturgy. It was responsible for the incredible changes to the Mass and the other sacraments following Vatican II.

What *Sacrosanctum Concilium* started, Pope Paul VI finished by suppressing the traditional Latin Mass and replacing it with an invalid Protestant service that is referred to as *the Novus Ordo Missae* (the New Order of the Mass). The "New Mass" alone has been responsible for the departure of millions from the Catholic Church. Pope Paul VI also changed the rites of all seven sacraments of the Church, making grave and possibly invalidating changes to the sacraments of Extreme Unction, Confirmation and Holy Orders, besides the changes to the Mass as stated above. But it all began with Vatican II's Constitution *Sacrosanctum Concilium*

The revolutionary intentions of Vatican II are clear in *Sacrosanctum Concilium*.

Sacrosanctum Concilium #63b: "There is to be a new edition of the Roman book of rites, and, following this as a model, each competent local church authority (see article 22.2) should prepare its own, adapted to the needs of individual areas, including those to do with language, as soon as possible."

Sacrosanctum Concilium #66: "Both rites of adult baptism are to be revised, the simpler one and the more elaborate one, the latter with reference to the renewed catechumenate."

Sacrosanctum Concilium #67: "The rite of infant baptism is to be revised, and adapted to the reality of the situation with babies."

Sacrosanctum Concilium #71: "The rite of confirmation is also to be revised." *Sacrosanctum Concilium #72:* "The rites and formulas of penance are also to be revised in such a way that they express more clearly what the sacrament is and what it brings about."

Sacrosanctum Concilium #76: "The rites for different kinds of ordination are to be revised - both the ceremonies and the texts."

Sacrosanctum Concilium #77: "The rite of celebrating marriage in the Roman book of rites is to be revised, and made richer, in such a way that it will express the grace of the sacrament more clearly...."

Sacrosanctum Concilium #79: "The sacramentals should be revised... the revision should also pay attention to the needs of our time."

Sacrosanctum Concilium #80: "The rite of consecration of virgins found in the Roman pontifical is to be subjected to review."

Sacrosanctum Concilium #82: "The rite of burying little children should be revised, and a special mass provided."

Sacrosanctum Concilium #89d: "The hour of prime is to be suppressed." *Sacrosanctum Concilium #93:* "... the hymns are to be restored to their original form. Things which smack of mythology or which are less suited to Christian holiness are to be removed or changed."

Sacrosanctum Concilium #107: "The liturgical year is to be revised."

Sacrosanctum Concilium #128: "The ecclesiastical canons and statutes which deal with the provision of visible things for worship are to be revised **AS SOON AS POSSIBLE**..."

Yes, the devil could not wait to destroy the precious liturgical heritage of the Catholic Church by means of the heretics at Vatican II. His goal was to leave as little of tradition remaining as he could. In *Sacrosantum Concilium* #37 and #40.1, the Council falls into heresy against the teaching of Pope Pius X in *Pascendi* on Modernist Worship.

Sacrosanctum concilium # 37: "... (the Church) cultivates and encourages the gifts and endowments of mind and heart possessed by various races in peoples... Indeed, **it sometimes allows them into the liturgy itself,** provided they are consistent with the thinking behind the true spirit of the liturgy." Please notice that Vatican II is allowing the customs of various peoples into liturgical worship. *Sacrosanctum concilium # 40.1:*

"The competent local Church authority should carefully and conscientiously consider, in this regard, **which elements from the traditions and particular talents of individual peoples can be brought into divine worship**. Adaptations which are adjudged useful or necessary should be proposed to the apostolic see, and introduced with its consent."

Notice again that Vatican II is calling for the customs and traditions of various peoples to be incorporated into the liturgy. This is exactly what Pope Pius X solemnly condemned in *Pascendi* as Modernist worship!

Pope Pius X, *Pascendi Dominici Gregis* (# 26), Sept. 8, 1907, On the Worship of **Modernists**: "**THEIR CHIEF STIMULUS IN THE DOMAIN OF WORSHIP WILL CONSISTS IN THE NEED OF ADAPTING ITSELF TO THE USES AND CUSTOMS OF PEOPLES**, as well as the need of availing itself of the value which certain acts have acquired by long usage."

The heresy of Vatican II on this point could not be any more clear. It had already been condemned word for word by Pius X in 1907! But Vatican II's heretical liturgical revolution wasn't finished there. In *Sacrosantum Concilium* #34 and #50, Vatican II felt the need to again contradict word for word a dogmatic constitution of the Church. In #34 and #50, Vatican II directly contradicted the teaching of the dogmatic constitution *Auctorem Fidei* of Pope Pius VI regarding the simplification of liturgical rites.

Sacrosanctum concilium # 34:

"The rites should radiate a rich simplicity; they should be brief and lucid, avoiding pointless repetitions; they should be intelligible for the people, and should not in general require much explanation."

Sacrosanctum concilium # 50:

"Therefore the rites, in a way that carefully preserves what really matters, should become simpler. Duplications which have come in over the course of time should be discontinued, as should the less useful accretions."

Pope Pius VI explicitly condemned the idea that the traditional liturgical rites of the Church should be simplified in his dogmatic Constitution *Auctorem fidei*!

Pope Pius VI, *Auctorem fidei*, Aug. 28. 1794, # 33:

"The proposition of the synod by which it shows itself eager to remove the cause through which, in part, there has been induced a forgetfulness of the principles relating to the order of the liturgy, '**by recalling it (the liturgy) to a greater simplicity of rites**, by expressing it in the *vernacular* language, by uttering it in a loud voice...'" - **Condemned as rash, offensive to pious ears, insulting to the Church, favorable to the charges of heretics against it**.

Besides everything stated above, *Sacrosanctum concilium* called for changing the rite of every sacrament, in addition to calling for "bodily self expression" in the liturgy (# 30):

Sacrosanctum concilium # 30:

"In order to encourage their taking an active share, acclamations for the people, together with responses, psalmody, antiphons and hymns, should be developed, as well as actions, movements and bodily self-expression."

Vatican II also called for "radical adaptation" to the liturgy (#40):

Sacrosanctum concilium # 40:

"However, in some places or in some situations, there may arise a pressing need for a more radical adaptation of the liturgy."

These clauses may form part of the reason why the modern churches of the Vatican II sect frequently conduct "Masses" at which one finds polka bands, electric guitars, balloons, drums, native American ceremonies, topless dancers and rock music. One might also find the "priests" celebrating such "Masses" dressed in anything from football jerseys to clown costumes. Yes, the "spirit of Vatican II" has truly touched the modern day churches of the Vatican II sect. Fortunately, Pope Gregory X at the *Second Council of Lyons* and Pope Clement V at the *Council of Vienne* authoritatively condemned all such abominations!

Pope Gregory X, *Second Council of Lyons*, 1274, Constitution 25:

"Churches, then, should be entered humbly and devoutly; behavior inside should be calm, pleasing to God, bringing peace to the beholders, a source not only of instruction but of mental refreshment... In churches the sacred solemnities should possess the whole heart and mind; the whole attention should be given to prayer. Hence where it is proper to offer heavenly desires with peace and calm, let nobody arouse rebellion, provoke clamour or be guilty of violence... Idle and, even more, foul and profane talk must stop; chatter in all its forms must cease. Everything, in short, that may disturb divine worship or offend the eyes of the divine majesty should be absolutely foreign to the churches, lest where pardon should be asked for our sins, occasion is given for sin, or sin is found to be committed... Those indeed who impudently defy the above prohibitions... will have to fear the sternness of divine retribution and our own, until having confessed their guilt, they have firmly resolved to avoid such conduct in the future."

Pope Clement V, *Council of Vienne*, Decree # 22, 1311-1312:

"There are some, both clergy and laity, especially on the vigil of certain feasts when they ought to be in church persevering in prayer, **who are not afraid to hold licentious dances in the cemeteries of the churches and occasionally to sing ballads** and perpetrate many excesses. **From this sometimes there follows the violation of churches and cemeteries, disgraceful conduct and various crimes**; and the liturgical office is greatly disturbed, **to the offense of the divine majesty and the scandal of the people nearby.**"

In the above words of Pope Gregory X, deep reverence and peace and silence is to be found in the church. This is why in all churches the last (3) rows are for parents with small children 10 years of age and below. In this way if the child makes noise or if the child must be taken out, it will not be seen or cause noticeable clamor. Nothing is as distracting as a person young or old coming and going in and out of church. This a great sign of irreverence to the Divine Majesty and His people which are in communion with each other. Saint Jerome had a great devotion to the Guardian Angels. He is a Doctor of the Church who assures us that all persons and places blessed have a Guardian Angel. There is a special angel in each church to record all distractions and irreverence that occur there. Let parents be on their guard of their children running in and out of the church, once the Mass or ceremony has begun, let all person be silent and reverent in the presence of the Divine Majesty. At the sermon of a priest leave before the sermon and do not re-enter the naive of the church until the sermon is over. Whenever the tabernacle door is open, whenever the consecration is begun and the bell is being rung, whenever the priest turns around holding or carrying the Sacred Host, you are to fall to your knees and remain until all is finished or past. Also **genuflexion on two knees** is a great show of reverence whenever the Divine Majesty is outside the tabernacle. I read of a saint who did not keep his eyes forward towards the tabernacle and look to the side at someone or something, his guardian angel slapped his face. That same thing happened to me, but it was my mother. God Bless her and my father for every spanking I received.

"The majority of adult Christians damn themselves." (St. Gregory the Great, St. Augustine, St. John Chrysostom, St. Basil) **Why?** Because they are not watch over their children, or in teaching them christianity and devotion to Mary. Teach the child to see and not have, learn to do without. Abstinence. Of course all child can not be like St. Philip Benizi, as a child he abstained from his mother's milk, only taking his mother's milk (3) times a week. A very good priest once told me eat in front of the child from time to time what the child may also want to have, but do not give it to him. Soon that child grow and learn that he can not always have what he wants. This child will learn to do without. And will develope into a decent person. St. Joseph, lover of poverty, pray for us.

> *Sacrosanctum concilium* # 119:

> "In some parts of the world, <u>especially in mission areas, peoples are found who have a musical tradition of their own</u>, a tradition which has great importance for their religious and cultural way of life... For this reason, special care should be taken in the musical training of missionaries, <u>so that, as far as possible, they will be able to encourage the traditional music of these peoples </u>in schools, in choirs, and <u>in acts of worship</u>."

Thankfully, the Council of Trent had already condemned any diabolical insertion of pagan musical tradition into the churches.

> Pope Pius IV, *Council of Trent*, Session 22, Decree on this to be observed and avoided at Mass:**" And they should keep out of their churches the kind of music in which a base and suggestive element is introduced** into the organ playing or singing, **and similarly all worldly activities**, empty and secular conversations, walking about, noises and cries, **so that the house of God may truly be called and be seen to be a house of prayer.**"

Is there any doubt that Vatican II tried to bring about a new apostate liturgy for its new apostate Church? Vatican II brings down the anathema of the Church on its head!

Pope St. Pius V, *Quo Primum Tempore*, July 14, 1570:

"Now, therefore, in order that all everywhere may adopt and observe what has been delivered to them by the Holy Roman Church, Mother and Mistress of the other churches, *it shall be unlawful henceforth and forever throughout the Christian world to sing or to read Masses according to any formula other than this Missal published by Us...* **Accordingly, no one whosoever is permitted to infringe or rashly contravene this notice of Our permission, statute, ordinance, command, direction, grant, indult, declaration, will, decree, and prohibition. Should any venture to do so, let him understand that he will incur the wrath of Almighty God and of the blessed Apostles Peter and Paul.**"[115]

Pope Paul III, *Council of Trent*, Session 7, Can. 13, ex cathedra:

"**If anyone shall say that the received and approved rites of the Catholic Church** accustomed to be used in the solemn administration of the sacraments, **may be disdained or omitted by the minister without sin** and at (their) pleasure, **or may be changed by any pastor of the churches to other new ones: let him be anathema.**"

8. *Gaudium et Spes* - Constitution on Church and the Modern World (The joy and hope)

Gaudium et Spes # 22:

"For by His incarnation the Son of God united Himself in some way with every human being. He labored with human hands, thought with a human mind, acted with a human will, and loved with a human heart."

One of the trademark heresies of the Vatican II sect is the idea that by His incarnation, Christ united himself with each man. Vatican II speaks of a union between Christ and each man that results from the incarnation itself. Pope John Paul has taken the baton of this heresy and run with it full speed ahead to its logical consequence - universal salvation.

Pope John Paul II, *Redemptor Hominis* (# 13), March 4, 1979:

"Christ the Lord indicated this way especially, when, as the Council teaches, '<u>by his</u> <u>Incarnation, he, the Son of God, in a certain way united himself with each man</u>.' (Gaudium et Spes, 22.)."

Pope John Paul II, *Redemptor Hominis* (# 13), March 4, 1979:

"We are dealing with each man, for each one is included in the mystery of the Redemption and **<u>with each one Christ has united Himself forever</u>** <u>through this</u> <u>mystery</u>."

Notice that Pope John Paul II teaches that Christ is united with each man forever. This means that no one can ever be separated from God in hell. And he bases this heresy on the teaching of Vatican II in *Gaudium et Spes* #22, that Christ has united himself with each man in the Incarnation. But the idea that God united himself to every man in the Incarnation is undeniably heretical. There is no union between Jesus Christ and each man that results from the incarnation itself. The whole point of the Catholic Church is to unite mankind to Jesus Christ. This is done through faith and baptism. But if the union between all of mankind and Jesus Christ occurred at the Incarnation, then the Church has no value and is in fact pointless.

The same would have to be said of the Crucifixion, the Resurrection, the seven sacraments, etc., which are all of no importance in uniting mankind to Jesus Christ according to Vatican II and Pope John Paul II. In this system, the Crucifixion of Christ by which the world was truly redeemed and given a chance to be saved becomes instead *merely a sign* of the union between Christ and each man that already exists and has existed since the Incarnation. The Redemption, then, has no saving value. One can see that in this system all of Catholic doctrine is simultaneously flushed down the toilet. Sounds like Fr. Portugal.

In fact, **this doctrine of Vatican II, which has been repeated and expanded upon countless times by Pope John Paul II, is actually worse than the heretical doctrine of Martin Luther.** Luther, heretic that he was, at least believed that to be united with Christ one had to possess faith in the Cross of Jesus Christ. But according to the doctrine of Vatican II and Pope John Paul II, faith in the Cross of Jesus Christ is of no value, as all of humanity has already been united to Christ "forever" through incarnation (Pope John Paul II, *Redemptor Hominis*, 13). We hope that the reader can see the incredible malice that lies behind the statements of Vatican II's Constitution *Gaudium et Spes* #22.

Now we will quote the Catholic dogmas surrounding the truth that union between sinful mankind and Christ only comes from faith and baptism; for original sin is not remitted in any other way.

> Pope Eugene IV, *Council of Florence*, Session 11, Feb. 4, 1442, "Cantate Domino":

> "**With regard to children**, since the danger of death is often present and **the only remedy available to them is the sacrament of baptism by which they are snatched away from the dominion of the devil and adopted as children of God ...**"

Pope Pius XI *Quas Primas* (# 15), Dec. 11, 1925:

"Indeed this kingdom is presented in the Gospels as such, into which men prepare to enter by doing penance; **moreover, they cannot enter it except through faith and baptism**, which, although **an external rite**, yet signifies and effects an interior regeneration."

Union with Christ is also lost by separation from the Church, something Vatican II doesn't bother to mention.

Pope Leo XIII, *Satis Cognitum* (# 5), June 29, 1896:

"**Whoever is separated from the Church is united to an adulteress**. He has cut himself off from the promises of the Church, and he who leaves the Church of Christ cannot arrive at the rewards of Christ."

Gaudium et spes # 58:

"At the same time the Church, which has been sent to all peoples of whatever age or region, is not connected exclusively and inseparably to any race or nation, to any particular pattern of human behavior, or to any ancient or recent customs."

Tradition is one of the two sources of revelation, Sacred Scripture being the other. Therefore, the Church is attached to ancient customs; for Tradition is one of the two sources of revelation! The Church is founded on the traditions of the apostles, in which is included, among other things, the traditional liturgical rites which the Church has "always been accustomed to use."

Pope Paul III, *Council of Trent*, Session 7, Can. 13:

"**If anyone shall say that the received and approved rites of the Catholic Church accustomed to be used**

in the solemn administration of the sacraments may be disdained or omitted by the minister without sin and at pleasure, or **can be changed into other new rites by any pastor in the Church whomsoever: let him be anathema."**

Pope Hadrian I, *Second Council of Nicaea*, 787:

"Those, therefore, who dare to think or to teach otherwise or to spurn according to the wretched heretics the ecclesiastical traditions and to invent anything novel, or to reject anything from these things which have been consecrated by the Church... or to invent perversely and cunningly for the overthrow of anyone of the legitimate traditions of the Catholic Church... if indeed they are bishops or clerics, we order them to be deposed; monks, however, or laymen, to be excommunicated."

Gaudium et Spes also expresses the heretical doctrine that dogma and all matters pertaining to the Church are in a state of evolution.

Gaudium et spes # 91:

"In view of the enormous diversities of conditions and human cultures in the world, what is proposed here is in many sections deliberately general in tone; in fact, although it expresses the received doctrine of the Church, yet, dealing as it often does with matters in a constant state of evolution, it must be pursued and expounded further."

This is one of the most important statements in Vatican II. It identifies what is really going on in this heretical council. It tells us that *"although"* the Church expresses the received doctrine of the Church - clearly implying that there is something more than just the received doctrine of the Church going on here - *it also deals with matters in a state of evolution*. In other words, the Church expresses a combination of the received doctrine and evolved doctrine. This is what is known as the "evolution of dogma," which was solemnly condemned by Pope Pius X in *Pascendi*. Those who believe in this heresy of the "evolution of dogma" do not possess the true faith and must be converted if they desire to be saved.

> Pope Pius X, *Pascendi Dominic Gregis* (# 26), Sept. 8, 1907, On the doctrine of the Modernists: **"To the laws of evolution everything is subject - dogma, Church, worship, the Books we revere as sacred, even faith itself,** and the penalty of disobedience is death. **The enunciation of this principle will not astonish anybody who bears in mind what the Modernists have had to say about each of these subjects**."

Besides this, *Gaudium et Spes* teaches that birth control is virtuous.

Gaudium et spes # 51:

> "The council is aware that in living their married life harmoniously, couples can often be restricted by modern living conditions and find themselves in circumstances in which the number of children cannot be increased, at least for a time, and the constant expression of love and the full sharing of life are maintained only with difficulty."

Gaudium et Spes # 52:

> "Those who are learned in the sciences, especially in the biological, medical, social and psychological fields, can be of considerable service to the good of marriage and the family, and to the peace of conscience, if they collaborate in trying to throw more light on the various conditions which favor the virtuous control of procreation."

Gaudium et Spes # 87:

"For, according to the inalienable human right to marriage and parenthood, the decision about the number of children to have, lies with the right judgment of the parents, and cannot in any way be entrusted to the judgment of public authority... In exploring methods to help couples regulate the number of their children, appropriate information should be given on scientific advances that are well proven and are found to be in accordance with the moral order."

Here we have Vatican II teaching that birth control can be virtuous and that couples can choose the number of children that are to be born. This is contrary to the natural law. God is the author of life. No human being is permitted to infringe upon God's will to bring new life into the world by controlling birth or limiting his family. Birth control is never allowed, regardless of whether it is performed by so-called "natural" or artificial methods.

Pope Pius XI, *Casti Connubii* (# 55): "As St. Augustine notes, '**Intercourse even with one's legitimate wife is unlawful and wicked where the conception of offspring is prevented.**"

Pope Pius XI, *Casti Connubii* (# 56):"... the Catholic Church, to whom God has entrusted the defense of the integrity and purity of morals, standing up in the midst of the moral ruin which surrounds her, in order that she may preserve the chastity of the nuptial union from being defiled by this foul stain, **raises her voice** in token of her divine ambassadorship **and through Our mouth proclaims anew: any use whatsoever of matrimony exercised in such a way that the act is deliberately frustrated in its natural power to generate life is an offence against the law of God and of nature, and those who indulge in such are branded with the guilt of a grave sin.**"

Family Planning must be supernatural - it must be controlled by God, not man. For man to assert that he will choose the number of children he wants to have, is the utmost arrogance and a grave insult to the Creator. Man should not be worried about whether or not God will send him a child. God will send one if it is in His will. And He will not send more than anyone can handle. "Seek first the kingdom of God and His justice and all things will be added unto you." (Mt. 6:33)

To prevent a conception by design (as Pius XI says) - no matter how it is deliberately prevented - is a sin, a lack of faith, and a circumvention of God's will. It is not a virtue, despite what Vatican II says. In fact, in *Humanae Vitae*, Pope Paul VI himself admitted that so-called natural family planning is birth control.

Pope Paul VI, *Humanae Vitae* (# 16), July 25, 1968:

"... the Church teaches that married people may then take advantage of the natural cycles immanent in the reproductive system and engage in marital intercourse **only during those times that are infertile, thus controlling birth** in a way which does not in the least offend the moral principles which We have just explained."

To control birth, by deliberately restricting the marriage act exclusively to the infertile periods - as in Natural Family Planning - is nothing other than to frustrate the primary *purpose* of the marriage act, conception.

Pope Pius XI, *Casti Connubii* (# 54), Dec. 31, 1930:

"**But no reason, however grave, may be put forward by which anything intrinsically against nature may become conformable to nature and morally good**. Since, therefore, the conjugal act is destined primarily by nature for the begetting of children, **those who in exercising it deliberately frustrate its natural powers and *purpose* sin against nature and commit a deed which is shameful and intrinsically vicious.**"

We can see that Pius XI condemns the frustration not only of the power, but also of the primary _purpose_ of the marriage act. This is an important point; for Natural Family Planning designedly frustrates the _primary purpose_ of the marriage act - as even Paul VI admits - and is therefore intrinsically vicious (Pius XI).

Moving on, we must cover Vatican II's **adoration of man**. The making man the center of things. This is why you see the Tabernacle off to the side altar, and the man seated in the center of the main high altar place where God should be adored. And the main altar unused. When the priest faces God to say Mass he leads the people to God.

> _Gaudium et Spes_ # 26:
>
> "There is also increasing awareness of the exceptional dignity which belongs to the human person, who is superior to everything and whose rights and duties are universal and inviolable."
>
> _Gaudium et Spes_ # 12:
>
> "According to the almost unanimous opinion of believers and unbelievers alike, all things on earth should be related to man as their center and crown."

This is blasphemy. There is no other word to describe it. If all things on earth should be related to man as their center and crown, this means that everything should be measured by man's law, not God's. This means that man is actually God, for all intents and purposes - everything is to be related to him. Man has been put in the place of God. This is actually Humanism. **This is why Archbishop Marcel Lefebvre said,** "The New Mass will make you a protestant." You can see the results of its decadence. The sleeves are rolled up, shirts hanging out and half the time wide open, blue jeans, shorts, and short dresses and shower shoes. Outside of church short sleeves are permissible, in church sleeves and shirts are to be buttoned up. Remember the words and example of St. Padre Pio, he would not give Holy Communion to any man or woman who approached the communion table with short sleeves. He was also heard to say that women's dresses are to be 8" below the knee. He said after he heard Hollywood say to raise the dress 8" above the knee. Modesty of dress is our culture and tradition.

I remember 1966 Sr. Vivian talking to me about how important it is to dress proper in public and before God. She showed me a picture of two boys. Shirt sleeves and rolled up, unbuttoned and one rolled up halfway and both had their shirt tails hanging out. One had his shirt front unbuttoned and the other half unbuttoned. She seemed appalled by it and said this is what the world is coming to the world will soon dress this way. And they were wearing tennis shoes, but they were not in church. *Your **not** suppose to wear tennis shoes to church.*

But we have become desensitized and decadent. Nobody cares. "If it feels good do it." I believe this one of Satan's mottos. Another one is: "It don't get any better than this." Satan is like Jimmy Dranty who used to say: 'I got a million of them.' The later times will be so lude in their manner of dress, fashions tight and never seen before.

Gaudium et Spes # 24: "This is why the first and greatest commandment is love of God and of neighbor."

Hold on a second. The first and greatest commandment **is <u>not</u> love** of God **and** of **neighbor**. The first and greatest commandment is **<u>love</u>** of **<u>God</u>**.

> Mark 12:28-31- "And Jesus answered him: The first commandment of all is, 'Hear, O Israel: the Lord thy God is one God. And thou shalt love the Lord thy God, with thy whole heart, and with thy whole soul, and with thy whole mind, and with thy whole strength. This is the first commandment.
>
> And the second is like to it: Thou shalt love thy neighbor as thyself."

The first commandment, as it is summarized by Our Lord, is love of God. The second is love of neighbor as thyself. Vatican II says that the first and greatest commandment is love of God and neighbor, which is contrary to a truth revealed in sacred scripture and it is a direct change of the commandments as Our Lord summarized them; for if the love of God and of neighbor is the greatest commandment, this means that love of God and neighbor is one and the same, which is to say man and God are one and the same.

There are many other errors in the documents of Vatican II. However, what is exposed above should be enough to convince anyone of good will that no Catholic can accept this heretical Council without compromising the the faith. And it is not sufficient merely to resist the heresies of Vatican II; **one must entirely condemn it and expose its errors. The above (8) points against Vatican II is just the tip of the iceberg. The Vatican II wording is so full of ambiguity that it open the definition to do whatever you personally think is proper.**

Pope Benedict XVI has shown clear displeasure with the *Novus Ordo*. In his book *The Spirit of the Liturgy* (written when he was the Cardinal Prefect of the Congregation for Doctrine of the Faith), he called the New Mass a *"fabricated liturgy...a banal on-the-spot product,"* which has divorced itself from the proper *"organic, living process of growth and development"* that takes place *"over centuries."* (Ratzinger, J., *The Spirit of the Liturgy*, pp. 165-6. San Francisco: Ignatius Press, 2000.) The end of Vatican II.

Our Lord made St. Peter His Vicar and Visible Head of the One True Church, outside of which there is no salvation.

Now when Our Lord said, "Thou art Peter, and upon this rock I will build My Church, and the gates of hell shall not prevail against it: and I will give to thee the Keys of the kingdom of heaven; and whatsoever thou shalt bind upon earth, it shall be bound in Heaven; and whatsoever thou shalt loose on earth, it shall be loosed also in Heaven."

Whose sins you shall forgive, they shall be forgiven, and whose sins you retain, they shall be retained."

Therefore when Our Lord says **My Church** this <u>does not</u> includes those churches that the first Catholics started when they protested against Christ and His Vicar and left the One True Church and started reformed churches which are now called Protestant Churches.

One of the early Protestant reformers was John Wycliffe, a theologian and an early proponent of reform in the 14th century. He influenced Jan Hus, a Czech priest from Prague, whose followers soon dominated the Kingdom of Bohemia. Hus in turn influenced German monk Martin Luther, who spread the Protestant Reformation throughout the world.

From there we have Anglicanism, Baptists, Calvinism, Methodism, Pentecostalism, Quakerism, Evangelicalism, Arminianism, Pietism, Modalism, Muslims, Christian Fundamentalism, Unitarianism, Latter Day Saints, Stone-Campbell Restoration Movement, Jehovah's Witnesses, etc. Over 700 Protestant religions today, claiming that they are the right church and true church of Christ. The only thing is that these are all started by men and not by God's Son, Jesus Christ.

Only the "ONE, TRUE, HOLY, CATHOLIC, AND APOSTOLIC CHURCH" is by Christ Himself.

IMPORTANT: Of all the reformation churches ever started, the most damaging and heretical, liberal, and modernist is the **reformation of VATICAN II WITH its FREEMASONS, LIBERALS, AND COMMUNIST INFILTRATORS.** They have fooled the people into believing that they are still Catholic and now they have lost the True Faith, and now have a new church. **OUR LADY'S WORDS AT LA SALETTE: "ROME WILL LOOSE THE FAITH." AND AT GARABANDAL: "MANY CARDINALS, MANY BISHOPS, AND MANY PRIESTS ARE ON THE ROAD TO PERDITION AND TAKING MANY SOULS WITH THEM." She also said: "THE MASS WILL BECOME VERY HARD TO SAY, (OR FIND)."**

Most Catholics today have a hard time believing Pope Francis is the true pope. Many believe Pope Benedict XVI is still the true pope. Why? They're many reasons: first, Pope Francis never genuflects before the Blessed Sacraments, which will profess the Divinity and true presents of God. He has rejected the Council of Florence and 90% of all Dogmas. He allows homosexuality and same sex marriage, and says who am I to judge? In Leviticus and 1Corinthians5 and other chapters you can read the necessity to judge right from wrong. If you do not speak out, but are silent, you are condoning the sin. Freemasons cheer him where ever he goes. We know he belonged to the Masonic Lodge in Argentina. Youtube: "Fr. Kramer: Apostate Antipope Francis & One World Religion"

Pope (Joseph Ratzinger) Benedict XVI said, "Pray for me so that I do not flee from fear of the wolves." The Cardinals are divided those for Pope Benedict and those for Pope Francis. Pope Benedict was only to be in office for (3) years according to the masonic plan. Pope Francis often is pictured giving the masonic hand signals. One third of the Cardinals are masonic.

Cardinal Martini privately met with Pope Benedict XVI and threatened him with "Either Resign or Die." This happened after he lifted the excommunication of "The Society of St. Pius X". We know that the Holy Spirit is going to stay with the true Pope. So what do you think?

One of the main branches of the Masons is the Illuminati branch, founded by German **Adam Weishaupt** stated: **"We will infiltrate that place (Vatican) and once inside, we will never come out. We will bore from within until nothing remains but an empty shell."**

The day after Francis was "elected?" as antipope, the Freemasonic Grand Orient Lodge of Italy released an announcement praising antipope Francis.

The Debate Between New and Old; Frogelent and Truth

The **Preface** in 1970 in the new mass consisted of (81)prefaces and (3) more added in 1975. The contents were to be from the ancient fathers of the church, with a modern twist of empty ill lukewarm feelings in them. The modernist say that the new prefaces had to be redone for pastoral needs, and adapted to the modern mentality. That the old original forms of text (that were better) were "unbearable" or "defective" for our times. In the Latin Mass we have the **Canon** of the Mass meaning **"the firm or fixed rule"** of prayer. In the New Mass you have (17) possibilities of choice called the **Eucharistic Prayer.** The new Eucharistic Prayer shorten the number of saints in the canon.

The old canon would not work because it disagreed with Ecuminism and Moderism. And so we have **"Liturgical Reform of the Canon of the Mass"** a 1966 book by Cipriano Vagaggini a modernist. This man attack the Canon as being "agglomeration of features with no apparent unity, lacking a logical connection of ideas, unsatisfactory with its intercessory prayers in full disorder of deficiencies."

Next the **Silent Stillness** reigns no more. In the new mass all prayers of the canon are recited in a loud, with speaker, voice so as to take away any mysticism of the mass. In the traditional Mass the priest recites the Roman Canon in what the **rubics** call the **"secret voice".** The priest pronounces the words of the **"Transubstantiation"** so that only he can hear himself. From one Mass to the other we have a change in Symbolism and Origin of the Holy Sacrifice of the Mass.

In this most beautiful book: **"The Holy Sacrifice of the Mass" by Rev. Dr. Nicholas Gihr.** Once in every seminary before Vatican II. Fr. Gihr tells of the Canon why this part of the Mass is in Silence: 1.) This is the priestly function for the priest. 2.) This silence harmonizes with the essence of the Mystery of the material elementals (bread and wine) changed without the human senses perceiving it into Christ's Body and Blood. 3.) This is the beautiful mystery of the Mass compounded with use Latin expresses awe and mystery. 4.) It Mystically represents Christ praying in silently during His Agony in the Garden of Olives. 5.) This Silence is due to the Sacred Presents and Mystery of Almighty God. This Silence implies a special spiritual privilege and status that only the priest enjoys and it sets him apart from all the rest of the Godly Christians.

The Council of Trent (1552) expressed...... "since the nature of men can not be lifted up except by external ads, it is for this reason that Holy Mother Church instituted certain rights, namely that some things or readings of the Mass be read in a low voice and others places in a louder voice. *Therefore the Council declare **anathema** on anyone who changes the silent readings of the Canon of the Mass.*

St. Pius V set this in perpetuity, never to be changed under pain of damnation (anathema). Now as I stated before when any pope makes a dogmatic declaration on morals and doctrine, no person or pope thereafter can change it without incurring anathema (Damnation). (The same went for changing the Mass into the vernacular.) This is why St. Catherine Emmerich was given a vision by Our Lord and saw all the bishops of the world marching along. And most all were **ipso facto excommunicated** and didn't even know it.

There have been many good laymen and priests from the mid 60's that have stood strong for the faith. Allow me to mention a few: Patrick Henry Omlor (1931 - 2013) in March 1968 he wrote the book: "Question of Validity" for two reason: Changing to all english and changing the words of Our Lord at the Transubstantiation. The forward in this book was written by Fr. Laurence Brey. (Whose Mass I attended for many yrs. in St. Cloud, Mn.) Fr. Stark, Fr. Wickens, Fr. Brey, Fr. Belland, Msgr. Durand, Fr. Gruner, Fr. Nelson, Msgr. Knap, many others I can't remember all dead. And some laymen such as Walter Matt, Michael Davis, Dennis McCoy and many other good men I came in contact with all dead, they have done Our Lady's work.

You all remember Uncle Dennis McCoy (God rest his soul): he started the Neumann Press. He printed many great Catholic books, this world famous book, entitled: "Lord of the World" a 1907 apocalyptic novel by Robert Hugh Benson. It is sometimes deemed one of the first modern dystopias, where things could possibly be true, but I hope not. Pope Benedict has read the book. And Pope Francis not only has read Benson's *The Lord of the World*, but refers to the book in homilies and has recommend it on three occasions. Let me tell you why I bring this up.

In this book there is a Senator Julian Felsenburgh (Obama) who is in his last year as senator and is traveling the world, setting up a New World Order for the golden age which is to come. Every where he goes he is accompanied and introduced by a Father Francis. In the book he stops at a Paris Convention where he talks. Eventually he becomes a one world leader and eventually is adored as the New Messiah over all the world.

Here's the make believe point. 2015 delegates from all over the world (including Obama I don't know where Pope Francis was) came together for a Paris Climate Convention to sign an agreement that has never been made public, and could never have any control over

the climate. **What was the signed agreement about?** *(This is not a ridel, this part is true.)*

One more thing before we go to Hell, in the next chapter. Just after Our Lady appeared at Guadalupe, She appeared in **Quito, Ecuador (1594)** as 'Our Lady of Good Success' to Sister Mariana de Jesus Torres. Here is a list of events as she is given by both Our Lady and Our Lord:

Our Lord made it known to her that the main devotion for all people is to His Passion, Sorrows, Blood, and to the Blessed Sacrament, and to Our Blessed Lady, especially Her Sorrows. Mother Mariana is given a secret, that God the Father was going to punish the world for it sins, and that this would begin in the second half of the 20th century. Sister Marianna is given the five meanings of why the Sanctuary Light was Extinguished in the chapel while she was praying. **First,** to signify that the light of Faith would be put out in the second half of the 20th century. **Second,** Sensuality will sweep through the world. Authentic vocations would be lost due to lack of discretion, prudence, and spiritual guidance. Injustice disguised as false charity would ruin many souls. **Third,** reason the lamp was extinguished is because of the spirit of impurity that will permeate the atmosphere in these times. Like an ocean filth, it's immodesty will fill the streets, squares, and all public places and even into the homes (through modern devices.) The flower of virginity will be lost. The innocence of little children will be lost. (Walt Disney films; How did people dress in the late 1800's and early 1900's? How did man lose his manners, baseball caps, shorts, shower shoes, earrings and necklaces. And eat with your hat on when he enters the building. Actually only the priest is allowed to leave his hat on when he enters any building to show his authority. (I forgot man is trying to be God.) And he is required to wear the biretta when entering the sanctuary vested to say Mass under pain of venial sin). **Fourth,** is the Crisis in the Clergy because of the infiltration of the twin sisters, communism and freemasonrieism. Against them the impious would rage a cruel war, corrupting the souls of both men and little children. Vocations to the priesthood would be lost. The true mass would become hard to find. By the pleading of the High Queen, the Blessed Virgin Mary to the Celestial Father of Heaven, and for the love of the Eucharistic Heart of His Most Holy Son and His Precious Blood shed with generosity, *God the Father took pity on the Church and upon the ministers and to bring an end to those ominous times, would send to the Church a prelate (bishop) to restore the true spirit of the priests.*

And This prelate would raise up an order of priests that would remain faithful to the Traditions of the One, True, Holy, and Apostolic Catholic Church to which many saint of the New Testament would die for (11 billion 36 to 306 A.D.) **(The Order of St. Pius X; Founded by Archbishop Marcel Lefebvre.)** They would hold true to Tradition and have nothing to do with Vatican II and Modernistic Rome. The stand against the Masons, Communism, and Modernistic Rome to insure the future of the restoration of the Church and the Triumph of the Immaculate Heart of Mary, which will come after the invasion.

There is no doubt by most all people agree that this the Archbishop Lefebvre who fulfilled the prophecy of Our Lady of Quito, Ecuador and has raised a group of priests who did keep the true spirit of priest firm in the True, Apostolic, Catholic Church, and which Pope Benedict XVI has said is more Catholic than any other Order in the Church, and Pope Francis has said similar things. The **Fifth,** reason for the extinguished lamp is the laxity and negligence of those who God's divine Providence had given great wealth too. These people would stand by and witness the Church being oppressed, persecuted, and torn down, would watch the demons triumph, without piously employing their riches for the reconstruction of this evil. (If it's a beautiful Church and looks Catholic, they destroy it.)

You can read in this beautiful book: "**Faith is greater than Obedience**" **Translated By Elizabeth Cattana from the diary of the Good Professor Fr. Albert Drexel (1889 - 1977), (his cause for canonization)** to whom Our Lord appeared and spoke to every First Friday of each month.

On two separate occasions Our Lord spoke of Marcel Lefebvre as being one of the most loyal of sons of My Church, to which one day I will raise him to the alter. (meaning Sainthood) This book is most interesting, let us quote a couple **words of Our Lord:** "Whoever denies the invisible creation of God, contradicts the revelation of God, loses the help and power of the holy angels, and delivers himself up to the power of the demons." _(Tell that to your friendly atheist.)_ "The angels and saints are mighty by the power of the triune God, but above them stands one creature without stain in soul, perfect in body and soul, and of sublime and divine beauty." _(Ok, my children all you 'J's listen up.)_

"This creature is My Virgin Mother Mary. '**Whosoever loves My Mother shall undoubtedly be saved! With the love you give to Her, I measure My love for you.**' For this reason, I bless you from the love of My Heart." pg 16 of this book: "Faith is Greater Than Obedience" _(Beautiful book.)_

Now do you understand why I want you to consecrate yourself to Mary the St. Louis De Montfort Way. _(U-tube: "True Devotion to Virgin Mary 1of 5")_ The Daily Rosary, Scapular, daily spiritual reading and Miraculous Medal. _(One has to be blind not to see this, or practice this.)_ But, then one will have eternity in Hell to ponder this. **(Why didn't I do it?)**.............................?

Another tid-bit from this book: "Once I said: My delights are to be with the children of men. From this delight My love has engendered the Eucharistic miracle, and has entrusted it to priests, to celebrate it and at the same time to offer it to all the faithful to be received and adored." _(In each host is a heartbeat.)_

"**Know**: _The measure of the love of God is gauged by the measure of reverence to the mystery of My Eucharistic Presence, and the manner and degree of love of the holy sacrifice,_ which is the mysterious but truly unbloody renewal and sacramental remembrance of the one and only bloody sacrifice on the cross."

"**Hear My Cry:** Sacrileges multiply among the faithful, *who take the Blessed Sacrament, like ordinary bread, in the hand, and with it they are not aware that this bread is no longer bread, but My Body, Flesh and Blood: it is My unbloody Presence!* Woe also to this sin!" *(Make more visits to Bl. Sacrament, in reparation for this great sin.)*

"Why have so many people, in receiving My Body in the hand, lost respect toward the Blessed Sacrament?" pg 40 (A very good question. Vatican II has dumbed it down to have less importance and meaning, the "Black Rubric" of the Anglican prayer book **Thomas Cranmer**. Pg. 160)

Remember Mother Teresa of Calcutta was asked, "What is the worst sacrilege today?" She answered, **"Communion in the hand."** Also remember, "The manner in which you dress is the respect you give to that person you go to visit." A cossack should be worn in the Sanctuary, no lay clothes, only clerical garb, no men should pass through the sanctuary, no bare arms. One time I came to make a visit to the Blessed Sacrament, and found the sacristain in shorts and 'T' shirt. He said God doesn't care. So do you wonder why St. Padre Pio would not give Holy Communion to people with bare arms and dresses not 8" below the knee. Our Lord speaks of the importance of modest, well dressed people.

About the Sacrament of **Matrimony**, which symbolizes the union of Christ with His Church, Our **Lady of Quito, Ecuador** said this: "Masonry, which will then be in power, will enact iniquitous laws with the objective of doing away with this Sacrament, making it easy for everyone to live in sin. The Christian spirit will rapidly decay, extinguishing the precious light of Faith until it reaches the point that there will be an almost total and general corruption of customs. In these unhappy times, there will be **unbridled luxury** that would conquer innumerable frivolous souls who will be lost. (*See New Houses, New Cars, Cell phones, Large TV's etc...*) Innocence will almost no longer be found in children, nor modesty in women. In this supreme moment of need of the Church, those who should speak will fall silent." (True, you never hear this from the pulpit.) *(More flesh and more tattoos, baseball caps and shower shoes. Another Satanic slogan.)*

Mother Mariana is given a vision of Christ suffering on the cross, and at the same time she sees the Church with smoke enveloping it.

Mother Mariana saw (3) swords above Our Lord's head: 1.) Heresy 2.) Impiety 3.) Impurity;

These three swords will be the main cause of corruption in the Church.

"To avoid the chastisement man must do penance, abstain from the pleasures and impurities of this world. Pray the Rosary daily.

"Satan would rein exclusively through the freemasons, even within the Church. Many would lose the Faith and their souls. And create a Great Crisis in the Church. Diabolical disorientation will happen."

We must do penance, but Satan fixed that, we don't have to do penance any more for Lent. Or any abstinence on Fridays during the year. So why weren't there many chastisements in the middle ages? Because we still had a penatinaul *Lent. True fasting with abstinence and the practice of virtue.*

Mother Mariana was told that customs would be lost both in the Church and outside the Church immodest dress, **no head covering**, no kneeing for Holy Communion, profanation of the Holy Eucharist, hosts would be stolen and trampled under foot which would be more possible with the New Mass introduced by the freemasons. (The Vicar of Christ (Pope Linus I) **forbid women** to enter the house of God without their head being covered. This is still in effect to this day. And of course masonic Vatican II has disallowed that. So men can look at the long beautiful hair of a woman and their minds will not be on God. Same with tight clothing and short dresses, must be 8" below the knee. In other words between ankle and knee. God came from Heaven putting on flesh to be seen by men, so we may be drawn by Him to Love the things unseen. And to live in a bright land of Heaven. The sacrament of Baptism, Penance, Confirmation, Extreme Unction, would fall into disuse. Matrimony would be profaned and many living together in sin. (Not to mention same (insane) sex marriage.)

The devil will corrupt priests and which would scandalize the faithful and lead many souls to Hell.

I hate to put off Hell, (actually, I hope to put it off for all eternally) but this is the **Great Sermon of St. Leonard of Port Maurice** consider to be one of the greatest missionary priests of the Church. _Now keep this in mind, the reason you may not go to Heaven is not because you are wick, but because you were not good enough to go to Heaven._ **Food for thought. Please Read the following:**

Saint Leonard of Port Maurice was a most holy Franciscan friar who lived at the monastery of Saint Bonaventure in Rome. He was one of the greatest missioners in the history of the Church. He used to preach to thousands in the open square of every city and town where the churches could not hold his listeners. So brilliant and holy was his eloquence that once when he gave a two weeks' mission in Rome, the Pope and College of Cardinals came to hear him. The Immaculate Conception of the Blessed Virgin, the adoration of the Blessed Sacrament and the veneration of the Sacred Heart of Jesus were his crusades. He was in no small way responsible for the definition of the Immaculate Conception made a little more than a hundred years after his death. He also gave us the Divine Praises, which are said at the end of Benediction. But Saint Leonard's most famous work was his devotion to the Stations of the Cross. He died a most holy death in his seventy-fifth year, after twenty-four years of uninterrupted preaching.

"The Little Number of Those Who Are Saved"
by St. Leonard of Port Maurice

Brothers, because of the love I have for you, I wish I were able to reassure you with the prospect of eternal happiness by saying to each of you: You are certain to go to paradise; the greater number of Christians is saved, so you also will be saved. But how can I give you this sweet assurance if you revolt against God's decrees as though you were your own worst enemies? I observe in God a sincere desire to save you, but I find in you a decided inclination to be damned. So what will I be doing today if I speak clearly? I will be displeasing to you. But if I do not speak, I will be displeasing to God.

Therefore, I will divide this subject into two points. In the **first** one, to fill you with dread, I will let the theologians and Fathers of the Church decide on the matter and declare that the greater number of Christian adults are damned; and, in silent adoration of that terrible mystery, I will keep my own sentiments to myself. In the **second** point I will attempt to defend the goodness of God versus the godless, by proving to you that those who are damned are damned by their own malice, because they wanted to be damned. So then, here are two very important truths. If the first truth frightens you, do not hold it against me, as though I wanted to make the road of heaven narrower for you, for I want to be neutral in this matter; rather, hold it against the theologians and Fathers of the Church who will engrave this truth in your heart by the force of reason. If you are disillusioned by the second truth, give thanks to God over it, for He wants only one thing: that you give your hearts totally to Him. Finally, if you oblige me to tell you clearly what I think, I will do so for your consolation.

Examine this great question: Is the number of Christians who are saved greater than the number of Christians who are damned?

First let us consult the theologians recognized as examining things most carefully and as not exaggerating in their teaching: let us listen to two learned cardinals, Cajetan and Bellarmine. They teach that the greater number of Christian adults are damned, and if I had the time to point out the reasons upon which they base themselves, you would be convinced of it yourselves. But I will limit myself here to quoting Suarez. After consulting all the theologians and making a diligent study of the matter, he wrote, *"The most common sentiment which is held is that, among Christians, there are more damned souls than predestined souls."*

Add the authority of the Greek and Latin Fathers to that of the theologians, and you will find that almost all of them say the same thing. This is the sentiment of Saint Theodore, Saint Basil, Saint Ephrem, and Saint John Chrysostom. What is more, according to Baronius it was a common opinion among the Greek Fathers that this truth was expressly revealed to Saint Simeon Stylites and that after this revelation, it was to secure his salvation that he decided to live standing on top of a pillar for forty years, exposed to the weather, a model of penance and holiness for everyone. Now let us consult the Latin Fathers. You will hear Saint Gregory saying clearly,

"Many attain to faith, but few to the heavenly kingdom." Saint Anselm declares, "*There are few who are saved.*" Saint Augustine states even more clearly, "*Therefore, few are saved in comparison to those who are damned.*" The most terrifying, however, is Saint Jerome. At the end of his life, in the presence of his disciples, he spoke these dreadful words: "*Out of one hundred thousand **people whose lives have always been bad**, you will find barely one who is worthy of indulgence.*"

But why seek out the opinions of the Fathers and theologians, when Holy Scripture settles the question so clearly? Look into the Old and New Testaments, and you will find a multitude of figures, symbols and words that clearly point out this truth: very few are saved. In the time of Noah, the entire human race was submerged by the Deluge, and only eight people were saved in the Ark. Saint Peter says, "*This ark was the figure of the Church,*" while Saint Augustine adds, "*And these eight people who were saved signify that very few Christians are saved, **because there are very few who sincerely renounce the world**, and those who renounce it only in words do not belong to the mystery represented by that ark.*" The Bible also tells us that only two Hebrews out of two million entered the Promised Land after going out of Egypt, and that only four escaped the fire of Sodom and the other burning cities that perished with it. All of this means that the number of the damned who will be cast into fire like straw is far greater than that of the saved, whom the heavenly Father will one day gather into His barns like precious wheat.

I would not finish if I had to point out all the figures by which Holy Scripture confirms this truth; let us content ourselves with listening to the living oracle of Incarnate Wisdom. What did Our Lord answer the curious man in the Gospel who asked Him, "*Lord, is it only a few to be saved?*" Did He keep silence? Did He answer haltingly? Did He conceal His thought for fear of frightening the crowd? No. Questioned by only one, He addresses all of those present. He says to them: "You ask Me if there are only few who are saved?" Here is My answer: "*Strive to enter by the narrow gate; for many, I tell you, will seek to enter and will not be able.*" Who is speaking here? It is the Son of God, Eternal Truth, who on another occasion says even more clearly, "*Many are called, but few are chosen.*" He does not say that all are called and that out of all men, few are chosen, but that many are called; which means, as Saint Gregory explains, that out of all men, many are called to the True Faith, but out of them few are saved. Brothers, these are the words of Our Lord Jesus Christ. Are they clear? They are true. Tell me now if it is possible for you to have faith in your heart and not tremble.

Look higher still, and see the prelates of the Holy Church, pastors who have the charge of souls. Is the number of those who are saved among them greater than the number of those who are damned? Listen to Cantimpre; he will relate an event to you, and you may draw the conclusions. There was a synod being held in Paris, and a great number of prelates and pastors who had the charge of souls were in attendance; the king and princes also came to add luster to that assembly by their presence. A famous preacher was invited to preach. While he was preparing his sermon, a horrible demon appeared to him and said, *"Lay your books aside. If you want to give a sermon that will be useful to these princes and prelates, content yourself with telling them on our part, 'We the princes of darkness thank you, princes, prelates, and pastors of souls, that due to your negligence, the greater number of the faithful are damned; also, we are saving a reward for you for this favor, when you shall be with us in Hell.'"*

Woe to you who command others! If so many are damned by your fault, what will happen to you? If few out of those who are first in the Church of God are saved, what will happen to you? Take all states, both sexes, every condition: husbands, wives, widows, young women, young men, soldiers, merchants, craftsmen, rich and poor, noble and plebeian. What are we to say about all these people who are living so badly? The following narrative from Saint Vincent Ferrer will show you what you may think about it. He relates that an archdeacon in Lyons gave up his charge and retreated into a desert place to do penance, and that he died the same day and hour as Saint Bernard. After his death, he appeared to his bishop and said to him, *"Know, Monsignor, that at the very hour I passed away, **thirty-three thousand** people also died. Out of this number, **Bernard and myself** went up to heaven without delay, **three** went to purgatory, and **all the others fell into Hell.***"

Our chronicles relate an even more **dreadful happening**. One of our brothers, well-known for his doctrine and holiness, was preaching in Germany. He represented the ugliness of the sin of impurity so forceful that a woman fell dead of sorrow in front of everyone. Then, coming back to life, she said, "*When I was presented before the Tribunal of God, **sixty thousand** people arrived at the same time from all parts of the world; out of that number, **three** were saved by going to Purgatory, and **all the rest were damned**.*"

I see almost all of you lowering your heads, filled with astonishment and horror. But let us lay our stupor aside, and instead of flattering ourselves, let us try to draw some profit from our fear. Is it not true that there are two roads which lead to heaven: innocence and repentance? Now, if I show you that very few take either one of these two roads, as rational people you will conclude that very few are saved. And to mention proofs: in what age, employment or condition will you find that the number of the wicked is not a hundred times greater than that of the good, and about which one might say, "*The good are so rare and the wicked are so great in number*"? We could say of our times what Salvianus said of his: it is easier to find a countless multitude of sinners immersed in all sorts of iniquities than a few innocent men. How many servants are totally honest and faithful in their duties? How many merchants are fair and equitable in their commerce; how many craftsmen exact and truthful; how many salesmen disinterested and sincere? How many men of law do not forsake equity? How many soldiers do not tread upon innocence; how many masters do not unjustly withhold the salary of those who serve them, or do not seek to dominate their inferiors? Everywhere, the good are rare and the wicked great in number. Who does not know that today there is so much libertinage among mature men, liberty among young girls, vanity among women, licentiousness in the nobility, corruption in the middle class, dissolution in the people, impudence among the poor, that one could say what David said of his times: "*All alike have gone astray... there is not even one who does good, not even one.*"

Go into street and square, into palace and house, into city and countryside, into tribunal and court of law, and even into the temple of God. Where will you find virtue? *"Alas!"* cries Salvianus, *"except for a very little number who flee evil, what is the assembly of Christians if not a sink of vice?"* All that we can find everywhere is selfishness, ambition, gluttony, luxury, and pleasure. Is not the greater portion of men defiled by the vice of impurity, and is not Saint John right in saying, *"The whole world –* if something so foul may be called – *"is seated in wickedness?"* I am not the one who is telling you; reason obliges you to believe that out of those who are living so badly, very few are saved.

But you will say: Can penance not profitably repair the loss of innocence? That is true, I admit. But I also know that penance is so difficult in practice, we have lost the habit so completely, and it is so badly abused by sinners, that this alone should suffice to convince you that very few are saved by that path. Oh, how steep, narrow, thorny, horrible to behold and hard to climb it is! Everywhere we look, we see traces of blood and things that recall sad memories. Many weaken at the very sight of it. Many retreat at the very start. Many fall from weariness in the middle, and many give up wretchedly at the end. And how few are they who persevere in it till death! Saint Ambrose says it is easier to find men who have kept their innocence than to find any who have done fitting penance.

St. Louis De Montfort, In True Devotion to Mary speaking of the race to Heaven in doing penance and prayer with Mary, also says, "some start our fast and than give up, some start slow and speed up, but towards the end of life give up, but those who start with a steady pace, that is regulated daily habit, because it is steady and habitual will become a daily necessity. Remember your habits follow you to your grave. An old man had the very bad habit of blaspheming the holy name of God in vain, on his deathbed he had not given it up. Ok, back to the sermon.

If you consider the sacrament of penance, there are so many distorted confessions, so many studied excuses, so many deceitful repentances, so many false promises, so many ineffective resolutions, so many invalid absolutions! Would you regard as valid the confession of someone who accuses himself of sins of impurity and still holds to the occasion of them? Or someone who accuses himself of obvious injustices with no intention of making any reparation whatsoever for them? Or someone who falls again into the same iniquities right after going to confession? Oh, horrible abuses of such a great sacrament! One confesses to avoid excommunication, another to make a reputation as a penitent. One rids himself of his sins to calm his remorse, another conceals them out of shame. One accuses them imperfectly out of malice, another discloses them out of habit. One does not have the true end of the sacrament in mind, another is lacking the necessary sorrow, and still another firm purpose. Poor confessors, what efforts you make to bring the greater number of penitents to these resolutions and acts, without which confession is a sacrilege, absolution a condemnation and penance an illusion?

Where are they now, those who believe that the number of the saved among Christians is greater than that of the damned and who, to authorize their opinion, reason thus: the greater portion of Catholic adults die in their beds armed with the sacraments of the Church, therefore most adult Catholics are saved? Oh, what fine reasoning! You must say exactly the opposite. Most Catholic adults confess badly at death, therefore most of them are damned. I say "all the more certain," because a dying person who has not confessed well when he was in good health will have an even harder time doing so when he is on his death bed with a heavy heart, an unsteady head, a muddled mind; when he is opposed in many ways by still-living objects, by still-fresh occasions, by adopted habits, and above all by devils who are seeking every means to cast him into hell. Now, if you add to all these false penitents all the other sinners who die unexpectedly in sin, due to the doctors' ignorance or by their relatives' fault, who die from poisoning or from being buried in earthquakes, or from a stroke, or from a fall, or on the battlefield, in a fight, caught in a trap, struck by lightning, burned or drowned, are you not obliged to conclude that most Christian adults are damned? That is the reasoning of Saint Chrysostom. This Saint says that most Christians are walking on the road to hell throughout their life. Why, then, are you so surprised that the greater number goes to hell? To come to a door, you must take the road that leads there. What have you to answer such a powerful reason?

The answer, you will tell me, is that the mercy of God is great. Yes, for those who fear Him, says the Prophet; but great is His justice for the one who does not fear Him, and it condemns all obstinate sinners.

So you will say to me: Well then, what is Paradise for, if not for Christians? It is for Christians, of course, but for those who do not dishonor their character and who live as Christians. Moreover, if to the number of Christian adults who die in the grace of God, you add the countless host of children who die after baptism and before reaching the age of reason, you will not be surprised that Saint John the Apostle, speaking of those who are saved, says, "*I saw a great multitude which no man could number.*" And this is what deceives those who pretend that the number of the saved among Catholics is greater than that of the damned... If to that number, you add the adults who have kept the robe of innocence, or who after having defiled it, have washed it in the tears of penance, it is certain that the greater number is saved; and that explains the words of Saint John, "*I saw a great multitude,*" and these other words of Our Lord, "*Many will come from the east and from the west, and will feast with Abraham and Isaac and Jacob in the kingdom of heaven,*" and the other figures usually cited in favor of that opinion. But if you are talking about Christian adults, experience, reason, authority, propriety and Scripture all agree in proving that the greater number is damned. Do not believe that because of this, paradise is empty; on the contrary, it is a very populous kingdom. And if the damned are "*as numerous as the sand in the sea,*" the saved are "*as numerous at the stars of heaven,*" that is, both the one and the other are countless, although in very different proportions.

One day Saint John Chrysostom, preaching in the cathedral in Constantinople and considering these proportions, could not help but shudder in horror and ask, "*Out of this great number of people, how many do you think will be saved?*" And, not waiting for an answer, he added, "*Among so many thousands of people, we would not find a hundred who are saved, and I even doubt for the one hundred.*" What a dreadful thing! The great Saint believed that out of so many people, barely one hundred would be saved; and even then, he was not sure of that number. What will happen to you who are listening to me? Great God, I cannot think of it without shuddering! Brothers, the problem of salvation is a very difficult thing; for according to the maxims of the theologians, **when an end demands great efforts, few only attain it.**

That is why Saint Thomas, the Angelic Doctor, after weighing all the reasons pro and con in his immense erudition, finally concludes that the greater number of Catholic adults are damned. He says, "*Because eternal beatitude surpasses the natural state, especially since it has been deprived of original grace, it is the little number that are saved.*"

So then, remove the blindfold from your eyes that is blinding you with self-love and a kind of self centered pride, that is keeping you from believing such an obvious truth by giving you very false ideas concerning the justice of God, "*Just Father, the world has not known Thee,*" said Our Lord Jesus Christ. He does **not** say "*Almighty Father, most good and merciful Father.*" He says "*just Father,*" so we may understand that out of all the attributes of God, none is less known than His justice, because men refuse to believe what they are afraid to undergo. Therefore, remove the blindfold that is covering your eyes and say tearfully: Alas! The **greater number of Catholics**, the greater number of those who live here, perhaps even those who are in this assembly, will be damned! What subject could be more deserving of your tears?

King Xerxes, standing on a hill looking at his army of one hundred thousand soldiers in battle array, and considering that out of all of them there would be not one man alive in a hundred years, was unable to hold back his tears. Have we not more reason to weep upon thinking that out of so many Catholics, the greater number will be damned? Should this thought not make our eyes pour forth rivers of tears, or at least produce in our heart the sentiment of compassion felt by an Augustinian Brother, Ven. Marcellus of St. Dominic?

One day as he was meditating on the eternal pains, Our Lord showed him how many souls were going to hell at that moment and had him see a very broad road on which twenty-two thousand reprobates were running toward the abyss, colliding into one another. The servant of God was stupefied at the sight and exclaimed, "*Oh, what a number! What a number! And still more are coming. O Jesus! O Jesus! What madness!*" Let me repeat with Jeremiah, "*Who will give water to my head, and a fountain of tears to my eyes? And I will weep day and night for the slain of the daughter of my people.*"

Poor souls! How can you run so hastily toward hell? For mercy's sake, stop and listen to me for a moment! **Either you understand what it means to be saved and to be damned for all eternity, or you do not.** If you understand and in spite of that, you do not decide to change your life today, make a good confession and trample upon the world, in a word, make your every effort to be counted among the littler number of those who are saved, I say that you do not have the faith. You are more excusable if you do not understand it, for then one must say that you are out of your mind. *To be saved for all eternity, to be damned for all eternity, and to not make your every effort to avoid the one and make sure of the other, is something inconceivable.* (Read: The 40 Dreams of St. John Bosco)

Hell is for being headstrong, bossy, overbearing, obnoxious, always wanting your way, and you never training yourself to be a quiet silent person like St. Joseph who prefers to speak to God rather than to men. If you know people like this pray for them, because that is about all you can do for them, if they are stubborn and will not listen to anyone.

Perhaps you do not yet believe the terrible truths I have just taught you. But it is the most highly-considered theologians, the most illustrious Fathers who have spoken to you through me. One of our brothers, Blessed Giles, was in the habit of saying that if only one man were going to be damned, he would do all he could to make sure he was not that man.

What must we do? Take the resolution to belong to the little number of those who are saved. You say: If Christ wanted to damn me, then why did He create me? Silence, rash tongue! God did not create anyone to damn him; but whoever is damned, is damned because he wants to be. Therefore, I will now strive to defend the goodness of my God and acquit it of all blame: that will be the subject of the second point.

Before going on, let us gather on one side all the books and all the heresies of Luther and Calvin, and on the other side the books and heresies of the Pelagians and Semi-Pelagians, and let us burn them. Some destroy grace, others freedom, and all are filled with errors; so let us cast them into the fire. All the damned bear upon their brow the oracle of the Prophet

Osee, "*Thy damnation comes from thee*," so that they may understand that whoever is damned, *is damned by his own malice and because he wants to be damned.*

First, let us take these two undeniable truths as a basis: "**God wants all men to be saved**," "**All are in need of the grace of God to be saved**." Now, if I show you that God wants to save all men, and that for this purpose He gives all of them His grace and all the other necessary means of obtaining that sublime end, you will be obliged to agree that whoever is damned must impute it to his own malice, and that if the greater number of Christians are damned, it is because they want to be. "*Thy damnation comes from thee; thy help is only in Me.*" "*Is it My will that a sinner should die, and not that he should be converted from his ways and live?... I live, saith the Lord God. I desire not the death of the sinner. Be converted and live.*"

When someone wants something so very much, it is said that he is dying with desire for it; it is a hyperbole. But God has wanted and still wants our salvation so much that He died of desire, and He suffered death to give us life.

This **will of God is** to save all men is therefore not an affected, superficial and apparent will in God; it is a real, effective, and beneficial will; for He provides us with all the means most proper for us to be saved. Seven sacraments, stations of the cross, Mass, daily Rosary, Scapular, medals, holy water, spiritual books and retreats on holiness. He gives them to us with a sincere will, with the intention that they may obtain their effect. And if they do not obtain it, He shows Himself afflicted and offended over it. He commands even the damned to use them in order to be saved; He exhorts them to it; He obliges them to it; and if they do not do it, they sin. Therefore, they may do it and thus be saved.

Saint Augustine exclaims, "*If, therefore, someone turns aside from justice, he is carried by his free will, led by his concupiscence, deceived by his own persuasion.*" But for those who do not understand theology, here is what I have to say to them: God is so good that when He sees a sinner running to his ruin, He runs after him, calls him, entreats and accompanies him even to the gates of hell; what will He not do to convert him? He sends him good inspirations and holy thoughts, and if he does not profit from them, He becomes angry and indignant, He pursues him. Will He strike him? No. He beats at the air and forgives him. But the sinner is not converted yet. God sends him a mortal illness. It is certainly all over for him. No, brothers, God heals him; the sinner becomes obstinate in evil, and God in His mercy looks for another way; He gives him another year, and when that year is over, He grants him yet another.

But if the sinner still wants to cast himself into hell in spite of all that, what does God do? Does He abandon him? No. He takes him by the hand; and while he has one foot in hell and the other outside, He still preaches to him, He implored him not to abuse His graces. Now I ask you, if that man is damned, is it not true that he is damned against the Will of God and because he wants to be damned? Come and ask me now: If God wanted to damn me, then why did He create me?

Ungrateful sinner, learn today that if you are damned, it is not God who is to blame, but you and your self-will. To persuade yourself of this, go down even to the depths of the abyss, and there I will bring you one of those wretched damned souls burning in hell, so that he may explain this truth to you. Here is one now: "*Tell me, who are you?*" "*I am a poor idolater, born in an unknown land; I never heard of heaven or hell, nor of what I am suffering now.*" "*Poor wretch! Go away, you are not the one I am looking for.*" *Another one is coming; there he is.* "*Who are you?*" "*I am a schismatic from the ends of Tartary; I always lived in an uncivilized state, barely knowing that there is a God.*" "*You are not the one I want; return to hell.*" *Here is another.* "*And who are you?*" "*I am a poor heretic from the North. I was born under the Pole and never saw either the light of the sun or the light of faith.*" "*It is not you that I am looking for either, return to Hell.*" Brothers, my heart is broken upon seeing these wretches who never even knew the True Faith among the damned. Even so, know that the sentence of condemnation was pronounced against them and they were told, "*Thy damnation comes from thee.*" They were damned because they wanted to be. They received so many aids from God to be saved! We do not know what they were, but they know them well, and now they cry out, "*O Lord, Thou art just... and Thy judgments are equitable.*"

Now if these infidels have no excuse, will there be any for a Catholic who had so many sacraments, so many sermons, so many aids at his disposal? How will he dare to say, *"If God was going to damn me, then why did He create me?"* How will he dare to speak in this manner, when God gives him so many aids to be saved? So let us finish confounding him.

You who are suffering in the abyss, answer me! Are there any Catholics among you? *"There certainly are!"* How many? Let one of them come here! *"That is impossible, they are too far down, and to have them come up would turn all of hell upside down; it would be easier to stop one of them as he is falling in."* So then, I am speaking to you who live in the habit of mortal sin, in hatred, in the mire of the vice of impurity, and who are getting closer to hell each day. Stop, and turn around; it is Jesus who calls you and who, with His wounds, as with so many eloquent voices, cries to you, "My son, if you are damned, you have only yourself to blame: *'Thy damnation comes from thee.'*** Lift up your eyes and see all the graces with which I have enriched you to insure your eternal salvation. I could have had you born in a forest in Barbary; that is what I did to many others, but I had you born in the Catholic Faith; I had you raised by such a good father, such an excellent mother, with the purest instructions and teachings. If you are damned in spite of that, whose fault will it be? Your own, My son, your own: *'Thy damnation comes from thee.'*

"I could have cast you into hell after the first mortal sin you committed, without waiting for the second: I did it to so many others, but I was patient with you, I waited for you for many long years. I am still waiting for you today in penance. If you are damned in spite of all that, whose fault is it? Your own, My son, your own: *"Thy damnation comes from thee."* You know how many have died before your very eyes and were damned: that was a warning for you. You know how many others I set back on the right path to give you the good example. Do you remember what that excellent confessor told you? I am the one who had him say it. Did he not enjoin you to change your life, to make a good confession? I am the One who inspired him. Remember that sermon that touched your heart? I am the One who led you there. And what has happened between you and Me in the secret of your heart, ...*that* you can never forget.

"Those interior inspirations, that clear knowledge, that constant remorse of conscience, would you dare to deny them? All of these were so many aids of My grace, because I wanted to save you. I refused to give them to many others, and I gave them to you because I loved you tenderly. My son, My son, if I spoke to them as tenderly as I am speaking to you today, how many others souls return to the right path! And you... you turn your back on Me. Listen to what I am going to tell you, for these are My last words: You have cost Me My blood; if you want to be damned in spite of the blood I shed for you, do not blame Me, you have only yourself to accuse; and throughout all eternity, do not forget that if you are damned in spite of Me, you are damned because you want to be damned: *'Thy damnation comes from thee.'*"

You are horror-struck at such a thought? Well then, cast yourself at the feet of Jesus Christ and say to Him, with tearful eyes and contrite heart: **"Lord, I confess that up till now I have not lived as a Christian. I am not worthy to be numbered among Your elect. I recognize that I deserve to be damned; but Your mercy is great and, full of confidence in Your grace, I say to You that I want to save my soul, even if I have to sacrifice my fortune, my honor, my very life, as long as I am saved. If I have been unfaithful up to now, I repent, I deplore, I detest my infidelity, I ask You humbly to forgive me for it. Forgive me, good Jesus, and strengthen me also, that I may be saved. I ask You not for wealth, honor or prosperity; I ask you for one thing only, to save my soul."**

In the **first Rules** on the discernment of spirits, Saint Ignatius shows that it is typical of the evil spirit to tranquilize sinners. Tranquilize and desensitize are the same thing. I will give you two examples: **First**, you commit a very bad sin, and you feel very, very bad about it, and you do it again and again. And you still feel very bad about it. Than after a few more times, you start to feel not so bad about it. the next time you commit it not bad at all. The next time you commit the sin, it completely OK.

You have become desensitized to it. This happen to when using bad language, or using God's name in vain, as you hear everyone doing today.

Second, way is when you a child, and you watch your first scary movie, maybe the 'Wizard of Oz'. It horrified you. As you grew older scary movies, westerns with killing and violence, video games with killing and language and violence, becomes easy listening music. DESENSITIZED!

Mother and Father's don't watch or teach their children high morals, little if any disciplinary action is seldom taken. God and prayer is not taught to the children from the first moment the child can talk and should learn to pray. As a result crime starts at an early age, lying and stealing. Between the ages of 10 and 17 they learn to steal, property damage, drugs and narcotics. All because the parents didn't think the child needed to know morality (God) before the age of reason. Thus the most important time of formation of a child is past up. I can not think of the communistic man's name who said, "Give me your children for the first six years of their life, after that you can have them back." Because what they learn in the earliest part of their formation when their mine is empty, what is taught sticks firm for ever." If God is not taught at an earliest of age the child's morals and ethics will be very low.

Russian author Fyodor Dostoevski (born 1821-1881) said, "The world and society are not economically determined, but theologically determined meaning (needing God). **What happens to any civilization entirely depends on the way it acts and lives and behaves toward God and morality. If you have no God, than you have no respect for man.** And man will be persecuted. Where there is no God then everything evil is allowable. The day will come when men will say, there is no crime there is no sin, there is no guilt, there is only hunger, and men will come to us saying make us slaves just give us bread. Then we will persuade them with lies that they will become free only by surrendering their freedom to us. And in their leisure hours we shall make there life like a child's game. We shall allow them to sin and they will love us because we allow them to sin. We shall tell them whether to marry or not to marry, whither to have children or not and they will submit to us gladly and cheerfully." This man foretold of communism and men like Marx and Lenin carrying it out. And the freemasons are stronger all over the world today. As a result war and chaos. This was written in 1871 and it was **not** called **communism** yet, it was called 'Shiga Lovism'.

Dostoevski suffered in prison and in Siberia he wrote two books: 'Crime and Punishment' and 'The Possessed' and in these works he describes communism, similar to Aleksandr Solzhenitsyn (1918-1956) in who does the same in a two volume work called, 'The Gulag Archipelago'. Solzhenitsyn writes these books to warn America of what is coming to her. Too late it's here. Communism is the bonding to atheism and Satanism. Marx studied satanism before he became a communist. These are the worst of possessed men. They care nothing for their neighbor. *Communism is the decay and foul stink of community wreckers.* It is a manure type fertilizer use by God to end all and bring back a Springtime of a new world. That is what is happening and is about to take place in the Chastisement soon to come.

This is where the **"Kingdom of the Divine Will" by Luisa Piccarreta** comes in. Paradise similar to that of Adam and Eve will be the second chance for mankind to start over. I know you've never heard of this before. I'll tell you more about it later.

These children grow up to be troubled parents. They can **not** get along because the upbringing from their mom and dad had no discipline, no morality, no dress code no manners. Their shirts are not tucked in, their sleeves are rolled up, instead of rolled down and buttoned. 'T' shirts, shorts, and shower shoes in public. They grow up with no manners, because their mom and dad had no manners. They have become the most disgusting of creators. They do not take their hat off in a building or house, and worse is that they eat with it on as if it were a sacred crown upon their head.

They do not give their best for God, as you see by what they wear to

Church. Remember: **'The way you dress is the respect you give to that person you go to visit,'** and it reflects your considerate or inconsiderate personality. As a result, we have a decadent society. This type of sociality is not deserving of God's grace. You don't think that Satan is more intelligent than you. *St. Perry Lamy said: "Satan compared to us is like a 25 year old man looking down at a 3 month old baby."*

Ever one thinks this is fine, just like everyone thinks they are going to Heaven. The truth is you're not wicked enough to go to hell and not good enough to go to Heaven. So why do catholics hate hats so much, especially the baseball and 'T' shirt, and the shower shoe revolution? Well it all goes back to the French Revolution and the **'Phrygian Cap.'** Sometimes called the **red liberty cap**, it was adopted as the symbol of liberty and freedom by the revolutionaries in May 1790.

Today's liberty cap is the baseball cap, a sure sign of today's revolution for comfort and of 'don't tell me what to do.' Along with the shorts, 'T' shirts, and shower shoes, which priests have told people not to wear in the church, are a sign of today's decadency.

The **Phrygian cap** was made famous by the "sans culottes". Many French citizen started to wear the Phrygian cap to show its acceptance of the revolutionaries power. Since then, Marianne, the national emblem of France, is still portrayed wearing the Phrygian cap. The most fundamental political ideals of the *sans-culottes* (Phrygian cap) 1787 were social equality, economic equality, and popular democracy. They never took it off, not even to eat. No manners like good catholics, who take their hat off when they enter a building and when they eat. My mother and grandmother would wrap my head if I walked in the house or sat down to eat with my hat on. The next time this **Phrygian 'liberty' Cap** was worn was Bullshivic or Lenin Communist Revolution 1917. These people always get away with everything. Communism + Atheism + Democracy = Satanism trying to get his foot in the door. The sans-culottes wore clothing of the poor so as to know one another. No fine clothing was worn or you were not one of them. To dress well was dangerous to be associated with anything counter-revolutionary, and was a sign of belonging to church and nobility.

A person who does not love God and His Mother can not be trusted. St. Augustine **Wait!!** I'm not finished. As a result the government, judges, and people in general, develop a 'false compassion'. What's that? I'll tell you. It's where the drug pushers are given a slap on the hand and let lose because their not bad people they're just sick. Now their arrested the second or third time for much worse crimes. IT'S WHERE THE CRIMINAL GETS OFF AND VICTIM GETS BURIED OR SUED.

It's where the girl has lived with several men in the last year. The judge has ordered that the house should be given to her. The two children should be care for by the state. Her husband is now made to pay her $300 or $500 a month, until she is emotionally restored, because she was to be pitied.

(What happened to the vows of matrimony, and to stay together til death?) **FALSE COMPASSION**

!!! It's where the devil says, "Don't judge people."

There is no right and there no wrong. Black becomes white and white becomes black.

God's laws must come back, reform of people, need of factories where people use their hands and crafts. The Farm life is always the best for the family up bring and moral standance. Of course this is why Satan pulled the family off the farm and into the city. Now we have Farm Corporations and sprayed canceler foods, like corn syrup with Aspartame in it. It ruins the body and the mind. They do what they want to control and reduce the population.

All people from youth on, must be given a plan, or develop a mission in life to restore responsibility. To distinguish the sin from the sinner. Where true justice prevails. Where we hate the sin and love the sinner this is **true compassion.** Where the child is spanked and loving, where discipline of wrong doing will brings back a good society. Bishop Fulton Sheen would say, "you must make a depression on the back side in order to make a lasting impression on the inside". I know I've mentioned this before.

Purgatory

Short stories of Purgatory -A remarkable collection of visits from the souls in Purgatory to various Saints and Mystics.

THE HOLY SOULS IN PURGATORY NEED OUR HELP. OUR TIME TO ASSIST THEM IS SHORT. ETERNITY IS FOREVER.

Now who can be in more urgent need of our charity than the **Poor Souls in Purgatory**? What hunger, or thirst, or dire sufferings on earth can compare to their dreadful torments? Neither the poor, nor the sick, nor the suffering, we see around us, have any such urgent need of our help as do these suffering souls in the fire pains of Purgatory. Yet we find many good hearted people who interest themselves in every other type of suffering, but, scarcely is there one who works for the **Holy Souls**.

Who can have more claim on us for our help, then our mothers and fathers, our friends and near of kin. When they are finally released from their pains will enjoy the beatitude of Heaven, which is to see God face to face.

By their prayers they will shield and protect those of us who have helped them in this painful place reparation. They will obtain whatever you ask of them.

If we Catholics and others only knew what powerful protectors we have in helping the **Poor Souls**, we would never be remised in praying for them though out the day.

Another very great grace that the Holy Souls obtain for their helpers is a shorter and easy Purgatory, or possibly its complete remission.

Seldom does anyone make it straight to Heaven without some remission of sins to pay for. Even St. Padre Pio was (6) hours in Purgatory before he was able to go into Heaven.

Spreading and having Mass said for the Poor Souls is the best way of having them in return help you with a special need you may have. If you have a limb or sore in need of healing this is the way to have your problem or need resolved.

In every Rosary, Mass and in all your daily and nightly prayers never failed to mention relief of the **Poor Souls**. *"I know when you pray for me, and it is the same with all of the other souls here in Purgatory. Very few of us here get any prayers; the majority of us are totally abandoned, with no thought or prayers offered for us from those on earth"* (Message from a soul in Purgatory)

Over the years of studying the lives of the mystics of the Church I have amassed a large number of eye witness accounts from various books and manuscripts of the appearances of the souls in Purgatory to a number of persons-- a good number of these accounts are not widely known, so I thought it would make a very interesting study to compile a number of shorter accounts from a variety of sources for those interested in this subject.

St Padre Pio's visions of the souls in Purgatory

In May, 1922, Padre Pio testified the following to the Bishop of Melfi, His Excellency Alberto Costa and also the superior of the friary, Padre Lorenzo of San Marco along with 5 other friars. One of the five friars, Fra Alberto D'Apolito of San Giovanni Rotondo wrote down the account as follows:

"While in the friary on a winter afternoon after a heavy snowfall, he was sitting by the fireplace one evening in the guest room, absorbed in prayer, when an old man, wearing an old-fashioned cloak still worn by southern Italian peasants at the time, sat down beside him. Concerning this man Pio states: 'I could not imagine how he could have entered the friary at this time of night since all the doors are locked. I questioned him: 'Who are you? What do you want?'

The old man told him, "Padre Pio, I am Pietro Di Mauro, son of Nicola, nicknamed Precoco." He went on to say, "I died in this friary on the 18th of September, 1908, in cell number 4, when it was still a poor house. One night, while in bed, I fell asleep with a lighted cigar, which ignited the mattress and I died, suffocated and burned. I am still in Purgatory. I need a holy Mass in order to be freed. God permitted that I come and ask you for help."

According to Padre Pio: "After listening to him, I replied, 'Rest assured that tomorrow I will celebrate Mass for your liberation.' I arose and accompanied him to the door of the friary, so that he could leave.

I did not realize at that moment that the door was closed and locked: I opened it and bade him farewell The moon lit up the square, covered with snow. When I no longer saw him in front of me, I was taken by a sense of fear, and I closed the door, reentered the guest room, and felt faint."

A few days later, Padre Pio also told the story to Padre Paolino, and the two decided to go to the town hall, where they looked at the vital statistics for the year 1908 and found that on September 18 of that year, one Pietro Di Mauro had in fact died of burns and asphyxiation in Room Number 4 at the friary, then used as a home for the homeless.

Around the same time, Padre Pio told Fra Alberto of another apparition of a soul from Purgatory which also occurred around the same time. He said:

One evening, when I was absorbed in prayer in the choir of the little church I was shaken and disturbed by the sound of footsteps, and candles and flower vases being moved on the main altar. Thinking that someone must be there, I called out, "Who is it?"

No one answered. Returning to prayer, I was again disturbed by the same noises. In fact, this time I had the impression that one of the candles, which was in front of the statue of Our Lady of Grace, had fallen. Wanting to see what was happening on the altar, I stood up, went close to the grate and saw, in the shadow of the light of the Tabernacle lamp, a young confrere doing some cleaning. I yelled out, "What are you doing in the dark?" The little friar answered, "I am cleaning."

"You clean in the dark?" I asked. "Who are you?"

The little friar said, 'I am a Capuchin novice, who spends his time of Purgatory here. I am in need of prayers.' and then he disappeared,"

Padre Pio stated that he immediately began praying for him as requested, and it is not known if he had any further dealings with this particular soul. However, in regards souls in Purgatory it is very interesting to note that later in life Padre Pio once said that 'As many souls of the dead come up this road [to the monastery] as that of the souls of the living." Without a doubt, many souls from Purgatory visited Padre Pio seeking his prayers, sacrifices and sufferings to obtain their release.

From the manuscript of Sister M. de L.C., written from 1874-1890

To get an idea of how Purgatory is arranged, we can get a good glimpse of it from a nun from France who had died on February 22, 1871 at the age of 36, and 2-1/2 years later (in November 1873) she began appearing from Purgatory to a fellow nun in her convent, named Sister M. de L.C (name kept anonymous in the manuscript to protect the nuns identity, as the manuscript was published while the nun was still living) as related in the booklet "An Unpublished Manuscript on Purgatory" published by The Reparation Society of the Immaculate Heart of Mary, Inc., 2002:

"I can tell you about the different degrees of Purgatory because I have passed through them. In the great Purgatory there are several stages. In the lowest and most painful, it is like a temporary hell, and here there are the sinners who have committed terrible crimes during life and whose death surprised them in that state. It was almost a miracle that they were saved, and often by the prayers of holy parents or other pious persons. Sometimes they did not even have time to confess their sins and the world thought them lost, but God, whose mercy is infinite, gave them at the moment of death the contrition necessary for their salvation on account of one or more good actions which they performed during life. For such souls, Purgatory is most terrible. It is a real hell with this difference, that in hell they curse God, whereas we bless Him and thank Him for having saved us.

Next to these come the souls, who though they did not commit great crimes like the others, were indifferent to God. They did not fulfill their Easter duties as prescribed by Christ's One True Church *(outside of which there is not salvation)* and were also converted at the point of death. Many were unable to receive Holy Communion. They are in Purgatory for the many long years of indifference. They suffer unheard of pains and are abandoned either without prayers or if they are said for them, they are not allowed to profit by them. There are in this stage of Purgatory religious of both sexes, who were tepid, neglectful of their duties, indifferent towards Jesus, also priests who did not exercise their sacred ministry with the reverence due to the Sovereign Majesty and who did not instill the love of God sufficiently into the souls confided to their care. I was in this stage of Purgatory. (Some priests don't want to give out their telephone number, because they don't want be bothered in any case of an emergency.)

In the second Purgatory are the souls of those who died with venial sins not fully expiated before death, or with mortal sins that have been forgiven but for which they have not made entire satisfaction to the Divine Justice. In this part of Purgatory, there are also different degrees according to the merits of each soul.

Thus the Purgatory of the consecrated souls or of those who have received more abundant graces, is longer and far more painful than that of ordinary people of the world.

Lastly, there is the Purgatory of desire which is called the Threshold. Very few escape this!!!! To avoid it altogether, one must ardently desire

Heaven and the vision of God. *That is rare, rarer than people think,* because even pious people are afraid of God and have not, therefore, a sufficiently strong desire of going to Heaven. This Purgatory has its very painful martyrdom like the others. The deprivation of the sight of our loving Jesus adds to the intense suffering."

Another explanation of the levels in Purgatory from this same book:

Retreat, August 1878: "Great sinners who were indifferent towards God, and religious who were not what they should have been, are in the lowest stage of Purgatory. While they are there [in the lowest realms of Purgatory], the prayers offered up for them are not applied to them. Because they have ignored God during their life, He now in His turn leaves them abandoned [without the aid of the prayers of others] in order that they may repair their neglectful and worthless lives. While on earth one truly cannot picture or imagine what God really is, but we (in Purgatory) know and understand Him for what He is, because our souls are freed from all the ties that fettered them and prevented them from realizing the holiness and majesty of God and His great mercy. We are martyrs, consumed as it were by love. An irresistible force draws us towards God who is our center, but at the same time another force thrusts us back to our place of expiation.

We are in the state of being unable to satisfy our longings. Oh, what a suffering that is, but how we desire it and there is no murmuring against God here. We desire only what God wants. You on earth, however, cannot possibly understand what we have to endure. I am much relieved as I am no longer in the fire. I have now only the insatiable desire to see God, a suffering cruel enough indeed, but I feel that the end of my exile is at hand and that I am soon to leave this place where I long for God with all my heart. I know it well, I feel more at ease, but I cannot tell you the day or the hour of my release. God alone knows that. It may be that I have still many years of longing for Heaven. Continue to pray; I will repay you later on, though I do pray a great deal for you now."

Why is it that I pray for you with less fervor than I pray for others and that often I forget to recommend you?

Do not trouble yourself about that. It is a punishment for me.

Even if you prayed more (for me) I should not be any the more relieved. God wills it thus. If He wants you to pray more He will inspire you to do so. I repeat again, do not be worried about me. You will never see me in my sufferings. Later on, when your soul is stronger, you will see souls in Purgatory and very awful ones, but let this not frighten you. God will then give you the necessary courage and all that you need to accomplish His holy will.

Is this not a punishment?

No, certainly not, I am here for my relief and for your sanctification. If you would but pay a little more attention to what I say.

That is true but these happenings are so extraordinary that I do not know what to make of them; it is not an ordinary thing to hear you in this way.

I understand well your difficulty and I am aware of your sufferings on this account. However, if God wishes it and it relieves me, you will have pity on me, will you not? When I am released you will see that I will do far more for you than you have ever done for me. I already pray much for you.

Where is Sister --?

In the lowest Purgatory, where she receives no benefit from anyone's prayers. God is often displeased, if one may speak thus, when many religious come to die, because He has called these souls to Himself that they might serve Him faithfully on earth and go straight to Heaven at the moment of death, but because of their infidelity, they have to stay long in Purgatory - far longer than people in the world who have not had so many graces.

1879, Retreat in September. We see St. Michael as we see the angels. He has no body. He comes to get the souls that have finished their purification. It is he who conducts them to Heaven. He is among the Seraphim as Monsignor said. He is the highest angel in Heaven. Our own Guardian Angels come to see us but St. Michael is far more beautiful than they are. As to the Blessed Virgin, we see her in the body. She comes to Purgatory on her feasts and she goes back to Heaven with many souls. While she is with us we do not suffer. St. Michael accompanies her. When he comes alone, we suffer as usual. When I spoke to you of the great and the second Purgatory, it was to try to make you understand that there are different stages in Purgatory. Thus I call that stage of Purgatory "great" or "worst" where the most guilty souls are, and where I stayed for two years without being able to give a sign of the torments I was suffering. The year when you heard me groaning, when I began to speak to you, I was still in the same place.

In the second Purgatory, which is still Purgatory but very different from the first, one suffers a great deal, but less than in the great place of expiation. Then there is a third stage, which is the Purgatory of desire, where there is no fire. The souls who did not desire Heaven ardently enough, who did not love God sufficiently, are there. It is there that I am at this moment. Further, in these three parts of Purgatory, there are many degrees of variation. Little by little, as the soul becomes purified, her sufferings are changed.

You sometimes say to me that the perfecting of a soul is a long process and you are also astonished that after so many prayers, I am so long deprived of the sight of God. Alas, the perfecting of a soul does not take any less time in Purgatory than upon earth. There are a number of souls, but they are very few, who have only a few venial sins to expiate. These do not stay long in Purgatory. A few well-said prayers, a few sacrifices soon deliver them. But when there are souls like mine - and that is nearly all whose lives have been so empty and who paid little or no attention to their salvation - then their whole life has to be begun all over again in this place of expiation. The soul has to perfect itself and love and desire Him, whom it did not love sufficiently on earth. This is the reason why the deliverance of some souls is delayed. God has given me a very great grace in allowing me to ask for prayers. I did not deserve it, but without this I would have remained like most of those here, for years and years more."

The Shepherd named Fritz —From the diary of Eugenie von der Leyen, 1923.

June 11, 1923. At awakening, a long grayish form was over me, completely nebulous; I can't say whether man or woman, but unsympathetic; I am very frightened.

June 14. The phantom was already in my room when I wanted to sleep. Then I said my evening-prayer aloud, during which it came very near to me. If it hadn't been for his arms, it rather would seem a walking tree-trunk. It stayed perhaps twenty minutes, then came back at four o'clock.

June 16. It was very bad. It shook my shoulder. That is a horrible moment. I struck him and said: "You may not touch me!" Whereupon it withdrew in a corner. At my push, I didn't feel a body, it was like a humid, warm towel. I believed I couldn't stand such terror any longer.

June 18. I prayed out of fear and took the particle of the Cross [a holy relic she possessed] in my hand. Then it remained with me, staying upright and big before me. It didn't answer questions," then it went out through the door, which it left open.

June 19. I can recognize now that it is a man; he was only there for a short while.

June 21. The horrible man more than an hour during the night, went back and forth continuously. He has disheveled black hair and horrific eyes.

June 22. This man from one o'clock until past five with me, it was very bad. He repeatedly bowed over me and sat down at my bedside. I really wept for fear, then prayed the "hours" so that I didn't need to see him. Then he went again back and forth and moaned horribly. Now it seems to me I must know him, however I cannot find out who it is. I have become very cowardly, for many times it is really a decision for me to go to my room in the evening. Yet ordinarily I am able to fall asleep very well.

June 24. He came back, seized me at my shoulder. I said: "Now tell me what you want and then don't come back."

No answer; he went again through the room a couple of times and then was gone. My rest however was completely destroyed. At six in the morning he came back. In daylight he even looked more horrific, belongs to the dirtiest category of ghosts who have already come. I said: "Don't disturb me, I want to prepare myself for holy Communion!" Then he drew very near to me and lifted his hands imploringly. I was so sorry for him that I promised him a lot. Then I said: "Can't you speak?" Whereupon he shook his head. "Do you have much to suffer?" Now he moaned terribly. I gave him much holy water" and then he was gone.

June 27. He was there again, in the night. Seems to know me; I racked my brains as to who he might be. He is very unsympathetic.?

June 29. He was again in the room when I went to bed. It could be the murdered shepherd Fritz. I asked him at once, but he didn't react. I prayed with him, during which he fixed his eyes on me so angrily that I was really frightened. I asked him to go and then he went indeed.

June 30. He came very briefly; his moaning waked me up.

July 1. Again, I really believe it was shepherd Fritz. However his face was so black that I had difficulty recognizing him. But figure, nose, and eyes are wholly "his," as I saw him so many times in life.

July 2. He came back, didn't look so terribly wild anymore and stayed not for a long time. I addressed him as "shepherd Fritz," which he apparently found quite natural.

July 3. He came very briefly. I asked: "Are you the murdered shepherd Fritz?" Then he said distinctly: "Yes!"

July 4. He came to me in the morning, looked sadly at me and went away soon, answered nothing, too. July 5. Now it struck me that everything about him is clearer. During prayer, he made the Sign of the Cross.

July 6. I am very happy for he can speak now. I asked him: "Why do you always come to me?" He: "Because you have always prayed for me." (That is right, for I had always been sorry for the poor fellow; he always looked so particular, even as a boy.) I: "Then what saved you?" He: "Insight and repentance." I: "Weren't you dead immediately?" He: "No." I: "Will you be released soon?" He: "Not by far." Then I gave him permission to continue coming to me, if it does him well. How remarkable it is, that someone who was so rude in life speaks like that when separated from his body. Now I am not frightened by him anymore, and would like to help him as best I can. How merciful is the good Lord!

July 8. He came very briefly.

July 9. He came at 6:00am and by doing so woke me up. Otherwise I had overslept. I: "Is it so important for you that I go to holy Mass?" He: "That way, you can help me a lot."

July 11. Only came very briefly.

July 12. We prayed together," then I: "Then what do you have to suffer?" He: "I am burning!" Then he came up to me and before I could defend myself, he pressed a finger on my hand. I was frightened so much and it hurt me so much, that I screamed. Now I have a red burn which I hope will heal soon. It is a very strange feeling, to have this visible mark from the other world.

July 24. Shepherd Fritz and the other one came two times in the night, all silent, but [the new one] not very pleasant.

July 29. Nothing special to mention. Now these two are coming every night. The new one looks horrible, while shepherd Fritz becomes ever more bright!!

August 10. Shepherd Fritz drew so near to me again, but looked very friendly. So I said to him, "Don't you have to suffer so much anymore?" He: "No." and I: "Can you pray for me yet?" He: "No." and I: "Where are you then all the time?" He: "In the forlornness." I: "Will you still come often to me?" He: "No." and I: "Why not?" He: "I am not allowed to any more!" and I: "Have I been able to help you?" He: "Yes." Then he was gone....

To close this remarkable account, Father Sebastian Wieser, Eugenie's parish priest and confessor, comments:

"The behavior of this apparition is like the echo of his earthly life. I have known shepherd Fritz well -he was like a "billygoat" in the parish. In him, the greatness of the mercy of God really manifests itself. Rarely did he come to church. He had an only son, who in school became well known for his meanness, falsehood, and deceptions and caused many troubles to his teachers and those in authority over him. When the boy had to be punished at school, the father pulled out all the stops of his indignation over the schoolmaster and priest. I prophesied at that time that someday the father himself would get a beating from this only son!

When this son was seventeen years old and was big and quite strong, he beat his father to death at around midnight .... Nobody knew if Fritz was dead immediately or if he came to for a moment. The latter seems to have been the case. The murderer had knocked him down in the hay-barn and abandoned him to his fate. Only in the morning was the dead man discovered ....On the sixth of July he states that: "...insight and repentance" have saved him from damnation! On the twelfth day of July he says, "I am burning!" and presses a finger on the hand of the princess, which leaves a red burn which I have seen myself." –Father Sebastian Wieser

"Oh! If people only knew what Purgatory is!"

In 1870, Belgium fought as an ally with France against Germany.

In September of that year, Sister Maria Serafina, a Redemptorist nun in Malines, Belgium, was suddenly seized with inexplicable sadness.

Soon after, she received the news that her father had died in that war.

From that day on, Sister Maria repeatedly heard distressing groans and a voice saying, "My dear daughter, have mercy on me!"

Subsequently, she was besieged with torments, which included unbearable headaches. While laying down one day, she saw her father surrounded with flames and immersed in profound sadness.

He was suffering in Purgatory and had received permission from God to beseech prayers from his daughter and relate Purgatory's suffering to her. Thus he said:

MISSING IMAGE

I want you to have Masses, prayers and indulgences said on my behalf. Look how I am immersed in this fire-filled hole! Oh! If people knew what Purgatory is, they would suffer anything to avoid it and alleviate the suffering of souls here. Be very holy, my daughter, and observe the Holy Rule, even in its most insignificant points. Purgatory for religious is a terrible thing!

Sister Maria saw a pit full of flames, spewing black clouds of smoke. Her father was immersed in the pit where he was burning, horribly suffocated and thirsty. Opening his mouth she saw that his tongue was entirely shriveled.

"I am thirsty, my daughter, I am thirsty."

The next day, her father visited her again saying, "My daughter, it has been a long time since I saw you last."

"My father, it was just yesterday . . ." "Oh! It seems like an eternity to me. If I stay in Purgatory three months, it will be an eternity. I was condemned for many years, but, due to Our Lady's intercession, my sentence was reduced to only a few months."

The grace of coming to earth was granted to him through his good works during his life and because he had been devoted to Our Lady receiving communion on all her feast days.

During these visions, Sister Maria Serafina asked her father several questions:

"Do souls in Purgatory know who is praying for them, and can they pray for us?" "Yes, my daughter."

"Do these souls suffer, knowing that God is offended in their families and in the world?"

"Yes."

Directed by her confessor and her superior, she continued to question her father:

"Is it true that the sufferings of Purgatory are much greater than all the torments of earth and even of the martyrs?"

"Yes, my daughter, all this is very true."

Sister Serafina then asked if everyone who belongs to the Scapular Confraternity of Carmel (those who wear the scapular), is freed from Purgatory on the first Saturday after death: "Yes," he answered, "but only if they are faithful to the Confraternity obligations." "Is it true that some souls must stay in Purgatory for as long as five hundred years?"

"Yes. Some are condemned until the end of the world. These souls are very guilty and entirely abandoned."

"Three main things draw God's malediction over men: failure to observe the Lord's Day through work, the very widespread vice of impurity, and blasphemy. Oh my daughter, how these blasphemies provoke the wrath of God!"

For over three months, Sister Serafina and her community prayed and offered penance for the soul of her tormented father who often appeared to her. During the elevation of the Host at Christmas Mass, Sister Maria saw her father shining like a sun with matchless beauty.

"I finished my sentence, and have come to thank you and your sisters for your prayers and pious exercises. I will pray for you in Heaven."

If Purgatory did not exist to remove the stain of sin from imperfect souls, the only alternative would be Hell. Therefore, Purgatory is a necessary place of expiation.

All personal sin carries two consequences: blame (which, in the case of mortal sin, destroys sanctifying grace and leads to Hell) and temporal

punishment warranted by the offense to God.

Although Confession frees us from blame and part of the punishment, we must still make additional reparation to God. In this life, this can be done through prayer, Mass intentions, alms, penance and acquiring indulgences. One who dies in a state of venial sin or without sufficient reparation goes to Purgatory.

Suffering Encouraged by Hope

According to Saint Thomas and Saint Augustine, the least pain of Purgatory is worse than the greatest of this life. This is due to the intensity of the desire souls have for God, Whose privation is extremely painful, and the magnitude of sensible pain, which, touching the soul directly, is worse than anything felt by the senses. Books on Hell and Purgatory convert more souls.

However rigorous the punishments of Purgatory may be, they are soothed by hope.

Saint Catherine of Genoa (1447-1510), a mystic who suffered Purgatory's torments on earth explained that one suffers simultaneously unspeakable torment and indescribable happiness.

She described the torment as stemming from a continually consuming interior fire, kindled by separation from God, for Whom the soul is aflame with love. This suffering is so intense that it transforms each instant into a martyrdom of pain.

Although surpassing all earthly suffering, it cannot be compared with the anguish of Hell where suffering is a despairing fruit of hatred while the suffering of Purgatory is a hope-filled suffering of love.

Consequently, Saint Catherine said that only in Heaven itself is there greater happiness than that amidst the torments of Purgatory. This is because the soul knows it is saved, in friendship with God, surrounded by holy souls, and thus aflame with love of God.

Your Mission is to Empty Purgatory

Saint Catherine explained:

> I believe no happiness can be found worthy to be compared with that of a soul in Purgatory except that of the saints in Paradise; and day by day this happiness grows as God flows into these souls, more and more as the hindrance to His entrance is consumed. Sin's rust is the hindrance, and the fire burns the rust away so that more and more the soul opens itself up to the divine inflowing. A thing which is covered cannot respond to the sun's rays, not because of any defect in the sun, which is shining all the time, but because the cover is an obstacle; if the cover be burnt away, this thing is open to the sun; more and more as the cover is consumed does it respond to the rays of the sun.

It is in this way that rust, which is sin, covers souls, and in Purgatory is burnt away by fire; the more it is consumed, the more do the souls respond to God, the true sun. As the rust lessens and the soul is opened up to the divine ray, happiness grows; until the time be accomplished the one wanes and the other waxes. Pain however does not lessen but only the time for which pain is endured. As for will: never can the souls say these pains are pains, so contented are they with God's ordaining with which, in pure charity, their will is united.

The Duration of Purgatory

The amount of time spent in Purgatory is very difficult to express in human terms. In accounts of private visions, we read of souls condemned for a number of years or even until the end of the world. Indeed, Our Lady revealed to the seers of Fatima that a girl who died shortly before the apparitions would remain there until the end of time.

Theologians explain that time in Purgatory can be gauged in two ways. The first is positive and corresponds to time as we measure it on earth; the other is fictitious or imaginary since it corresponds to the amount of time that souls judge they suffered which is distorted since this very suffering causes them to lose track of time.

Thus, we see souls, who after mere hours in Purgatory complain about years or even centuries of suffering.

Saint Anthony tells the story of a sick person who suffered so atrociously that he considered it beyond human nature and thus continually prayed for death. One day, an angel appeared to him and said, "God sent me here to offer you a choice. You can spend one year of suffering on earth, or one day in Purgatory." Choosing the latter, he died and went to Purgatory.

When the angel went to console him, he was greeted with this groan of pain, "Deceitful angel!

At least twenty years ago, you said that I would spend only one day in Purgatory . . . My Dear God, how I suffer!"

To which the angel said, "Dear soul, it has been but one hour, and your body is not even buried."

The man replied, "Please allow me the one year to suffer on earth."

The holy souls have repeatedly told her Maria Simma (1915-2004) that the greatest help for them that they can obtain from those here on earth is the offering of holy Mass. Next to the Mass, the holy Rosary and the Stations of the Cross are very beneficial to them. Any sacrifice we make-- even the smallest ones-- offered specifically for them have a great value in the eyes of God, and greatly lessen their sufferings and time in purgatory. The poor souls have told her that even the smallest prayer or sacrifice is like giving a cool glass of water to a parched sojourner travelling in the driest desert.

When St. James the Greater was dying, he had a vision of Our Lady, and he begged to Her his death to Her Son for him. She did. Our Lord appeared to Our Lady and told Her that anyone who at their death, would as St. James has done, ask you My Mother for your help to offer their soul to Me, I will grant them eternal salvation.

In times of temptations Our Lord gave Our Lady the power to help anyone who call upon Her for help in time of temptation.

Our Lady told Mary of Agreda that the most important virtue implanted in Her, and should be in all men's hearts is namely to have a great fear of God's Judgement. Asking yourself, "am I in God's favor or have I lost it." "And to have a constant hate for sin and all that is evil."

Hell

St. Padre Pio (Stigmatist) Meeting a man; the man said, 'I do not believe in Hell.' St. Padre Pio said, 'You will, when you get there'.

In the 1500's there was a **Nun** by the name of **Sr. Magdalena of the Cros**s, she was thought to be of very high sanctity. She performed miracles and prophecy. So loved by her followed sisters that they made her abbess. She was told by St. Francis in a vision that she did not need to confess to a priest any more, but directly to God. She told the rest of her convent that they did not have to go confession, but if they did feel the need they could go. She felt it was not necessary to confess to the priest from behind the grille, and that it should be eliminated, so they could confess **face to face** with the priest. This made it harder for them to tell, and accuse themselves of severe sins.

This horrified the bishop and priests. Soon she was found to have made a pact with the devil at an early age 40 years long. She was found to be possessed by two demons named: Balban and Patorrio. Now to die soon.

In all this she and the devil had fooled the nuns, the priests, bishop and nearly all of Spain, except a couple of priests by the names: St. Ignatius Loyola and St. John of Avila who was discreetly denied access to her.

An old priest, a Franciscan monk Rev. Don Juan of Cordova won her back to Christ. She was than 61. Balban was very reluctantly dislodged from Magdalena, it is discovered that the most wicked and hideous means were used to undermine Magdalena's soul as a child. It was believed that he originally chose her because she was in fact very pious and devoted to God, and so in his terrible wickedness he earnestly sought to despoil God of one of His favorites. The infernal creature is repulsive and the possessed nun describes in horror his wide, flat nose, his twisted horns and his toothless mouth. But, God wins triumphantly in the end. She dies at 74.

Fr. Nieremberg relates the story of a noble lady, who was exceedingly pious, asked of God to make known to her what displeased His Divine Majesty most in persons of her sex. The Lord vouchsafed in a miraculous manner to hear her. He opened under her eyes the Eternal Abyss There she saw a woman prey to cruel torments and in her recognized one of her friends, a short time before deceased. This sight caused her as much astonishment as grief, the person whom she saw damned did not seem to her to have lived badly. Then that unhappy soul said to her; "It is true that I practiced religion, but I was a slave of vanity. Ruled by the passion to look pleasing, <u>I was not afraid to adopt indecent fashions to</u> <u>attract attention</u> and I kindled the fire of impurity in more than one heart. Ah! If Christian women knew

how much immodesty in dress displeases God!" At the same moment, this unhappy soul was pierced by two fiery lances, and plunged into a caldron of liquid lead." One can only imagine the screams of pain and cries of despair she emitted in this vision, screams and cries that will last forever, in the "everlasting fire." St. Matt. 25:41

Our Blessed Mother warned over 80 years ago to Blessed Jacinta that "certain fashions would be introduced that would greatly offend Our Loud very much."

St. Paul warned that the immodest would not be saved. Gal. 5:19-21

Now the works of the flesh....immodesty, meaning the young men and women who do not cover their arms in church, or wear blouses that cling tightly to show the form of the body and do not go up to the base of the neck, which cause men to look at them instead of paying attention to God, or the dress is not 8" below the knee, or sandals are worn instead of socks with modest shoe wear. St. Padre Pio told women do not paint your fingers and toes and body, because this is not pleasing to God. Jacinta, who was one of the three who had the vision of hell, had this to say: "If people only knew what awaits them in eternity, they would do everything in their power to change their lives!" "Many are called," said Jesus, "but few are chosen."

"I assure you, My child, could man look into purgatory, he would beg to find--he would search out every moment of his life upon earth a manner to purge himself by penance and suffering. The years are few upon your earth; time beyond the veil is forever and endless." - Our Lady to privileged soul.

Cry of a Lost Soul...and the lessons that it teaches.

Clara and Annette, both single Catholics in their early twenties, worked adjacent to each other as employees of a commercial firm in Germany.

Although they were never very close friends, they shared a courteous mutual regard which lead to an exchange of ideas and, eventually, of confidences. Clara professed herself openly religious, and felt it her duty to instruct and admonish Annette when the latter appeared excessively casual or superficial in religious matters.

In due course, Annette married and left the firm. The year was 1937. Clara spent the autumn of that year on holiday at Lake Garda. About the middle of September she received a letter from her mother: "Annette is dead. She was the victim of an auto accident and was buried yesterday at Wald-Friedhof."

Clara was frightened since she knew her friend was not very religious. Was she prepared to appear before God? Dying suddenly, what had happened to her?

The next day she attended Mass, received Holy Communion, and prayed fervently for her friend. The following night, at ten minutes after midnight the vision took place.

"Clara, do not pray for me! I am in Hell. If I tell you this and speak at length about it, do not think it is because of our friendship. We here do not love anyone. I do this under constraint. In truth, I should like to see you too come to this state where I must remain forever.

"Perhaps that angers you, but here we all think that way. Our wills are hardened in evil -- in what you call 'evil'. Even when we do something 'good', as I do now, opening your eyes about Hell, it is not because of a good intention.

"Do you still remember our first meeting four years ago at the firm? You were then 23 and had been there already half a year. Because I was a beginner, you gave me some helpful advice. Then I praised your love of your neighbor. Ridiculous! Your help was mere coquetry. Here we do not acknowledge any good -- in anybody.

"Do you remember what I told you about my youth? Now I am painfully compelled to fill in some of the gaps. According to the plan of my parents, I should not have existed. A 'misfortune' brought about my conception. My two sisters were 14 and 15 when I was born.

"Would that I had never existed! Would that I could now annihilate myself and escape these tortures! No pleasure would equal that with which I would abandon my existence, as a garment of ashes which is lost in nothingness. But I must continue to exist as I chose to make myself -- as a ruined person.

"When father and mother, still young, left the country for the city, they had lost touch with the Church and were keeping company with irreligious people. They had met at a dance, and after a year and a half of companionship they had to get married.

"As a result of the nuptial ceremony, so much holy water remained on them that my mother attended Sunday Mass a couple of times a year. But she never taught me to pray. (Yes, this is happening even in my own descendants, they take no time, or they think the children are too young. Soon formation time is past.) (The Asperges at the beginning of High Mass when holy water is sprinkled in abundance, some saints say they have seen the demons fleeing out through the walls to get a way.)

Instead, she was completely taken up with daily cares of life, although our situation was not that bad."

"My mother attended Sunday Mass a couple of times a year. But she never taught me to pray. Instead, she was completely taken up with the daily cares of life, although our situation was not bad."

"I refer to prayer, Mass, religious instruction, holy water, church with a very strong repugnance. I hate all that, as I hate those who go to church, and in general every human being and everything.

"From a great many things do we receive torture. Every knowledge received at the hour of death, every remembrance of things lived or

known is, for us, a piercing flame. In each remembrance, good and bad, we see the way in which grace was present - the grace we despised or ignored. What a torture this is!

"We do not eat, we do not sleep, we do not walk. Chained, with howling and gnashing of teeth, we look appalled at our ruined life, hating and suffering.

"Do you hear? We here drink hatred like water. Above all we hate God. With great reluctance do I force myself to make you understand.

"The blessed in Heaven must love God because they see Him without veil, in all His dazzling beauty. That makes their bliss indescribable. We know this and the knowledge makes us furious.

"Men on earth, who know God from nature and from revelation, can love Him, but they are not compelled to do so. The believer - I say this with gnashing of teeth - who contemplates Christ on the cross, with arms extended, will end by loving Him.

"But he whom God approaches only in the final storm, as punisher, as just avenger, because He was rejected by him, such a person cannot but hate Him with all the strength of his wicked will. We died with willful resolve to be separated from God.

"Do you now understand why Hell lasts forever? It is because our wills were fixed for eternity at the moment of death. We had made our final choice. Our obstinacy will never leave us.

"Under compulsion, I must add that God is merciful, even towards us. I affirm many things against my will and must choke back the torrent of abuses I should like to vomit out.

"God was merciful to us by not allowing our wicked wills to exhaust themselves on earth, as we should have been prepared to do. This would have increased our faults and our pains. He caused us to die before our time, as in my case, or had other mitigating circumstances intervene.

"Now He shows Himself merciful towards us by not compelling a closer approach than that afforded in this remote inferno. Every step bringing us closer to God would cause us a greater pain than that which a step closer to a burning furnace would cause you.

"You were scared when once, during a walk, I told you that my father, a few days before my first Communion, had told me: 'My little Annette, the main thing is your beautiful white dress, all the rest is just make-believe.' Because of your concern, I was almost ashamed. Now I sneer at it.

"The important thing is that we were not allowed to receive Communion until the age of (12). By then I was already absorbed in <u>worldly amusements</u> *and found it easy to set aside, without scruple, the things of religion. Thus, I attached no great importance to my first Communion."*

"We are furious that many children go to Communion at the age of seven. We do all we can to make people believe that children gave insufficient knowledge at that age. (Yes I know people who think this way.)

"They must first commit some mortal sins. Then the white Particle will not do so much damage to our wick cause as when faith, hope, and charity - oh, these things! - received in Baptism, are still alive in their hearts." (I have heard of parents who take their children to Mass, but never teach them them their religion or prayers or why they genuflect before the tabernacle. And I was told the true story of a five year old child that was taught by his parents to blaspheme God and his Mother. The Child die before the age of six, and is in Hell forever.)

"Maria and you induced me to enter The Association of the Young Ladies. The games were amusing. As you know, I immediately took a directive part. I liked it. I also liked the picnics. I even let myself be induced to go to confession and Communion sometimes.

"Once you warned me, 'Anne, if you do not pray, you will go to perdition.' I used to pray very little indeed, and even this unwillingly. You were then only too right. All those who burn in Hell did not pray or did not pray enough.

"Prayer is the first step towards God. And it is the decisive step. Especially prayer to her who is the Mother of Christ, whose name we never pronounce. Devotion to her rescues from the devil numberless souls whom sin would infallibly give to him.

"I continue my story, consumed with rage and only because I have to. To pray is the easiest thing man can do on earth. And God has tied up the salvation of each one exactly to this very easy thing.

"To him who prays with perseverance, little by little God gives so much light, so much strength, that even the most debased sinner will at the end come back to salvation.

"During the last years of my life I did not pray any more, so I lacked those graces without which nobody can be saved. Here we no longer receive graces. Moreover, should we receive them, we would cynically refuse them. All the fluctuations of earthly existence have ceased in this other life.

"For years I was living far away from God. In the last call of Grace, I decided against God. I never believed in the influence of the devil. And now I affirm that he has strong influence on the persons who are in the condition in which I was then. Only many prayers, those of others and my own, united with sacrifices and penances, could have snatched me from his grip. And even this only little by little. If there are only few externally obsessed, there are very many internally possessed. The devil cannot steal the free will from those who give themselves to his influence. But in punishment of their, so to speak, methodical apostasy from God, He allows the devil to nest in them.

"I hate the devil, too. And yet I am pleased about him, because he tries to ruin all of you; he and his legions, the spirits fallen with him at the *beginning of time. There are millions of them. They roam around the earth, as thick as a swarm of flies, and you do not even notice it. It is not reserved to us damned to tempt you; but to the multitude of fallen spirits. In truth, every time they drag down here to Hell a human soul, their own torture is increased. But what does one not do for hatred?*

"Deep down I was rebelling against God. You did not understand it; you thought me still a Catholic. I wanted, in fact, to be called one. I even used to pay my ecclesiastical dues. Maybe your answers were right sometimes. On me they made no impression, since you must not be right. Because of these counterfeited relationships between the two of us, our separation on the occasion of my marriage was of no consequence to me. Before the wedding I went to confession and Communion once more. It was a precept. My husband and I thought alike on this point. Why not comply with this formality? So we complied with this, as with the other formalities.

"Our married life, in general, was spent in great harmony. We were of the same idea in everything. In this too -- that we did not want the burden of children. In truth, my husband would have liked to have one -- no more, of course. In the end I succeeded in dissuading him even from this desire. Dresses, luxurious furniture, places of entertainment, picnics and trips by car and similar things were more important for me. It was a year of pleasure on earth, the one that passed from my marriage to my sudden death. Internally, of course, I was never happy, although externally at ease. There was always something indeterminate inside that gnawed at me.

"Unexpectedly, I had an inheritance from my aunt, Lottie. My husband succeeded in increasing his wages to a considerable figure. And so I was able to furnish our new home in an attractive way. Religion did not show its light but from afar off, pale, feeble, and uncertain.

"I used to give free vent to my ill humor about some medieval representations of Hell in cemeteries, or elsewhere, in which the devil is roasting souls in red burning coals, while his companions with

long tails, drag new victims to him. Clara! One can be mistaken in depicting Hell, but never can one exaggerate.

"I tell you; the fire of which the Bible speaks, does not mean the torment of the conscience. Fire is fire! What He said: 'Away from Me, you accursed ones, into eternal fire', is to be understood literally. Literally!

'How can the spirit be touched by material fire?' you will ask. How can your soul suffer on earth when you put your finger on the flame? In fact the soul does not burn, and yet what complete torture the whole individual feels!

"Our greatest torture consists in the certain knowledge that we shall never see God. How can this torture us so much, since on earth we are so indifferent? As long as the knife lies on the table, it leaves you cold. You see how keen it is, but you do not feel it. Plunge the knife into the flesh and you will start screaming for pain. Now we feel the loss of God; before we hardly thought of it. Not all the souls suffer to the same degree. With how much greater wickedness and how much more systematically one has sinned, the more weighs on him the loss of God and the greater the torment he suffers, which is increased even more by the number of souls with whom he sinned, who now curse him. The lost Catholics suffer more than those of other religions, because they, mostly, received and despised more graces and more light. He who knew more suffers more cruelly than he who knew less. He who sinned out of malice suffers more keenly than he who sinned out of weakness. But nobody suffers more than he deserves. Oh, if that were not true, I would have a motive for hate!

"My death happened this way: A week ago -- I am speaking according to your reckoning, because according to the pain, I could very well say that it is already ten years that I am burning in Hell -- a week ago, then, my husband, and I, on a Sunday, went on a picnic, the last one for me. The day was glorious. I felt very well. A sinister sense of pleasure, that was with me all the day long, invaded me. When lo,

suddenly, during the return, my husband was dazzled by a car that was coming full speed. He lost control.

"The name of JESUS escaped from my lips with a shivering. Not as a prayer, but as a shout. A lacerating pain took hold of the whole of me. (In comparison with the present one only a trifle.) Then I lost consciousness. Strange! That morning this thought had come to me in an inexplicable way: 'You could go to Mass once more.' It seemed like the last call of Love.

"Clear and resolute, my 'NO' cut off that train of thought. You will know already what happened after my death. The lot of my husband and that of my mother, what happened to my corpse and the proceedings of my funeral are known to me through some natural knowledge we have here. What happens on earth we know only obscurely. But we know what touches us closely. So I see also where you are living.

"I myself awoke from the darkness suddenly, in the instant of my passing. I saw myself as flooded by a dazzling light. It was in the same place where my dead body was lying. It was like a theater, when suddenly the lights in the hall are put out, the curtains are rent aside and an unexpected scene, horribly illuminated, appears. The scene of my life.

"My soul showed herself to me as in a mirror; all the graces despised from my youth until my last 'NO' to God. I felt myself like an assassin, to whom his dead victim is shown during his trial at court. Should I repent? Never! Should I feel ashamed? Never!

"However, I could not even stand before the eyes of God, rejected by me. There was only one thing for me -- flight! As Cain fled from the dead body of Abel, so my soul rushed from that sight of horror.

"This was the particular judgment; the invisible Judge said: 'Away from Me.' Then my soul, as a yellow brimstone shadow, fell headlong into the place of eternal torture."

Most important Chapter - READ This!

The book the "Four Last Things", is very essential for your salvation. However you can go:(youtube: The Four Last Things: Death; Judgement; Heaven; Hell) you will not be sorry if you listen to these (4) talks.

You know my children, one of the most absolute important things you can do to save your soul, according to St. Thomas and St. Augustine, is to read the book of Hell and Purgatory. According to these two saints more people are brought closer to God and save their souls by the daily meditation and thinking of what it would be like to be in Hell. This very sober thought of the existence of Hell and the giant ugly demons that torture you in smoke and darkness endlessly. The above (youtube) talk on *death* tells that your ability to move or be mobile in not given you in Hell by Almighty God, you are totally helpless forever. And because you were catholic and had the true Faith but did not practice it to the fullest, your pain will worse than those not catholics. Perhaps you stood around in the back of church or never became close to God at Mass not using a missal or during the day in work or play. You never from time to time whispered a word of love to God. you never grew close to His Mother. If you had at least shown a little love for Her you She would have helped you into Heaven.

If you could the demons flying around outside, you would not be able to see the light of the sun.

A touch of Hell. Sr. Josefa Menendez's Description of Hell. Our Lady told her on October 25, 1922: "Everything that Jesus allows you to see and to suffer of the torments of Hell, is..........that you may make it known to your Mother Superiors. So forget yourself entirely, and think only of the glory of the Heart of Jesus and the salvation of souls."

She repeatedly dwelt on the greatest torment of Hell, namely, the soul's inability to love. One of these damned souls cried out: "This is my torture... that I want to love and cannot; there is nothing left for me but hatred and despair. If one of us could so much as make a single act of love (contrition)..... this would no longer be Hell.... But we cannot, we live on hatred and malevolence...." (March 23, 1922).

Another of these unfortunates said: "The greatest of our torments here is that we are not able to love Him whom we are bound to hate. Oh! How we hunger for love, we are consumed with desire of it, but it is too late.... You too will feel this same devouring hunger, but you will only be able to hate, to abhor, and to long for the loss of souls....nothing else do we care for now!" (March 26, 1922).,

The following passage was written in obedience, though it was extremely repugnant to Josefa's humility: "Every day now, when I am dragged down to Hell and the devil orders them to torture me, they answer: 'We cannot, for her members have undergone torture for Him....' (then they blaspheme His name)..... then he orders them to give me a draught of sulfur .....and again the reply is: 'She has voluntarily deprived herself of drink....'

'try to find some part of her body to which she has given satisfaction and pleasure.'

"I have also noted that when they shackle me to take me down to Hell, they never can bind me where I have worn instruments of penance. I write all this simply out of obedience." (April 1, 1922).

"Some in Hell are thieves and their hands burn ......others curse their tongues, their eyes, ...whatever the occasion of their sin.....'Now, O body, you are paying the price of the delights you granted yourself!...... and did it of you own free will......"(**illegitimate delights**).

"It seemed to me that the majority accused themselves of sins of impurity, of stealing, of unjust trading; and that most of the damned are in Hell for these sins." (April 6, 1922).

"I saw many worldly people fall into Hell, and no words can render their horrible and their terrifying cries:

'Damned forever.... I deceived myself; I am lost.....I am here forever....There is no remedy possible..... a curse on me...' **(There was the daily Rosary and scapular, and true devotion to Mary the St. Louis De Montfort way. The Doctors of the Church say you can <u>not</u> save your soul without devotion to Mary.)**

"Today, I saw a vast number of people fall into the fiery pit... they seemed to be worldlings and a demon cried vociferously: 'The world is ripe for me..... **I know that the best way to get hold of souls is to rouse their desire for enjoyment....** Put me first.... me before the rest.... no humility for me!!..... but me first..... **but let me enjoy myself.....** This sort of thing assures victory for us.... and they tumble headlong into Hell'". (October 4, 1922).

Saint Faustina and her visit to Hell: Today, I was led by an angel to the chasms of hell. It is a place of great torture; how awesomely large and extensive it is!

"The kinds of tortures I saw: the first torture that constitutes hell is loss of God; the **second** is perpetual remorse of conscience; the **third** is that one's condition will never change; the **fourth is the fire** that will penetrate the soul without destroying it, a terrible suffering since it is a purely spiritual fire, lit by God's anger; **the fifth torture is continual darkness** and a terrible **suffocating smell,** (St. Bonaventure Doctor of the Church says that if one soul from hell were cast upon the surface of the earth, the smell would be enough to kill anyone who came near), despite the darkness, the devils and the souls of the damned see each other and all the evil, both of others and their own; the **sixth** torture is the constant company of Satan; **the seventh torture is the horrible despair, hatred of God, vile words, curses** and blasphemies. (Read the 'Forty Dreams of St. John Bosco'). These are the tortures suffered by all the damned together, but that is not the end of the sufferings. There are special tortures destined for particular souls. These are the torments of the senses. Each soul undergoes terrible and indescribable sufferings related to the manner in which it has sinned. There are caverns and pits of torture where one form of agony differs from another. I would have died at the very sight of these tortures if the omnipotence of God had not supported me. Let the sinner know that he will be tortured throughout all eternity, in those senses which he made use of to sin. I am writing this at the command of God, so that no soul may find an excuse by saying there is no hell, or that nobody has ever been there, and so no one can say what it is like. **I, Sister Faustina, by the order of God**, have visited the abysses of hell so that I might tell souls about it and testify to its existence. I cannot speak about it now; but I have received a command from God to leave it in writing. The devils were full of hatred for me, but they had to obey me at the command of God. But I noticed one thing: that most of the souls there are those who disbelieved that there is a hell. I could hardly recover from the fright. How terribly souls suffer there! Consequently, I pray even more fervently for the conversion of sinners. I incessantly plead God's mercy upon them. O my Jesus, I would rather be in agony until the end of the world, amidst the greatest sufferings, than offend You by the least sin." (A very good ideal to help your daily meditation is to go to: **Youtube**: 'Four Last Things: Hell; or Death; or Judgement; or Heaven.')

"In the Great Deluge in the days of Noah, nearly all mankind perished, eight persons alone being saved in the Ark. In our days a deluge, not of water but of sins, continually inundates the earth, and out of this deluge very few escape. Scarcely anyone is saved." **Saint Alphonsus Liguori – Doctor of the Church**

"I do not speak rashly, but as I feel and think. I do not think that many **priests** are saved, but that those who perish are for more numerous." **Saint John Chrysostom Doctor of the Church**

"Defeat Modernism Ep 2: The Link between the Prophecies of Blessed Elena Aliello" (Youtube)

"It is certain that few are saved. If you wish to imitate the multitude, then you shall not be among the few who shall enter in by the narrow gate." **St. Augustine Doctor of the Church**

"Out of one hundred thousand sinners who continue in sin until death, scarcely one will be saved." **St. Jerome Doctor of the Church**

"One out of ten thousand are saved." **St. Louis de Montfort** (*He speaks of those in the Church.*)

"There are a select few who are saved. Those who are saved are in the minority." **St. Thomas Aquinas**

"The majority of men shall <u>not</u> see God, excepting those who live <u>justly</u>, purified by righteousness and by every other <u>virtue</u>." **St. Justin the Martyr (I wish my Justin had said this! He has many young ones to save as do all of you and to set good example to those around you by good language and humility and the Rosary every day.) Life will soon be over, teach them well, and read to them nightly of the saints. You to John and James. Young people just like you 100 years ago didn't, and where are they today.**

Our Lady told Conchita at Garabandal: "Few will see God." And Our Lord: "Many are called, but few are chosen." and to Luisa; "It's not that your bad enough to go to Hell, it's just that your not good enough to go to Heaven." (I absolutely plead with you to have some kind of daily spiritual reading in front to read every day to become closer to God. Especially the book of Hell and Purgatory and Imitation of Christ.

A holy priest was exorcising a **demoniac**, and he asked the demon what pains he was suffering in Hell. "An eternal fire," he answered, "an eternal malediction, an eternal rage, and a frightful despair at being <u>never able</u> to <u>gaze upon Him who created me.</u>" "*What would you do to have the happiness of seeing God?*" "**To see Him but for one moment**, I should willingly consent to endure my torments for 10,000 years. But vain desires! I shall suffer forever and never see Him!"

On a like occasion, the exorcist inquired of the demon what was his greatest pain in Hell. He replied with an accent of indescribable despair: "Always, always! Never; never!"

Unhappy sinners who are lulled to rest by the illusions of the world and who live as if there were no Hell will be suddenly stripped of their illusions by the most frightful of catastrophes. From the midst of their pleasures they shall fall into the Pit of Torments. (No Scapular and no Rosary.) (My Children take heed of this, don't be fooled!)

Children are very innocent in their youth, but as they grow older they lose that innocence because Original Sin starts to take hold and grip the heart and soul of the child. You will notice they are no longer as willing to help or work for you as they did when younger. As they grow older this can develop into hatred for their duties, their work, and even authority. The mention of things they don't want to do become repugnant to them. Parents must give them chores around the house and yard and teach them charity; to do all they do out of love for God and neighbor. At the very moment they are asked to do anything, they must learn to immediately drop whatsoever they are doing out of obedience and go to the task they are asked to do. One thing you should always remember is what Our Lord said: "he who labors hard and prefers to live in poverty is most pleasing to Me."

St. Padre Pio: Met a man who said, "I don't believe in hell," Padre Pio answer, "you will when you get there."

Heaven and Hell were made as real as middle earth where we stand today, free will, two eternal rewards.

They who deny Hell will be forced to admit it sooner or later; but alas! It will be too late. Father Nieremberg, in his work "**The Difference between Time and Eternity**", speaks of an unfortunate sinner, who, as the result of his evil ways, had lost the Faith. His virtuous wife exhorted him to return to God and reminded him of Hell, but he would answer obstinately: "**There is no Hell.**" One day his wife found him dead and from strange circumstance, he held in his hand a mysterious paper on which in large characters was traced this terrifying avowal: "**I now know that there is a Hell!**"

"But I say to you, that whosoever is angry with his brother, shall be in danger of the judgment. And whosoever shall say to his brother, Raca, shall be in danger of the council. And whosoever shall say, Thou fool, shall be in danger of hell fire." (Matt. 5:22). *My children if you are angry* *with any person whoever or are not on good terms with them, get it so you are or you will never see Heaven!!!!*

The Grudge You Should Not Hold Against Any Man

In the Book of Hell it tells the story of a very good catholic man, who's family is around him and praying for him as he is dying. The priest hears his confession gives him last rites, "Extreme Unction" give him the 'HolyVaticum' and 'Apostolic Blessing'. The man dies and all are happy that he has received all the church can give from the hand of a priest. That night the man appears to the priest, and tell him <u>do not pray for me</u>, I'm in Hell. How can this be, you have received all the rites and blessings of the church. I am in Hell because I held a *slight grudge* against a man and never sought to reconcile with him." (Did you hear that my sons?)

Our Lord said, "If thou hatest thy brother, thy neighbor, or mother or father, thou shall not enter Heaven."

<u>Charity</u> towards our neighbor is one of the <u>primary</u> fundamentals of getting to Heaven. (Always humble yourself to the will of others as is stated in the 'Imitation of Christ'.) (And as God has regarded the humility of His hand Maid, Mary.) (True knowledge of God and knowledge of yourself equals Humility.) (Meditate daily on your sins and on the pains of Hell, as the saints have done, or you will never be one.)

Another incident:

There would not be one so crazy as to accept this bargain: During the year, you may yield to all your passions, gratify all your whims, on the condition of spending one day, only one day, or even one hour, in fire. I repeat, not a single person would accept the bargain. Will you have a proof of it? Listen to the history of the three sons of an old usurer: A father of a family who grew rich only by doing wrongs had fallen dangerously ill. He knew that the final stages of death had already set in, and nevertheless he could not decide to make restitution. "If I make restitution," he said, "what will become of my children?" His confessor, a man of sagacity, had recourse to a singular stratagem to save this poor soul. He told him that if he wished to be cured, he was about to give him an extremely simple, but costly remedy. "Should it cost a thousand, two thousand, even ten thousand francs, what odds?" answered the old man briskly. "What is it?" "It consists in pouring the melted fat of a living person on the dying parts. It does not need much. If you find anyone willing, for ten thousand francs, to suffer one hand to be burned for less than a quarter of an hour that will be enough."

"Alas!" said the poor man, sighing, "I am very much afraid I can find no such person." "I will help you," said the priest quietly. "Summon your eldest son; he loves you; he is to be your heir; say to him, 'My dear son, you can save your old father's life if you consent to allow one hand to be burned only for a small quarter of an hour.' If he refuses, make the proposal to the second, pledging yourself to make him your heir at the expense of his elder brother. If he refuses in this turn, the third will no doubt accept."

The proposition was made successively to the three brothers, who, one after the other, rejected it with a shudder. Then the father said to them: "What! To save my life, an instant's pain alarms you? And I, to procure your comfort, would go to Hell - to be burned eternally! Indeed, I should be quite mad." And he hastened to restore all he owed without regard to what should become of his children. He was quite right, and so were his three sons. To suffer a hand to be burned, a short quarter of an hour, even to save a father's life, is a sacrifice above human strength. A true story.

"It is granted too few to recognize the true Church amid the darkness of so many schisms and heresies, and to fewer still so to love the truth which they have seen as to fly to its embrace." **St. Robert Bellarmine Doctor of the Church**

"I had the greatest sorrow for the many souls that condemned themselves to Hell, especially those Lutherans, I saw souls falling into Hell like snowflakes. **St. Teresa of Avila Doctor of the Church's**

"The number of the saved is as few as the number of the grapes left after the vineyard-pickers have passed." **St. John Marie Vianney**

"Notwithstanding assurances that God did not create any man for Hell, and that He wishes all men to be saved, it remains equally true that only few will be saved; that only few will go to Heaven; and that the greater part of mankind will be lost forever." **St. John Neumann**

"So vast a number of miserable souls perish, and so comparatively few are saved!" **St. Philip Neri**

"Get out of the filth of the horrible torrent of this world, the torrent of thorns that is whirling you into the abyss of eternal perdition... This torrent is the world, which resembles an impetuous torrent, full of garbage and evis odours, making a lot of noise but flowing swiftly passed, dragging the majority of men into the pit of perdition." **St. John Eudes**

"Meditate on the horrors of Hell, which will last for eternity because of one easily committed mortal sin. Try hard to be among the few who are chosen. Think of the eternal flames of **Hell**, and how few there are that are saved." **St. Benedict Joseph Labre**

"Live with the few if you want to reign with the few." **St. John Climacus**

"The number of the damned is incalculable." **St. Veronica Giuliani**

"Among adults there are few saved because of sins of the flesh.... With the exception of those who die in childhood most men will be damned." **St. Regimius of Rheims**

"The greater numbers of Christians today are damned. The destiny of those dying on one day is that very few – not as many as ten went straight to Heaven; many remained in Purgatory; and those cast into Hell were as numerous as the snowflakes in mid – winter." **St. Anna Maria Taigi**

Apparitions of the Damned

St. Antoninus (1389--1459), Archbishop of Florence, relates in his writings a terrible fact which about the middle of the 15ᵗʰ century, spread fright over the whole North of Italy. A young man of good stock, who, at the age of 16 or 17, had had the misfortune of concealing a mortal sin in Confession, and, in that state, of receiving Communion, had put off from week to week and month to month, the painful disclosures of his sacrileges. Tortured by remorse, instead of discovering with simplicity his misfortune, he sought to gain quiet by great penances, but to no purpose. Unable to bear the strain any longer, he entered a monastery; there, at least, he said to himself, I will tell all, and expiate my frightful sins. Unhappily, he was welcomed as a holy young man by his superiors, who knew him by reputation, and his shame again got the better of him. Accordingly, he deferred his confession of this sin to a later period; and a year, two years, three years passed in this deplorable state; he never dared to reveal his misfortune. Finally, sickness seemed to him to afford an easy means of doing it. "Now is the time," he said to himself; "I am going to tell all; I will make a general confession before I die." But this time, instead of frankly and fairly declaring his faults, he twisted them so artfully that his confessor was unable to understand him. He hoped to come back again the next day, but an attack of delirium came on, and the unfortunate man died.

The community, who were ignorant of the frightful reality, was full of veneration for the deceased. His body was borne with a certain degree of solemnity into the church of the monastery, and lay exposed in the choir until the next morning when the funeral was to be celebrated.

A few moments before the time fixed for the ceremony, one of the Brothers, sent to toll the bell, saw before him, all of a sudden, the deceased, encompassed by chains that seemed aglow with fire, while something blazing appeared all over his person. Frightened, the poor Brother fell on his knees, with his eyes riveted on the terrifying apparition. Then the damned soul said to him: "Do not pray for me, I am in here for all eternity." And he related the sad story of his false shame and sacrileges. Thereupon, he vanished, leaving in the church a disgusting odor, which spread all over the monastery, as if to prove the truth of all the Brother just saw and heard. Notified at once, the Superiors had the corpse taken away, deeming it unworthy of ecclesiastical burial.

After having cited the preceding example, Monsignor de Segur adds what follows (from Opuscule on Hell): "In our century, three facts of the same kind, more authentic than some others have come to my knowledge.

The first happened almost in my family.

"It was in Russia, at Moscow, a short while before the horrible campaign of 1812. My maternal grandfather, Count Rostopchine, the Military

Governor of Moscow, was very intimate with General Count Orloff, celebrated for his bravery, but as godless as he was brave.

"One day, at the close of a supper, Count Orloff and one of his friends, General V., also a disciple of Voltaire, had set to horribly ridiculing religion, especially Hell. 'Yet,' said Orloff, 'yet if by chance there should be anything the other side of the curtain?' 'Well,' took up General V., 'whichever of us shall depart first will come to inform the other of it. Is it agreed?' 'An excellent idea,' replied Count Orloff, and both interchanged very seriously their word of honor not to miss the engagement.

"A few weeks later, one of those great wars which Napoleon had the gift of creating at that time, burst forth. The Russian army began the campaign, and General V. received orders to start out forthwith to take an important command.

"He had left Moscow about two or three weeks, when one morning, at a very early hour, while my grandfather was dressing, his chamber door was rudely pushed open. It was Count Orloff, in dressing gown and slippers, his hair on end, his eyes wild, and pale like a dead man. 'What? Orloff, you? At this hour? And in such a costume? What ails you? What has happened?' 'My sir,' replied Count Orloff, 'I believe I am beside myself. I have just seen General V.' 'Has General V., then, come back?' 'Well, no,' rejoined Orloff, throwing himself on a sofa, and holding his head between his hands; 'No, he has not come back, and that is what frightens me!'

"My grandfather did not understand him. He tried to soothe him. 'Relate to me,' he said to Orloff, 'what has happened to you, and what all this means.' Then, striving to stifle his emotion, the Count related the following: 'My dear Rostopchine, some time ago, V. and I mutually swore that the first of us who died should come and tell the other if there is anything on the other side of the curtain. Now this morning, scarcely half an hour since, I was calmly lying awake in my bed, not thinking at all of my friend, when all of a sudden, the curtains of my bed were rudely parted, and at two steps from me I saw General V.

Standing up, pale, with his right hand on his breast, and saying to me: "What do we do now? There is a Hell, and I am there! What do we do now?" And he disappeared. I came at once to you. My head's splitting! What a strange thing! I do not know what to think of it.'

"My grandfather calmed him as well as he could. It was no easy matter. He spoke of hallucinations, nightmares; perhaps he was asleep... There are many extraordinary unaccountable things... and other commonplaces, which constitute the comfort of freethinkers. Then he ordered his carriage, and took Count Orloff back to his hotel.

"Now, ten or twelve days after this strange incident, an army messenger brought my grandfather, among other news, that of the death of General V. The very morning of the day Count Orloff had seen and heard him, the same hour he appeared at Moscow, the unfortunate General, reconnoitering the enemy's position, had been shot through the breast by a bullet and had fallen stark dead."

"There is a Hell, and I am there!" These are the words of one who came back.

Mgr. de Segur relates a second fact, which he regards as alike free from doubt. He had learned it in 1859, of a most honorable priest and superior of an important community. This priest had the particulars of it from a near relation of the lady to whom it had happened. At that time, Christmas Day, 1859, this person was still living and little over 40 years.

She chanced to be in London in the winter of 1847-1848. She was a widow, about 29 years old, quite rich and worldly. Among the gallants who frequented her salon, there was noticed a young lord, whose attentions compromised her extremely and whose conduct, besides, was anything but edifying!

One evening, or rather one night, for it was close upon midnight, she was reading in her bed some novel, coaxing sleep. One o'clock struck by the clock; she blew out her taper. She was about to fall asleep when, to her great astonishment, she noticed that a strange, wan glimmer of light, which seemed to come from the door of the drawing-room, spread by degrees into her chamber, and increased momentarily. Stupefied at first and not knowing what this meant, she began to get alarmed, when she saw the drawing-room door slowly open and the young lord, the partner of her disorders, enter the room. Before she had time to say a single word, he seized her by the left wrist, and with a hissing voice, whispered to her in English: "There is a Hell!" The pain she felt in her arm was so great that she lost her senses.

When, half an hour after, she came to again, she rang for her chambermaid. The latter, on entering, noticed a keen smell of burning. Approaching her mistress, who could hardly speak, she noticed on her wrist so deep a burn that the bone was laid bare and the flesh almost consumed; this burn was the size of a man's hand. Moreover, she remarked that, from the door of the salon to the bed, and from the bed to that same door, the carpet bore the imprint of a man's steps, which had burned through the stuff. By the directions of her mistress, she opened the drawing-room door; there, more traces were seen on the carpet outside.

The following day, the unhappy lady learned, with a terror easy to be divined, that on that very night, about one o'clock in the morning, her lord had been found dead-drunk under the table, that his servants had carried him to his room, and that there he had died in their arms.

I do not know, added the Superior, whether that terrible lesson converted the unfortunate lady, but what I do know is that she is still alive and that, to conceal from sight the traces of her ominous burn, she wears on the left wrist, like a bracelet, a wide gold band, which she does not take off day or night. I repeat it, I have all these details from her near relation, a serious Christian, in whose word I repose the fullest belief. They are never spoken of, even in the family; and I only confide them to you, suppressing every proper name.

Notwithstanding the disguise beneath which this apparition has been, and must be enveloped, it seems to me impossible, adds Mgr. de Segur, to call into doubt the dreadful authenticity of the details.

Here is a third fact related by the same writer. "In the year 1873," he writes, "a few days before the Assumption, occurred again one of those apparitions from beyond the grave, which so efficaciously confirms the reality of Hell. It was in Rome. A brothel, opened in that city after the Piedmontese invasion, stood near a police station. One of the bad girls who lived there had been wounded in the hand, and it was found necessary to take her to the hospital of Consolation. Whether her blood, vitiated by bad living had brought on mortification of the wound, or from an unexpected complication, she nonetheless died suddenly during the night. At the same instant, one of her companions, who surely was ignorant of what had happened at the hospital, began to utter shrieks of despair to the point of awaking the inhabitants of the locality, creating a flurry among the wretched creatures of the house, and provoking the intervention of the police. The dead girl of the hospital, surrounded by flames, had appeared to her and said: 'I am damned! And if you do not wish to be like me, leave this place of infamy and return to God.'

"Nothing could quell the despair of this girl, who, at daybreak, departed, leaving the whole house plunged in a stupor, especially as soon as the death of her companion at the hospital was known.

"Just at this period, the mistress of the place, an exalted Garibaldian and known as such by her brethren and friends, fell sick. She soon sent for a priest to receive the Sacraments. The ecclesiastical authority deputed for this task a worthy prelate, Mgr. Sirolli, the pastor of the parish of Saint-Saviour in Laura. He, fortified by special instructions, presented himself and exacted of the sick woman, before all, in presence many witnesses, the full and entire retraction of her blasphemies against the Sovereign Pontiff and the discontinuance of the infamous trade she plied. The unhappy creature did so without hesitation, consented to purge her house, then made her confession and received the Holy Viaticum with great sentiments of repentance and humility. "Feeling that she was dying, she besought the good pastor with tears not to leave her, frightened as she always was by the apparition of that damned girl. Mgr. Sirolli, unable to satisfy her on account of the properties which would not permit him to spend the night in such a place, sent to the police for two men, closed up the house and remained until the dying woman had breathed her last.

"Pretty soon, all Rome became acquainted with the details of these tragic occurrences. As ever, the ungodly and lewd ridiculed them, taking good care not to seek for any information about them; the good profited by them, to become still better and more faithful to their duties."

The Denial of Hell is Foolish Bravado

There are some miserable men, let us rather say, fools, who in the delirium of their iniquity make bold to declare that they laugh at Hell.

They say so, but only with their lips; their consciences protest and give them the lie. Collot de Herbois, famous for his impiety as much as for his sanguinary ferocity, was the chief author of the massacres of Lyons in 1793; he caused the destruction of 1,600 victims. Six years after, in 1799, he was banished to Cayenne, and used to give vent to his infernal rage by blaspheming the holiest things. The least act of religion, the slightest show of Christian piety, became the subject of his jests. Having seen a soldier make the Sign of the Cross, he said to him, "Imbecile! You still believe in superstition! Do you not know those gods, the Holy Virgin, Paradise, Hell, are the inventions of the accursed tribe of priests?" Shortly after, he fell sick and was seized by violent pains. In an excess of fever he swallowed, at a single draught, a bottle of liquor. His disease increased; he felt as if burned by a fire that was devouring his bowels. He uttered frightful shrieks, called upon God, the Holy Virgin, a priest, to come to the relief. "Well, indeed," said the soldier to him, "you ask for a priest? You fear Hell, then? You used to curse the priests, make fun of Hell!" "Alas!" he then answered, "my tongue was lying to my heart." Pretty soon, he expired, vomiting blood and foam.

The following incident happened in 1837. A young second lieutenant, being in Paris, entered the Church of the Assumption near the Tuileries and saw a priest kneeling near a confessional. As he made religion the habitual subject of his jokes, he wished to go to Confession to while away the time and went into the confessional. "Monsieur l'Abbe," he said, "would you be good enough to hear my confession?"

"Willingly, my son; confess unrestrained." "But I must first say that I am a rather unique kind of sinner." "No matter, the Sacrament of Penance has been instituted for all sinners." "But I am not very much of a believer in religious matters." "You believe more than you think." "Believe? Me? I am a regular scoffer." The confessor saw with whom he had to deal and that there was some mystification. He replied, smiling: "You are a regular scoffer? Are you, then, making fun of me too?"

The pretended penitent smiled in like manner. "Listen," the priest went on, "what you have just done here is not serious. Let us leave confession aside; and, if you please, have a little chat. I like military people very much, and then you have the appearance of a good, amiable youth. Tell me, what is your rank?" "Second lieutenant." "Will you remain a second lieutenant long?" "Two, three, perhaps four years." "And after?" "I shall become a first lieutenant." "And after?" "I hope to become a captain." "And after?" "Lieutenant colonel." "How old will you be then?" "Forty to forty-five years." "And after that?" "If I rise higher, I shall be general of a division." "And after?" "After! There is nothing more except the Marshal's baton, but my pretensions do not reach so high." "Well and good. But do you not intend to get married?" "Yes, when I shall be a superior officer." "Well! There you are married; a superior officer, a general, perhaps even a French marshal, who knows? And after?" "After? Upon my word, I do not know what will be after."

"See, how strange it is!" said the abbe. Then, in a tone of voice that grew more sober: "You know all that shall happen up to that point, and you do not know what will be after. Well, I know, and I am going to tell you. After, you shall die, be judged, and, if you continue to live as you do, you shall be damned, you shall go and burn in Hell; that is what will be after."

As the second lieutenant, dispirited at this conclusion, seemed anxious to steal away, the abbe said,

"One moment, sir. You are a man of honor. So am I. Agree that you have offended me and owe me an apology. It will be simple. For eight days, before retiring to rest, you will say: 'One day I shall die, but I laugh at the idea. After my death I shall be judged, but I laugh at the idea. After my judgment, I shall be damned, but I laugh at the idea. I shall burn forever in Hell, but I laugh at the idea!' That is all. But you are going to give your word of honor not to neglect it, eh?"

More and more wearied, and wishing at any price to extricate himself from this blunder, the second lieutenant made the promise. In the evening, his word being given, he began to carry out his promise. "I shall die," he said. "I shall be judged." He had not the courage to add, "I laugh at the idea." The week had not passed before he returned to the Church of the Assumption, made his confession seriously and came out of the confessional, his face bathed with tears and with joy in his heart. END

A young person who had become an unbeliever in consequence of her dissipation kept incessantly shooting sarcasm at religion and making jests of its most awful truths. "**Juliette**," someone said to her one day, "this will end badly. God will be tired of your blasphemies, and you shall be punished." "Bah," she answered insolently, "it gives me very little trouble.

Who has returned from the other world to relate what passes there?" Less than eight days after, she was found in her room, giving no sign of life, and already cold. As there was no doubt that she was dead, she was put in a coffin and buried.

The following day, the gravedigger, digging a new grave beside that of the unhappy Juliette, heard some noise; it seemed to him that there was a knocking in the adjoining coffin. At once, he put his ear to the ground and in fact heard a smothered voice, crying out: "Help! help!" The authorities were summoned; by their orders, the grave was opened, the coffin taken up and unnailed. The shroud was removed; there was no further doubt, Juliette had been buried alive. Her hair, her shroud was in disorder, and her face was streaming with blood.

While they were releasing her and feeling her heart to be assured that it was still beating, she heaved a sigh, like a person for a long time deprived of air; then she opened her eyes, made an effort to lift herself up, and said: "My God, I thank Thee." Afterward, when she had got her senses well back and, by the aid of some food, recovered her strength, she added: "When I regained consciousness in the grave and recognized the frightful reality of my burial, when after having uttered shrieks, I endeavored to break my coffin, and struck my forehead against the boards, I saw that all was useless; death appeared to me with all its horrors; it was less the bodily than the eternal death that frightened me. I saw I was going to be damned. My God, I had but too well deserved it! Then I prayed, I shouted for help, I lost consciousness again, until I awoke above ground. Oh, the goodness of my God!" she said, again shedding tears. "I despised the truths of Faith; Thou hast punished me, but in Thy mercy, I am converted and repentant."

They who deny Hell will be forced to admit it soon; but alas! It will be too late. Father Nierenberg, in his work The Difference between Time and Eternity, speaks of an unfortunate sinner, who, as the result of his evil ways, had lost the Faith. His virtuous wife exhorted him to return to God and reminded him of Hell, but he would answer obstinately: "There is no Hell." One day his wife found him dead, and strange circumstance, he held in his hand a mysterious paper on which in large characters was traced this terrifying avowal: "I now know that there is a Hell!"

Unhappy sinners who are lulled to rest by the illusions of the world and who live as if there were no Hell will be suddenly stripped of their illusions by the most frightful of catastrophes. From the midst of their pleasures they shall fall into the Pit of Torments.

The disaster of the Café Kivoto supplies an image of the catastrophe still more terrible which awaits them sooner or later.

The Kivoto was a theatrical café at Smyrna, built upon piles in the sea. The extremely stout stakes that kept the house above the waves--water and time-eaten--had lost their solid contents. It was on February 11, 1873, at 10 p.m. Two hundred persons had assembled to witness a comic spectacle. They were amusing themselves, when all at once a frightful crash was heard. At the same moment everything gave way and was turned topsy-turvy; the house, with the theater and spectators, was pitched forward and swallowed up in the sea. What an awful surprise for those amusement amateurs! But a more tragic surprise awaits the worldling! A day will come when, from the center of his pleasures, he shall all of a sudden behold himself cast headlong into a sea of sulphur and fire.

On the night of March 31-April 1, 1873, a stately and magnificent steamship, the Atlantic, foundered on the Canadian banks near Halifax. The number on board, passengers and crew, reached 950, of whom 700 were lost in the shipwreck. Most of them were wrapped in sleep when the vessel, striking some rocks, sank almost instantaneously. Swallowed up by the sea in the middle of their repose, they awoke in the waters and were suffocated before being able to account for the terrible accident which had just happened. Frightful awaking! But more frightful by far will be the awaking of the atheist when he shall see himself suddenly engulfed in Hell.

On December 28, 1879, there occurred the Tay Bridge accident. The train from London to Edinburgh crosses the Tay, near Dundee, over an iron bridge half a league long. A dreadful storm, which had swelled the waves and broken the bridge during the day, ended by sweeping away several arches, despite the iron cross- bars and piers. These arches, when falling, left an empty space, which was not perceived in the darkness. At 7:30 p.m., the express train out from Edinburgh thundered along, carrying a hundred travelers; it mounted the fatal bridge, and soon coming on the empty space, was hurled into the waves. Not a cry was heard; in the twinkling of an eye, the victims were in the depths below. What a surprise! What a sudden change! But what will it be, when the sinner shall see himself, in the twinkling of an eye, in the pit of Hell?

The Truth of Hell

This is how the Son of God speaks to us of Hell:

"Woe to the world because of scandals. For it must needs be that scandals come: but nevertheless woe to that man by whom scandal cometh." "And if thy hand or thy foot scandalizes thee, cut it off and cast it from thee. It is better for thee to go into life maimed or lame, than having two hands or two feet to be cast into everlasting fire."

"And if thy eye scandalizes thee, pluck it out, and cast it from thee. It is better for thee, having one eye to enter into life, than having two eyes to be cast into hell fire." (Matt. 18: 7-9; compare 5:29-30).

"And fear ye not them that kill the body, and are not able to kill the soul: but rather fear him that can destroy both soul and body in hell." (Matt. 10:28).

"The rich man also died: and he was buried in hell."

"And lifting up his eyes when he was in torments, he saw Abraham afar off and Lazarus in his bosom."

"And he cried, and said, Father Abraham, have mercy on me, and send Lazarus, that he may dip the tip of his finger in water to cool my tongue: for I am tormented in this flame." (Luke 16:22-24).

"Then he shall say to them also that shall be on his left hand: Depart from me, you cursed, into everlasting fire which was prepared for the devil and his angels." (Matt. 25:41).

"And I say to you that many shall come from the east and the west, and shall sit down with Abraham, and Isaac, and Jacob in the Kingdom of heaven."

"But the children of the kingdom shall be cast out into the exterior darkness: there shall be weeping and gnashing of teeth." (Matt. 8:11-12).

"The King went in to see the guests: and he saw there a man who had not on a wedding garment.

"And he saith to him: Friend, how camest thou in hither not having on a wedding garment? But he was silent. "Then the King said to the waiters: Bind his hands and feet, and cast him into the exterior darkness: there shall be weeping and gnashing of teeth." (Matt. 22:11-13).

"The unprofitable servant cast ye out into the exterior darkness. There shall be weeping and gnashing of teeth."

(Matt. 25:30).

"But I say to you, that whosoever is angry with his brother, shall be in danger of the judgment. And whosoever shall say to his brother, Raca, shall be in danger of the council. And whosoever shall say, Thou fool, shall be in danger of hell fire." (Matt. 5:22).

"The Son of man shall send his angels, and they shall gather out of his kingdom all scandals, and them that work iniquity:

"And shall cast them into the furnace of fire. There shall be weeping and gnashing of teeth." (Matt. 13:41-42).

"And if thy hand scandalizes thee, cut it off: it is better for thee to enter into life, maimed, than having two hands to go into hell, into unquenchable fire.

"Where their worm dieth not, and the fire is not extinguished.

"And if thy foot scandalizes thee, cut it off. It is better for thee to enter lame into life everlasting than having two feet, to be cast into the hell of unquenchable fire. "Where their worm dieth not, and the fire is not extinguished.

"And if thy eye scandalizes thee, pluck it out. It is better for thee with one eye to enter into the kingdom of God, than, having two eyes to be cast into the hell of fire.

"Where their worm dieth not, and the fire is not extinguished." (Mark 9:42-47).

"Every tree that bringeth not forth good fruit, shall be cut down, and shall be cast into the fire." (Matt. 7:19).

"I am the vine; you the branches; he that abideth in me, and I in him, the same beareth much fruit: for without me you can do nothing.

"If any one abides not in me, he shall be cast forth as a branch, and shall wither, and they shall gather him up, and cast him into the fire, and he burneth." (John 15:5, 6).

"But Jesus turning to them, said: Daughters of Jerusalem, weep not over me; but weep for yourselves, and for your children.

"For behold, the days shall come, wherein they will say: Blessed are the barren, and the wombs that have not borne, and the paps that have not given suck.

"Then shall they begin to say to the mountains: Fall upon us; and to the hills: Cover us.

"For if in the green wood they do these things, what shall be done in the dry?" (Luke 23:28, 30-31). That is to say, what will sinners be, destined, like the dry wood, to be burned.

"For now the axe is laid to the root of the trees. Every tree therefore that doth not yield good fruit, shall be cut down and cast into the fire.

"I indeed baptize you in water unto penance, but he that shall come after me, is mightier than I, whose shoes I am not worthy to bear, he shall baptize you in the Holy Ghost and fire.

"Whose fan is in his hand, and he will thoroughly cleanse his floor and gather his wheat into the barn; but the chaff he will burn with unquenchable fire." (Matt. 3:10-12). Words of St. John the Baptist.

"And the beast was taken, and with him the false prophet, who wrought signs before him, wherewith he seduced them who received the character of the beast, and who adored his image. These two were cast alive into the pool of fire, burning with brimstone." (Apoc. 19:20).

Where they were tormented day and night, for ever and ever.

"And whosoever was not found written in the book of life, was cast into the pool of fire." (Apoc. 20:15).

To doubt about Hell is to doubt the infallible word of God; it is to give ear to the speech of libertines rather than to the infallible teachings of the Church. The Church teaches that there is a Hell; a libertine tells you that there is not; and should you prefer to believe a libertine? An honorable Roman, Emilius Scaurus, was accused by a certain Varus, a man without word or honor. Being obliged to prove his innocence, Scaurus addressed the people in this short speech: "Romans, you know Varus, and you know me; now, Varus says I am guilty of the crime charged against me, and I protest that I am not guilty. Varus says yes, I say no; whom will you believe?" The people applauded, and the accuser was confounded.

Natural reason confirms the dogma of hell. An atheist was boasting that he did not believe in Hell. Among his hearers, there was a sensible young man, modest, but who thought that he ought to shut the silly speaker's mouth. He put him a single question: "Sir," he said, "the kings of the earth have prisons to punish their refractory subjects; how can God, the King of the Universe, be without a prison for those who outrage His majesty?" The sinner had not a word to answer. The appeal was presented to the light of his own reason, which proclaims that, if kings have prisons, God must have a Hell.

The atheist who denies Hell is like the thief who should deny the prison. A thief was threatened without sentenced to prison. The foolish fellow replied: "There is no court, there is no prison." He was speaking thus when an officer of justice put his hand on his shoulder and dragged him before the judge. This is an image of the atheist who is foolish enough to deny Hell. A day will come when, taken unawares by divine justice, he shall see himself dashed headlong into the Pit which he stubbornly denied, and he shall be forced to acknowledge the terrible reality of hell.

The truth of Hell is so clearly revealed that heresy has never denied it. Protestants, who have demolished almost all dogmas, have not dared to touch this dogma. This fact suggested to a Catholic lady this witty answer. Anxiously importuned by two Protestant ministers to pass over into the camp of the Reformation, she replied, "Gentlemen, you have indeed achieved a fine reformation. You have suppressed fasting, confession, Purgatory. Unfortunately, you have kept Hell; put Hell away, and I shall be one of you."

Yes, Messrs. Freethinkers, remove Hell, and then ask us to be yours. But know that an "I do not believe in it" is not sufficient to do away with it.

Is it not the most inconceivable folly to rely on a "perhaps" at the risk of falling into Hell? Two atheists went one day into an anchorite's (hermit's) cell. At the sight of his instruments of penance, they asked him why he was leading so mortified a life. "To deserve paradise," he replied. "Good Father," they said, smiling, "you would be nicely caught if there is nothing after death!" "Gentlemen," rejoined the holy man, as he looked at them with compassion, "you will be quite otherwise if there is!"

A young man belonging to a Catholic family in Holland, as a consequence of imprudent reading, had the misfortune to lose the treasure of faith and to fall into a state of complete indifference. It was a subject of the bitterest grief for his parents, especially his pious mother. In vain did this "other Monica" give him the most solid lectures; in vain did she admonish him with tears to come back to God; her unhappy son was deaf and insensible. Yet at last, to satisfy his mother, he was pleased to consent to spend a few days in a religious house, there to follow the exercises of a retreat, or rather, as he put it, to rest a few days and smoke tobacco, an enjoyment he loved. So he listened with a distracted mind to the instructions given to those making the retreat and speedily after began again to smoke without thinking further of what he had heard. The instruction on Hell, to which he seemed to listen to like the rest, came on, but being back again in his little cell, while he was taking his smoke as usual, a reflection arose in his mind in spite of himself: "If, however, it should be true," he said to himself, "that there is a Hell! If there be one, clearly it shall be for me! And in reality, do I know myself that there is not a Hell? I am obliged to acknowledge that I have no certainty in this behalf; the whole basis of my thinking is only a perhaps. Now, to run the risks of burning for eternity on a perhaps, frankly speaking, as a matter of extravagance, would be to go beyond bounds. If there are some who have such courage, I have not sufficiently lost my senses to imitate them." Thereupon, he began to pray; grace penetrated his soul; his doubts vanished; and he rose up, converted.

A pious author relates the history of the tragic punishment that befell an ungodly scoffer of hell. This was a man of quality whom the author through respect for his family, does not name; he designates him by the fictitious name of Leontius. This unfortunate man made it a boast to brave Heaven and Hell, which he treated as chimerical superstitions. One day, when a feast was about to be celebrated at his castle, he took a walk, accompanied by a friend, and wished to go through the cemetery. Chancing to stumble against a skull lying on the ground, he kicked it aside with profane, blasphemous words: "Out of my way," he said, "rotten bones, worthless remains of what is no more." His companion, who did not share in his sentiments, ventured to say to him that he did "wrong to use this language. The remains of the dead," they added, "must be respected on account of their souls, which are always alive, and which will assume their bodies again on the day of the Resurrection."

Leontius answered by this challenge, spoken to the skull: "If the spirit that animated thee still exists, let it come and tell me some news about the other world. I invite it for this very evening to my banquet." Evening came; he was at table with numerous friends and telling his adventure of the cemetery, while repeating his profanations, when all at once, a great noise was made, and almost at the same time a horrible ghost appeared in the dining room, and spread fright among the guests. Leontius, especially, losing all his audacity, was pale, trembling, out of his wits. He wanted to flee; the spectre did not give him time, but sprang upon him with the swiftness of lightning, and smashed his head to pieces against the wainscot (wall). A day will come when the pride of the ungodly shall be dashed down, and their heads broken by the judge of the living and the dead:

"The Lord shall judge among nations, he shall fill ruins; he shall crush the heads in the land of many." (Psalm 109: 6).

Here is a another fact almost contemporaneous and related by a trustworthy author: Two young men, whose names, through respect for their families, must remain secret, but whom I shall call Eugene and Alexander, old schoolmates and college friends, met again later in life after a long separation. Eugene, having stayed at home, used to occupy himself with works of charity, according to the spirit of the Society of St. Vincent de Paul, of which he was a member. Alexander had entered the army and obtained the rank of colonel, but unhappily, there lost every spark of religion.

Having procured a leave of absence of a few days, he had returned to his family and wished to see Eugene. The interview happened on a Sunday. After they had chatted together for a time, Eugene said, "Alexander, it is time to leave you." "Where do you wish to go? It cannot be there is anything pressing?" "I am going first after the business of salvation; then I must attend a benevolent reunion." "Poor Eugene; I see it; you still believe in Paradise and Hell. It is all a chimera, superstition, fanaticism." "Dear Alexander, do not speak so; you, like me, learned that the dogmas of faith rest on unexceptionable facts." "Chimeras, I tell you, which I believe no longer. If there be a Hell, I am willing to go there today. Come with me to the theater." "Dear friend, use your liberty, but do not brave God's justice."

Eugene spoke to a deaf man, who was unwilling to heed salutary advice. He left him with a sore heart. That very day, in the evening, Eugene was already in bed, when he was awakened. "Quick," they said to him, "rise, go to Alexander's; he has just been brought back from the theater, seized by a frightful pain." Eugene ran there, and found him tossed by violent convulsions, with foam in his mouth and rolling his wild eyes. As soon as he saw Eugene, he shouted, "You say there is a Hell; you say truly there is a Hell, and I am going there; I am there already; I feel its tortures and fury."

In vain did Eugene try to calm him; the unhappy man answered only by yells and blasphemies. In the transports of his rage, he tore with his teeth the flesh off his arms and cast the bleeding fragments at Eugene, his mother, and sisters. It was in this paroxysm of agony that he expired. His mother died of grief, his two sisters entered religion, and Eugene also quitted the world; owner of a brilliant fortune, he forsook all to consecrate himself to God and avoid Hell.

Pains of Hell

What predominates in the words of Scripture when it exhibits to us the pains of Hell is the terrible torture of the fire. The Scriptures call Hell a "pool of sulfur and fire," the gehenna of fire," the eternal fire," a "fiery furnace where the fire shall never be extinguished." But this fire, kindled by divine justice, will possess an activity incomparably superior to that of all the furnaces, all the fires, of this world. Alas! Do we understand how it shall be possible to bear it? How it will be necessary to dwell in it as in an everlasting habitation? "Which of you," demands the Prophet, "can dwell with devouring fire? Which of you shall bear everlasting burnings?" (Isaiah 33:14).

In 1604, in the city of Brussels, there occurred the celebrated apparition of a damned soul, attested by Blessed Richard of St. Ann, of the Order of St. Francis, who suffered martyrdom at Nagasaki, in Japan, on September 10, 1622. Blessed Richard related the fact to a theologian of the Spanish Inquisition, Father Alphonsus of Andrada, of the Company of Jesus; he, in turn, communicated it to Adrian Lyroeus, who has inserted it in his Trisagium Marianum, Book III. Saint Alphonsus Liguori, who cites the same fact in his Glories of Mary, has made Blessed Richard one of the two actors in this frightful drama; he (Bl. Richard) was only a witness, like many others who were living at Brussels, but the impression he experienced was so lively that it became the determining cause of his entrance into the Seraphic order.

This is how the occurrence is related, after authentic documents in the Annals of Franciscan Missions, for the years 1866-67.

It was not without a terrible, though merciful interposition of God's justice, that Blessed Richard was brought to demand the habit of St. Francis. It was in 1604. There were at Brussels, where Richard was at that time, two young students who, instead of applying themselves to study, thought only of how to live in pleasure and dissipation. One night, among others, when they had gone to indulge in sin in a house of ill-fame, one of the two left the place after some time, leaving his miserable companion behind him.

Having reached home, he was about to lie down in bed, when he remembered that he had not recited that day the few Hail Marys which he had the habit of saying every day in honor of the Holy Virgin. As he was overpowered by sleep, it was troublesome for him; however, he made an effort and said them, although without devotion; then he went to bed. In his first sleep he heard all of a sudden, a rude knocking at the door; and immediately afterward he saw before him his companion, disfigured and hideous.

"Who are you?" he said to him. "What? Don't you know me?" replied the unhappy youth. "But how are you so changed? You look like a devil?" "Ah, pity me; I am damned!" "How is that?" "Well, know that upon leaving that accursed house a devil sprang upon me and strangled me. My body has remained in the middle of the street, and my soul is in Hell. Know, moreover, that the same chastisement awaited you, but the Virgin preserved you from it, thanks to your practice of reciting every day a few Hail Marys in her honor. Happy are you if you know how to profit by this information, which the Mother of God gives you through me."

While finishing these words, the damned soul partly opened his garment, allowed the flames and serpents that were tormenting him to be seen, and vanished. Then the young man, melting into tears, threw himself on his face on the floor to thank the Holy Virgin Mary, his deliverer. Now, while he was praying in this manner and reflecting upon what he ought to do to change his life, he heard the Matins bell ring at the Franciscan Monastery.

That very moment he cried out, "There it is that God calls me to do penance." The next day indeed, at a very early hour, he went to the monastery and begged the Father Guardian to receive him. The Father, who was aware of his bad life, having presented difficulties at first, the young student, shedding a torrent of tears, related to him all that had taken place. And really, two religious, having repaired to the street indicated, found the corpse of the wretched youth, black as a coal. Then the postulant was admitted among the Brothers, whom he edified by a life altogether devoted to penance.

Such is the terrible fact which struck dismay and fright into many souls and which induced Blessed Richard also to consecrate himself entirely to God in the same Order into which the young student, so wonderfully protected by Mary, had just been received.

The following fact is related by Father Martin del Rio, from the Annals of the Company of Jesus. It is an apparition that occurred in 1590 and was vouched for by trustworthy witnesses: Not far from Lima, dwelt a Christian lady who had three maid-servants, one of whom, called Martha, was a young Indian of about sixteen years. Martha was a Christian, but little by little she grew cool in the devotion she had at first displayed, became negligent in her prayers, and light, coquettish, and wanton in her conversations.

Having fallen dangerously ill, she received the Last Sacraments. After this serious ceremony, during which she had evinced very little piety, she said, smiling to her two fellow servants, that in the confession she had just made she had taken good care not to tell all her sins to the priest. Frightened by this language, the girls reported it to their mistress, who by dint of exhortations and threats, obtained from the sick girl a sign of repentance and the promise to make a sincere and Christian confession. Martha confessed then, over again, and died shortly afterward.

Scarcely had she breathed her last, when her corpse emitted an extraordinary and intolerable stench. They were obliged to remove it from the house to a shed. The dog in the courtyard, usually a quiet animal, howled piteously, as if he were undergoing torture. After the interment, the lady, according to custom, was dining in the garden in the open air, when a heavy stone fell suddenly onto the center of the table with a horrible crash and caused all the table settings to bounce, but without breaking any article. One of the servants, having occupied the room in which Martha had died, was awakened by frightful noises; all the furniture seemed to be moved by an invisible force and thrown to the floor.

We understand how the servant did not continue to occupy that room; her companion ventured to take her place, but the same scenes were renewed. Then they agreed to spend the night together there. This time they distinctly heard Martha's voice, and soon that wretched girl appeared before them in the most horrible state, and all on fire. She said that by God's command she had come to reveal her condition to them, that she was damned for her sins of impurity and for the sacrilegious confessions she had continued to make until death. She added, "Tell what I have just revealed to you, that others may profit by my misfortune." At these words she uttered a despairing cry and disappeared.

The fire of Hell is a real fire, a fire that burns like this world's fire, although it is infinitely more active. Must not there be a real fire in Hell, seeing that there is a real fire in Purgatory? "It is the same fire," says St. Augustine, "that tortures the damned and purifies the elect." A number of indisputable facts demonstrate the reality of the fire in the place of expiation. This is what Mgr. de Segur relates:

"In the year 1870, in the month of April," he writes, "I saw, or at least, touched at Foligno, near Assisi, in Italy, one of those frightful imprints of fire, caused sometimes by souls that appear and prove that the fire of the other life is a real fire. On November 4, 1859, there died of a stroke of apoplexy, at the Convent of the Tertiary Franciscans of Foligno, a good Sister named Theresa Gesta, who had been many years mistress of novices and at the same time in charge of the poor little clothes room of the convent. She was born at Corsa in Bastia in 1797, and she entered the convent in February, 1826. It need not be said that she was well prepared for death.

"Twelve days afterward on the 6th of November, a sister named Anna Felicia, who replaced her in her office, went up to the wardrobe and was about to enter, when she heard moans which seemed to come from the interior of this room. Somewhat alarmed, she hastened to open the door; no one was there. But new moans resounded, so clearly articulated that, despite her usual courage, she felt seized by fear. 'Jesus, Mary!' she exclaimed, 'what is this?' She had not finished when she heard a plaintive voice accompanied by this mournful sigh: 'Oh, my God, how I suffer!' ('Oh! Dio che peno tanto.')

The shocked sister recognized at once the voice of poor Sister Theresa. Then the whole hall was filled with a dense smoke, and the ghost of Sister Theresa appeared, moving toward the door, while gliding along by the wall. Having almost reached the door, she exclaimed forcibly: 'This is a sign of the mercy of God.' And saying that, she struck the highest panel of the door, leaving hollowed in the charred wood a most perfect stamp of her right hand; then she disappeared.

"Sister Anna Felicia had remained half dead with fear. All confused, she began to cry out and call for help. One of her companions hastened to her, then another, then the whole community; they pressed eagerly around her, and they were all astonished at finding a smell of burnt wood. Sister Anna Felicia told them what had just taken place, and showed them the terrible stamp on the door. They immediately recognized the shape of Sister Theresa's hand, which was remarkably small. Alarmed, they took flight, ran to the choir, began to pray, spent the night praying and doing penances for the deceased, and the next day all received Communion for her.

"The news spread abroad, and the different communities of the city joined their prayers to those of the Franciscans. The next day following, November 18, Sister Anna Felicia, having retired to her cell to go to bed, heard herself called by her name and recognized perfectly the voice of Sister Theresa. At the same instant an all-resplendent sphere of light appeared before her, lighting up the cell as if at noonday, and she heard Sister Theresa, who, with a joyous, triumphant voice, uttered these words: 'I died on Friday, the day of the Passion, and behold, on a Friday I depart for glory! Be brave in carrying the Cross; be courageous in suffering; love poverty.' Then, adding affectionately, 'Adieu, Adieu, Adieu!' she became transfigured into a thin, white, dazzling cloud; she flew away to Heaven and vanished.

"A canonical inquest was immediately held by the Bishop of Foligno and the magistrates of the city. On November 23, in the presence of a great number of witnesses, the grave of Sister Theresa was opened, and the stamp burned into the door was found exactly to correspond with the hand of the deceased. The result was an official judgment that established the perfect certainty and authenticity of what we have just narrated. The door with the burned mark is preserved with veneration in the Convent. The Mother Abbess, a witness of this fact, deigned to show it to me herself."

St. Peter Damian speaks of a worldling who lived only for amusement and pleasure. To no purpose was he advised to think of his soul; to no purpose was he warned that, by following the life of the wicked rich man, he should reach the same end; he continued his guilty life unto death. He had scarcely ceased to live when an anchorite (hermit) knew of his damnation. He saw him in the midst of a fiery pool; it was an immense pool like a sea, in which a great number of people, howling with despair, were plunged. They were striving to gain the shore, but it was guarded by pitiless dragons and demons, which prevented them from coming near it, and hurled them far back into that ocean of flames.

Nicholas of Nice, speaking of the fire of Hell, says that nothing on earth could give an idea of it. If, he adds, all the trees of the forests were cut down, piled up into a vast heap and set to fire, this terrible pile would not be a spark of Hell.

Vincent of Beauvais, in the 25th book of his history, narrates the following fact, which he says happened in the year 1090: Two young libertines, whether seriously or through mockery, had made a mutual promise: whichever of the two died first would come and tell the other in what state he was. So one died, and God permitted him to appear to his companion. He was in a horrible state, and seemed to be the prey of cruel sufferings, which consumed him like a burning fever and covered him with sweat. He wiped his forehead with his hand and let a drop of his sweat fall onto his friend's arm, while saying to him: "That is the sweat of Hell; you shall carry the mark of it till death." That infernal sweat burned the arm of the living man, and penetrated his flesh with unheard-of pains. He profited by this awful information and retired to a monastery.

Peter, the venerable Abbot of Cluny, tells an incident of the same kind. A dying man persisted in sin and was about to die impenitent. Burned by fever and tortured by thirst, he asked for some cold water to cool himself. God permitted, thanks to prayers offered for this wretched man, two infernal spirits to appear to him under a visible form. They bore a goblet containing a liquid, a drop of which they threw on the sick man's hand, saying: "This is the cold water used for cooling Hell!" The infernal liquid went through and through the hand, burning the flesh and bones. The attendants saw with astonishment this terrible phenomenon, as well as the convulsions of the sinner, who twisted and turned in his unspeakable sufferings. If the cold water of Hell burns like that, what will the boiling water and blazing sulfur do?

In 1870, the city of New York witnessed a conflagration, the circumstances of which offered an image of Hell. The Barnum menagerie became the prey of flames. It was stocked with tigers, lions and other wild beasts. All these animals were burned alive in their iron cages, the bars of which grew to a white heat. As the fire and the heat became more intense, the beasts became more enraged. With extreme violence they sprang at the bars of their prisons, and fell back like inert heaps, only to leap again at the insuperable obstacle which held them captive. The awful roars of the lions, the screams of the tigers, the howls of all the animals, which betrayed supreme despair, were blended together and formed a frightful chorus, bringing to mind what the damned must hear resounding in Hell. But the sounds of their terrible concert grew weaker and weaker, until the lion having uttered his last roar, the silence of death succeeded the most doleful din.

Fancy in these shining iron cages, not animals, but men, and men who, instead of dying in the fire, continue to live in it, as if their bodies were harder than iron; this would be an image of Hell, but an imperfect one, for all of that.

On Friday, February 18, 1881, there was a carnival ball given at Munich by the young artist-painters.

They were numerous and masked, some as monks, priests, comical pilgrims, carrying grotesque-looking beads, and making a parody of religious usages; others like Esquimaux, covered with tow, pitch and hemp. A cigar, imprudently lighted, set fire to one of these inflammable costumes. The unfortunate person, seeing himself in flames, rushed headlong among his companions; in a minute all these tow and pitch garments were on fire. Twelve of the dancers, like living torches, ran about crazy, unable to receive help.

They flung themselves onto one another, roamed around uttering mournful wails, rushed blazing into all the corners of the hall, spreading around a disgusting odor. Soon three of them were only charred corpses. Nine others died shortly after; thirteen were transported to the hospital. Among these last was Joseph Schonertzer; he expired when skillful hands were proceeding with the first bandaging. The skin peeled off his chest and arms; it came off partly in rolls, leaving the living flesh bare, scorched also by the fire. This dreadful death was regarded, not without reason, as a chastisement of the Divine Justice, which these unhappy young people had provoked by their excesses of impiety and dissipation. It presents at the same time an image of Hell, but with two great differences; it is far less cruel, and it lasts only a short time.

On March 24, 1881, a catastrophe threw the city of Nice into a state of fright and dismay; the municipal theater became a prey to flames. This theater had doors exceedingly narrow and absolutely insufficient for passage in case of a great rush. On March 24, a brilliant presentation, which had drawn numerous spectators, was given.

The curtain had just risen for the first act when, at the expiration of a few minutes, there was an explosion among the footlights; all at once the flames were seen to issue from the frail boards and gain the stage. The shouts, "Fire! Fire!" came from all parts of the theater, and the panic became general, especially when new explosions were heard.

The orchestra and the stage were in complete darkness. Only the glimmer of the great fire, which was rapidly spreading, revealed to the gave a few unfortunate actresses crossing the stage, crazy, wild with terror, and seeking an outlet, which the flames barred against them. The audience in the galleries, with a frenzied violence, rushed headlong down the winding starts to the corridors.

The women, the children, were trampled underfoot. Only shouts of terror and despair were heard, the shouts of all those human beings, who were struggling to save their lives and who felt themselves dying, suffocated by the smoke, or ground beneath the feet of their neighbors.

When the firemen, soldiers and marines could penetrate the interior, the spectacle was horrible. There was a pile of corpses, black, hideous, some almost entirely reduced to cinders. These were the bodies of the unfortunate spectators, who rushed down, all at once, by the narrow stairways. Men, women and children, hanging on to one another, had rolled into this place. What poignant, frightful dramas must have been enacted during these few supreme minutes, when safety was possible no more.

At three in the morning, 63 corpses were borne to the Church of St. Francis of Paola. They were half burned. The anguish of the most harrowing agonies might be detected in their faces and postures.

What will it be in Hell? There also, all outlet is closed in the midst of the great fire; there too, is the anguish of direct agony; but there death does not come to end it. Were these unhappy people ready to die? Alas! It is not to the theater that we go to prepare for death! Is it not to be feared that this place may have literally been the gate of Hell for them?

On the occasion of the dreadful catastrophe of the Ring Theater, which happened in Vienna in 1881, an estimate of the theaters burned during the previous century was made; the figure rose to several hundred. Is there not a lesson of Providence here, upholding the warning which the Church does not cease to give the faithful? Since the contemporary theater is generally a school of irreligion and immorality, a hotbed of corruption for nations, do not the continual great fires point out sufficiently that these edifices, given up to fire, are for souls the gates of Hell?

The sight of a soul that falls into Hell is of itself alone an incomparable pain. St. Margaret Mary, as her history relates, beheld the apparition of one of her sisters in religion, recently deceased. That sister implored her prayers and suffrages; she was suffering cruelly in Purgatory. "See," she said to St. Margaret, "the bed I lie on, where I am enduring intolerable pains." I saw that bed, writes the saint, and it still makes me shudder; it was bristling with sharp and fiery spikes which entered the flesh. The deceased added that she was suffering this torture for her sloth and negligence in observing the rule. "This is not all," she said again; "My heart is torn in my bosom to punish my murmurs against my superiors; my tongue is eaten by worms for my words contrary to charity and my breaches of silence. But all this is a small matter in comparison with another pain which God made me experience; although it did not last long, it was more painful to me than all my sufferings." The saint, having desired to know what this dire pain was, she replied, "God showed me one of my near female relatives who had died in a state of mortal sin sentenced by the Supreme Judge and dashed into Hell. That sight caused me a fright, horror, pain that no tongue could communicate."

Surius, in the Life of St. Lydwina, relates that, in an ecstasy, this servant of God saw an abyss, the wide opening of which was bordered with flowers, and the great depth of which, when the eye pierced it, chilled with terror. There issued from it an indescribable noise, a frightful mixture of yells, blasphemies, tumult, ringing blows. Her Angel Guardian told her that it was the abode of the damned, and he wanted to show her the torment they suffer. "Alas!" she replied, "I could not bear the sight of them. How could I, as the mere noise of these despairing yells caused me an unbearable horror?"

If the damned suffered no other pain in Hell than to remain there always, without motion, without changing place or position, that alone would be an insupportable torment. A wealthy voluptuary, loaded down with crimes and dreading Hell, did not have the courage either to break off with his evil habits or to expiate his sins by penance. He had recourse to St. Lydwina, who at that time was edifying the world by her patience, and begged her to do penance for him. "Willingly," she replied. "I will offer my sufferings for you on condition that for the space of one night you keep the same position in your bed, without changing sides, budging or stirring."

He readily consented. But, having lain down in bed, he had scarcely rested half an hour when he felt uncomfortable and wished to move. Nevertheless, he did not do it and remained immovable, but the discomfort went on increasing, so much so that at the end of an hour it seemed intolerable to him. Then a salutary reflection sprang up in his mind: "If it is such a torture," he said to himself, "to remain without motion upon a comfortable bed for the space of one night, what would it be, if I were bound down on a bed of fire for the space of a century, of an eternity? And do I fear to redeem such a punishment by a little penance?"

St. Christina, a virgin, justly surnamed "The Admirable," born at St. Trond in 1150, after her death came to life again and lived afterward for 42 years, enduring unheard of sufferings for the relief of the souls in Purgatory and the conversion of sinners.

After a youth spent in innocence, patience and humility, Christina died in the odor of sanctity at the age of 32 years (1182). Her body was borne to the Church of Notre Dame, in which her obsequies were to be celebrated, and it was placed in the middle of the nave, after the manner of that period, in an open coffin. The great throng of people, who were present, was praying devoutly, when at the time of the Agnus Dei, the deceased lifted herself up in her coffin, and a few seconds after, with the lightness of a bird, shot up toward the dome and sat calmly on a cornice. At this sight the whole congregation took to flight in a panic; the eldest sister of Christina alone stayed in the church with the priest, who finished the Sacrifice. As soon as he came down from the altar, having ascertained what had happened, he commanded Christina to descend. She obeyed instantly, came down softly, as if her body had no weight, and calmly returned home with her sister.

There, being questioned by her friends and relations, she spoke to them thusly: "When I had given my last sigh, my soul, gone out of my body, found itself surrounded by a troop of angels, who bore it to a dark and frightful place in which there was an innumerable multitude of human souls. There I saw pains and torments which no tongue could express. Among those who were enduring them I noticed many whom I had known on earth. At the sight of their cruel sufferings, I was penetrated with the liveliest compassion, and I asked my guides what this place was. I scarcely doubted that it was Hell, but they replied that it was Purgatory.

"Afterward, they showed me the tortures of the damned; there I saw, also, a few unhappy creatures I had once known.

"Then the angels bore me to the heights of Heaven, before the eternal throne of God. The look, full of love, with which the Most High greeted me, filled my soul with an unspeakable joy. I felt that for all eternity I should enjoy His Blessed Presence. Answering my thoughts, the Lord said to me: 'Yes, My daughter, you will be eternally with Me, but for the moment, I leave you the choice either to enjoy beatitude from now on, or to return again to earth, there to suffer in a mortal body the pains of the immortal souls (in Purgatory), these pains, however, being unable to cause any damage to your body. By these sufferings you will deliver the souls that have inspired you with so lively a pity, and you will contribute powerfully to the conversion and sanctification of the living. When you shall have filled up the time of this mission, you shall return here again, and enter into the possession of My kingdom.'

"Such was the choice of God proposed to me. I did not hesitate; I chose the part of charity; and God, visibly satisfied with my choice, commanded the angels to bring me to earth.

"My friends," added the saint, "be not astonished at the excess of the wonders which you shall see wrought in my person. They will be the work of God, who does what He pleases, and who acts in everything by designs often hidden, but always adorable."

Upon hearing these words, it may well be understood that the hearers were struck with a holy dread; they looked at Christina with astonishment and trembled at the thought of the sufferings which this woman, returned to life, was going to endure. Indeed, from that moment on, quite different from what she had been before her death, Christina seemed to be a soul from Purgatory in a mortal body. Her life was nothing more than a tissue of unheard-of marvels and sufferings.

She abandoned human society and lived habitually in solitude. After having assisted in the morning at Mass--at which she often approached the Holy Table--she was observed fleeing to the woods and wild places, there to spend days and nights in prayer. Endowed with the gift of agility, she flew from one place to another with the speed of lightning, darted to the tops of trees, the roofs of houses, the towers of churches and castles. Often passersby would see her resting on the branches of a tree, then taking flight and disappearing at their approach.

Using no shelter, she lived like the birds of the woods, exposed to all the hardships of the weather, even in the most severe season. Her dress was modest, but excessively coarse and poor. She ate, like animals, what she found in the streets. If she saw a fire lighted, she would plunge her hands or feet into it, or if she could, her whole body altogether, and would endure as long as possible this torture. She used to watch for the opportunity of entering glowing furnaces, red-hot limekilns, and sink as deeply as she could into hot boilers. In winter, she spent the night in the icy water of the rivers; at times she would allow herself to be borne by the current upon mill-wheels, cling to them, suffering herself to be dragged by the machine which struck and broke her against obstacles. Another ingenuity of her passion for torments was to tease packs of dogs so as to be bitten and torn by these animals. At times she rolled in the bushes and thorns until she was covered with blood.

These are some of the means by which she tortured her body; and wonderful circumstance, but conformable to the promise which God had made to her, as soon as she emerged from her torture, she retained no wound of it; her body was untouched and without the least lesion.

This life of sufferings served for the edification of a countless multitude of the faithful who were witnesses of it for the space of 42 years, during which the saint still lived. She also converted a great number of sinners, and finally went to enjoy the glory of the elect in the year 1224.

If such mortification makes us shudder, what are we to think of the tortures of the other life? "There," says the author of the Imitation, "one hour in torment will be more terrible than a hundred years spent here below in the most rigorous penance." (Book 1, Chap. 24).

The history of Japan speaks of the horrible abysses of Mount Ungen, situated not far from Nagasaki. Its lofty summit is divided into three craters, the intervals between which form frightful pits; forth from these shoot momentarily into the air eddies of flames, corroding waters and burning mud, which carry such stinking exhalations with them that these abysses pass in the country for the sewers of Hell. All the animals shun them with horror, and the very birds do not fly with impunity over them, however high they soar. The tyrant, Bungondono, the Prince of Ximbara, resolved to dash the Christians head-foremost into these frightful chasms. Let the frightful agony they must suffer there be imagined! It was an agony to which death was not to come and put an end, for the consolation of dying was not left to them. Before they were suffocated, they were carefully drawn out to let them regain their breath. Then, soaked as they were by the sulphurous waters, the bodies of the martyrs were covered with frightful pus sacs and were soon but one wound; all their flesh dropped into putrefaction. In this condition they were abandoned like corpses, cast into the common sewer. Are these torments the torments of Hell? They are only a shadow of them.

The same Bungondono devised unheard of tortures to combat Christianity in Japan. One day seven Christians were led before him; they displayed great joy to suffer for the name of Jesus Christ. At this sight, inflamed with rage, the tyrant caused seven ditches to be dug, in which seven crosses were erected; he had the martyrs bound to them and ordered their limbs to be sawed with sharp-edged canes and at the same time salt thrown into their wounds. This torture was executed with a cruel slowness; it lasted five whole days. By an abominable use of the art destined for the preservation of men, the physicians had cordials taken to the martyrs to prolong their sufferings. Is this one of the tortures of Hell? It is only a shadow of them.

At the time of the inroads of the Calvinists into Holland in the 16th century, those sectaries, having seized at Maastricht some priests of the Company of Jesus, resolved to practice all the cruelty of their fanatical hatred upon them. After having overwhelmed them with contempt and outrages, they put round their necks iron collars provided with knives and sharp spikes, they encircled their arms and legs with similar rings, then seated them on seats bristling with nails, so that the martyrs could neither rest nor move without pain. They surrounded them with flames, to burn them slowly. What torture! If the sufferers remained motionless, they were burned; if they moved, they were torn by the spikes and knives. The servants of God triumphed by the help of grace over all this barbarity; it is true, nevertheless, that their torments were atrocious. Now, are these the torments of Hell? They are but the shadow of them.

Antiquity has preserved the names of three tyrants: Mezentius, Actiolinus and Phalaris. The first, Mezentius, it is said, chained his victims to corpses and left them in that revolting state until the infection and putrid inhalations of the dead killed the living. Actiolinus had such frightful dungeons that the condemned used to ask as a favor to be strangled, not to enter them. This grace would be denied; they were lowered with ropes into these stinking caves, there to be buried alive in putrefaction. Phalaris used to shut up his victims in a brazen bull, which he then surrounded with flames to burn them in this manner, while alive. All these pains are horrible, but they are only a shadow of the pains of Hell.

The Romans punished parricides (i.e., those who murdered their parents) by a special kind of torture. The guilty person was tied up in a sack with serpents, and thus cast into the depth of the sea; a feeble image of the torture reserved for those who are guilty of parricide toward God.

We shudder when reading in history the description of the frightful torments which the assassin of William, Prince of Orange, had to endure. His body was lacerated by iron rods.

Sharp spikes were driven into his flesh; then he was exposed to the action of a slow fire, which caused him inexpressible pains, and, just as he was on the point of expiring, after his hands had been burned with a red iron, he was torn asunder by horses. That unhappy man committed an enormous crime, but he attacked only a mortal prince. What will not be the chastisement of one who has assailed the King of Kings?

According to certain historians, the Emperor Zeno, a prince as impious as he was dissolute, died by a most tragic death. On the night of April 9, 491, after an excess at table, he fell into so violent a coma that he was believed to be dead, and he was hurriedly buried in the imperial burial vault. There, having regained consciousness, he called in vain for his servants and his guards; no one answered his shouts; he beheld himself in darkness, shut up with the dead on all sides, meeting only cold walls and iron doors. Then giving way to all the transports of rage and despair, he dashed himself against his surroundings and broke his skull against the walls. It was in this terrible state that his corpse was discovered. What a horrible situation for that prince, buried alive! Is that the situation of the reprobate?

Hell is the sink of the world and the receptacle of all the moral filth of humanity. There, impurity, intemperance, blasphemy, pride, injustice and all the vices which are like the rottenness of souls are found heaped up. To this moral filth a corporal stench is added more insupportable than all the stenches of hospitals and corpses. If the body of a damned person, says St. Bonaventure, were deposited on the earth, that of itself alone would be sufficient to make the earth uninhabitable; it would fill it with its infection, as a corpse that might be left to rot in a house would infect it all the way through.

A man at Lyons had gone into a burial vault in which a corpse lately buried was found wholly putrefied. Scarcely had he gone down when he fell dead. The poisonous exhalations caught him so violently that he was suffocated.

Sulpicius Severus narrates in the life of St. Martin of Tours that towards the end of the saint's life the demon came to tempt him under a visible form. The spirit of lies appeared before him with royal magnificence, a crown of gold on his head, and said he was the King of Glory, Christ, the Son of God. The holy bishop recognized the tempter under these appearances of human grandeur and chased him away with contempt.

Proud Satan was confounded; he disappeared, but for his revenge, he left the holy man's room filled with a stench that did not allow him to remain there anymore.

Another torture of hell is the horrible society of the devils and the damned. There are some wretched sinners who, seeing plainly that they are walking toward Hell, are comforted by saying, "I shall not be there alone!" Sad consolation! It is that of the convicts sentenced to wear irons together in the galleys. Still it is intelligible how a convict finds a certain life in the company of his kind. Alas! It will not be thus in Hell, in which the damned will be mutual executioners. "There," says St. Thomas, "the associates of his wretchedness, far from alleviating the lot of the damned soul, will make it more intolerable for him." (Suppl. 9, 86, A. 1). The society of even those persons who on earth were their best friends is insupportable to the damned in Hell. They would esteem themselves happy to have tigers and lions for companions, rather than their relatives, brothers, or their own parents.

Do you wish to see the poverty of hell and the privations that are suffered there by those who made the goods of this world their god? Consider the wicked rich man of the Gospel. Accustomed during his life to eat delicate meats served in silver utensils, to drink exquisite wines in goblets of gold, to wear purple and fine linen, having become an inhabitant of Hell, he found himself brought down to the last extremity of need. He who refused poor Lazarus the crumbs from his table, was obliged to beg in his turn. He asks, not delicacies, but a drop of cold water, which he will be happy to receive from a leper's finger. Now, this drop of water is refused to him. Has not the Savior said: "Woe to you that are rich, for you have your consolation. Woe to you that are filled, for you shall hunger." (Luke 6:25).

"There is no light," **writes St. Teresa** (Autobiography, Chapter 25), "in the eternal pit, only darkness of the deepest dye; and yet, O mystery! Although no light shines, all that can be most painful to the sight is perceived. Among those objects which torture the eyes of the damned, the most frightful are the demons, who reveal themselves in all their hideousness. St. Bernard speaks of a religious who, being in his cell, uttered all of a sudden frightful cries, which attracted the community. He was found beside himself and uttering only these sorrowful words: "Accursed be the day I entered religion!" Terrified and troubled by this curse, the cause of which they did not understand, his brethren questioned and encouraged him and spoke to him of confidence in God. Soon, being quieted, he replied, "no, no, it is not the religious life that I should curse. On the contrary, blessed be the day I became a religious! My brethren, do not be astonished at seeing my mind disturbed. Two devils have appeared to me; their horrible appearance has put me out of my senses. What monstrosity! Ah! Rather all torments than again to endure the sight of them!"

A holy priest was exorcising a demoniac, and he asked the demon what pains he was suffering in Hell. "An eternal fire," he answered, "an eternal malediction, an eternal rage, and a frightful despair at being never able to gaze upon Him who created me." "What would you do to have the happiness of seeing God?" "To see Him but for one moment, I should willingly consent to endure my torments for 10,000 years. But vain desires! I shall suffer forever and never see Him!"

On a like occasion, the exorcist inquired of the demon, 'what was his greatest pain in Hell.' He replied with an accent of indescribable despair: "Always, always! Never, never!"

One day, a holy soul was meditating upon Hell, and considering the eternity of the pains, the frightful "always... never," she was thrown into complete confusion by it, because she was unable to reconcile this immeasurable severity with the divine goodness and other perfections. "Lord," she said, "I submit to Thy judgments, but do not push the rigors of Thy justice to far." "Do you understand," was the answer, "what sin is? **To sin is to say to God, I will not serve Thee! I despise Thy law, I laugh at Thy threats!"**

"I understand, Lord, that sin is an outrage to Thy Majesty." "Well, measure, if you can, the greatness of this outrage." "Lord, this outrage is infinite, since it attacks infinite Majesty."

"Must it not, then, be punished by an infinite chastisement? Now, as the punishment could not be infinite in its intensity, justice demands that it be so at least in its duration. Accordingly, it is the divine justice that wills the eternity of the pains: the terrible 'always,' the terrible 'never.' The damned themselves will be obliged to render homage to this justice, and cry out in the midst of their torments: 'Thou art just, O Lord, and thy judgments are equitable.'" (Psalm 118: 137).

St. John Damascene relates, in the life of **St. Josaphat,** that this young prince, being one day exposed to violent temptations, prayed to God with tears to be delivered from them. His prayer was graciously heard; he was caught up in an ecstasy, and he beheld himself led to a dark place, full of horror, confusion, and frightful specters. There was a pool of sulfur and fire in which were plunged innumerable wretches, a prey to devouring flames. Amid the despairing howls and shouts, he heard a heavenly voice, which uttered these words: "Here it is that sin receives its punishment; here it is that a moment's pleasure is punished by an eternity of torments." This vision filled him with new strength, and enabled him to triumph over all the assaults of the enemy.

The most bitter regret of the damned will be, says St. Thomas, to be damned for "nothing," while they might have so easily obtained everlasting happiness.

Jonathan was condemned to death for having eaten a little honey, against the prohibition of Saul. In his misfortune he said, while moaning, "Alas! I did but taste a little honey... and behold I must die!" (1 Samuel 14:43).

More bitter will be the regrets of the damned when they shall see that, for a "honeycomb," for a fleeting enjoyment, they have incurred everlasting death.

King Lysimachus, besieged by the Scythians, who had cut off all the springs, beheld himself reduced to the last extremity by lack of water. Yielding to the craving of his thirst, he surrendered to the enemy, who left him only his life safe. Then a cup of water was given him to quench his thirst. When he had drunk it, he said, "Oh, how quickly has the pleasure passed for which I have lost my throne and my liberty!" It is in this manner that the damned will speak, but with far more bitterness: Oh, how quickly passed the guilty pleasure for which I forfeited an eternal crown and happiness!

Esau returned faint from the chase, and seeing Jacob, who was cooking lentils, he sold him his birthright for a dish of the pottage. "And so taking bread and the pottage of lentils," says the Scripture, "he ate and drank, and then went his way, making little account of having sold his birthright." But when the time came to receive his inheritance when he saw the large portion given to his brother and the small portion that was left to him, "He was filled with consternation, and uttered a great cry." Then, having sought in vain to better his lot, he yielded to the bitterest regrets and filled the air with his doleful cries; they were less cries than roars.

"Irriguit clamore magno." ("He roared out, with a great cry." (Gen. 25, 27:34). What will be the cries of the damned when they shall see that they have sold their heavenly inheritance for less than "a dish of pottage"-- when they shall see that for a trifle they have sold everlasting benefits and incurred everlasting torments?

The prophet Jeremias had warned Sedecias King of Juda, of the future that awaited him; he had spoken to him on behalf of God. "Behold life, and behold death; if you observe my words, you shall remain quiet on your throne; if you trample them under foot, I will deliver you into the hands of the King of Babylon." (Jerem. 29:39). Sedecias paid no attention to these warnings of God, and soon the chastisements foretold fell upon him; he was delivered to Nebuchadnezzar, blinded, loaded with chains, and thrown into the prison of Babylon. Then, what were not his regrets, his grief, at the remembrance of the words of Jeremias? A weak image of the tardy regrets, the cruel sorrows that devour the damned.

They weep for the time they lost in vain amusements and in forgetfulness of their salvation. "One hour," they say, "would have given us what an eternity could give us back no more!" Father Nieremberg relates that a servant of God, finding himself in a secluded place into which no other man had ventured, heard mournful wails, which could proceed only from a supernatural cause. He demanded, then, who were the authors of these piteous cries and what they meant. Then a sad voice replied to him: "We are the damned. Let it be known that we are deploring in Hell the time lost, the precious time which we waste on earth in vanities and crime. Ah! One hour would have given us what an eternity could restore to us no more."

Many people have been converted by this phase such as **St. Simeon Stylites (459)**: "Woe to you what now laugh, for you shall mourn and weep" (Luke 6:25) Abstain from today's pleasures, learn to do with out.

Many Christians unfortunately commit mortal sins during their lives, but though they confess their sins, they make no due satisfaction for them.

The Venerable Bede appears to be of the opinion that those who pass a great part of their lives in the commission of grave sins and confess them on their deathbed may be detained in Purgatory even until the Last Day. *(For some of us it's good we're so close to the last day.)*

St. Gertrude in her revelations states that those who have committed many grave sins and have not done due penance may not share in the ordinary suffrages of the Church for a very considerable time!

All those sins, mortal and venial, are accumulation for the 20, 30, 40, 50, 60, years of our lives. Each and every one has to be atoned for after death, if not before.

Is it any wonder that souls have to remain so long in Purgatory? The Length of time souls are in Purgatory depends on:

a.) the number of their faults;
b.) the malice and deliberation with which these have been committed;
c.) the penance done, or not done, the satisfaction made, or not made for sins during life;
d.) Much, too, depends on the suffrages offered for them after death.

What can safely be said is that the time souls spend in Purgatory is, as a rule, very much longer than people commonly imagine.

St. Louis Bertrand's father was an exemplary Christian, as we should naturally expect, being the father of so great a Saint. He had even wished to become a Carthusian monk until he learned that it was not God's will for him.

When he died, after long years spent in the practice of every Christian virtue, his saintly son, fully aware of the rigors of God's Justice, offered many Masses and poured forth the most fervent supplications for the soul he so dearly loved.

A vision of his father still in Purgatory forced him to intensify a hundred fold his suffrages. He added most severe penances and long fasts to his Masses and prayers. Yet eight whole years passed before he obtained the release of his father.

St. Malachy's sister was detained in Purgatory for a very long time, despite the Masses, prayers, and heroic mortifications the Saintly brother offered for her!

It was related to a holy nun in Pampluna, who had succeeded in releasing many Carmelite nuns from Purgatory, that most of these had spent their terms of from 3 to 60 Years!

At Fatima, Lucia asked Our Lady about a friend who had recently died. Our Lady told Lucia that she had committed an impure act, and would be in purgatory until the end of time.

It's like spending a 2nd life to get yourself sanctified for God and Heaven, because you didn't get it right the first time on earth and did not make up for your sins.

Do you go to daily Mass, are you wearing the scapular, are you praying the daily Rosary. Examine your conscience each night. Never say a thing against any man, priest or other wise. You should think daily on burning in Hell. St. Teresa said to meditate daily on Hell as she did.

St. Anthony saw in a vision the whole world entangled in a net of sin. "O Lord," he cried out, "who will escape these snares?" And a voice from Heaven answered: "ONLY THOSE WHO ARE HUMBLE OF HEART."

A Salutary Fear of Hell

We ought to believe in Hell, because we may fall into it. Alas! It is very easy to be damned, and the damned are very numerous. St. Teresa compares them to the flakes of snow which fall in the dreary days of winter. The servant of God, Anthony Pereyra, in a very authentic vision with which he was favored (see Ch. 2), saw the souls of sinners descending into the pit like corn beneath the millstones, like stones cast in heaps into a huge limekiln. God showed one day before a large multitude that they fall into it as the dead leaves in autumn fall from the trees under the breath of the wind. The venerable Father Anthony Baldinucci, a celebrated missionary of the Company of Jesus, who died in the odor of sanctity in the year 1717, was preaching in the open air, because the church could not contain the faithful who came in crowds to hear him.

Speaking of Hell, he said, "My brethren, would you know how great the number of those who are damned is? Look at that tree." All eyes were turned to a tree that was there, covered with leaves. At the same moment a gust of wind, rising, shook all the branches of the tree, and caused the leaves to fall so plentifully that there remained only a certain number of them, thinly scattered and easy to count. "See," went on the man of God, "what souls are lost, and what souls are saved. Take your precautions to be among the latter."

Father Nieremberg speaks of a bishop, who by a special permission of God, received a visit from an unhappy sinner who had died impenitent, a short time before. Addressing the prelate, this damned soul demanded if there were men still on earth. As the bishop seemed astonished at this question, the lost soul added: "Since I have been in that melancholy abode, I have seen such a prodigious multitude arrive, that I am at a loss to conceive that there are men still on earth." This speech recalls that of the Savior in the Gospel. "Enter ye in at the narrow gate; for wide is the gate, and broad is the way that leadeth to destruction, and many there are who go in thereat. How narrow is the gate and strait is the way that leadeth to life; and few there are that find it!" (Matt. 7:13-14).

To avoid Hell, it is necessary to avoid the road to it, and to destroy the cause of damnation, that is, sin, under all its forms. Men permit themselves to be allured to their ruin by different bonds of iniquity, sometimes by one, sometimes by another. There are many who die in their sins because they are deprived of the Last Sacraments, and among those who receive them, there are not a few who are lost because they lack sincerity in the accusation of their sins. Here is an incident which we read in the Annals of Paraguay, during the year 1640. In the Reduction (Jesuit mission plantation) of the Assumption, a woman died who had left a son of about 20 years. This young man beheld his mother appear to him in the most frightful condition. She told him that she was damned for not having made a sincere Confession, and that many others were damned like her for having concealed their sins in Confession. "And you," she added, "do profit by the example of your unfortunate mother."

Father Nieremberg mentions also another damned person who revealed the cause of his damnation. A young man was leading an apparently Christian life, but he had an enemy whom he hated, and while frequenting the Sacraments, he all the while harbored in his heart sentiments of ill-will and revenge, which Jesus Christ commands to be discarded. After his death, he appeared to his father and told him that he was damned for not having forgiven his enemy, after which he exclaimed with an accent of unutterable sorrow: "Ah! If all the stars in Heaven were so many tongues of fire, they could not express what torments I endure!"

Let us listen again to the same author. An unhappy man who had the habit of taking pleasure in immodest thoughts fell sick and received the Last Sacraments. The next day his confessor, going to visit him again, saw him on the road coming to meet him. "Go no further," he said to him, "I am dead and damned." "How?" demanded the priest. "Did you not make a good confession of your sins?" "Yes, I made a good confession, but afterwards the devil represented to me sinful pleasures, and asked me whether in case of a cure I should not return again to my pleasures? I consented to these evil suggestions, and at the same moment death surprised me." Then, opening his garment, he showed the fire that was devouring him and disappeared.

We read also in Father Nieremberg that a noble lady, who was exceedingly pious, asked God to make known to her **what displeased His Divine Majesty** most in persons of her sex. The Lord vouchsafed in a miraculous manner to hear her. He opened under her eyes the Eternal Abyss. There she saw a woman a prey to cruel torments and in her recognized one of her friends, a short time before deceased. This sight caused her as much astonishment as grief: the person whom she saw damned did not seem to her to have lived badly. Then that unhappy soul said to her: "It is true that I practiced religion, but I was a slave of vanity. Ruled by the passion to please, **I was not afraid to adopt indecent fashions to attract attention**, and I kindled the fire of impurity in more than one heart. Ah! If Christian women knew how much immodesty in dress displeases God!" At the same moment, this unhappy soul was pierced by two fiery lances, and plunged into a cauldron of liquid lead.

Thomas of Cantimpre, a learned religious of the Order of St. Dominic, relates that there was at Brussels an unhappy sinner, the slave of intemperance and the other vices which it foments. He had a friend, the companion of his dissipation, to whom he was greatly attached. A sudden death put an end to his disorders. His sorrowful companion, after having accompanied him to the grave, had returned home and was alone in his chamber, when he heard moans underground. Frightened at first and not knowing what to do, he ventured at length to ask who it was that he heard moaning. "It is I, your companion, whose body you attended to the grave. Alas! My soul is buried in Hell." Then, uttering a cry, or rather a dreadful roar, he added, "Woe to me! The abyss has swallowed me, and the pit has closed its mouth upon me."

Louis of Granada speaks of a young woman whose damnation had no other source than **vanity** and the desire to please. She led a regular life, but her passion to attract attention by the charm of her beauty was the moving cause of her whole conduct (St Bridget of Ireland (Kildare)prayed to God to take away her beauty and God did this for her.) Having fallen sick, she died, and having received all the Sacraments. While her confessor was praying for her soul, she appeared to him, saying that she was damned, and that the cause of her damnation was vanity. "I sought," she added, "only to please the eyes of men. This passion caused me to commit a multitude of sins; it prevented me from receiving the Sacraments well, and it has led me to everlasting torments."

A usurer (banker) had two sons who followed the evil example of their father. One of the two, touched by God, forsook his guilty profession and retired to the desert. Before setting out, he exhorted his father and brother with tears to think, like him, of the salvation of their souls. It was to no purpose; they persevered in sin, and died in a state of impenitence. God permitted the solitary to know their unhappy condition. In an ecstasy he saw himself on a high mountain at the foot of which was a sea of fire, from which arose confused cries, like a tempest.

Soon, in the midst of these burning waves, he perceived his father and brother, furiously raging against each other, mutually upbraiding and cursing each other and holding this dreadful dialogue: "I curse thee, detestable son! It is for thee that I did injustice and lost my soul." "I curse thee, unworthy father, who ruined me by thy bad example." "I curse thee, foolish son, who joined thy father in his sins." "I curse thee, the author of my life, who reared me up for damnation!" Behold how wicked parents and wicked children will eternally rend one another by reciprocal maledictions. (Lives of the Fathers of the Desert).

What is Liberalism or who is a Liberal?

Thoughts of Catherine Clarke from the book "The Boston Heresy Case"

"We have been asked many times what we mean by a 'Liberal'....
we do not mean a Liberal in the political sense, but in the religious
sense, and as pertaining to the Catholic Religion. A Catholic Liberal
is one who, having taken all his cultural standards from a non-
Catholic society, tries to make his Catholic dogmas square (or meant)
society standards. Liberal Catholicism can occur in any country....

in the United States many non- Catholics induce the Catholic to reconcile his beliefs with the humanitarian, utilitarian, pragmatic and political ideals of the new world into which they now live.

As a result, Catholics stopped being interested in Christ, and started being interested in Christianity. This term Christianity quickly became hyphenated with the various secular group movements, and it ended up by leaving Catholics with a set of relative standards towards religion, and caused them to little by little, abandon their dogmatic certitudes, or dogmatic beliefs of past popes and councils of tradition. (Soon making them protestants.)

A Liberal Catholic is one who always knows how God should behave. God's behavior is invariably made to conform with the Liberal's own feelings in any situation. (So whatever the Liberal wants to do is always going to be OK with God, even if it's wrong.)

So if past councils, popes, or tradition says things like "Outside the Church there is No Salvation" or "If latin is not used, let them be anathema" all these things must be done away with.

What past popes and councils have defined as dogmatic certitudes are for the good of your soul and for your salvation. Don't be fooled by this New Church. **"Many are called, but few are chosen."** **U-tube: Fr. Hesse, "Exposing the Worst Statements of Vatican II" and "Vatican II vs. Syllabus of Errors"**

How to begin your day in the Divine Will.

The following is from Our Lord to a favored Soul. Luisa Piccarreta of Corato Italy. I will give you her history after you read this. Also I will give you Our Lady's words on how to live in the Divine Will.

In order to help you live daily life in the Divine Will, Jesus has given you the **Prevenient Act** to begin your day, and the **Current Act** to keep you attentive throughout the day. He explains these two acts in the following passage:

There is both a prevenient act and a current act. The prevenient act is when the soul, at the break of dawn, sets its will in Mine and decides and affirms that it wants to live and act only in My Will. With this act it prepares all its acts and makes them flow in My Will. With this predisposing consent My Sun surges and My life is replicated in all your acts as if in one single current act. But the prevenient act can be eclipsed and clouded by certain human ways: by self-will, by self-esteem, by carelessness, by neglect, etc. All these things are like clouds that interfere with the sun and render its light less vivid as it falls on the face of the earth.

The current act, on the other hand, is not subject to the possible interference of clouds but rather clears away any clouds that may exist. It makes rise other suns in which my Life is replicated with ever-more-intense light and heat, each more beautiful than the other. Both acts are necessary; the prevenient act assists, creates the disposition and makes room for the current act. The current act preserves and enlarges the disposition of the prevenient act (May 27, 1922).

The Prevenient Act, then, can be compared to the Morning Offering. For ages, Catholics have been making the Morning Offering to express to God their desire to make every act of the day an act of love for Him. In a similar manner, by the Prevenient Act, the Child of the Divine Will renews each morning his desire to make all his acts flow in God's Will. And just as the effect of the Morning Offering is easily spoiled by self-love and thoughtlessness, and thus needs to be renewed throughout the day by many loving aspirations, so the Prevenient Act is easily spoiled *"by certain human ways,"* and also needs to be renewed throughout the day. Therefore Jesus has given the **Current Act**.

The importance of **Being Faithful And Attentive** to the **Current Act** can be summarized in the following illustration. **In the early morning a farmer asks his two sons to go out and work in the field**; the weather is going to turn soon and he needs to get the harvest in quickly. Both boys agree to go to the field and work. The **first boy** begins by working hard, but is soon distracted by field mice, butterflies and the nearby children flying a kite. The **second boy**, knowing that, he too, like his brother, is easily distracted, ties a string to his finger. And, in fact, he frequently begins to be distracted. But as soon as he sees the string on his finger, he remembers his purpose, and with a strong act of his will, turns away from the distractions and becomes attentive to his duty. Both boys spent the whole day in the field, but it is only the second boy who, *by frequently remembering his purpose and being attentive to his duty*, actually makes his day in the field a **fruitful one**.

A Method for Making the Current Act

The Prevenient Act (as mentioned at the beginning of <u>Chapter 4</u>) is included in the <u>Rounds to Begin the Day</u> of Book 2 — *Advéniat Regnum Tuum*. Having made this act at the beginning of the day, it's now up to you to continue making Current Acts throughout the day. In the following passage, Jesus gives a beautiful method for making the **Current Act**:

In order for the soul to be able to forget herself, everything she does or has to do must be done as if I wanted to do it in her. If she prays, she should say "It is Jesus Who wants to pray, and I pray together with Him." If she works: "It is Jesus Who wants to work; it is Jesus Who wants to walk; Who wants to get up; Who wants to enjoy Himself." And it should be like that in everything for the rest of her life, excluding errors. Only in this manner is the soul able to forget herself. For not only will she do everything because I want it; but, because I want to do it, she will need Me (August 14, 1912). Luisa and the Divine Will

For this reason, in another place Our Lord says:

*...from now on between you and Me, I **don't** want "you" and "I" to exist. Therefore, it will no longer be said "you will do," or "I will do," but **"we will do."** Also, that "<u>yours</u>" and "<u>mine</u>" must <u>disappear</u>. Instead, we will say **"ours,"** as in all things...* (Chapter 39).

Acquiring the habit of offering short prayers for routine activities can also be helpful in your effort to do everything *for* and *in* Jesus. By offering a certain prayer for every act of your daily routine, your attention will be brought back to Him Who wants to do all these simple acts in you. Examples:

— <u>When making your bed in the morning</u>: Lord, as I put my bed in order in your Will, I call all souls to put their day in order in You by making their Morning Offering. I call the Children of the Divine Will to do so, by making their Prevenient Act. I also beseech You for true order in the world through the coming of your Kingdom.

— When dressing: While dressing in your Will I call all souls to discard the gloomy garment of sin, and to dress themselves in the beautiful and bright garment of your grace, or still better, in the "Royal Vestments" of Your grace (Vol. 16: Jan. 14, 1924) in your Holy Divine Will.

— When brushing your teeth: While brushing my teeth in your Will I call all sinners to repentance so that we may brush away their sins. I call chosen souls to greater faithfulness so that we may brush away everything in them that could displease You in the least. Thus let us prepare the world for the coming of your Kingdom.

— When writing: Lord, as we write, let us write names in the Book of Life and in the Kingdom of your Will on earth. As we make this ink flow, let us make your Blood flow over the souls in Purgatory to purify them.

— When taking a walk: Lord as we walk, let us walk in your Will above all the acts of all creatures, and cover them with the mantle of your Will. By this means let us make them perfect and complete in the eyes of the Supreme Majesty.

Ask the Holy Spirit to inspire you with similar prayers for your other routine, daily activities.

All things come from Me, this includes your work. Your is to be offered to Me for all creatures, which will always include yourself.

Be aware, dear soul, that by learning to act and live in this "divine way" (as Jesus calls it) you will be working *in favor of all creatures*. That is, God will receive the perfect glory that would be His, if all creatures — past, present and future — were doing what you are doing in accordance with His Will. Thus, in return, God will pour out his grace on everyone universally; and the creatures will benefit from this grace *according to their dispositions*. Jesus explains this in the following passage:

...I want you closely united with Me. But do not believe that you should do this only when you pray or when you suffer. No, but rather always and forever in

*all you do. If you move, if you breathe, if you work, if you eat, if you sleep —
all this you must do as if you were doing it in My Humanity, (in His Person)
as if all of your work came out of Me."*

*You must do everything like this — and in favor and for the good of all
creatures — as if My Humanity were in the midst of all creatures. Hence, by
doing everything with this intention of receiving life from Me, even the most
indifferent and small actions acquire the merits of My Humanity."*

When I was on earth I humble Myself working with wood, hammering
nails, helping my foster father, Joseph, in his carpentry labors. I was
divinizing all human actions; I was sanctifying them, giving divine merit
to each. Through the movements of my fingers, I was calling all the
movements of your fingers as well as all other creatures. And if I saw them
laboring for Me, because they wanted Me to perform these acts in Me, for
Me, and by Me. I offered them the merits of my own Life. *And while you
are working — working because I want to work — look at your fingers as if
they are mine. How many do I call and how many others do I sanctify, correct,
chastise, etc.? You, then, are also here with Me to create, to call, to correct,
and more. And since you are not working alone, neither am I in all my works.
Could I have given you a greater honor?*

In the last page of Vol. III "Book of Heaven," Our
Lord tells Luisa that He has a bitterness in His stomach that comes from
impurities and **insipid foods** which are good works done badly, or
carelessly. He almost despises receiving them, and is unable to bear them,
He wants to vomit them out of His mouth.

They are like the lukewarm people who are neither hot or cold in their
love, their work, their prayers, and actions in which they were created to
do and offer to their God.

This is called the continuation of the work of God on earth, that we
catholics are called to offer and do this daily work, starting with our
Morning Offering. On Judgement Day we must show up with our hands
full of good works. (And have died in the state of Sanctifying grace.)

In a beautiful book **"Meditations for Religious"** I read on pg **103**, a chapter "The Repercussion of My Acts". A young Twenty-one year old girl wrote, "The thought that every one of our actions has its effect upon the whole human race is both consoling and terrifying. The smallest act of virtue raises even without our knowledge the low-water mark of morality, but the contrary, alas, is also true and how disturbing is this thought."

So the repercussions of your actions in thought, word, and deed, either appease God's wrath or brings it down upon us a chastisement of some kind. INTERESTING? Bad language and too many masons and not enough interior virtue and peace. Learn The Necessity of Practicing the Lesser Forms of Holiness. The virtues which need to be put *"in order"* to maintain this interior peace in the trials and storms of life are, **obedience** and **abandonment (resignation)**. But, to practice these two virtues, you also need **humility, trust (confidence) in God, mortification** and **detachment and habitual perseverance.** ("Learn to do without." Fr. Brey)

Again, the two commandment which bring the chastisements upon us is breaking the 2nd and 3rd commandments. Which is using God's name in vain and working on Sundays. *(Below I will go over a catechism reviewing each commandment, and you will be greatly surprised at what you should and should not being doing.)*

Do not grow impatient with yourself. It takes time to form this habit, and Jesus understands this. What He wants is your constant effort, *"Fickleness escapes from the steadiness of the Divine behavior."* Strive then always to **Be Faithful And Attentive.** Let me whisper from time to time be a word of love to Him. May my life be lived always in the supernatural, with the Divine Will, full of power for good and strong in its purpose of sanctity.

This the same thing, only through Mary you offer all to Jesus, the St. Louis De Montfort way.

To have the knowledge that you have the gift of the true Faith is the most wonderful thing. Show me something better, if you can. There is nothing. This is called the 'Joy of the Truth'.

A writer who was far from the truth but who was tormented by a desire to possess it, put these words on the lips of two of his characters to express the state of his soul:

"Speak to me, tell me what is on your mind. What do you need?" The other lowered his eyes and answered: "What I need you cannot give me." "What is it then?" "Peace, joy, an immortal soul and God."

How can a man exist in this world of torment, perpetually groping in the dark from day to day and have nothing to hope for, nothing to eternally youth, happiness, joy of knowing the truth will set you free as long as you practice the One, True, Holy, Catholic, and Apostolic Faith. I could not exist if I was not told by certain saints that God exist in Heaven, in the tabernacle, and deep within my soul. That I must constantly think of Him and speak with Him as I work. Because God dwells in us and comes to us sacramentally, this is why it is wrong to burn the body or destroy a church building.

One day St. Teresa of Avila was reflecting that her soul was more pure when she had nothing to do with business, and that she then committed fewer sins than when she was engaged in affairs. Then Our Lord said to her: "It can be otherwise, My child, and for that reason you must continually endeavour to have a RIGHT INTENTION in all things and to be **detached** (of worldly things). THEN KEEP YOUR EYES ON ME, SO AS TO MAKE ALL YOUR ACTIONS CONFIRMED TO MINE."

TORMENTS OF THOSE WHO HAVE NEVER LOVED THEIR GOD

While in prayer, St. Mechtilde saw hell open beneath her, and in it infinite wretchedness and horror, as it were serpents and toads, lions and dogs and every kind ferocious animal, who were cruelly tearing at each other. The saint asked: "O Lord, who are those unfortunates?" The Lord answered: "Those are the people who never thought tenderly of me for even one hour." *(Learn who God is and you will find Him very Loving.)*

BRIDLE YOUR TONGUE

"When I delivered Myself up to the wicked," said the Lord to St. Mechtilde, "They bound My hands and did as they pleased with Me. They could not, however, BIND MY TONGUE; but I Myself fettered it that I spoke only what was useful for them. In the same way man, though he can say good things or evil at his pleasure, ought to RETRAIN HIS

TONGUE THAT HE NEVER SAYS ANYTHING TO WOUND OR EVEN TO DISTURB HIS NEIGHBOR."

THE CROSS AND THE EUCHARIST

"When I want to lead a soul to the summit of perfection," said her Divine Master to St. Gertrude, "I give her the **CROSS** and the **EUCHARIST**. The Eucharist first makes the soul accept the Cross and afterwards love it, and lastly long for it. The Cross purifies the soul and disposes and prepares the soul for the Divine Banquet. The Eucharist nourishes and fortifies the soul and helps the soul to carry her cross; it supports her on the road to Calvary. What precious gifts the CROSS and the EUCHARIST are! They are the gifts of God's true friends."

"If we always kept in mind that God is Present everywhere we are, we should never, or hardly ever, commit a sin." **St. Thomas Aquinas**

Now I give you a Special Secret, but now meant to be a secret. From the book: "Fresh Flowers for our Heavenly Crown." pg. 116 It is a book on the teaching of virtue. You know that the highest achievement of man's maturity is **virtue**. Universal and Perpetual Intention According to the Custom of St. Gertrude.

St. Gertrude borrows first from the Blessed Trinity, praise, joy, thanksgiving, which she pours out afterwards on every creature. Then, through the bond of charity, she appropriates merits, grace, praise, all the riches of the Saints, who are only too eager to grant her desires. The following is of the most remarkable example of this: (Fom the Life of St. Gertrude) One year, on the feast of the Assumption as preparation for Holy Communion, Gertrude repeated three times the *Laudate Dominum omnes gentes* asking **first** of these, all the saints to offer to Our Lord all their merits as her own: **second** Laudate, St. Gertrude made the same petition to the Blessed Virgin, and by the **third** Laudate to Our Lord, St. Gertrude saw the Blessed Virgin rise at once and offer for St. Gertrude to the Blessed Trinity, the incomparable merits which raised Her above the Angels on the Day of the Assumption. Immediately St. Gertrude felt the joy of the Lord within her, and the Angels and Saints came near to do her honour. Having received Holy Communion, St. Gertrude offered It to

Our Lord to increase the joy and glory of His Blessed Mother in return for the gift of Her merits. Then Jesus, seeming to give a present to His tender Mother, said: "My Dear Mother, I return you double in what belongs to you, without taking anything from her to whom you have shown favour through love of Me." St. Gertrude gained the goods from brethren on earth, from the nuns in her Monastery, and lastly the goods from the entire universe as in this beautiful prayer which she frequently said: "Hail, Jesus! my fair spouse, full of the love of the entire universe, and I kiss the wounds which love has caused thee." (Kiss your crucifix.)

Offer your day for the Church and for the salvation of souls. Here is what the saints have to say on this:

Pope St. Gregory the Great (590 - 604): "No sacrifice is more acceptable to God than zeal for souls."

St. Rose Of Lima, (1586 - 1617): We read that her confessor offered himself to go to the missions, but he feared because of the dangers it would entail. After consulting the saint, he heard these words: "Go Father, and do not fear. Leave all to labor for the conversion of the infidel, and know that the greatest service that man can offer to God is to convert souls, for this is a work proper of the Apostolate. What greater happiness could there be than to baptize, be it only a little Indian child who would enter Heaven through the gates of Baptism?"

St. John de Brebeuf (1593 - 1649), one of the eight North American Martyrs, was heard to say, after pouring the saving waters of Baptism on a dying Indian child, "For this one single occasion I would travel all the way from France; I would cross the great ocean to win one little soul for Our Lord!"

St. Margaret Mary (1647 - 1690): "My divine Savior has given to understand that that those who work for the salvation of souls will have a gift of touching the most hardened hearts, and will labor with marvelous success, if they themselves are penetrated with a tender devotion to His Divine Heart."

St. Cardinal John Newman (1801 - 1890): "How can we answer to ourselves for the souls who have in our times lived and died in sin; the souls that have been lost and are now waiting for the judgment, seeing that for what we know NOT daily help them."

So offer your prayers, penance, and sacrifices to God in union with the Mass and all that have great merits of all the greatest of saints to join to your own merits and glory in Heaven and gain whatever you ask of God for good of souls. This method would be good to incorporate into your morning offering. Remember Grandpa McCoy told me upon opening his eyes each morning he would greet Jesus, Mary, and Joseph. When you can get to the point of talking to Jesus at each moment of the day about what ever you are doing and uniting it to the Divine Will, you will Divinize your actions making them divine, this is what Our Lord tells will happen. This is what Our Lady did and Adam and Eve. Always be in conversation with Christ as if you are talking it over to yourself, but of course you are talking to God, now you are becoming closer to God. He keeps Himself invisible, to test your faith in Him truly He is beside you, and He is always there listening, to when you say good or bad of Him, He is listening.

Gabrielle Bossis (1874-1950) was a Catholic Mystic and layperson who lived in France in the 20th century. Born in Nantes, France in 1874, she was the youngest child of a family of four children. In her later years Our Lord spoke interiorly with her:

"Can you measure this love that made Me give Myself up when I could have escaped into the invisible? It was My love that went out to meet the torture. Don't you believe that I paid for the right to have at least your **friendship**? You recall what the thief said: *'Remember me when You come into Your kingdom'?* And I say to you, *'Remember Me during your life'*. Place Me as a lighthouse in the center of your mind, not just a lighthouse that illumines, but one that gives warmth. Where can you be where I am not? When you are hunting for Me, I am already there, and when you love Me, I love Myself in you. I am your Source. Give everything back to Me in joy and simplicity. So few stop to think about this.

Then tell Me now, do you want Me to knock at the door of your soul?"

April 8, 1948

"Have you thanked Me for all I did for you, for mankind, for the angels, for My mother? What a concert of blessings, My child! Gather them all as though they were yours and join in the symphony of thanksgiving. Sing your part in the choir of numberless voices, and I'll know it from all the others. Are there two voices alike in the whole world? Aren't you struck by the diversity in human creation? In heaven too, each saint differs from the other, and if you are enchanted by the variety of colors in your garden, you may be sure that Paradise flashes with a myriad of countless splendid things, all for My glory. There too, I know the voices, for I know you all. My children, I atoned for all of you and I know My redeemed ones.

November 4, 1948

"I knock at your door. You don't believe that I need my children, do you? And yet, My God-Love needs your love. That is how it is. Always. You remember My words, 'I thirst'? I am always thirsty. If you knew this thirst, more intense than the thirst of men, you would devise every means in your power to quench it. That is why I knock at your door.

Do you remember the heat of the Sahara? The desert burns less than I. Can you understand My thirst for your awareness of Me, for your desire to be pleasing to Me, for your gratitude for My pitiable sufferings, your compassion for all the disgrace, the filth and the hatred I received during the night before My crucifixion and on the morning of My death? And for the blows, and the torture of My body and mind. Do you sometimes think of it?

This Book of St. Gabrielle Bossis is entitled **"He and I"** and it is great thoughts from God Himself to think about and become closer to God, which is the most important thing you can do to develop a relationship.

"...Ask Me for love. Ask Me; I am burning with desire to give it to you".... "Talk to Me. For Me, there is no sweeter prayer." -Words of our Lord for all who listen

Words of our Lord to Sister Mary of the Holy Trinity (1901-1942)

"To find Me, to know Me, to receive Me, then to come to Me -that is the only meaning of every life. All activities, all zeal are subordinate to that, and have only the value of means, in the measure in which they lead to Me. I am the Alpha and Omega, your God and your All. How is it then that in so many lives, I am accepted and treated merely as something supplementary?

"People come to Me in distress, beseeching... and I always, always give...Where are those who love Me simply because I am the Savior, because I am your God and your All?...because I am the Alpha and the Omega...?"

"Those who love Me a little, have a little confidence in Me. Those who love Me much, have great confidence in Me. Those who place no limit to their love have a confidence in Me without bounds or limit. I cannot disappoint them. You honor Me more by the confidence you show Me than by all that you could give Me. And notice, I respond at once by putting joy into the heart that honors Me with confidence."

"People have a false idea of Me. They take Me for a master who distributes his favors at his caprice and who enforces His will. Do you understand that I enforce nothing? I am powerless before your liberty. It is I who beg for your love. Look at Me gasping for breath upon the Cross; behold My royalty! I have expiated your sins, but I do not even force you to believe it. I show you My Passion -does it speak to you? -and I wait.

Behold My Divinity; -an indefatigable patience. Throughout the centuries I await souls. I never refuse them. Ask to know Me better.

Do the same with your life. Make reparation; expiate; love without asking for anything in return; and wait patiently until you too are loved. Never refuse to give love. It is I whom you honor and serve so tenderly; I have such need of it."

"I am sought after as so far away, whereas I am so near. You have only to descend into your heart and listen. Do you understand how much I am with you, *in you*? As soon as you call me, I answer. I am always present. What do you lack?"

Our Lord tells us that those souls who each morning and throughout the day unit their thoughts, words, and deeds, and every little thing from moment to moment to My Divine Will, will give the highest places in Heaven. But all this He says depends on how much knowledge you acquire of the Divine Will. You must agree with me that all knowledge is acquired with studying. In order to love God, you must know Him, in order to love God, you must study. After you do these things than can you say with the saints and angels, I will serve You, because I love You. And He said He would give this great gift to whoever sincerely wants it. So ask for it and study it. Buy the Book: **"Virgin Mary in the Kingdom of the Divine Will"** *(This book is a wealth of understanding.)*

When you use His name in vain, or when you are speaking to Him. Religion means to bond with God. This bond is a similar bond to that you have with your spouse. Only your spouse is not with you all the time and God is. So the bond between you and God should be much greater, because your every moment should be speaking and conversing with Him about what you're doing and what your next move should be. (This is also part of the practice of Divine Will by Our Lord to Luisa.)

Who is Luisa?

The Servant of God Luisa Piccarreta was born in Corato in the Province of Bari, Italy on April 23, 1865 and died there in the odor of sanctity on March 4, 1947. She was a 3rd Order Dominican, like Saint Catherine of Siena.

Luisa from her very birth was given a mystical life, for example, at the age of 17 she received the Mystical Union that Saint John of the Cross, Saint Teresa of Avila and Saint Catherine of Siena received right before they died. After this mystical Union Jesus asked Luisa if she would suffer in bed and because of her "Fiat!", He taught Luisa about the Life of the Divine Will, forming It first in her. As in Adam, Eve, and in Our Lady Mary.

For the next 64 years until her death, Luisa stayed in bed basically not eating, drinking or sleeping. Luisa was nourished by receiving the Most Holy Eucharist during the Holy Sacrifice of the Mass daily said in her room. This special blessing was given by Pope Saint Pius X and Pope Leo

XIII his predecessor. Luisa also lived on the food of the Divine Will, which Jesus said in the Gospels, "a food that you do not know of…."

During that time through great sufferings and a sublime call to holiness, Jesus taught Luisa about the fulfillment of the Our Father, the prayer that Jesus taught His Apostles.

Jesus taught Luisa that now is the time for the Kingdom of God to reign on earth as in Heaven. Jesus dictated 36 Volumes of the doctrine of the Divine Will, which He gave the title "The Kingdom of the Fiat in the Midst of Creatures. **Book of Heaven** – The Recall of the Creature into the Order (the very same as Adam and Eve before the fall), to its place and into the purpose for which he was Created by God", to teach Luisa how to "<u>Live</u>" in the "Divine Will." This is different than the devotional life of the Saints which is "<u>doing</u>" the Will of God.

These Volumes were basically dictated in three sections: in the **first section**, Volumes 1-10, Jesus shows Luisa how to become a Divine Mirror of Jesus Himself. In the **second section**, Volumes 11-19, Jesus shows Luisa how to "Live" in the Divine Will through the Power of the Holy Spirit. In the **third section**, Volumes 20-36, Jesus shows Luisa how to receive the Divine Inheritance of the Father. (This begins after the Chastisement.)

In humble obedience Luisa, under the constant direction of the Church, faithfully wrote all that Jesus Himself wanted her to put down on paper. *This would be <u>not</u> only for herself but for those who would read it*, so that they too could "**Live**" in the Divine Will as Luisa (also Adam and Eve, and Our Lady) learned how to "Live" in the Divine Will, by putting into practice these "**Truths**" taught by Jesus and Mary. (*All souls are called to enter into the state of sanctity or perfection and can enter into the mystical world. In the two vols. "The Three Ages of the Interior Life" by Garrigou Lagrange, this is a different direct or way of jumping across Purgatory into Heaven, he points out the (3) stages one must go through to obtain this mystical union with God. This type of purification enters into Ascetical Theology and Mystical Theology. First you must enter into the Purgative Way, the Illuminative Way, and then the Unitive Way, This is somewhat difficult because we are in still in the world and not in a convent or monastery. I have read and tried it. The hard part is the Purgative Way, where you purge yourself of the pleasures and enjoyments of the world. It's actually very easy at first and almost a pleasure you look forward to doing for love of God and His Mother.*

But I have learned that this is because God hold your hands and gives you the graces to walk in this state at first. I did this for seven years when I consecrated myself the Mary the St. Louis de Montfort Way. Than being in the world and seeing the things I was missing and had given up, I started to fall back into old habits. If you do not enter into this state of perfection in this life, you will have to do so in Purgatory. Just so you know the definition of Ascetical Theology is simply the practice of strict self-denial. And Mystical Theology is docility to the Holy Ghost of infused contemplation of the mysteries of the Faith or graces, visions, or revelations. And you can look for these two theologies anywhere and not find the correct definition, except in these books.

But in the "Divine Will or Book of Heaven" seem to be a different approach to perfection and is basically the denial of your own free will and the practice and learning of God's. Before you read the (36) small vols. You need to read the **"Virgin Mary in the Kingdom of the Divine Will"** *to Luisa. Our Lady will explain to you that She never practiced Her own will, and that your* **'human will'** *is considered a dark and stormy and leads you away from God into the sins and pleasures of the world, the devil, and the flesh.*

After the Chastisement, in the 6th period of the world or Church, our passions will be made weaker and it will be easier to stay united to God on an exceptionally high level. This will be because God the Father wants to start over, all the way back to the beginning to before Adam and Eve had sinned. This is new and is being studied by the Church. Jesus tell Luisa that this has been hidden from the Fathers of the Church for our time, and is the first true meaning of the part of **"Our Father"; "Thy Kingdom come Thy Will be done, on earth as it is in Heaven."**

In addition to the **36 Volumes** Jesus dictated the book, **"The Hours of the Passion"** and Our Lady dictated the book, **"Virgin Mary in the Kingdom of the Divine Will"** to Luisa. Jesus told her Confessor, St. Annibale Maria Di Francia, through Luisa, that these 36 Volumes are to be called: **"The Book of Heaven."** (*Small books ½" thk.*)

Our Lord told Luisa that, anyone who reads this book: "The Hours of the Passion" which is dictated by Our Lord to Luisa, who would reads it with true Love, Sincerity, and Compassion for all he suffered, He would grant them for every _word_ they read, He would _save_ one soul. Our Lord has never made such a generous promise before. (*I don't think we understand that God is Pure True Love and

wants us to live with Him to show us all of His most beautiful creation and share with us His hidden secrets. And will do anything to get us to get us to Heaven if only we will freely give up our human will for the Divine Will.)

Now the Explanation of the giving up of your human will for doing the Will of God, The Divine Will. Which is actually the secret to perfection and sanctification and true happiness. Now from the Book: "Virgin Mary in the Kingdom of the Divine Will" a Lesson from the Queen of Heaven: "Child of my maternal Heart, do not fear, I will never forget you. On the contrary, if you always do the Divine Will and live in Its Kingdom, we will be inseparable, I will always carry you clasped in my hand, to lead you and to be your guide, in order to teach you how to live in the Supreme Fiat. Therefore, banish fear; in It, everything is peace and security. The human will is the disturber of souls, and puts in danger the most beautiful works, the holiest things. Everything is unsafe in it: sanctity, virtues, and even the salvation of the soul are in danger; and the characteristic of one who lives of human will is volubility. Who could ever trust one who lets himself be dominated by the human will? No one - neither God, nor man! You become like those empty reeds that turn at every blow of the wind. Therefore, dearest child of mine, if a blow of the wind wants to render you inconstant, plunge yourself into the sea of of the Divine Will, and come to hide on the lap of your Mother, that I may defend you from the wind of the human will; and holding you tightly in my arms, I may render you firm and confident along the path of Its Divine Kingdom.

Now, my child, follow Me before the Supreme Majesty, and listen to Me. With my rapid flights, I would reach Their Divine Arms, and upon arriving, I would feel Their overflowing love which, like mighty waves, covered Me with Their love. Oh! How beautiful it is to be loved by God. In this love one feels happiness, sanctity, infinite joys, and one feels so embellished, that God Himself feels enraptured by the striking beauty He infuses into the creature in loving him or her.

I wanted to imitate Them (The Trinity), and, though little, I did not want to remain behind in returning Their love. So, from the waves of love They had given Me, I would form my waves of love, in order to cover my Creator with my love. In doing this, I would smile, because I knew that my love could never cover the immensity of Their love. But in spite of this, I would try, and my innocent smile would arise on my lips. The Supreme Being would smile at my smile, making feast and amusing Himself with my littleness.

Now, in the middle of our loving stratagems, I remembered the painful state of my human family upon earth *(She talking the whole human race)*, for I too was of their offspring - and how I grieved and prayed that the Eternal Word would descend and put a remedy to it. And I would say this with such tenderness as to reach the point of changing smile and feast into crying. The Most High was so moved by my tears, more so, since they were the tears of a little one; and pressing Me to the Divine Bosom, They dried my tears and said to Me: "My Daughter, do not cry, pluck up courage. Into your hands We have placed the destiny of mankind; We gave You that mandate, and now, to console You more, We make of You the Peacemaker between Us and the human family. So, to You it is given to reconcile Us. The power of Our Will that reigns in You compels Us to give the kiss of peace to poor humanity, which is decayed and unsafe."

Now My child, who can tell you what My Heart felt at this Divine condescension? My love was so great that I felt faint and, in delirium, I was restless, looking for more love as relief for My love.

Now a word to you, My child: If you listen to Me by banishing your own will and giving the royal place to the Divine Fiat, you too will be loved with the striking love of your Creator; you will be His smile, and your smile, will put Him in feast, and will bond peace between the world and God." End of Our Lady's talk.

What is being said in all these 36 vols. Is that to enter into the Kingdom of the Divine Will (which is the innermost part of Heaven, actually Heaven itself) You must become like the Saints and Angels and completely submit your will to the Divine Will, which is to become one with God. And which is what Lucifer would not do. When you give up your will to God's Will, you will begin to give up the things of this world. And begin to become closer to God and His world, and to desire it. In Chapter One this is the way Our Lady asks and invites you to enter into this Kingdom: *"Dearest child, I come to invite you to enter into the Kingdom of your Mother - that is, the Kingdom of the Divine Will; and I knock at the door of your heart, that you may open it to Me. You know? With My own hands I bring you this book as a gift; This book is of gold, my child. I offer it to you with maternal care, so that, in your turn, in reading it, you may learn to live of Heaven and no longer of earth."*

Take the above seriously in this world, so you don't have learn of it in Purgatory. Satan did his own will instead of God's and where did that get him. Now this is going to take some studying, and you have 36 vols. to study. Remember this is all brand new in the Church. Luisa Piccarreta would already be canonized, but Rome is still studying her book dictated by Christ to her. Most of the first books have all been given the Nihil Obstat and the Imprimatur.

So few will see Heaven because they rush through every day life, going to work, making a dollar, searching for pleasure. And never, if ever, first stopping to think of why they were created. Study God, and cause your children to study GOD and learn the science of saints, or you will see none of them in Heaven. AND IT IS SAID THAT IN HELL THE GREATEST AGONY WILL BE TO SEE YOUR LOVED ONES THERE WITH YOU!

Words of Our Lady: "A soul can not have virtue if it does not love God with all it's heart."

Again Our Lady: "No grace descends into the soul except through prayer and mortification of the body."

Words of Our Lady: "Without tribulation few will reach Heaven." (Therefore don't expect things to always go well for you. And the more you love God the more you will long for these crosses.)

Our Lady's words: "Voluntary poverty is the greatest gift you can give to God."

"O child of My Everlasting Love! Whom I have loved more than My own Life; if thou loveth Me and thyself, sin no more. Give up your will and do My Divine Will." Words of Our Lord and King Words of Baby Jesus in the Crib in the Stable to Mary and Joseph: **"I have come from Heaven to earth in order to exsult humility and discredit pride. To Honor poverty and scorn riches and to destroy vanity and establish truth and to enhance the value of labor. Therefore it is My Will that exteriorly you treat Me accordingly to the humble position that I have**

assumed as if I were your natural child. And that you love and revere Me as the Man - God, Son of the Eternal Father." *(In other words no special favors.)*

(When Jesus became a year and half old, Mary made for Him a seamless gray/brownish gown. This clothing never became dirty or soiled and grew with Him. He never removed it until they took it off of Him at the scourging.) For all info: on the "Kingdom of the Divine Will" call: 305-864-1683 or email to: "fjalbas@athlanticbb.net" His books are cheaper than anywhere else. Also go to U-tube: Thomas Fahy and the Divine Will. Also another must listen to is: **I have seen the new world. (Fr. Adam Skwarczynski)"** This very holy priest has been shown by Almighty God the coming time of Kingdom on Earth as it is in Heaven. This is what I have tried to explain above, which will come after the Russian War and the Warning which will kill millions of people who see how far from God and their sins look like. After the Great Miracle and the coming Comet. He will help you understand how deeply you must love and be in union with God when this time comes.

(It is related in the annals of Clairvaux that St. Bernard asked Our Lord which was His greatest unrecorded suffering, and Our Lord answered: "I had on My Shoulder, while I bore My Cross on the Way of Sorrows, a grievous Wound, which was more painful than the others, and which is not recorded by men. Honor this Wound with thy devotion, and I will grant thee whatsoever thou dost ask through its virtue and merit. And in regard to all those who shall venerate this Wound, I will remit to them all their venial sins and will no longer remember their mortal sins.") Here is that Prayer:

PRAYER TO THE SHOULDER WOUND OF CHRIST

O loving Jesus, meek Lamb of God, I, a miserable sinner, salute and worship the most Sacred Wound of Thy Shoulder on which Thou didst bear Thy heavy Cross, which so tore Thy Flesh and laid bare Thy Bones as to inflict on Thee an anguish greater than any other wound of Thy Most Blessed Body. I adore Thee, O Jesus most sorrowful. I praise and glorify Thee, and give Thee thanks for this most sacred and painful Wound; beseeching Thee by that exceeding pain, and by the crushing burden of Thy heavy Cross to be merciful to me, a sinner, to forgive me all my mortal and venial sins, and to lead me on towards Heaven along the Way of Thy Cross. Amen. think St. Bernard asked the Holy Father for 1000 yrs. indulgence for this prayer.

St. Annibale Maria di Francia – Apostle of the Divine Will

Pope John Paul II canonized St. Annibale and declared him to be the Saint for our times to pray to him for Vocations.

"...Know that I no longer occupy myself with anything of my Institutes, since I dedicated myself completely to the great work of the "Divine Will." I talk about It with people of (docile) spirit; I engage in conversation about this topic with whomever I best can; I promote It as much as I can, even in my Institutes." St. Annibale – Feb. 14, 1927

As Father Annibale penetrated into Luisa's spirituality, he came to realize just how necessary it was to make known to the world all the writings on the Divine Will that our Lord made Luisa record, to accelerate the coming of the Kingdom of God on earth for a second try, and so that the Divine Will would be done on earth as it is in Heaven. In fact, he was providentially appointed not only spiritual director in all matters concerning her writings and their publication, but their ecclesiastical censor as well, as we see by this document. St. Annibale Maria di Francia put the 'Imprimatur' and the Bishop of Bari gave it his 'Nihil Obstat' to the first (19) vols. and Rome is finishing reading the rest of her writings for the canonization of Luisa Piccarreta. Who according to **St. Padre Pio** will the greatest saint in Heaven after Our Lady. Why? Because she has been shown how to practice the 'Divine Will' as Adam and Eve and the Blessed Virgin Mary. (Read it.)

The Second Coming of Christ in Glory

"Finally, the power of the serpent will be broken, it will be powerless, it will no longer be able to seduce creatures to say no to the Divine Will. The creatures will say YES to the Divine Will of God.

"In this complete fulfillment of the Divine Will the creation will be almost transposed into an original state, in a state of a new earthly paradise, in which all creatures will say YES to the Divine Will of the Heavenly Father.

"Here in Italy, a certain woman named Luisa Piccarreta, [Servant of God,] whose beatification is in progress, wrote a great book about Divine Will. Once when I was in Mexico, I was shown passages of the book, which related to so many topics about which our book [To the Priests: Our Lady's Beloved Sons] also speaks.

"Let me cite a passage from this book [The Book of Heaven] by the Servant of God, Luisa Piccarreta. She says that **2000** years after creation came the Great Flood so that the water would cleanse mankind; and **2000** years later, came the flood of the Blood: the Redemption; and still **2000** years hence, there will be the flood of fire—a real and spiritual fire, I believe—and finally the Kingdom of [the] Divine Will will come upon this world: because every creature will fulfill the Divine Will of God in a complete way.

"This is what I think, that the Second Coming of Christ in glory will bring this Kingdom of [the] Divine Will. Every creature will fulfill the Will of the Father completely and the Heavenly Father will be glorified in His children, who will say YES to His Divine Will. Christ will bring His Kingdom, the Kingdom of holiness and of humble obedience to the Will of the Heavenly Father."

This a brief explanation of the great secrets of the small part of the "Our Father," namely **"Thy Kingdom come thy will be done on earth as it is in heaven".** *It's amazing the treasure of understanding hidden in this phase. This* secret meaning of the "Our Father" Jesus hid from the father's of the Church for this ending time. Jesus told Luisa that the Father wanted to start all over again, as at the time of Adam and Eve. Jesus told Lusia that the Father would allow the world to satisfy itself with sin as it no longer wants God, which would cause the coming of atheist communist invasion.

When God created Adam & Eve, God gave them the ability to practice, use, and be one with the Divine Will of God. In uniting with God in His Will they took on the attributes of God, to become as little gods. They could see, practice, and understand God and His Will. They were able to have a true union with God that was on going wherever they went and in whatever they did. God was truly present in them in a very real living way. The only time we have God really truly in us is when he comes to us in Holy Communion for a few moments.

This combination of being Immaculate and doing or living in the Divine Will brought them closer to God than any other creature. This is true also for the Blessed Virgin Mary, who also received the altima gift from God.

Luisa Piccarreta was created for this special mission from birth. At the age of 24 she was taken to heaven and a very great ceremony was give in her honor, because of this great work she was about to receive from Jesus. Jesus would dictate all (36) vols. to her. On Sept. 7, 1889 God gave to Lusia that same gift He gave to Adam & Eve and to Mary. This gift will cause her and any one of us who ask for this great gift, to live in common with God.

I hear your question. So what does that mean? Well, before the Chastisement we can ask for this gift and live in close union with God and meriting a very high merit. But not until the Chastisement (or if God chooses to do this after the Judgement Day) those people we walk in a world without sinning. They will be forgiven Original Sin and there will be no effects of original sin. There will no sickness, understanding of the universe and all creation will be infused knowledge. This would be a sacramental gift above the (7) sacraments and greater.

All will be as God wanted it to be in the beginning before the fall of Adam. When the time of death comes for a person. There will be no death. God will tell them to prepare yourself, because I am taking you home to Heaven.

St. Luisa is given by God this similarity, that the Will of God is a very **big river** and our will is like a **little stream** or small river flowing into and with God's Will. Now the the little river takes on the characteristics of the big river and do what the waters of the big river do, now everywhere we go we do God' Will and we take on the colour and beauty and holiness the waters of the Divine Will. This is Divine Sanctity, above ordinary sanctity if that is possible to say. You must understand that their is three person in One God, but there is **not** three wills in One God. There is only One Will in God. If there were more than one will in God, there would be **confusion**.

Likewise the husband is the head of the house and his will is the only will in the house and family. If the wife or child wants their will instead, now there is confusion. Thus you have problem families, troubled families, and divorce in families. If the father of the family is not educated in the ways of God and Catholicism, you will still have problems in the family, especially in raising of children in love and strict discipline and getting them home to Heaven, the Divine Kingdom. You can see much in a man by the way he dresses. Especially when he is goes before God or in public before his neighbor. Why do the police have uniforms, the nuns have habits, the nurses have uniforms, soldiers have uniforms, the boys and girls in a private school have uniforms? It's so they don't show up in baseball caps, 'T' shirts, shorts, shower shoes or tennis shoes. We are a slave to comfort and to today's fashions. Which is today's casual comfortable dress and decadent society.

*One of the very best **youtube** to hear is:* '**Thomas Fahy Garabandal**' You will learn all that is to soon happen. He also tells of the **Divine Will** which automatically comes up right away after the Chastisement.

Climate temperature will be very mild all over the world.

Another great way to gather merits is to make reparation to God by the many Revelations God has given us through his saints. Here is the revelations to Sr. Mary of St. Peter, Discalced Carmelite Nun of Tours 1840's, France, in favor of those who honor **His Holy Face**. Details of these revelations are found in the book named

'The Golden Arrow'

May the most Holy, most Sacred, most Adorable, Most Incomprehensible and Ineffable Name of God.

Be always Praised, Blessed, Loved, Adored and Glorified, In Heaven, on Earth and in Hell, By all the Creatures of God, And by the Sacred Heart of Our Lord Jesus Christ, In the most Holy Sacrament of the Altar. Amen

Our Lord also revealed to Sister Maria Pierina of the Daughters of the Immaculate Conception on May 16,1916 the same "Devotion to the Holy Face". As a novice she was permitted to do all night adoration. On the night between Holy Thursday and Good Friday, while she was praying before the Crucifix, she beard it say "Kiss Me." Sister Maria Pierina obeyed and her lips felt not the contact with the image of plaster but the soft face of Jesus.

Blessed Maria Pierina de Micheli was a holy nun who died in 1945, was urged in many visions by the Blessed Mother and Jesus Himself to spread the devotion to the Holy Face of Jesus, in reparation for the many insults that Jesus suffered in His Passion, such as to be slapped, spit upon and kissed by Judas, as well as now being dishonoured in many ways in the Blessed Sacrament by neglect, sacrileges and profanations.

She was given a medal, which on one side, bore a replica of the Holy Shroud of Turin and the inscription, "Illumina, Domine, vultum tuum super nos." (Psalm 66: "May, O Lord, the light of Thy countenance shine upon us"). On the reverse, was a radiant host with the words, "Mane nobiscum, Domine." ("Stay with us, O Lord").

After great difficulties, she obtained permission to have the medal cast. Even the expenses for the casting were miraculously met when she found on her desk an envelope with the exact amount of the bill, 11,200 lire. The evil spirit showed his chagrin and rage at the medals by flinging them down and burning the pictures of the Sacred Face, and beating Mother Pierina savagely.

In 1940, when the Second World War had the world in turmoil, Italy saw a wide distribution of this medal. Relatives and friends saw that their soldiers, sailors and aviators were provided with the replica of the Holy Face of Jesus since the medal was already famous for its miracles and countless spiritual and temporal favours.

Blessed Maria Pierina de Micheli was beatified on the Solemnity of the Most Holy Trinity, Sunday, May 30th, 2010 at the Basilica of Santa Maria Maggiore in Rome by His Excellency, Archbishop Angelo Amato.

On the Tuesday following Passion Sunday, Jesus returned to her and said, "every time my face os contemplated, I will pour out my love into the heart of those persons and by means of My Holy Face the salvation of many souls will be obtained."

On the First Tuesday of 1937, while she was at prayer Our Lord told her: "Perhaps, some souls fear that the devotion to My Holy Face will diminish that to My Heart. On the contrary it will be a completion and augmentation of that devotion. Souls contemplation My Face participate in My Sorrow. They feel the necessity of love and reparation. Is this not the true devotion to My Heart?"

In May 1938, whilst at prayer on the step of the Altar, a beautiful Lady appeared to her carrying in her hand a Scapular, made of two pieces of flannel joined by a cord. One of these pieces bore the image of the Holy face of Jesus with the words "Let Thy Face shine upon us, O Lord" and the other a Host surrounded by rays and the words "Remain with us, Lord." Gently the Lady approached and said: *Listen carefully and report everything to the Father: This Scapular is an armour of defence, a shield of strength, a token of the love and mercy which Jesus wishes to give the the would in these times of lust and hatred against God and His Church. Diabolical nets are thrown to wrench the Faith from hearts, evils abound, true apostles are few, and the remedy is the Holy Face of Jesus. All who wear a Scapular like this and make, if possible, every Tuesday a visit to the Blessed Sacrament, in order to repair the outrages which the face of my son Jesus received during His Passion and receives every day in the Holy Eucharist,*

Will be strenghtened in Faith, prompt to defend it,

And to overcome all difficulties internal and external.

Further they will have a peaceful death under the loving gaze of my Divine Son."

The same year Jesus appeared again covered with blood and with much sadness said: *"See how I suffer. Nevertheless I am understood by so few. What ingratitude on the part of those who say they love Me. I have given my heart as a sensible object of My great Love for man and I give My Face as a sensible object of my sorrow for the sins of man, I desire that it be honoured by a special feast on Tuesday in Quinquagesima, the feast will be preceded by a novena in which the faithful make reparation with Me uniting themselves with My Sorrow."*

In 1939 Our Lord said to Mother Pierina: *"I wish that My Holy Face be honoured in a particular manner on Tuesdays."*

Money was needed to make the scapulars, and Our Lady promised She would help, and so She did. One morning Mother Pierina saw on a little table an envelope: she opened it to find L. 11,200.

The devil was madden at this and tried to frighten her from distributing the medals. The devil threw her down in the corridor and than down the steps. The devil tore up the pictures of the Holy Face.

Mother Pierina was wondered because she got medals made instead scapulars. She turned to Our Lady and our Lady appeared April 17, 1943 and said to her: *"My daughter, be calm, the Scapulars have been substituted by the medal with the same promises and favours, but it only remains to be widely distributed. Just now my heart is set on the feast of the Face of My Divine Son. Tell the Pope that it preoccupies Me."* She blessed her and departed.

This Metal of the Holy Face has obtained, dangers have been averted, cures, conversion, liberality condemned.

"O Holy Face of my Sweet Jesus, by that tenderness of love and unspeakable grief with which the Blessed Virgin Mary beheld Thee in Thee in Thy painful Passion, grant sorrow, and fulfill more perfectly the Holy Will of God. Amen."

Prayers and Promises of Our Lord Jesus Christ

1.) By offering My Face to My Eternal Father, nothing will be refused, and the conversion of many sinners will be obtained.

2.) By My Holy Face, they will work wonders, appease the anger of God and draw down mercy on sinners.

3.) All those who honor My Face in a spirit of reparation will by so doing perform the office of the pious Veronica.

4.) According to the care they take in making reparation to My Face disfigured by blasphemers, so will I take care of their souls which have been disfigured by sin. My Face is the Seal of the Divinity, which has the virtue of reproducing in souls the image of God.

5.) Those who by words, prayers or writings defend My cause in the Work of Reparation, especially My priests, I will defend before My Father, and will give them My Kingdom.

6.) As in a kingdom they can procure all that is desired with a coin stamped with the King's effigy, so in the Kingdom of Heaven they will obtain all they desire with the precious coin of My Holy Face.

7.) Those who on earth contemplate the wounds of My Face, shall in Heaven behold it radiant with glory.

8.) They will receive in their souls a bright and constant irradiation of My Divinity, that by their likeness to My Face they shall shine with particular radiance in Heaven.

9.) I will defend them, I will preserve them and I assure them of Final Perseverance.

10.) I will grant them contrition so perfect, that their very sins shall be changed in My sight into jewels of precious gold.

11.) None of these persons shall ever be separated from Me.

12.) In offering My Face to My father, they will appease His anger and they will purchase as with a celestial coin, pardon for poor sinners.

13.) I will open My Mouth to plead with My Father to grant all the petitions that they will present to Me.

14.) I will illuminate them with My light, I will consume them with My love I will render them fruitful of good works.

15.) They will, as the pious Veronica, wipe My adorable Face outraged by sin, and I will imprint My divine Features in their souls.

16.) At their death, I will renew in them the image of God effaced by sin.

17.) By resemblance to My Face, they will shine more than many others in eternal life and the brilliancy of My Face will fill them with joy.

Saint Mechtilde asked Our Lord if those who celebrate and honor the memory of His Holy Face should never be deprived of His amiable company. Our Lord replied, "Not one of them shall be separated from Me."

"By my Face you shall work miracles."

The Things to Remember and Live By:

Only One Thing is Necessary the SALVATION of YOUR SOUL. Work keeps you alive to do this.

1.) Receive frequently the Sacraments of Penance and Holy Communion.

2.) Say your morning and evening prayers. Make acts of Faith, Hope, and Charity every day; at night before retiring, examine your Conscience and make an act of Contrition. (*Always before you falls to sleep.*)

3.) Attend Mass devoutly, especially on all Sundays and Holy Days of Obligation. (Receive Holy Communion at every Mass if possible, it helps enlighten to avoid sin, take away temporal punishment, and cleans your soul of venial sins.)

4.) If there exists any Church Societies in your parish, join at least one of them. (*Anything done for God, Church, or the community will raise yourself before God and take away temporal punishment.*)

5.) It is an obligation binding under pain sin to contribute to the support of the Church.

6.) You are obligated to avoid any Occasion of sin, which can be any person, place, or thing which will likely lead you into sin.

7.) Practice Daily Devotion to the Blessed Virgin Mary, pray to Her particularly for the grace of a Holy and Happy Death. *(It is impossible to save your soul without Our Lady. St. Alphonsus Liguori)*

8.) **Remember:** Death - Judgment - Heaven - Hell - (On a daily meditation.) and you will persevere unto the end.

Practice the most precious of all devotions: Meditations on the **Wounds and Blood of Christ** and How He got them. There is so many promises and indulgences attached to praying (5) Our Father, (5) Hail Marys, (5) Glory Be's. Our Lord made (5) promises or graces by reciting for (3) years in honor of His Blood:

1.) The plenary indulgence and remittance of your sins at death.

2.) you will be free from the pains of Purgatory.

3.) If you should die before completing the said (3) years, for you it will be the same as if you had completed them.

4.) It will be upon your death the same as if you had shed all your blood for the holy Faith.

5.) I will descend from Heaven to take your soul and that of your relatives, until the fourth generation.

THE PROMISES OF OUR LORD

To Those Who Devotedly Pray the Chaplet of the Precious Blood

1. I promise to protect any person who devoutly prays this Chaplet against evil attacks.

2. I will guard his five senses.

3. I will protect him from sudden death.

4. Twelve hours before his death, he will drink. My Precious Blood and eat My Body.

5. Twenty-four hours before his death, I will show him my five wounds that he may feel a deep contrition for all his sins and have a perfect knowledge of them.

6. Any person who makes a novena with it will get their intentions. His prayer will be answered.

7. I will perform many wonderful miracles through it.

8. Through it, I will destroy many secret societies and set free many souls in bondage, by My mercy.
9. Through it, I will save many souls from Purgatory.
10. I will teach him My way, he who honors My Precious Blood through this Chaplet.
11. I will have mercy on them who have mercy on My Precious Wounds and Blood.
12. Whoever teaches this prayer to another person will have an indulgence of four years.

To Those Who Devotedly Pray the Consolation and Adoration Prayers

1. My children, I promise to protect anyone who devotedly consoles and adores Me with this prayer against evil attacks. He will not die a sudden death. He will not be burned by fire.
2. My children, I promise to protect anyone against the attacks of evil spirits who devotedly consoles and adores Me.
3. Any soldier who prays this prayer before entering a battlefield will not be defeated. No bullet will have any effect on him.
4. If this prayer is said to a woman in labor, she will have lesser pains and any woman who devotedly says these prayers will deliver safely.
5. Put this prayer on the head of any child disturbed by evil spirits, My Cherubim will protect him.
6. I promise to protect any family from lightning and thunder effects, and any house where this prayer is will be protected against storms.
7. If this prayer is said to the dying before his death, I promise that his soul will not be lost.
8. Any sinner who consoles and adores Me through this prayer will obtain conversion.
9. I promise to protect them with My Precious Blood and hide them in My Holy Wounds all who console and adore Me. Poison will have no effect on them. I will guard their five senses.

10. I promise to baptize aborted children who are killed daily in the world, and put a deep contrition on the hearts of their parents through the power of My Precious Blood.
11. All who devotedly console and adore Me with this prayer until death will join the heavenly Armies and Choirs. I will give them the Morning Star.

To Those Who Hear or Pray These Anguished Appeals Receive the following:

1. Children, whenever the Reparation Prayer is said with love, I promise to convert the twelve most hardened sinners in the world.
2. I will allow my Precious Blood to flow into every soul that hears this prayer said. Their love for Me will grow.
3. I will forgive the sins of a nation that turns back to Me through this prayer. They will not suffer the weight of the curses due to their sins.

For All Those Who Devoutly Observe the Gethsemane Hours

1. All who remain in Gethsemane with Me will receive a special grace from Me to withstand hard trials. I promise to sustain them with a special grace of faith and love.
2. During their hour of trials, I will console them, because they console me, now that I am in agony.
3. Those who are faithful to this hour will have nothing to fear from the antichrist.

On the Crown of Thorns

1. I will heal the wounds of their hearts, those who adore My Sacred Head through this Crown.
2. I will console those who console Me through this Crown.
3. I will open the ocean of the Divine Mercy on those who adore the wounds of My Sacred Head through this Crown.
4. All who adore the Most Precious Blood from My Sacred Head through this Crown will receive the grace of Divine Wisdom.

5. I will guard their five senses.

6. When you touch this Crown with love, I will allow a drop of My Blood to fall on your head.

7. I will renew the love of a repented sinner who can mercifully adore My Sacred Head with this Crown.

8. There is always a sprinkle of My Most Precious Blood wherever this thorn is, I am not far; I am near.

9. I will crown his head with a victorious crown, anyone who adores the Sacred Wounds and Blood of My Sacred Head through this Crown.

10. I promise to show them My Sacred Head one day before they die, all who love their crown and adore My Sacred Head through it, so as to have perfect knowledge of their sins and repent.

11. On 15 September 2001, Our Lady asked her Son Jesus to bless the Crown of Thorns with healing power.

To Those Who Devotedly Venerate
The Agonizing Crucifix

1. To prepare you for the battle, I give you My Agonizing Crucifix. I promise to protect anyone who has this Crucifix against the evil forces.

2. Through this Crucifix, I will deliver many from captivity.

3. Whenever you raise this Crucifix against evil power, I will open heaven and let My Precious Blood flow to subdue the evil power.

4. I will let My Precious Blood flow from all My Sacred Wounds and cover all who venerate My Wounds and Blood through this Crucifix.

5. I promise to protect any house where this Crucifix is against any destructive power in the hour of darkness.

6. I promise to perform numerous miracles through this Crucifix.

7. I will break their hearts of stone and pour My love on them that venerate My Agonizing Crucifix.

8. I promise also to draw straying souls closer to Myself through this Crucifix.

9. Children, in the days of the evil one you will be able to go freely without any harm through this Crucifix.

Finally, Our Lord emphasized; "Children, through this Cross I will conquer. This Cross will soon be a victorious Cross."

After This Devotion is none other than the **Devotion to Our Lady of Sorrows.** Our Blessed Lady revealed to St. Mechtilde and St. Bridget that those who practice a tender devotion to her Sorrows will enjoy the following advantages:

1.) Contrition at the hour of death.
2.) Assistance in all their afflictions, and especially at the hour of death.
3.) Jesus Christ will imprint in their hearts compassion for His sufferings and the sorrows of Mary, that He may hereafter reward them for it in Heaven.
4.) Jesus promised His Mother, who had suffered of much on His account, that He would grant whatever grace may be to the advantage of those amongst Her Children who are devout to Her Sorrows.

There is no grace more precious than that of a good and holy death; it is, we may say, the grace of graces. Its gives the crown to all other graces, and without it the most precious gifts are forever useless.

Here are **Seven Graces** the Blessed Virgin Grants to the Souls Who Honor Her Daily by saying Seven Hail Mary's and Meditating on Her Tears and Sorrows. The Devotion was passed to us by St. Bridget:

1. I will grant peace to their families.
2. They will be enlightened about the divine mysteries.
3. I will console them in their pains and I will accompany them in their work.
4. I will give them as much as they ask for as long as it does not oppose the adorable will of my Divine Son or the sanctification of their souls.

5. I will defend them in their spiritual battles with the infernal enemy and I will protect them at every instant of their lives.
6. I will visibly help them at the moment of their death, they will see the face of their Mother.
7. I have obtained (This Grace) from my Divine Son, that those who propagate this devotion to my tears and dolors, will be taken directly from this earthly life to eternal happiness since all their sins will be forgiven and my son will be their eternal consolation and joy.

The Fifteen Secret Tortures and Suffering of Our Lord and Savior Jesus Christ, Chaplet Prayer

"I Look for one that would comfort me, and I found none."

This chaplet consists of 15 beads + 3 beads at the beginning.

Revealed to the pious, God-loving Sister Mary Magdalen of Sancta Clara Order, Franciscan, who lived, died and was beatified in Rome. Jesus fulfilled the wish of this Sister, who desired to ardently know something about the secret sufferings which He endured the night before His death.

This devotion is approved and recommended by His Holiness Clement II, (1730-1740)

On the first 3 beads is said:

"I looked for one that would comfort me, and I found none" followed by an Our Father, Hail Mary and Glory be....

On each single bead meditate upon the secret tortures and sufferings.

On the Crucifix say the prayer that Jesus gave to Sister Mary Magdalen of Santa Clara. Then, Jesus added,

"My daughter, I desire that you let everybody know the Fifteen Secret Tortures in order that everyone of them be honored."

"Anyone who daily offers Me, with love, one of these sufferings and says with fervor the following prayer, will be rewarded with eternal glory on the day of judgement."

The Fifteen Secret Tortures and Suffering of Our Lord and Savior Jesus Christ

1. They fastened My feet with a rope and dragged Me over the stepping stones of the staircase, down into a filthy, nauseating cellar.
2. They took off My clothing and stung My body with iron joints.
3. They attached a rope around My body and pulled Me on the ground from end to end.
4. They hanged Me on a wooden piece with a slip knot until I slipped out and fell down. Overwhelmed by this torture, I wept bloody tears.
5. They tied Me to a post and pierced My body with various arms.
6. They struck Me with stones and burnt Me with blazing embers and torches.
7. They pierced Me with awls; sharp spears tore My skin, flesh and arteries out of My body.
8. They tied Me to a post and made Me stand barefoot on an incandescent metal sheet.
9. They crowned Me with an iron crown and wrapped My eyes with the dirtiest possible rags.
10. They made Me sit on a chair covered with sharp pointed nails, causing deep wounds in My body.
11. They poured on My wounds liquid lead and resin and, after this torture, they pressed Me on the nailed chair so that the nails went deeper and deeper into My flesh.
12. For shame and affliction, they drove needles into the holes of My uprooted beard. They tied my hands behind My back and led Me walking out of prison with strikes and blows.
13. They threw Me upon a cross and attached Me so tightly that I could hardly breathe anymore.
14. They threw at My head as I lay on the earth, and they stepped on Me, hurting My breast. Then, taking a thorn from My crown, they drove it into My tongue.
15. They poured into My mouth the most immodest excretions, as they uttered the most infamous expressions about Me.

Then, Jesus added,

"My daughter, I desire that you let **everybody** know the **Fifteen Secret Tortures** in order that everyone of them be honored." "Anyone who daily offers Me, with love, one of these (15) sufferings and says with fervor the following prayer, will be rewarded with eternal glory on the day of judgment." *(If you have no time to say the Chaplet Rosary, at least meditate on one torture, and say the prayer.) (Another great way to please God is to Make the Stations of the Cross. There are many ways of making the Stations, the best way is according to Doctor of the Church St. Alphonsus liguori. He said, "If you can not meditate, than pray while looking at a picture." The 'Our Father, Hail Mary, Glory Be, which should be said because of the hidden mystery, power, the deep meaning, and the great honor they give the Blessed Trinity in the Our Father and to Mary in the Angelic Salutation, and the abundant grace they give us, the accidental joy it gives the angels. To neglect them is to rob the honor and joy they give to God and Mary. Also alway finish the Stabat Mater to Mary in Her sorrows. Indulgence is attached to this prayer.)*

~ P R A Y E R ~

My Lord and My God, it is my unchangeable will to honor and compassionate you in these Fifteen Secret Torments when You shed Your Most Precious Blood; as many times as there are grains of sand around the seas and the waters of the earth, grains of sands in all desserts, fruit in orchards, leaves on trees, flowers in gardens and fields, stars in the sky, angels in Heaven, creatures from the beginning to the end of time on earth. So many thousands of times may you be glorified, praised and honored, O Most love-worthy Lord Jesus Christ in - Your Most Sacred Heart, Your Most Precious Blood, Your Divine Sacrifice for mankind, Your Sacramental presence in Tabernacles on all the altars, Your Most Holy Virgin Mother, the nine glorious choirs of Angels and the Blessed Phalanx of the Saints, from myself and everyone, now and forever, and unto all eternal ages.

I desire, my dear Jesus, to give You thanksgiving, to love, and to serve you, to make repair and atonement for all my sins and ignominies, and to offer You my soul and body through the Immaculate Heart of Mary as Your possession forever. Likewise, I regret all my sins and beg Your pardon, O my Lord and my God. And I offer You all the merits of Your Passion to repair for my sins and all sins of mankind, to obtain a holy and happy death at the last hour of my life. The deliverance of the poor souls from Purgatory especially those dearest to me, and those dearest to You my Lord, and thy Mother. I desire this prayer be renewed at each hour of my life until death, O my lovable Jesus, and Sweet Savior, fortify my resolution and never permit it to be destroyed by any wretched men nor Satan. **Amen**.

The Way You Prayer shows the way You Believe. When Driving by a Church, make the sign of the Cross? God **sees** You. He is always watching to see what **quality** of man you are. Make the sign of the Cross as you drive. And before all your work, play, eating, or whatever you do. Think of God at all times.

A very beautiful and extraordinary devotion to the Wounds and Blood of Our Lord: This Prayer is called

The Heavenly Court of Saint Lutgarde

INTRODUCTION By Father JOHANN LUDWIG a MUSIS, Provincial of the Franciscan Order for the Province of Strasburg, 1662.

This Way of Prayer, already so widely known, has brought light and comfort to innumerable human hearts during the long years of its existence. The blessed and wonder-working virgin Lutgarde it was who made the Prayer, a Sister of the Third Order of St. Francis, the Foundress and first Reverend Mother of the Convent of St. Clare at Wittichen in the Black Forest; but it was I, Father Johann Ludwig a Musis, who gave to the Prayer it's written and printed life. This was at Freiburg in the year 1635.

"There were two unmarried sisters who had lived together for forty years. To these, about two years ago, I showed the Devotion of the Heavenly

Court, and gave them a copy of the book which I had brought with me from Germany.

Thereupon they set to work in good earnest and with faith and diligence went through the Prayer, perhaps even twice.

These two sisters have just died and this is the manner of their dying: The elder of the two fell ill on the very day on which she finished the Devotion of the Heavenly Court. On the fourth day of her illness the Lord Christ appeared to her, and with Him His Blessed Mother, and the entire heavenly host. She saw them all full clearly, and spoke of them to those who were standing around the bed. Some among the heavenly company she recognized, and these she named.

Most earnestly did she charge the bystanders to make use of the Devotion of the Heavenly Court, saying that the Wicked Enemy could not approach those who used it, with so great and special a power did the holy Guardian Angels defend them. Lastly, she turned to her sister, who was standing there as yet all cheerful and vigorous and spoke these words: "I beg of thee likewise to finish the holy Prayer, for then thou shalt come with me." And the next day the sister ended the Prayer and fell ill and died just as had the elder; and the whole house was filled with a sweet and rare and costly perfume."

Thus ran the writing of the aforesaid noble lady, and her words are of a truth to be believed, for many similar instances are reported in other places from the use of this Devotion. I myself was present at the deathbed of a devout virgin named Katharina Neidinger, daughter of a burgher-baker of Villingen, whose name was the first to be inscribed by me in my register of the Heavenly Court. While as yet there was no sign of her immediate death, she suddenly exclaimed in a clear voice: "O Joy of Joys! O Grace of Graces!" And in this very outburst of rejoicing did she unexpectedly render her soul to God. Other similar instances I pass over, for indeed those I have given are amply sufficient to show how pleasing is the Devotion of the Heavenly Court to Christ our Lord.

For the Heavenly Father was shown to them surrounded by all the heavenly Spirits; but His only-begotten Son, Jesus Christ, was in the midst of a company of His dear Saints, who by their valiant lives had deserved to be chosen for His courtiers, and some to be His faithful counselors.

The Holy Ghost appeared to the Sisters surrounded by those souls who on earth had burned with zeal for the Glory of God, and had been consumed with longing to extend His Kingdom. Furthermore, they saw the Mother of God as Queen of Heaven reigning over all pure and virgin souls.

And the four-and-twenty Ancients sat there as clerks of the Court, the four Evangelists as chancellors and keepers of the archives, the holy Apostles as judges and privy councilors, and all the holy Angels as attendants and noble stewards. The holy Mother Lutgarde sees how Mary, the Queen of Heaven, founds a Heavenly Court also on earth then (continues Father Musaus) the two devout Sisters saw how he Queen of Heaven held a Court, after the fashion of the great on earth. And they understood that the Court was held in praise of God, the Eternal King, and in honor of the Most Holy Trinity. And at the same time they were shown what manner of men are to be admitted to the Holy Court of the glorious Queen of Heaven.

These men are indeed diverse: **Firstly**, those who give themselves up to contemplating, imitating, and tenderly pitying the all-holy life and sufferings and death of our Saviour Christ, and who have a heartfelt and compassionate devotion to the sorrowful Mother of God, Mary of Many Sorrows.

Secondly, those who lead an exemplary and edifying life, detached from all the passions of earth, whose whole desire and longing, will and heart, are fixed upon Eternity alone.

Thirdly, those who are patient in adversity, and place all their trust and confidence and hope in God.

Fourthly, those who are peaceable, loving, humble of heart, despisers of their own selves.

Such as these are qualified to enter the Heavenly Court. These are they who in the world beyond the grave will merrily come to the Heavenly Court and there be crowned by God with a crown of honour.

And on St. Lutgarde the task fell (as once on St. John the Baptist) to serve her Lord by preparing a path. "It is not enough," said He to her, "that men should learn through thee the excellence of the reward of Heaven; thou must also point out the road which leads to their eternal possession."

One day, as St. Lutgarde earnestly besought God that He would show her the Way of Prayer that pleased Him best of all, a very beautiful Prayer was infused into her, which comprised in itself the whole of the life and sufferings of Christ. And forthwith her memory retained it' so accurately that she repeated it every day with the greatest devotion. The Blessed Virgin told Lutgarde that she herself had begged the grace of this Prayer for her. The Prayer, as recorded by Father Musaus, runs thus:

THE PRAYER OF THE HEAVENLY COURT

O, all-holy and all-merciful Redeemer, Source of all graces, and our most kind Jesus! Out of incomprehensible love for us poor children of Eve, has Thou left Thy seat on the right hand of Thy Heavenly Father, and willed to clothe Thyself with our helplessness and poverty.

Nay, the more surely to win us to love Thee in return, Thou hast made Thyself helpless and poor beyond us all. No possible trouble, no possible toil, has Thou spared Thyself in order to save us from the wicked enemy, and make us the children of Thy Father in Heaven.

Bitterly do I grieve that up till now, 1, a valueless and wretched worm of earth, have so little understood the excess of Thy Love, and have given Thee such poor thanks for all the hardships, pains and martyrdom Thou has borne for me.

And therefore do 1 now offer up to Thee this my unworthy prayer, in honor of Thy most holy life and sufferings and death, and of every year and day and hour Thou didst spend on earth for the salvation of lost and sinful men.

And I offer Thee too, from the inmost depths of my heart, all the myriad acts of praise and love and gratitude of the nine Choirs of holy Angels, and indeed of all creatures from the first moment of their creation until now, and all the acts made by the Most Blessed Virgin Mary with the greatest possible love and devotion since her Immaculate Conception to this very day, together with those she will not cease to make through all the instants of Eternity. *(At this point the Heavenly Court center will send you which number mystery you are say for the next six months. Roll call is every February. They send you a File #; a Group # ; a patron saint to be under.)*

And I offer Thee these acts that 1 may thank Thee perfectly for all Thou hast done for me:

1. For Thy choice from all Eternity of the Most Blessed Virgin Mary to be the Mother of God;
2. For her Immaculate Conception, and her preservation from every spot of original sin, in which all other mortals are conceived and born;
3. For the most pure nativity of Thy Immaculate Mother, which shed alight over the whole world and caused joy in Heaven.
4. For Thine own wonderful Conception by the power of the Holy Ghost in the virgin womb of Thy chosen Mother which was announced by the Archangel Gabriel;
5. For the first journey Thou didst take, hidden in the most pure womb of Thy Holy Mother, a journey over the hills to Thy cousin Elizabeth and her child John-John who., even as Thou didst, then lay hidden;
6. For Thy holy Nativity, when Thou didst come into the world in the greatest poverty and wast born in a stable amid senseless beasts, without even a pillow on which to lay Thy Sacred Head, or clothes wherewith to warm and protect Thy tender limbs;

7. For the great honor Thou didst vouchsafe to receive from the Adoration of the Three Wise Men and from their costly symbolic gifts gold and frankincense, and myrrh;

8. For Thy first blood-shedding at the Circumcision, which Thou didst suffer for our sakes and out of humble obedience to the Law of Moses;

9. For Thy most holy Presentation in the Temple at Jerusalem by Thy Blessed Mother, in accordance with the Law of Moses;

10. For the bitter persecution which began even with Thy tenderest years, and which drove Thee into the godless land of Egypt and kept Thee there for a long space of time;

11. For Thy most dear Mother's anxious search for Thee, and then her joyful finding of Thee amid the doctors in the Temple, after She had sought Thee for three days with bitter grief and pain;

12. For the submission Thou didst show to Mary and Joseph at Nazareth rendering them all manner of humble, filial services;

13. For all Thy teaching and preaching, for Thy hard and dangerous journeys, and especially for all the fatigue and toil Thou didst undergo for our salvation;

14. For Thy most holy fast of forty days, and Thy constant, fervent prayers in the desert;

15. For Thy great and glorious miracles, worked to convince the stubborn Jews;

16. For Thine agonized prayer and bloody sweat in the Garden of Gethsemane, when shuddering and sorrowful unto death, Thou wert yet perfectly resigned to Thy Father's Will;

17. For the false kiss with which the faithless Judas betrayed Thee and delivered Thee into the hands of wicked men;

18. For the painful bands and cruel cords of Thine infamous captors, and for their grievous dragging and pulling of Thee over stones and through water and briars;

19. For the many false accusations devised and brought against Thy most holy Person before Annas and Caiaphas, Pilate and Herod;

20. For the most painful treatment meted out to Thee when Thou wast ignominiously drawn from one unjust Judge to another;

21. For the hard and worse than blasphemous blow Thou didst receive on Thy most Holy Face from a servant of the High Priest;
22. For the copious and most painful blood-shedding when every part of Thy most holy Body was torn by the rods and scourges of the executioners;
23. For Thy nakedness, and the bitter shame Thou didst experience when most of Thy garments were torn from Thee and Thou wert thus bound to the pillar before all the crowd;
24. For the jeering, scoffing, and mock genuflections by which godless Jews ridiculed Thee to Thy holy Face;
25. For the sharp pressure on Thy sacred Head of the crown of thorns, which caused Thy Precious Blood to flow down over Thy Face;
26. For Thy piteous appearance before Pilate, who by his exclamation BEHOLD THE MAN tried to move the people to compassion;
27. For the sentence pronounced on Thee by Pilate, for the manner in which Thou wast led forth to die, and for the heavy weight of the Cross;
28. For Thy dolorous meeting with Thy sorrow-stricken Mother and the other holy women who had followed Thee on the Path to Calvary and shed tears of pity over Thee;
29. For the painful removal of most of Thy clothing to the renewal of Thy wounds, and for the merciless nailing to the wood of the Cross, as also for all the priceless words spoken on the Cross, and the final surrender of Thy Spirit;
30. For Thy glorious Resurrection on the third day after Thy sufferings, when Thou didst appear to Thy Mother, Thy Disciples and Apostles, and after that to many others;
31. For Thy wonderful Ascension into Heaven and glorious return to Thy Heavenly Father, when Thine earthly pilgrimage was ended and Thou hadst triumphed victoriously over the world and Satan;
32. For the wonderful fiery Descent of the Holy Ghost on Thy Disciples and Apostles and Thy most beloved Mother on the holy Day of Pentecost.
33. For the lordly triumph Thou didst celebrate when Thou didst assume Thy beloved Mother, body and soul, into Heaven;

34. For Thy festival of joy, in which were associated the Father and the Holy Ghost, at the exaltation of Thy most glorious Mother over all the Choirs of Angels, and at her Coronation as the Queen of Heaven;

For all these, and more especially for every beat of Thy Heart and every act of love, for all Thy thoughts and desires, for all the silent and the uttered prayers which Thou didst offer while on earth, and still dost offer in the Most Holy Sacrament of the Altar - for all these I tender Thee a thousand thanks, and ask Thee most humbly that Thou wouldst grant to me and to all who have commended themselves to my prayers, or for whom I ought to pray, perfect contrition for our sins and a firm determination never again to offend Thy Divine Majesty, together with the grace of final perseverance. Grant that I and all men may enjoy Thy grace here, and after this toilsome life is over may be received into the company of Thine elect, and be united with them to the Source of Eternal Joy - which is none but Thou Thyself, O dearest Lord. And may we be permitted to gaze at last on Thy most holy Face, Who with the Father and the Holy Ghost livest and reignest, God, forever and ever. **Amen.**

A number of men despised these rivers of grace and turned away from them, and these the holy Mother saw hurled with ignominy into a deep abyss. A nun of the Order founded by St. Francis, presumably attached to the Convent of Wittichen, had grave doubts of the **Prayer of the Heavenly Court** and of its efficacy, and she besought God to enlighten her on the matter and to remove the temptation. And in truth her doubts were soon resolved by a secret and Divine communication, which she did indeed keep hidden, but which had the result that she afterwards took every opportunity of seeking out persons who would follow in common with her the Devotion of the Heavenly Court. She even made an occasion of speaking of this Prayer, so rich in graces, to the Abbess of a neighboring Convent, who, however, gave but little credence to her words. "In good sooth" (so ran her answer), "we have a number of more beautiful and more spiritual prayer s in our Convent, and, my daughters can make use of these at choice; nor have we any time to devote to so long and troublesome a Prayer."

But during the ensuing night, the Holy Mother of God appeared to the Abbess, reproved her for those words, and herself instructed her as to the great power of this Prayer.

The result was that not only did the Abbess and all her daughters make use of the Prayer from that day forth, but they did all that in them lay to induce others to do the same.

Once the holy Mother Lutgarde saw Our Dear Lord Jesus Christ in a vision after the following manner: He hung on a Cross, and fresh Blood was streaming from all His Sacred Wounds. And men were turning towards this stream of the Precious Blood, in such fashion that some received that which flowed from the Heart, and others again that which flowed from the Feet of the Saviour. By means of this picture God taught the Saint that through the Prayer of the Heavenly Court many men should be saved and brought to eternal blessedness.

The main purpose of this devotion then is to make Christ live in the lives of men. By contemplating the 34 Mysteries over and over again, the Life of Christ becomes a Reality, the main focus-point and a pattern for our lives. For subject matter on the 34 Mysteries, use the Sacred Scriptures, especially the Gospels, "Way of Divine Love," "Divine Mysteries of the Most Holy Rosary," "The Path to Glory," etc.

THE HEAVENLY COURT

In giving this prayer to St. Lutgarde in 1246 Jesus said, "Whosoever shall piously and devoutly recite this Prayer, to him will I in My great mercy give 34 human souls; rescue from everlasting death 34 human souls who would otherwise die in sin . . . For his sake too, I will release 34 souls from Purgatory. As for the man himself who had made this prayer, his reward shall be multiplied as the grass of the field whose blades no one can number." Dividing His life and suffering into 34 Mysteries Our Lord requested that we say 1000 Our Fathers, Hail Marys and Glory be's for each Mystery and for the most spiritual merit picture in our mind the Mystery as we say the prayers. No time limit was set but our intention must be to complete it in our lifetime. You are to say (5) Our Fr., Hail Marys, and Glory Be's each day, which spreads out to a little over six months.

Go to TAN Books for this little RED booklet. The address to enroll is in the booklet, and you will be told how to say it correctly. And given a mystery to start with. March is roll call to give a new mystery.

The **Seven Dolors of Mary Rosary**
(Say Seven Hail Marys ea. Day)

1.) The Prophecy of Simeon.
2.) The Flight into Egypt.
3.) The Loss of the Child Jesus in the Temple.
4.) The Meeting of Jesus and Mary on the Way to Calvary.
5.) The Crucifixion.
6.) The taking down of the Body of Jesus from the Cross.
7.) The Burial of Jesus.

A Prayer to Start the Day

My God, I offer Thee, all Thou appointest me, all the day may bring, of joy or suffering. All Thou givest today, all Thou takest away, all Thou wouldst have me be, my God, I offer Thee in union with your Divine Will. Teach me, my Lord, to live in the Divine Will, to be sweet and gentle in all the events of life. In the disappointments and the thoughtlessness of some; in wrongs and injuries I must bear patiently. Let me put myself aside to think of the happiness of others to hide my little pains and heartaches, so that I may be the only one to suffer from them, and unite my sufferings with Thine. Teach me to profit by the sufferings that come across my path. Let me so use them that they may mellow me, not harden or embitter me ; to make me patient, not irritable to be broad in my forgiveness, not marrow, haughty, or overbearing. May no one be less good for having come within my influence, no one less pure, less true, less noble, for having been a companion on our journey towards eternal life. As I go my rounds of daily life and duties, let me whisper from time to time a word of love to

Thee. May my life be lived always in the Divine Will, the supernatural, full of power for good and strong in its purpose of sanctity. Amen.

A Prayer to End the Day

Jesus thank you for this day, the food, the water, all drink. For having created me. For my work. That I am a Roman Catholic, outside of which there is no salvation. For have died for me on the cross and shed Thy Precious Blood. For having given me to thy most Holy Mother Mary, and Her to me in this devotion of holy bondage. May She be for me, my advocate in the presence of the Thy Divine Majesty. My support in my extreme misery. For without this dear Lady I would certainly be lost. Mary is necessary for me that I may alway do Thy Holy Will, seek Thy greater glory in all things. Would that I could proclaim throughout the whole world, the grace and mercy thou hast shown unto me. Would that everyone might know that I would already be damned were it not for Mary. And I would rather die than to live without belonging to Mary. May my mind be made up of peace, goodness, purity, and truth, and good thoughts always. Help me to understand the nothingness of this world, the greatness of heaven, the shortness of time, and the length of eternity. And that I must constantly prepare for death. That I may fear your judgements, escape Hell and in the end uptain Heaven through the merits of Jesus Christ my Lord, God, and Redeemer. Amen.

The Rosary Chaplet of St. Michael

One day St. Michael appeared to Antonia d' Astonac, a most devout Servant of God. And told her that he wished to be honored by nine salutations corresponding to the nine Choirs of Angels, which should consist of one Our Father, and three Hail Marys in honor of each of the angelic choirs.

The Promises of St. Michael

Whosoever would practice this devotion in his honor would have, when approaching the Holy (Communion) Table, and have an escort of nine angels chosen from each one of the nine choirs.

In addition, for the daily recital of these nine salutations he promised his continual assistance and that of all the angels during life, and after death deliverance from purgatory for themselves and their relations. (You see how many ways there are to avoid purgatory, and these are just a few.)

Many Great Devotions, **But the Best** of all is **THE MOST HOLY ROSARY.** And I will prove why this grace to pray it is the grace of predestination.

In the year 1214, Holy Mother Church received the Rosary in its present form and according to the method we use today. It was given to the Church by Saint Dominic who had received it from the Blessed Virgin as a powerful means of converting the Albigensians and other sinners.

The Albigensians a neo-Manichaean sect (started by, Mani (c.216–c.276) associated with the Catharist (Puritan) movement, that flourished in southern France in the 12th and 13th centuries. They believed in a good spirit who created the spiritual world, and that an evil spirit created the material world, including the human body, which is therefore under his control and is evil. They believed the Jesus was a creature only.

They commended suicide especially by starvation, their endura, to release the good spirit (soul) from the body which was evil to them. Some of these people also believed in Buddhism which is one of the major false religions in the world. It began around 2,500 years ago in India when Siddhartha Gautama who believed he could bring happiness into the world. He was born around 566 BC, in the small kingdom of Kapilavastu. His father was King Suddhodana and his mother was Queen Maya. He the founder of Buddhism.

The following are the words and stories of St. Louis De Montfort

From the book "Secret of the Rosary" (Read this book often.)
Whosoever loves the Rosary truly loves God. And
is absolutely certain of obtaining Heaven.
Mary's faithful servants grow to perfect and
despise this world and it's pleasures.
I will tell you the story of how he received it, which is found in the
very well-known book "De Dignitate Psalterii" by Blessed Alan de
la Roche. Saint Dominic, seeing that the gravity of people's sins was
hindering the conversion of the Albigensians, withdrew into a forest near
Toulouse where he prayed unceasingly for three days and three nights.
During this time he did nothing but weep and do harsh penances in
order to appease the anger of Almighty God. He used his discipline
so much that his body was lacerated, and finally he fell into a coma.
At this point Our Lady appeared to him,
accompanied by three angels, and she said:

*"Dear Dominic, do you know which weapon the Blessed
Trinity wants to use to reform the world?"*

Then Our Lady replied:

*"I want you to know that, in this kind of warfare, the battering ram has
always been the Angelic Psalter (Hail Mary) which is the foundation stone
of the New Testament. Therefore if you want to reach these hardened
souls and win them over to God, preach my Psalter." (Rosary)*

This miraculous way in which the devotion to the Holy Rosary was
established is something of a parallel to the way in which Almighty
God gave His "Ten Commandments" to Moses and the world on
Mount Sinai and obviously proves its value and importance.

Alphonsus, King of Leon and Galicia, very much wanted all his servants to honor the Blessed Virgin by saying the Rosary. So he used to hang a large rosary on his belt and always wore it, but unfortunately never said it himself. Nevertheless his wearing it encouraged his courtiers to say the Rosary very devoutly.

One day the King fell seriously ill and when he was given up for dead he found himself, in a vision, before the judgement seat of Our Lord. Many devils were there accusing him of all the sins he had committed and Our Lord as Sovereign Judge was just about to condemn him to hell when Our Lady appeared to intercede for him. She called for a pair of scales and had his sins placed in one of the balances whereas she put the rosary that he had always worn on the other scale, together with all the Rosaries that had been said because of his example. It was found that the Rosaries weighed more than his sins.

Looking at him with great kindness Our Lady said: "As a reward for this little honor that you paid me in wearing my Rosary, I have obtained a great grace for you from my Son. Your life will be spared for a few more years. See that you spend these years wisely, and do penance."

When the King regained consciousness he cried out:
"Blessed be the Rosary of the Most Holy Virgin Mary, by which I have been delivered from eternal damnation!"
After he had recovered his health he spent the rest of his life in spreading devotion to the Holy Rosary and said it faithfully every day.
People who love the Blessed Virgin ought to follow the example of King Alphonsus and that of the saints whom I have mentioned so that they too may win other souls for the Confraternity of the Holy Rosary. They will then receive great graces on earth and eternal life later on. "They that explain me shall have life everlasting life." [1] Ecclus. 24:31

Blessed Alan De la Roche who was so deeply devoted to the Blessed Virgin had many revelations from her and we know that he confirmed the truth of these revelations by a solemn oath.
Three of them stand out with special emphasis: **the first**, that if people fail to say the Hail Mary (the Angelic Salutation which has saved the world) out of carelessness, or because they are lukewarm,

or because they hate it, this is a sign that they will probably and indeed shortly be condemned to eternal punishment.

The second truth is that those who love this divine salutation bear the very special stamp of predestination. **The third** is that those to whom God has given the signal of grace of loving Our Lady and of serving her out of love must take very great care to continue to love and serve her until the time when she shall have had them place in heaven by her divine Son in the degree of glory which they have earned. (Blessed Alan, chapter XI, paragraph 2).

The heretics, all of whom are children of the devil and clearly bear the sign of God's reprobation, have a horror of the Hail Mary. They still say the Our Father but never the Hail Mary; they would rather wear a poisonous snake around their necks than wear a scapular or carry a rosary.

Among Catholics those who bear the mark of God's reprobation think but little of the rosary (whether that of five decades or fifteen). They either fail to say it or only say it very quickly and in a lukewarm manner.

Jesus and Mary have always said: "We love those who love us; we enrich them and fill their treasuries to overflowing." "He who soweth in blessings, shall also reap blessings."

St. Louis De Montfort said, "That when you pray the Rosary, you receive **(15)** of the most precious jewels or stones for each well said Hail Mary."

- **One day Saint Gertrude** had a vision of our Lord counting **gold coins**. She summoned the courage to ask him what he was doing, and he answered, "I am counting the Hail Marys that you have said; this is the money with which you purchase (your entrance into) heaven."

A fault commonly committed in saying the **Rosary** is to have **no intention** other than that of getting it over with as quickly as possible. Name all your <u>intentions</u> before you begin.

Small wonder, then, that the most sacred prayers of our holy religion seem to bear no fruit, and that, after saying thousands of Rosaries, we are still no better than we were before. No intentions.

Some say it astonishingly fast, slipping over part of the words. We could not possibly expect anyone, even the most important person, to think that a slipshod address of this kind was a compliment, and yet we imagine that Jesus and Mary will be honoured by it! Read the story of the three sisters and what happened to them for saying the Rosary to fast.

Take great care to avoid the two pitfalls that most people fall into during the Rosary. The first is the danger of not asking for any graces at all, so that if some good people were asked their Rosary intention they would not know what to say. So, whenever you say your Rosary, be sure to ask for some special grace or virtue, or strength to overcome some sin.

Dear friend of the Confraternity, I beg you to restrain your natural precipitation when saying your Rosary, and make some pauses in the middle of the Our Father and Hail Mary, and a smaller one after the words of the Our Father and Hail Mary which I have marked with a cross, as follows:

Our Father who art in heaven, + hallowed by thy name, + thy kingdom come, + thy will be done + on earth as it is in heaven. + Give us this day + our daily bread, + and forgive us our trespasses + as we forgive those who trespass against us, + and lead us not into temptation, + but deliver us from evil. Amen. + Hail, Mary, full of grace, + the Lord is with thee, + blessed art thou among women, + and blessed is the fruit of thy womb, Jesus. + Holy Mary, Mother of God, + pray for us sinners, now + and at the hour of our death. Amen. + At first, you may find it difficult to make these pauses because of your bad habit of saying prayers in a hurry;

but a decade said recollectedly in this way will be worth more than thousands of Rosaries said in a hurry, without pausing or reflecting.

A certain pious but self- willed lady in Rome, so often referred to by speakers on the Rosary. She was so devout and fervent that she put to shame by her holy life even the strictest religious in the Church. Having decided to ask St. Dominic's advice about her spiritual life, she made her confession to him. For penance he gave her one Rosary to say and advised her to say it every day. She excused herself, saying that she had her regular exercises, that she made the Stations of Rome every day, that she wore **sackcloth** as well as a **hair-shirt**, that she gave herself the discipline several times a week, that she often fasted and did other penances.

Saint Dominic urged her over and over again to take his advice and say the Rosary, but she would not hear of it. She left the confessional, horrified at the methods of this new spiritual director who had tried so hard to persuade her to take up a devotion for which she had no taste. Later on, when she was at prayer she fell into ecstasy and had a vision of her soul appearing before the Supreme Judge.

Saint Michael put all her penances and other prayers on one side of the scales and all her sins and imperfections on the other. The tray of her good works were greatly outweighed by that of her sins and imperfections. Filled with alarm, she cried for mercy, imploring the help of the Blessed Virgin, her gracious advocate, who took the one and only Rosary she had said for her penance and dropped it on the tray of her good works. This one Rosary was so heavy that it weighed more than all her sins as well as all her good works. Our Lady then **reproached** her for having refused to follow the counsel of her servant Dominic and for **not** saying the Rosary every day.

This is the time to say a little about the indulgences which have been granted to Rosary Confraternity members, so that you may gain as many as possible.

An indulgence, in general, is a remission or relaxation of temporal punishment due to actual sins, by the application of the superabundant satisfactions of Jesus Christ, of the Blessed Virgin and all the saints, which are contained in the treasury of the Church.

A **plenary indulgence** is a remission of the whole punishment due to sin; a **partial indulgence**, for instance, a hundred or a thousand years can be explained as the remission of as much punishment as could have been expiated during a hundred or a thousand years, if one had been given a corresponding number of the penances prescribed by the Church's ancient Canons.

Now these Canons exacted seven and sometimes ten or fifteen years' penance for a single mortal sin, so that a person who was guilty of twenty mortal sins would probably have had to perform a seven year penance at least twenty times, and so on.

Members of the Rosary Confraternity who
want to gain the indulgences must:

1. Be truly repentant and go to confession and communion, as the Papal Bull of indulgences states.
2. Be entirely free from affection for venial sin, because if affection for sin remains, the guilt also remains, and if the guilt remains the punishment cannot be lifted.
3. Say the prayers and perform the good works designated by the Bull. If, in accordance with what the Popes have said, one can gain a partial indulgence (for instance, of a hundred years) without gaining a plenary indulgence, it is not always necessary to go to confession and communion in order to gain it. Many such partial indulgences are attached to the Rosary (either of five or fifteen decades), to processions, blessed rosaries, etc. Do not neglect these indulgences. (They cut your suffering down in Purgatory.)

Flammin and a great number of other writers tell the **story of a young girl of noble station** named Alexandra, who had been miraculously converted and enrolled by St. Dominic in the Confraternity of the Rosary. After her death, she appeared to him and said she had been **condemned** to

seven hundred years in purgatory because of her own sins and those she had caused others to commit by her worldly ways (and fashions). So she implored him to ease her pains by his prayers and to ask the Confraternity members to pray for the same end. St. Dominic did as she had asked. Two weeks later she appeared to him, more radiant than the sun, having been quickly delivered from purgatory **by the prayers of the Confraternity members.** She also told St. Dominic that she had come on behalf of the souls in purgatory to beg him to go on preaching the Rosary and to **ask their relations** to offer their Rosaries for them, and that they would reward them abundantly when they entered into glory (Heaven).

A Spanish countess who had been taught the holy Rosary by St. Dominic used to say it faithfully every day, with the result that she was making marvellous progress in her spiritual life. Since her only desire was to attain to perfection, she asked a bishop who was a renowned preacher for some practices that would help her to become perfect. The bishop told her that, before he could give her any advice, she would have to let him know the state of her soul and what her religious exercises were. She answered that her most important exercise was the Rosary, which she said every day, meditating on the Joyful, Sorrowful and Glorious Mysteries, and that she had profited greatly by so doing. The Bishop was overjoyed to hear her explain what priceless lessons the mysteries contain. "I have been a doctor of theology for twenty years," he exclaimed, "and I have read many excellent books on various devotional practices. But never before have I come across one better than this or more conformed to the Christian life. From now on I shall follow your example, and I shall preach the Rosary." He did so with such success that in a short while he saw his diocese changed for the better.

(Jeremy pay attention to this below.)

The victories of Count Simon de Montfort won against the Albigensians under the patronage of Our Lady of the Rosary. They are so famous that the world has never seen anything to match them.

One day he **defeated ten thousand heretics** with a force of **five hundred men**; on another occasion he overcame three thousand with only thirty men; finally, with eight hundred horsemen and one thousand infantrymen he completely routed the army of the King of Aragon, which was a hundred thousand strong, and this with the loss on his side of only one horseman and eight soldiers.

Our Lady also protected Alan de l'Anvallay, a Breton knight, from great perils. He too was fighting for the faith against the Albigensians.

One day, when he found himself surrounded by enemies on all sides, our Lady let fall a hundred and fifty rocks upon his enemies and he was delivered from their hands. Another day, when his ship had foundered and was about to sink, this good Mother caused a hundred and fifty small hills to appear miraculously above the water and by means of them they reached Brittany in safety.

In thanksgiving to our Lady for the miracles she had worked on his behalf in answer to his daily Rosary, he built a monastery at Dinan for the religious of the new Order of St. Dominic and, having become a religious himself, he died a holy death at Orleans.

Othère, also a Breton soldier, from Vaucouleurs, often put whole companies of heretics or robbers to flight, wearing his rosary on his arm and on the hilt of his sword. Once when he had beaten his enemies, they admitted that they had seen his sword shining brightly, and another time had noticed a shield on his arm on which our Lord, our Lady and the saints were depicted. This shield made him invisible and gave him the strength to attack well.

Another time he defeated twenty thousand heretics with only ten companies without losing a single man. This so impressed the general of the heretics' army that he sought out Othère, abjured his heresy and declared that he had seen him surrounded by flaming swords during the battle. (No doubt the angels of Our lady that She had sent to help him.)

In 1578, a woman of Antwerp had given herself to the devil and signed a contract with her own blood. Shortly afterwards she was stricken with remorse and had an intense desire to make amends for this terrible deed. So she sought out a kind and wise confessor to find out how she could be set free from the power of the devil. She found a wise and holy priest, who advised her to go to Fr. Henry, director of the Confraternity of the Holy Rosary, at the Dominican Friary, to be enrolled there and to make her confession. Accordingly, she asked to see him but met, not Fr. Henry, but the devil disguised as a friar. He reproved her severely and said she could never hope to receive God's grace, and there was no way of revoking what she had signed. This grieved her greatly but she did not lose hope in God's mercy and sought out Fr. Henry once more, only to find the devil a second time, and to meet with a second rebuff. She came back a third time and then at last, by divine providence, she found Fr. Henry in person, the priest whom she had been looking for, and he treated her with great kindness, urging her to throw herself on the mercy of God and to make a good confession. He then received her into the Confraternity and told her to say the Rosary frequently. One day, while Fr. Henry was celebrating Mass for her, our Lady forced the devil to give her back the contract she had signed. In this way she was delivered from the devil by the authority of Mary and by devotion to the holy Rosary.

Another beautiful devotion from Our Lord to St. Bridget of Sweden is the:

The Twelve-year Prayer of S. Bridget of Sweden

They consist of (7) short prayers with very Great Promises of Our Lord.

Saint Bridget of Sweden, the great 14th century Mystic and Visionary, was given a set of Prayers by Our Divine Lord, to be prayed for 12 years. These prayers are meditations on **the seven times that Christ shed His Precious Blood on our account.** To the one who will say the set of prayers daily for 12 years, **these graces are promised:**

1.) The soul who prays them suffers no purgatory.
2.) The soul who prays them will be accepted among the Martyrs as though he had spilled his blood for his faith.
3.) The soul who prays them can choose three others whom Jesus will then keep in a state of grace sufficient to become holy.
4.) No-one in the four successive generations of the soul who prays them will be lost.
5.) The soul who prays them will be made conscious of his death one month in advance.

If the suppliant should die before the allotted span, God the Father will accept them as having been prayed in their entirety, as the genuine intention was there. If a day or a few days are missed for a valid reason, they can be made up later.

This devotion was pronounced good & profitable, and recommended by both the Sacro Collégia de propagánda fide, the Sacred Congregation for the Propagation of the Faith – The Holy Office – and by Pope Clement XII. Pope Innocent X declared that they are from God.

+++++++++++++++++++++++++++++++

Start with this Prayer:

O Jesus, I now wish to pray the Lord's Prayer seven times in unity with the love with which Thou sanctified this prayer in Thy Heart. Take it from my lips into Thy Divine Heart. Improve and complete it until it brings as much honour and joy to the Blessed Trinity as Thou granted it on Earth with this prayer. May these prayers pour upon Thy Holy Humanity the glorification due to Thy painful Wounds and the Precious Blood Thou spilled from them.

1.) **The Circumcision** *[The First Mortal sin]* Our Father. Hail Mary.

Eternal Father, through Mary's unblemished hands and the Divine Heart of Jesus, I offer to Thee the first wounds, the first pains and the first bloodshed, as atonement for my sins & all of humanity's sins of youth, as protection against the first mortal sin, especially among my relatives.

2.) **The Suffering on the Mount of Olives** *[Sins of the heart]* Our Father. Hail Mary.

Eternal Father, through Mary's unblemished hands and the Divine Heart of Jesus, I offer to Thee the terrifying suffering of the Heart of Jesus on Mount of Olives, and every drop of His Sweat of Blood, as atonement for my sins and all of humanity's sins of the heart, as protection against such sins, and for the spreading of Divine and Brotherly Love.

3.) **The Scourging** *[Sins of the flesh]* Our Father. Hail Mary.

Eternal Father, through Mary's unblemished hands and the Divine Heart of Jesus, I offer to Thee the many thousands of Wounds, the gruesome Pains and the Precious Blood of the Scourging, as atonement for my sins and all of humanity's sins of the Flesh, as protection against such sins and the preservation of innocence, especially among my relatives.

4.) **The Crowning with Thorns** *[Sins of pride]* Our Father. Hail Mary.

Eternal Father, through Mary's unblemished hands and the Divine Heart of Jesus, I offer to Thee the Wounds, the Pains and the Precious Blood of the Holy Head of Jesus from the Crowning with Thorns, as atonement for my sins and all of humanity's sins of the spirit, as protection against such sins and for the spreading of the Kingdom of Christ here on Earth.

5) **The Carrying of the Cross** *[Sins of the tongue, against the Cross]* Our Father. Hail Mary.

Eternal Father, through Mary's unblemished hands and the Divine Heart of Jesus, I offer to Thee the Sufferings on the Way of the Cross, especially the Holy Wound on

His Shoulder and its precious Blood, as atonement for my sins and all of humanity's rebellion against the Cross, every grumbling against Thy Holy Providence, and all other sins of the tongue, as protection against such sins and for true love of the Cross.

6.) **The Crucifixion of Jesus** *[For the Church and the Jews]* Our Father. Hail Mary.

Eternal Father, through Mary's unblemished hands and the Divine Heart of Jesus, I offer to Thee Thy Son on the Cross, His nailing and being lifting on high, the Wounds on His Hands and Feet, and the three streams of His Precious Blood that poured forth for us from these wounds, the extreme tortures of His Body and Soul, His precious death and its unbloody renewal in all Holy Masses on Earth, as atonement for all wounds against vows and regulations within Religious Orders, as reparation for my sins and all the world's sins, for the sick and dying, for all holy priests and laymen, for the intentions of the Holy Father toward the restoration of Christian families, for the strengthening of Faith, for our country, for unity among all nations in Christ and His Church, and the Diaspora *(Outside)*.

7.) **The Piercing of Jesus' Side** *[All of mankind and the Holy Souls]* Our Father. Hail Mary.

Eternal Father, accept as worthy for the needs of Holy Mother Church, and as atonement for the sins of all Mankind, the precious Blood and Water which poured forth from the Wound of the Divine Heart of Jesus. Be gracious and merciful towards us. Blood of Christ, the last precious content of His Holy Heart, wash me of all my sins and other's guilt of sin! Water from the Side of Christ, wash me clean of all punishments for sin and extinguish the flames of Purgatory for me and for all the Poor Souls. Amen.

Problems on Dress, and Manners of Attending Mass

1.) Teach your children to genuflect towards the tabernacle on the right Knee, which is for God only. The left knee is for kings, queens, bishops, and the Virgin Mary.

2.) Complete Silence is demanded by God and His angels in the Church, in the presence of God. Each Church has a <u>guardian angel that records all distractions and irreverences that occur in Church</u>. This is why the pews in the back are reserved for the parents with children seven years and under. If the child is making any noise what so ever, the child is to be taken out for fear of displeasing God and the conversation He is having with the people around you. This is a grave irreverences to Almighty God. The only talking in church should be to God and nothing else should be heard, but the whisper of God's voice in your ear.

3.) Stand for the priest when he enters the sanctuary and knee and bless yourself when he starts the foot of the altar prayers. Do not leave Mass **after** this point, and train your children to stay attentive and read the words in the missel.

4.) If you must leave, go out by the **side aisle**. If you leave at the time of the sermon, do not re-enter the church (out of respect for the priest speaking and the people listening) **until the Creed**, when everyone stands. (Re-enter by side aisle.) This is an old custom. Today people run in and out like a grocery store. Sit in the back, as the child learns to set still and read the Missal, he can go to the front pew and as he comes to know what the is about. The time for instruction is not in the front pew, it is at home.

5.) At the **time of the Consecration** (elevation) you are to fall to your **knees** even if you are in the aisle or back of the church standing. Children must learn to do this too. Keep your eyes on the elevated spices and whisper a word of praise and love to God until lowered. (Normally "My Lord and My God.") There are (14) miracles at the Mass, according to an old Irish priest who lived at the turn of the century. And it is no place for noisy little people who don't know what is going on. (They are yet still catechumens, who normally would have to leave at the time of the Offertory.)

6.) On the way up to the Communion Rail (table) you are to follow the example of the angels with your hands folded towards heaven and not towards hell, and eyes downward asking Mary and Joseph to clean your heart and soul as they did at the stable for the coming of Jesus. Our Lord wants each family to receive Holy Communion as a family. So, older children set together with your mother and father, not in the back so no one can see what they're doing, someone is always watching you from the invisible side of eternity. In the old days women sat on the left and men set on the right. Some places a family were assigned a pew so the priest new if he had lost any of his sheep. Say, if they are missing Mass for a couple weeks. He would go looking for them.

7.) When receiving Holy Communion, always kneel before your God and Creator and Savior, tip your head back as far as you can, and stick your tongue **out** as far as you can, and not just a little to where the priest can not place the host on your tongue, and possibly drop the host.

8.) When you go to receive Holy Communion, it is a daily antidote against sin. It is the antidote to venial sin. You make your guardian angel very happy when you receive Holy Communion.

9.) Modest dress in Church yes, Immodest and Indecent dress no, do **not** wear tennis shoes in God's house, Nor shower shoes, shorts, slacks, blue jeans, jacket with symbols or words, a smartly dressed Catholic will wear nice polished pear of shoes.

10.) Women's' dress is to be 8" below the knee. No bare arms in church, outside of church short sleeves is permissible, but not encouraged. (*St. Padre Pio would not give Communion to anyone with bare arms or not buttoned up to the base of the neck, and dress 8" below the Knee.*) Aunt Regina said she never saw her father or grandfather in short sleeve shirts. For that matter I never saw my father or either of my grandfathers or mother in short sleeve shirts.

11.) Short sleeve shirts in church kicked in after Vatican II, outside of church short sleeves were here.

12.) Men are to should show their devotion to God by dressing in your Sunday best. No bare arms in church, and always a buttoned long sleeved shirt, which traditionally is covered with a jacket of some kind, dress jacket, or dinner jacket, or whatever will cover the physique and but-ox of the man is covered. Many saints would not give Communion to men and women with bare arms or legs.

13.) Women are commanded by the vicar of Christ to wear something on their head, preferably to cover all their beautiful hair (her glory is in her hair and her fortune is in body which belong only to the man she marries.) All attention is to be given to God, not on your neighbor. Nothing is to be wore that is tight to the body, to show off your beautiful figure. All clothing should be very loose on all people.

The following is taken from the book, **"A CATECHISM OF CHRISTIAN DOCTRINE"** by Rev. Jos. Deharbe, S.J. specially adapted for use in the parochial schools of the United Stated, by a Father of the Society of Jesus. With Imprimatur: March 15, 1902. I will touch briefly some important issues.

There are questions and answers according to this book, and mainly after a set a questions I will just state the Practical Conclusion. The first question is most important, because many are outside the catholic church in hersey because there own interpretation.

Is faith necessary for salvation?

Faith is absolutely necessary for salvation, for Christ says: "He that doth not believe is already judged" (John 3, 18) and: "He that believeth not shall be condemned." (Mark 16, 16.)

Practical Conclusion: Always firmly believe in the teaching of the Holy Catholic Church, for, believing in her teachings, you believe in the Word of God and in His Vicar on earth.

Why has the Catholic Church alone have the true faith taught by Christ?

Because the Catholic Church alone received her faith from Christ and His Apostles and has always kept it incorrupt. (Until Vatican II.)

Practical Conclusion: Rejoice and often thank God, that you are a child of the Catholic Church; for there is no wealth so great, no treasure so precious then to that Great Peril the Catholic Faith." (St. Augustine) The Council of Trent is the guiding light in these later times, and has set down in writing all that is most necessary to believe in for our salvation.

The sign of the Cross is the profession of our True Faith in the principal mysteries namely: The Most Holy and Blessed Trinity and the Redemption through the death of Christ on the Cross for those who belong to the One True Faith outside of which no one is saved. The Sign of the Cross is not found outside the True Church.

When is our entire?

Our faith is entire when we believe not only some but all the truths which the Catholic Church teaches.

When is our faith constant?

Our faith is constant when we are ready to lose all, even life itself, rather than renounce it.

When is our faith "living"?

Our faith is "living" when we live up to it, that is, when we shun evil and do good, as faith requires. "As the body without the spirit is dead, so also faith without works is dead." (James 2, 26.)

When should we make the Sign of the Cross?

It is good and wholesome to make the Sign of the Cross frequently, especially in the morning when we rise and in the evening when we retire, before and after prayer, before important actions, in temptations and in all dangers, at before work and play.

Practical Conclusion: never be ashamed of the Catholic Faith nor of the Sign of the Cross. Shun everything that may endanger you faith; especially beware of vainly prying into the mysteries of Religion, of reading bad books and papers and of making friends with unbelieving and wick persons.

Remember your Salvation as follows:

From the Catechism of Christian Doctrine by Rev.
Jos. Deharbe, S.J. New Edition 1902

Never be ashamed of the Catholic Faith nor of the 'Sign of the Cross.' Shun everything that may endanger your faith; especially beware of vainly prying into the mysteries of Religion, of reading bad books and papers and of making friends with unbelieving and wicked persons. (Today we have movies and vanity and the flesh in Disney movies.)

Never forget how grateful you should be to the Most Holy Trinity for the inestimable benefits of Creation, Redemption and Sanctification and what you have solemnly promised in Holy Baptism.

Thank God Who for the love of becoming man; adhering firmly to Him and His Holy Doctrine, for He says: "I am the way, the Truth and the Life. No man cometh to the Father, but by Me." (John 14: 6)

Never forget the exceedingly great love of Our Lord Jesus Christ; love Him with your whole heart; because He suffered for you the most cruel death. Take up your cross (daily duties) without complaint and follow Jesus. (Devotion in honor of the bitter Passion; Stations of the Cross; Agony in the Garden; Visit to the Holy Sepulchre in Holy Week; Abstinence on all Fridays.) Always show great respect and submission to our Holy Father, the Pope, and to the Bishops, Priests united with him. (As long as they are holding firm to Sacred Tradition.) Christ said to them: "He that heareth you, heareth Me, and he that despiseth you, despiseth Me."

Sometime before the Jews crucified Our Lord gave them the
chance to believe in Him as the Son of God. They closed
their minds the truth and few were saved. Today is the same
thing they have closed their mind to the truth and will not
believe in the Old Ways. (Tradition of nearly 2000 yrs.)

Thank God with your whole heart, that you can obtain through the
Church forgiveness of your sins, but never forget that, in order to obtain
pardon, you must have sincere contrition and an earnest will to amend
your life.

"The hour cometh wherein all that are in the **grave** shall hear the voice
of the Son of God. And they that have done good things, shall come forth
unto the resurrection of life; but they have done evil, unto the resurrection
of judgment."(John 5: 28;29)

Never abuse the members and senses of your body to commit sin, so
that you may one day rise to everlasting glory. Your body's a temple of God.
It is against the law of God and Church to cremate it.

"Love your enemies, do good to them that hate you, and pray for them
that persecute and calumniate you, that you may be the children of your
Father who is in Heaven, who maketh His sun to rise upon the good and
bad, and raineth upon the just and the unjust." (Matt. 5: 44;45)

Honor devoutly the Saints, particularly the Blessed Virgin, St.
Joseph, your Patron Saint, and your guardian Angel. Love to read
the lives of the Saints and faithfully follow their example.

Never use God's name in vain. In the Old Testament death was the
penalty for blasphemy. "He that blasphemeth the name of the Lord,
dying let him die, all the multitude shall stone him." (3 Mos. 24;16)

Carefully guard against the shameful habit of cursing and swearing.
Invoke the names of Jesus and Mary devoutly, especially in the time of
temptations. Do not watch movies with cursing and obscene language.

What are we expressly commanded to do on Sunday and Holy Days?

To keep Holy this Day (Sabbath) by spiritual readings; attending
Mass; keeping from all servile works. The fear of temporal
and eternal punishment which God has threatened to inflict
on those who violate the Sabbath Day. The thought, that the
desecration of the Sunday is a disgrace to our fellow-christians.

"They grievously violated my Sabbaths. I said therefore that I
would pour out my indignation upon them in the desert, and
would consume them." (Ezech. 20;13) (This goes for our time
too. Using God name in vain and working on Sunday were
the main cause of WWI & WWII. **Our Lady of Fatima**)

He that shall profane the Sabbath (Sunday),
shall be put to death." (2 Mos. 31;14)

Always keep the Day of the Lord religiously Holy. Never allow
carelessness or the passion for amusement or the wicked example of
irreligious companions to influence you to desecrate the Sunday.

"If a man hath a stubborn and unruly son, who will not hear the
command of the father or mother, (he begrudges them) and being corrected,
slighteth obedience, (maybe he doesn't remove his hat in the house) the
people of the city shall stone him, and all Israel (Church) hearing it maybe
afraid." (5 Mos. 21; 18,21)

"With all thy soul fear the Lord, and reverence his priests." (Ecclus. 7:
31) "Let every soul be subject to higher powers: for there is no power
but from God: and those that are, are ordained for God." Rom. 13; 1)

Withhold not correction from a child, for if you strike him with the
rod, he will not die. Thou shalt beat him with the rod, and deliver
his soul from Hell." (Col. 4: 1) (Foolish parent fail to spank or
reprimand their children for their boisterousness and disobedience, the
child always gets what he asks for and becomes spoiled and become
demanding the rest of his life, instead of becoming humble.)

Honor your parents, pastors, teachers, and all who by authority, rank or age, are placed over you. Obey cheerfully and promptly after the example of Our Divine Saviour.

Be temperate and peaceable. Shun the seducer and beware of ever becoming the murderer of the soul of your neighbor.

Do you know that you are a temple of God, and that the Spirit of God dwelleth in you? But if any man violate the temple of God, him shall God destroy. (Murder and cremation.) For the temple of God is holy, which you are." (1 Cor. 3, 16. 17.) "He that joineth himself to harlots, will be wicked. Rottenness and worms shall inherit him." (Ecclus. 19, 3) "They shall have their portion in the pool, burning with fire and brimstone."

(This goes for the people pay no attention to the Sacrament Matrimony, and live together.)

Never steal anything, be it ever so small, not even from your parents. Think well of the true sayings: "Small beginnings end in greater things." (Things just get worse and Lying is the next sin.)

Injustice never prospers." "Woe to him that builds up his his house by injustice......that will oppress his friend without cause, and will not pay him his wages." (Jer. 22, 13)

"Go to the ant, O sluggard, and consider her ways and learn wisdom." (Prov. 6, 6)

Of spiritual sloth or lukewarm, in the service of God, the Lord says: "I would thou were hot or cold. But because thou are lukewarm, and neither hot nor cold, I will begin to vomit thee out of my month." (Apoc. 3: 15,16)

"My son, all the days of thy life have God in thy mind; and take heed, that thou never consent to sin

..... We shall have many good things if we fear God, and depart from all sin and do what is good." (Tob. 4:6, 23)

Pray to God everyday for His grace, and take heed not to shut Him out of your heart. "Behold, I stand at the gate and knock. If any man shall hear my voice and open to Me his door, I will come in to him, and will sup with him and he with Me. "(Apoc. 3:20)

"Remember thou thy sins with alms, and thy iniquities with works of mercy to the poor; perhaps he will forgive thy offences." (Daniel 4:24)

Sanctifying grace is the most precious gift of God. Avoid sin, in order not to lose grace, and practice good works in order to increase it. Pray **often** and **fervently** for the great grace of final perseverance.

The sacraments are the most sacred and most efficacious means of grace. Be careful never to despise the sacraments or to desecrate them either by blasphemous language or by receiving them unworthily.

Never forget your promise to God in Holy Baptism, of which the priest reminded you when giving you the white garment he said: "Receive this white garment, which mayest thou carry without stain before the judgment-seat of our Lord, that thou mayest have life eternal."

Always remember that as a soldier of Christ you should uphold the cause of God, and consider it an honor to suffer humiliation and persecution for the sake of the faith.

The Holy Eucharist is also called the Sacrament of the Altar, the Blessed Sacrament, Corpus Christi, the Eucharist, the Sacred Host, the Lord's Table, the Viaticum.

Beware of all the irreverence in the Church of talking of adults and the screaming of children in the presence of the Eucharist.

May many visits to Our Eucharistic King, and show always, even outside the Church, due veneration for the Blessed Sacrament.

Attend Mass with all the reverence and devotion which so sublime a mystery demands. At the Offertory, offer yourself in union with Jesus to His Eternal Father: at the Consecration, adore your Savior humility, by falling on your knees wherever you are in the church, even if in the ilsi or standing in the back, at Holy Communion ask Mary and Joseph to clean your heart and soul as they did at the stable for the coming of Jesus and may a spiritual communion several times a day. Adore God most humbly and say the Magnificat.

"He who eateth My Flesh and Drinketh My Blood will hath everlasting life; and I will raise him up on the last day." (John 6:55,57)

"Let a man prove himself, and then let him eat of that Bread and drink of the Chalice." (1 Cor. 11,28)

Frequently approach the table of the Lord, and partake of the Bread of Angels with a pure heart and fervent desire.

Remember that on earth there is no more Precious time, then the time following your Holy Communion. Do not consider it too much to spend at least fifteen minutes with your Saviour in prayer and thanksgiving.

The Fathers and Doctors of the Church have alway taught that we can hope for no forgiveness of our sins from God if we be ashamed to confess them to the priest. Confessing sins was always in practice in the Church. It is certain that no one would have consented to do so, if Christ Himself had not instituted Confession.

What is Contrition?

Contrition is heartfelt sorrow and hatred for our sins. Our contrition must be: 1.) Interior, 2.) Universal, 3.) Supernatural.

When is contrition imperfect?

Contrition is imperfect, when the motive of our sorrow is principally fear of God or of temporal or eternal punishments we have deserved at His hands, and not because He is your dearest Friend.

What should we do to obtain the required contrition?

We should pray earnestly ask for the grace
of a true contrition and consider:

1.) That we deserve to be punished by God;

2.) That we are the cause of Christ's suffering and death;

3.) That we have offended our God, our greatest benefactor and our best of father and friend, the greatest, most amiable Good.

Perfect Contrition may not be necessary for a worthy confession, imperfection is sufficient, nevertheless we should strive to have perfect contrition, because of greater merit and most of all to please God.

What is an indulgence?

An indulgence is the remission of the temporal punishments of our sins, which the Church grants outside the Sacrament of Penance.

We must believe that the Catholic Church has the power
to grant indulgences, because Christ Himself has given
to the Church the power to remit all punishments due
to sin, not only the eternal, but also temporal.

"Whatsoever thou shalt loose on earth, it shall be
loosed also in heaven." (Matt. 16:19, and 18:18)

Go to confession frequently, it strengthen you. Why every two weeks, because indulgences are gained every (8) before or after confession. St. Padre Pio said to go every week. Some saints when ever day.

Always make a good preparation for confession and make it as carefully as though you were about to die.

Value indulgences highly and endeavor to gain as many as possible for yourself and for the poor souls in Purgatory. In your morning prayers make the intention of gaining all the indulgences, which are attached to your pious practices.

Do not delay to receive the last sacraments, especially the Sacrament of Extreme Unction, until the last moment, but rather prepare yourself in due time for death, that it may not take you unaware and send you unprepared before the Judge.

Always show to the priest the respect and submission due to him: for he is God's representative, and the minister of His mysteries, without him you can not get to Heaven. Pray for priests especially on Ember Day.

In choosing a state of life, keep in mind God and the salvation of your soul. If after mature deliberation and you believe yourself called to the married state, prepare yourself for this step by prayer, good works and, above all, by a worthy general confession, and do not act like those who by their sins and vices call down God's curse upon themselves.

Never treat irreverently any blessed objects by the Church; always show due veneration and devotion when using them, who make use of the Church.

Remember that in your prayers you are talking with God, Who is deep inside your soul and hears all you say to Him, think of what a blessing it is, to be allowed to speak to God, as a child to his father. Honor and deeply love the Blessed Virgin Mary with a true child like disposition. Because you will never see Heaven without Her. Call upon Her in all your needs and dangers. If your devotion is to Her, She will save you on your judgment day.

You have but one soul to Save, One God to Love and to Serve, Death will come soon, Judgment will follow and then, Heaven or Hell forever. "For the man who does not seek Jesus does himself Much greater harm than the whole world and all his Enemies together could do." Church is the gate of Heaven, when ever any ceremonies are going on in the church attend them. We are created by God to Know, Love and Serve Him and to be Happy with Him in Heaven. Avoid Sin, keep the Commandments, lead a Virtuous Life, receive the Sacraments and Pray always.

Marie Ann Taigi was shown in a vision the large box with the moving pictures. It would be found in every family's home. Our Lord told her this box would be the damnation of many people and families, because they would spend their time in front of it, instead of in front of God or with God in the tabernacle. This the way Satan tricks many into Hell for all eternity with the pleasures of the world. Daily think of your **death**, this will help you to pray and do sacrifice. People who forget to think of death, usually forget to think of God.

PRAYER FOR A CLEAN HEART AND FOR HEAVENLY WISDOM

Strengthen me, O God, by the grace of the Holy Ghost. Give me power to grow stronger spiritually and to empty my heart of every useless care; not to be carried away by different desires of anything whether worthless or valuable, but to look on all things as passing away, and I too passing with them, since nothing under the sun is permanent. O how wise is he who thus looks upon all earthly things! O Lord, give me heavenly wisdom that above all I may learn to seek You and to find you, to taste and love above all, ordering Your eternal wisdom. Give me discretion to avoid flattery; patience to endure opposition. This great wisdom, not to be moved by every kind of word, nor to give in to the flattering siren, for otherwise the road of safety is missed.

PRAYER FOR THE GRACE OF DEVOTION

O Lord my God, You are my only good. Who am I that dare speak to You? I am Your lowest servant a vile worm, much more contemptible than I realize. Yet remember me, Lord, because I am nothing; I have nothing, and can do nothing. You alone are good, just, and holy. You can do all things, You give all things, You fill all things, only the sinner You send away empty handed. Remember Your compassion,(Ps. 24:6), and fill my heart with Your grace, You Who will not allow any of Your works to be in vain. How can I bear this wretched life unless Your mercy and grace support it? Do not turn Your face from me. Do not delay Your visit. Do not withdraw Your consolation, my soul thirsts for you like the parched lands for rain, (Ps. 142:6) Lord, teach me to do Your will (Ps. 142:10). Teach me to live worthily and humbly in Your presence, for You are Wisdom Who knows me well, and Who knew me before the world was made, and before I was born into it. Count me amongst Your own. Let not Thy Passion be in vain on my account.

Altar Boys

1.) Light Candles five minutes before Mass. After you put on your cassock and surplice, this is the cleric garb for an Acolyte issued by the Church. (The Epistle Side (right side) candles closest to the tabernacle are lit first and are put out last from the outside in. Walk down the side and around to the center and genuflect. Go to other side and light the other candles)

2.) (The Sanctuary where the Saints adore the King and the Angels fear to trend. Only the Priest and Sacristan may step on the top platform step. The Sacristan wears a cossack or the habit of his the Order, as before Vatican II. All layman in lay clothes went around outside or through the basement to get to the sacristy. No lay clothes or persons in the sanctuary From the book "Holy Sacrifice of the Mass by Fr. Nicholas Gihr. A book studied in all seminaries before Vatican II.) Normally the priest is the sacristan. If you knew how holy, truly real and present God is in the tabernacle, as He has proved in many miracles, if you knew the awesome magnificent powers of God. Remember Old Testament one priest for a year was chosen. He along with a rope tied around him would enter the sanctuary. If anyone else dared to enter he would die instantly. The Sacristan should have everything set up before the altar boy gets dressed. The sisters when I was a boy would never let us go into the sanctuary without a cassock on.

All Catholic boys in school were instructed by the <u>Nuns </u>to first put a Cassock on, before trespassing into the Sanctuary amongst the angels. Check yourself to be sure your surplus is on straight. If you are to serve Mass you are required to wear a white shirt and polished black shoes. (No girls or women are allowed to serve Mass, lecture, or lead public pray. "Let your women be silent" St Paul. Since Vatican II the Catholic Church has turned protestant and all religious habits have turned to lay clothing in the Sanctuary and elsewhere. Many a Saint have foretold that after the year 1900 young and old men would dress like women in earrings, necklaces and marriage would be disregarded. Women would wear men's clothing and dresses would go up and shorts and pants, and shower shoes and 'T' shirts and baseball caps would take the place of the modest dress of middle 1900's. As the dresses of the women went up so did the pant legs of men go up to show off their hairy legs and destroy man's dignity. Women would hold the place of men at work and leave the children at home. Our Lord at Fatima said, He would be greatly appalled by the dress at the end of the 1900th century. All men and women are required to cover their arms and legs when entering the Church. Saint Padre Pio would refuse Holy Communion to any person whose arms or legs were not covered. The Vicar of Christ ordered that the heads of women would be covered when entering the house of God, which is and always has been in effect to this day. Pope Linus)

3.) A good Altar Boy never allows his eyes to cross the Communion Rail. And when in procession your eyes should be down cast. (Saints tell us that the Angels always keep their eyes downcast looking forward. Do not be looking at the people as you walk down the aisle. All genuflections should be done before the tabernacle at the bottom three steps on the right knee, Left knee is for the bishop or king or queen.)

4.) Silence in the sacristy no talking. (In fact, the only talking in church should be to God. The eyes should never be looking around. The eyes should be forward towards the tabernacle in deep prayerful thought. Some Saints have told that if they looked away from the tabernacle their guardian angel would slap their face.)

5.) Answer the prayers loudly and distinctly for the priest.

6.) During the Sermon sit still and hands on lap. No one should sleep during the sermon or leave the church (Considered a grievous sin.) (Parents with little children should sit in the back, so as not to distract the priest or the people if they must leave the church. If people must leave the church during the sermon they should be within hearing range of the sermon. Out of courtesy for both the priest and the people do not re-enter the church until the Credo is started. Always use the side aisle.)

7.) The Priest is to wear his Beretta when entering the sanctuary; this shows his authority as a priest under any Roof. As the Pope wears his Tiara and Bishop's miter in any ceremonies. However, as mere men and to show our manners and good catholic courtesy, we men are required to remove their hat when entering a building or house. The worst of men eat with their hats on. **The Priest's Beretta goes on the priest's chair, never on the Credence Table.** (Only sacramentals and sacred vessels can go on the Credence Table and this table is to be cleared after each Mass.) Read Sacristans Hand book.

8.) The bell is either left <u>under</u> the credence table or left on the <u>middle step</u> at the altar after Mass as well as the ending Mass card. Credence table should be cleared after Mass. (In some places the bell is rang (3) times at the elevation, the Council of Trent has state that wherever one is all of the three persons in Divinity are present.

9.) It is up to the Sacristan to change the flowers which are left on the Communion Rail by the women of the "Alar Society". Also to clean both the Court of Our Lord (the Sanctuary) and the Sacristy and to care for the candles. He should also keep track of hosts and wine on hand. (Read where the priest is always to remove the Blessed Sacrament from the Altar when any work or a practice of any kind is to be done. This is very important. Some Churches have an extra tabernacle for to put into the sacristy.

10.) Lay clothing should not be worn in the sanctuary.
(Read sacristan's handbook, normally the sacristan is the priest. Like the priest and the altarboy always wear a cossack into sanctuary. The NEW CHURCH doesn't care if there is lay clothes worn in the serve of God. I can't image an angel or God wearing pants in the sanctuary or anywhere else for that matter.)

11.) Use side door to avoid going with the sanctuary. (All the things that happened in the Old Testament is type and an example for the New Testament. There was elected one man to enter the sanctuary of the Temple where the Ark of the Covenant was kept. This one man had a rope tied around him, so if he died while he was in this sanctuary, they could pull him out. Because if any man walked into this sanctuary he would be killed instantly. And this was the Ark of the Covenant, not the true God. Today boys, girls, men, and women just walk through the sanctuary, where the most holy angels and saints are in constant adoration of the Blessed Sacrament, God.

This is why you should enter by the side door and put on your cossack before entering into the sanctuary, never trespass through the Court of the Divine Majesty.

Our Lord said to St. Bridget of Sweden; "do not think that because I am merciful that My justice will not demand strict punishment of those who act with a less and lukewarm attitude in My House of Worship. My strictness we be no different than was My Father's in the Old Testament." (on Judgement Day) (Read Book of Rev. Fr. Nicholas Gihr and Sacristan's Handbook.)

ACT OF CONSECRATION TO OUR LADY OF SORROWS

Most immaculate Virgin Mary, Mother of God, Mother of Sorrows, I (   ) though most unworthy to be thy Servant and Slave, am encouraged by thy Great Mercy, moved by a desire to serve Thee. I choose Thee this day and for all eternity, as my Special Sovereign, Advocate, and Mother.

I firmly resolve henceforth to Love, Serve, and Compassionate Thee, and do all within my power to make others Love Thee too. As I kneel before Thee receive me a Thy Special Servant and as a partaker in thy sufferings.

Give me strength always to remain close to the cross of your Son and to carry my cross after Him without complaint. Help me to overcome my nature, Temptations, and deny myself the pleasures of this would, to mortify my passions and to expiate my sins. Help me to perfect perfection that my mind may be made up of Peace, Goodness, Purity, Truth, and Good Thoughts always. Increase in me the Living Sentiments of Faith, Hope and Charity. To have True Humility, Purity, Patience, Obedience, and Perseverance in Loving Thee always and in doing God's Holy Will. And to walk in the Divine Will, on earth as it is in Heaven. To be Meek, Gentle, and Mild of Heart and to practice True Sincerity towards others.

Help me to be a Good Father and Husband, to accept all things as coming from God and to have complete Uniformity to the Will of God. Accept all I am and all that I have as being Thine. Take all my merits and use them for the Salvation of Poor Souls, especially those dearest to me, those who have asked my prayers, and for those for whom I ought to pray, and for those you would have me pray for, and for those who have done me any good whatsoever.

DEAR MOTHER HELP ME TO BE MOST WORTHY OF THIS TITLE: "SERVANT AND SLAVE OF OUR LADY OF SORROWS"

For I would rather die than to live without belonging entirely to thee my Sorrowful Mother. Teach me to understand the Nothingness of this World, the Greatness of Heaven, the Shortness of Time, and the Length of Eternity. That I must constantly prepare for Death through prayer, penance, sacrifice, and practicing silence, never to speak of myself to others.

I beg of Thee my Sorrowful Mother to plead continually for me and mind to thy Son, since He can not refuse Thee nothing because You ask nothing contrary to His Honor. Offer to Jesus one drop of His Precious Blood and remind Him that Thou art our Life, our Sweetness, and our Hope. Assist me to remain constant in virtue as the sun is constant, never changing like the moon.

Stand by me in all my actions as you stood by your Son at the Foot of the Cross. Touch His Sacred Heart that I may obtain my requests, Oh Thou Who Art The Advocate of the Living and the Salvation of the dying. Be with me in the last three hours of my life. Obtain for me perfect sorrow, Sincere Contrition and Remission of all my sins so that I will not go to Purgatory. Help me to receive most worthly the Holy Viaticum and a strengthening effect of the Sacrament of Extreme Unction.

Jesus, Mary, and Joseph I give you my heart and my soul. O Jesus, Mary, and Joseph be with me in my last agony. O Jesus, Mary, and Joseph may I breathe forth my spirit to you, and may my last words, be Jesus, Mary, and Joseph.

God the Father made me, God the Son died to save me, God the Holy Ghost come to sanctify me, O Most Holy Trinity, take me to Heaven when I die. **Amen.**

Consecration to Jesus Christ, the Incarnate Wisdom, through the Blessed Virgin Mary

O Eternal and incarnate Wisdom! 0 sweetest and most adorable Jesus! True God and true man, only Son of the Eternal Father, and of Mary, always virgin! I adore Thee profoundly in the bosom and splendors of Thy Father during eternity; and I adore Thee also in the virginal bosom of Mary, Thy most worthy Mother, in the time of Thine incarnation.

I give Thee thanks for that Thou hast annihilated Thyself, taking the form of a slave in order to rescue me from the cruel slavery of the devil. I praise and glorify Thee for that Thou hast been pleased to submit Thyself to Mary, Thy holy Mother, in all things, in order to make me Thy faithful slave through her. But, alas! Ungrateful and faithless as I have been, I have not kept the promises which I made so solemnly to Thee in my Baptism; I have not fulfilled my obligations; I do not deserve to be called Thy child, nor yet Thy slave; and as there is nothing in me which does not merit Thine anger and Thy repulse, I dare not come by myself before Thy most holy and august Majesty. It is on this account that I have recourse to the intercession of Thy most holy Mother, whom Thou hast given me for a mediatrix with Thee. It is through her that I hope to obtain of Thee contrition, the pardon of my sins, and the acquisition and preservation of wisdom.

Hail, then, 0 immaculate Mary, living tabernacle of the Divinity, where the Eternal Wisdom willed to be hidden and to be adored by angels and by men! Hail, 0 Queen of Heaven and earth, to whose empire everything is subject which is under God. Hail, 0 sure refuge of sinners, whose mercy fails no one. Hear the desires which I have of the Divine Wisdom; and for that end receive the vows and offerings which in my lowliness I present to thee.

I; (Name), a faithless sinner, renew and ratify today in thy hands the vows of my Baptism; I renounce forever Satan, his pomps and works; and I give myself entirely to Jesus Christ, the Incarnate Wisdom, to carry my cross after Him all the days of my life, and to be more faithful to Him than I have ever been before. In the presence of all the heavenly court I choose thee this day for my Mother and Mistress. I deliver and consecrate to thee, as thy slave, my body and soul, my goods, both interior and exterior, and even the value of all my good actions, past, present and future; leaving to thee the entire and full right of disposing of me, and all that belongs to me, without exception, according to thy good pleasure, for the greater glory of God in time and in eternity.

Receive, 0 benignant Virgin, this little offering of my slavery, in honor of, and in union with, that subjection which the Eternal Wisdom deigned to have to thy maternity; in homage to the power which both of you have over this poor sinner, and in thanksgiving for the privileges with which the Holy Trinity has favored thee. I declare that I wish henceforth, as thy true slave, to seek thy honor and to obey thee in all things.

O admirable Mother, present me to thy dear Son as His eternal slave, so that as He has redeemed me by thee, by thee He may receive me! 0 Mother of mercy, grant me the grace to obtain the true Wisdom of God; and for that end receive me among those whom thou lovest and teachest, whom thou leadest, nourishes and protects as thy children and thy slaves.

0 faithful Virgin, make me in all things so perfect a disciple, imitator and slave of the Incarnate Wisdom, Jesus Christ thy Son, that I may attain, by thine intercession and by thine example, to the fullness of His age on earth and of His glory in Heaven. Amen.

Youtube: Life of the Blessed Virgin Mary pt 1-8 (By St. Mary of Agreda) *This will bring you closer to Mary.*

"O God, I thank You for having been until this time the sunshine of my life. It is like the gift of sight. I have enjoyed it without remembering to thank You for it. In the future I want to be more attentive, and even more exultant in my joy and thanksgiving. I wish to sing praise Your infinite Goodness, for this true joy of the True Faith and to know the Divine Will which is like a pearl or precious gift, the highest ultimate gift You can give. Thank you for my existence and chance to know, love, and serve You."

Remember that every drop of Christ's Blood, every wound and mark on his body was unbearable pain for Him, each cried out to YOU, saying: 'I do this for you, so you may enjoy the delights of the land of Heaven, and become children of My Father. So why do you neglect Me by chasing after the fleeing short joys of this world, to become children of Satan? You know you will not last here forever, see where ancestors are in the cemetery. They walked this earth just like you are doing now. Soon you will be 100's of years beside them. And your descendants will be walking where you have walked. Let's get out of this world alive.

We will all receive our just reward according to how many points we have on report card. You gain high points for your love firstly by getting out of bed and going to Mass, the Rosary each night, visits to the Blessed Sacrament, putting yourself aside to think of perform good works for others, offering your daily duty's each morning to God, etc........ So what's in your report card?

A TRUE LETTER OF OUR SAVIOUR JESUS CHRIST

Consecrating to the Drops of Blood which Our Lord Jesus lost on His way to Calvary

Copy of a letter of the Oration found in the Holy Sepulchre of Our Lord Jesus Christ in Jerusalem, preserved in a silver box by His Holiness and by the Emperors and Empresses of the Christian Faith.

St. Elizabeth, Queen of Hungary, with St. Matilda and St. Bridget, wishing to know something of the Passion of Jesus Christ, offered fervent and special prayers, upon which there appeared to them Our Lord Jesus Christ who spoke to them in the following manner: *"I descended from Heaven to the Earth in order to convert you.*

In olden times, people were religious, and their harvests were abundant; at present, on the contrary, they are scanty.
If you want to reap an abundant harvest you must not work on Sunday, for Sunday you must go to Church and pray to God to forgive your sins. He gave you six days in which to work and one for rest and devotion and to tender your help to the poor and assist the Church. Those people who brawl against My Religion and cast slurs on this Sacred Letter will be forsaken by Me. On the contrary, those people who shall carry a copy of this letter with them shall be free from death by drowning and from sudden death. They shall be free from all contagious diseases and lightning; they shall not die without confession, and shall be free from their enemies and from the hand of wrongful authority, and from all their slanderers and false witnesses.

386 | *Jerald James*

Women in peril at child-birth will, by keeping this Oration about them, immediately overcome the difficulty. In the houses where this Oration is kept, no evil thing will ever happen: and forty days before the death of a person who has this Oration about him or her, the Blessed Virgin will appear to him or her. So said St. Gregorious.

To all those faithful who shall recite for three years, each day, 2 Paters, Glorias, and Aves, in honor of the drops of blood I lost, I will concede the following five graces:

1ˢᵗ The plenary indulgence and remission of your sins.

2ⁿᵈ You will be free from the pains of Purgatory.

3ʳᵈ If you should die before completing the said 3 years, for you it will be the same as if you had completed them.

4ᵗʰ It will be upon your death the same as if you had shed all your blood for the Holy Faith.

5ᵗʰ I will descend from Heaven to take your soul and that of your relatives, until the fourth generation.

Be it known that the number of armed soldiers were 150; those who trailed me while I was bound were 23. The number of executioners of justice were 83; the blows received on my head were 150; those on my stomach, 108; kicks on my shoulders, 80. I was led, bound with cords by the hair, 24 times; spits in the face were 180; I was beaten on the body 6666 times; beaten on the head, 110 times. I was roughly pushed, and at 12 o'clock was lifted up by the hair; pricked with thorns and pulled by the beard 23 times; received 20 wounds on the head; thorns of marine junks, 72; pricks of thorns in the head, 110; mortal thorns in the forhead, 3. I was afterwards flogged and dressed as a mocked king; wounds in the body, 1000. The soldiers who led me to the Cavalry were 608; those who watched me were 3, and those who mocked me were 1008; the drops of blood which I lost were 28,430.

Benedetta DA S.S.; Pope Leo XIII, in Roma 5 Aprile 1890

Those who will not believe this Letter was written by divine hand and dictated by the Holy Mouth of Christ, and who will hide it to other people, will be cursed by God and damned on the Day of Judgment; and those who will publish it, though they may have gravely sinned and offended their fellow beings, on condition they are truly repentant of having offended me and ask for my forgiveness, they will have their sins wiped away by me:

those who will copy this Letter, or will read it, or will get others to read it, will be free of any temptation".

A Spanish Captain, travelling near Barcelona, saw on the ground a head detached from its body, who spoke to him like this: "Since you are on your way to Barcelona, dear traveler, send a Priest to me, so that I may be confessed. It is three days since I was attacked by thieves and cannot die before being confessed". The Captain took a Confessor to the place; the living head was confessed and died. On the body from which the head was detached was this Oration found, and on that occasion it was approved by many Inquisition Tribunals and by the Queen of Spain. The said Pater, Ave and Gloria can be recited in favor of any soul.

At the time of the earthquake in Northern Italy and France, a little girl named Natalina was for three days buried under the debris. When she was rescued, they found her asleep, with a copy of this letter on her, though she could not read or write.

On 12 march 1821 many emigrants left San Giovanni Incarico, province of Caserta, for America in search of work. During the sea passage the ship was caught by a violent storm and sank. This happened on the 19th, the feast of St. Joseph. Out of 667 people on board, only 9 survived, and each of them had one letter of Jesus Christ like this one! The survivors were found, wearing their waistcoats, in whose pockets the Letter was found, dry and thoroughly intact. Two of the survivors, Luigi Ceccaccio and Francesco Nero, from the same town, supplied ample evidence of the miracle.

Another miracle of the Holy Letter of Jesus Christ took place on the island of Liri, always in Italy. A man was peacefully asleep in his bed, when a mysterious hand shook him abruptly and a voice thundered: "Rise and run into a corner of your home!" the man obeyed hastily just in time to see the floor disappear into an abyss.

Miracle made by the Vergine Addolorata: - Three miles from Castelpetroso, in the province of Campobasso, 13-year-old Maria Grazia Estasia Bibiana was guarding her sheep in the company of her mother near an old monastery when suddenly the Vergine Addolorata (Virgin of Sorrows) appeared to them and said: "Come with me into the old Church, where my Son is celebrating Mass and I have to serve". The two women went and, once the Divine Service (Mass) was over, the Virgin spoke like this: "My Son is disgusted with the people of this world, since they make too many sins, vice reigns everywhere and religion is forgotten; terrible earthquakes, plague, hunger and war will come as great trials for the mankind. Go to Church, do not sin, confess regularly and take Communion (often) at least once a year, so that He will forgive your sins". And with these words the Virgin disappeared.

A more recent miracle took place on 30 June 1889. At Ancona station, when the train to Rome was about to leave, there was a lady, who, not having any money for the trip, could not get on the train. The train started, but a short while it stopped. (5) more engines were added, so the train could start again. Cavaliere Morelli, who had noticed that mourning the lady at the station, he came back and offered to pay her ticket, she accepted the offer on condition she was allowed to travel alone. The gentleman paid 47 lire for a first-class ticket and, as soon as the lady got on the train it left almost magically, to the awe of all. When they came in Rome, since Cavaliere Morelli wanted to give his regards to the lady, he came into the waggon where she had been seated, but the compartment was empty; on the seat he found money for 2000 Lire and a note written in golden letters saying: "I am the Lady of Sorrows, and I want to say to the sinners of the world who want to convert, believe in God and serve Him, or a terrible calamity will soon come over Christianity."

His Holiness the Pope, on 2 October 1889, received a letter where he found that if, in the future, people should not forsake the devil and ill actions, and should not solemnly promise to live well, according to God's law, according to the Law of God they would be destroyed. This letter, sent to the Pope by Our Lord Jesus Christ, confirmed the miracle of Our Lady of Sorrows of Ancona and said that on Good Friday no visitor had gone to the Holy Sepulchre; it also said that the people should be reminded of the Day of Judgement, when the Faithful will be rewarded with the glory of Heaven and the evil souls will be cast into the tortures of fire and unimaginable sufferings.

On 2 July 1889, when a terrible flood destroyed everything, making innumerable victims, the very few survivors were those who had this Letter on themselves.

During the terrible earthquake in Southern France, which caused great disaster and claimed innumerable lives, one Giovanni Saltarello was buried alive under the debris of a collapsing house. He was saved after four days and nights of terrible agony, and he too was in possession of this Holy Letter.

On the solemn occasion of the Last Jubilee Our Lord Jesus Christ appeared to the Pope, who was at the moment sitting in his Throne, surrounded by Cardinals, Bishops and Great Authorities of the Church. And the Holy Spirit spoke as follows: "Ye people of the world, abandon your sins, or the world will be near to its end!" And at these words disappeared. Then all those who were present fell on their knees before the Pope, begging for pardon and mercy.

Let us then all believe in the Holy Letter of Our Lord Jesus Christ, who can obtain so many graces and perform so many miracles!

CHRIST'S LAST WILL AND TESTAMENT

When The Holy Wood of The Cross had been Raised on Mount Calvary, Bearing Aloft With it the Incarnate Word Crucified Before Speaking Any of The Seven Words, Christ Prayed Interiorly to His Heavenly Father and Said:

"My Father and Eternal God, I Confess and Magnify Thee From This Tree of The Cross, and I Offer Thee a Sacrifice of Praise in My Passion and Death; For, by The Hypostatic Union With The Divine Nature, Thou Hast Raised My Humanity to The Highest Dignity, That of Christ, the Godman, Anointed With Thy Own Divinity.

I Confess Thee on Account of The Plenitude of The Highest Possible Graces and Glory, Which from the First Instant of My Incarnation Thou Hast Communicated to My Humanity, and Because from All Eternity up to This Present Hour Thou Hast Consigned to Me Full Dominion of The Universe Both in The Order of Grace and of Nature.

Thou Hast Made Me The Lord of The Heavens and of The Elements (Matth. 28, 18), of The Sun, The Moon and The Stars; of Fire and Air, of The Earth and The Sea, of All The Animate and Inanimate Creatures Therein; Thou Hast Made Me The Disposer of The Seasons, of The Days and Nights, With Full Lordship and Possession According to My Free Will, and Thou Hast Set Me as The Head, The King and Lord of All Angels and Men (Ephes. 1, 21), to Govern and Command Them, to Punish The Wicked and to Reward The Good (John 5, 22) ; Thou Hast Given Me.

The Dominion and Power of Disposing All Things from Highest Heavens to Deepest Abysses of Hell (Apoc. 20, 1). Thou Hast Placed in My Hands The Eternal Justification of Men, The Empires, Kingdoms and Principalities,

The Great and The Little, The Rich and The Poor; and of All That are Capable of Thy Grace and Glory, Thou Hast Made Me The Justifier, The Redeemer and Glorifier, The Universal Lord of All The Human Race, of Life and Death, of the Holy Church, its Treasures, Laws and Blessings of Grace: All Hast Thou, My Father, Consigned to My Hands, Subjected to My Will and My Decrees, and For This I Confess,

Exalt and Magnify Thy Holy Name. Now, at This Moment, My Lord and Eternal Father, When I Am Returning From This World to Thy

Right Hand Through This Death on The Cross, by Which I Completed The Task of The Redemption of Men Assigned to Me, I Desire That This Same Cross Shall be The Tribunal of Our Justice and Mercy. Nailed to it, I Desire to Judge

Those For Whom I Give My Life. Having Justified My Cause, I Wish to Dispense The Treasures of My Coming into The World and of My Passion and Death to The Just and The Reprobate According as Each One Merits by His Works of Love or Hatred.

I Have Sought to Gain All Mortals and Invited Them to Partake of My Friendship and Grace ; From The First Moment of My Incarnation I Have Ceaselessly Labored For Them; I Have Borne Inconveniences, Fatigues, Insults, Ignominies, Reproaches, Scourges, a Crown of Thorns, and Now Suffer The Bitter Death of The Cross; I Have Implored Thy Vast Kindness Upon All of Them;

I Have Watched in Prayer, Fasted and Wandered About Teaching Them The Way of Eternal Life. As Far as in Me Lay I Have Sought to Secure Eternal Happiness For All Men, Just as I Merited it For All, Without Excluding Any One.

I Have Established and Built Up The Law of Grace and Have Firmly and Forever Established The Church in Which All Human Beings Can Be Saved. But in Our Knowledge and Foresight We Are Aware, My God and Father, That On Account of Their Malice and Rebellious Obstinacy Not All Men Desire to Accept Our Eternal Salvation, nor Avail Themselves of Our Mercy and of The Way I Have Opened to Them By My Labors, Life and Death; but That Many Will Prefer to Follow Their Sinful Ways Unto Perdition. Thou Art Just, My Lord and Father, and Most Equitable Are Thy Judgments (Ps. 68, 137) ; and Therefore it is Right, Since Thou Hast Made Me The Judge of The Living and The Dead, of The Good and The Bad (Act 10, 3),

That I Give to The Good The Reward of Having Served and Followed Me, and to Sinners The Chastisement of Their Perverse Obstinacy; That The Just Should Share in My Goods, and The Wicked be Deprived of The Inheritance, Which They Refuse to Accept. Now Then, My Eternal Father, in My and Thy Name and For Thy

Glorification, I Make My Last Bequest According to My Human Will, Which is Conformable to Thy Eternal and Divine Will. First Shall be Mentioned My Most Pure Mother, Who Gave Me Human Existence; Her I Constitute My Sole and Universal Heiress of All The Gifts of Nature, Of Grace and Of Glory That Are Mine.

She Shall be Mistress and Possessor of Them All. The Gifts of Grace, of Which as a Mere Creature She is Capable, She Shall Actually Receive Now, While Those of Glory I Promise to Confer Upon Her in Their Time.

I Desire That She Shall be Mistress of Angels and Men, Claim Over Them Full Possession and Dominion and Command The Service and Obedience of All. The Demons Shall Fear Her and Be Subject to Her. All The Irrational Creatures, The Heavens, The Stars, The Planets, The Elements With All The Living Beings, The Birds, The Fishes and The Animals Contained in Them, Shall Likewise be Subject to Her and Acknowledge Her as Mistress, Exalting and Glorifying Her With Me. I Wish Also That She Be The Treasurer and Dispenser of All The Goods in Heaven and On Earth.

Whatever She Ordains and Disposes in My Church For My Children, The Sons of Men, Shall Be Confirmed by The Three Divine Persons; and Whatever She Shall Ask For Mortals Now, Afterwards and Forever, We Shall Concede According to Her Will and Wishes. To The Holy Angels, Who Have Obeyed Thy Holy and Just Will, I Assign as Habitation The Highest Heavens as Their Proper and Eternal Abode, and With it The Joys of Eternal Vision and Fruition of Our Divinity. I Desire That They Enjoy its Everlasting Possession Together With Our Company and Friendship. I Decree, That They Recognize My Mother as Their Legitimate Queen and Lady.

That They Serve Her, Accompany and Attend Upon Her, Bear Her Up in Their Hands in All Places and Times, Obeying Her in All That She Wishes to Ordain and Command. The Demons, Rebellious to Our Perfect and Holy Will.

I Cast Out and Deprive of Our Vision and Company; Again Do I Condemn Them to Our Abhorrence, to Eternal Loss of Our Friendship and Glory, to Privation of The Vision of My Mother, of The Saints and of My Friends, The Just. I Appoint and Assign to Them as Their

Eternal Dwelling The Place Most Remote From Our Royal Throne, Namely The Infernal Caverns, The Centre of The Earth, Deprived of Light and Full of The Horrors of Sensible Darkness (Jude 6).

I Decree This to Be Their Portion and Inheritance, as Chosen by Them in Their Pride and Obstinacy Against The Divine Being and Decrees. In Those Eternal Dungeons of Darkness They Shall be Tormented by Everlasting and Inextinguishable Fire. From The Multitudes of Men, in The Fulness of My Good Will, I Call, Select and Separate All The Just and The Predestined, Who Through My Grace Save Themselves by Imitating Me, Doing My Will and Obeying My Holy Law.

These, Next to My Most Pure Mother, I Appoint as The Inheritors of All My Mysteries, My Blessings, My Sacramental Treasures, of The mysteries Concealed in The Holy Scriptures; of My Humility, Meekness of Heart; of The Virtues of Faith, Hope, and Charity; of Prudence, Justice, Fortitude and Temperance; of My Divine Gifts and Favors; of My Cross, Labors, Contempt, Poverty and Nakedness.

This Shall be Their Portion and Inheritance in This Present and Mortal Life. Since They Must Choose These in Order to Labor Profitably, I Assign to Them The Trials I Have Chosen For Myself in This Life, as a Pledge of My Friendship, in Order That They May Undergo Them With Joy. I Offer Them My Protection and Defense, My Holy Inspirations, My Favors and Powerful Assistance, My Blessings and My Justification, According to Each One's Disposition and Degree of Love.

I Promise to be to Them a Father, a Brother and a Friend, and They Shall be My Chosen and Beloved Children, and as Such I Appoint Them as The Inheritors of All My Merits and Treasures Without Limitation. I Desire That All Who Dispose Themselves, Shall Partake of The Goods of My Holy Church and of The Sacraments; That, if They Should Lose My Friendship, They Shall Be Able to Restore Themselves and Recover My Graces and Blessings Through My Cleansing Blood.

For All of Them Shall be Open The Intercession of My Mother and of The Saints, and She Shall Recognize Them as Her Children, Shielding Them and Holding Them as Her Own. My Angels Shall Defend Them, Guide Them, Protect Them and Bear Them Up In Their Hands Lest They Stumble, and If They Fall, They Shall Help Them to Rise (Ps. 90, 11, 12).

Likewise it is My Will That My Just and Chosen Ones Shall Stand High Above The Reprobate and The Demons, That They Shall Be Feared and Obeyed by My Enemies; That All The Rational and Irrational Creatures Shall Serve Them; That All The Influences of The Heavens, The Planets and The Stars Shall Favor Them and Give Them Life; That The Earth, its Elements and Animals, Shall Sustain Them; All The Creatures, That Are Mine and Serve Me, Shall be Theirs, and Shall Serve Also Them as My Children and Friends (I Cor. 3, 22; Wis. 16, 24), and Their Blessing Shall be in The Dew of Heaven and In The Fruits of The Earth (Genes. 27, 28). I Wish to Hold With Them My Delights. (Pros. 8, 31)

Communicate to Them My Secrets, Converse With Them Intimately and Live With Them in The Militant Church in The Species of Bread and Wine, as An Earnest and An Infallible Pledge of The Eternal Happiness and Glory Promised to Them; of it, I Make Them Partakers and Heirs, in Order That They May Enjoy it With Me in Heaven by Perpetual Right and In Unfailing Beatitude. I Consent That The Foreknown and Reprobate (Though They Were Created For Another and Much Higher End), Shall be Permitted to Possess as Their Portion and Inheritance The Concupiscence of The Flesh and The Eyes (John 1, 2-16), Pride in All its Effects;
They Eat and Are Satisfied With The Dust of The Earth, Namely, With Riches (They make their belly their god); With The Fumes and The Corruption of The Flesh and Its Delights, and With The Vanity and Presumption of The World.

For Such Possessions Have They Labored, and Applied All The Diligence of Their Mind and Body; in Such Occupations Have They Consumed Their Powers, Their Gifts and Blessings Bestowed Upon Them by Us, and They Have of Their Own Free Will Chosen Deceit, Despising The Truth I Have Taught Them in The Holy Law (Rom. 2, 8).

They Have Rejected The Law Which I Have Written In Their Hearts and The One Inspired by My Grace; They Have Despised My Teachings and My Blessings, and Listened to My and Their Own Enemies; They Have Accepted Their Deceits, Have Loved Vanity (Ps. 4, 3), Wrought Injustice, Followed Their Ambitions, Sought Their Delight in Vengeance, Persecuted The Poor, Humiliated The Just,

Mocked The Simple and The Innocent, Strove to Exalt Themselves and Desired to Be Raised Above All The Cedars of Lebanon in Following The Laws of Injustice. Since They Have Done All This in Opposition to Our Divine Goodness and Remained Obstinate in Their Malice, and Since They Have Renounced The Rights of Sonship Merited For Them by Me, I Disinherit Them of My Friendship and Glory.

Just as Abraham Separated The Children of The Slave, Setting Aside Some Possessions For Them and Reserving The Principal Heritage for Isaac, The Son of The Freedwoman Sarah (Gen. 25, 5),

Thus I Set Aside Their Claims on My Inheritance by Giving Them The Transitory Goods, Which They Themselves Have Chosen. Separating Them From Our Company and From That of My Mother, Of The Angels and Saints, I Condemn Them To The Eternal Dungeons and The Fire of Hell in The Company of Lucifer and His Demons, Whom They Have Freely Served, I Deprive Them Forever of All Hope of Relief.

This is, O My Father, The Sentence Which I Pronounce As The Head and The Judge of Men and Angels (Eph. 4, 15; Col. 2, 10), and This is The Testament Made at My Death, This is The Effect of My Redemption, Whereby Each One is Rewarded With That Which He Has Justly Merited According To His Works and According to Thy Incomprehensible Wisdom in The Equity of Thy Strictest Justice: (II Tim. 4, 8)."

Such Was The Prayer of Christ Our Savior On The Cross to His Eternal Father. It Was Sealed and Deposited in The Heart of The Most Holy Mary as The Mysterious and Sacramental Testament, in Order That Through Her Intercession and Solicitous Care it Might at its Time, and Even From That Moment, Be Executed in The Church, Just as it Had Before This Time Been Prepared and Perfected by The Wise Providence of God, In Whom All The Past and The Future is Always One With The Present. (The End)

"Smile at everyone. I'll make your smile a blessing to others." When praying, or thinking of Me, or just speaking or when working through the day: "Guard Your imagination, it is like a house dog

that wanders from place to place, from here to there. Be severe with this wandering house dog." **Our Lord to St. Gabrielle Bossis**
Think about this: When you finish a long hard race and you take first place, everyone is waiting to greet you and congratulate you. Yes, it will be the same when you finish your short lived earthly course, when you have beat the devil and his temptations.

Everyone will be waiting in Heaven to meet you and congratulate you for not having been deceived by the most beautiful and witty masterful deception that devil has ever come up with in the history of this world.

Yes! The infiltration of the Church and turning it totally protestant, the time consuming pleasures of new technology devices, the decency of the fashions which unveil the flesh on both men and especially women. The saints and relatives will greet you, and new wonderful life time friends will greet you, and never will there be an unpleasant person in your life again.

The best knowledge of the 3rd Secret that I have ever heard or read is giving by Fr. Nicholas Gruner on Youtube: God will Punish the World - 3rd Secret of Fatima - Apocalypse (Much is revealed. Listen to it.) And again please hear this priest: Youtube: "I have seen the new world. (Fr. Adam Skwarczynski)"
And: "Fatima and the Sacrament of Confession" - Father Isaac Relyea And: "Fr. Malachi Martin on Poisoned Popes & Cardinal Siri" (very very informative)

Remember God took you out of His ocean of souls, put you here, to see just how close you will bond in friendship with Him, your reward will be for all eternity up or down. "You may not be bad enough to go to Hell, but you're not good enough to go to Heaven."
Wisdom of God is a grace to know right from wrong, but grace is like water to the soul to do virtue. When grace dries up in the soul it is because you have stopped watering your soul with grace by praying. Now you are more prone to evil.
Wear the Our Lady's Miraculous Medal (*The bullet that kills evil.*) and attach it to your scapular.

Remember to Reject: THE WORLD, THE FLESH, AND THE DEVIL

Remember: DEATH, JUDGMENT, HELL, OR HEAVEN
The Four Keys to Heaven: THE LATIN MASS, ROSARY (Daily), SCAPULAR (Always), CONFESSION (every two weeks)

Always Remember the Nothingness of this Would; the Greatness of Heaven; the Shortness of Time; and Length of Eternity; and to Constantly Prepare for Death, Through Prayer, Penance, and Sacrifice. Be slow to speak and slow to anger. God helps them who help themselves and pray.

One more thing; Do not be fooled by the few traditional groups that still say the Latin Tridentine Mass. One of those who are called "Old Roman Catholic Church" they are heretics for either being "sedevacantist" or they believe in the Holy Father being the Pope and Vicar of Christ, but they do not believe he is infallibility in matters of "Faith and Morals" which he is. This church is called the ICCA = "Independent Catholic Church of America." This group stems back to Utrecht, Holland in 1718 when Bishop Varlet was consecrated in Paris by Bishop Guyon de Montignon. Bishop Varlet refused to believe in the Bull of Pope Clement XI's 1713 condemning Jansenism, Unigenitus. Varlet joined up with the rebel Canons of the cathedral of Utrecht and became their bishop, in the place of the one who had been named by the Pope.

In 1725 Bishop Varlet consecrated Steenoven. At that time Pope Benedict XIII described these consecrations as "illegitimate and sacrilegious." In 1739 Bishop Steenoven consecrated Meindaert. And the list of consecrations goes on and on and on, until 1908 pure Jansenism changed a little. Vatican I definition the dogmatic of Papal "Infallibility." These people rejected it. At this time Bishop Gul consecrated Bishop Matthew who consecrated bishop De Rache in 1913. This continues up to 1971 Bishop Brown consecrates Bishop Schuckardt who changed the name of the ICCA to the "Tridentine Church of the Latin Rite" which has since become the "Congregation of Mary Immaculate Queen," in Spokane, WA. This Bishop has caused several serious scandals, which have forced his priests to separate themselves from him in 1984. Now there are two Bishops this later one is Bishop Musey, Bishop McCormick. The stem from Canada and Florida. These people believe that clergy can be married. And Women maybe ordained.

So stay clear of these groups. It seem the only one which is recognized by Rome is the "Society of Pope Pius X" and they have stayed on the straight and narrow even after Vatican II. And they are recognized by Rome, but they have not followed Rome into "Heresy."

May you live happily ever after.
He who chases after God, catches God.
"Religion", a greek word meaning to "bond with."
If you do not bond with God (befriend Him).
He will say to you on the last day, "Amen I
say to you, I do not know you."
Watch Daily, never failing to say your prayers kneeling at your bedside.
Blessed be the Holy Name of God.
I Love You All.
Pray for me, and all our deceased relatives, daily.
We are Adam and Eve's children and all of us God's children.
God created Adam and Eve, and the world just over 6000 years ago.
Daily think of where you will be 100 years from now.
Daily struggle to get to that place you want to be 100 years from now,
no matter what it takes to get there.
Inside the door of the church or outside of it.
JMJ

Our Lady of Sorrows, Pray for us.

Is this **The End?**

Remember Our Lord's words to Luisa Piccarreta: "You may not be bad enough to go to Hell, but your just not good enough to go to Heaven." (The Rosary said daily and slowly and well.)

To Love God is to Fear to hurt Him. **"To Fear God is the beginning of Wisdom."** This great grace is obtained chiefly in the Most Holy Rosary. Aaahhh! The Secret of the Holy Rosary. **Knee, pray, while looking at and studying the crucifix. My best and final recommendation is to find a copy of the most beautiful book: "Divine Mysteries of the Most Holy Rosary" by St. Mary of Agreda, Spain, (2 April 1602 – 24 May 1665), was a Franciscan abbess By JMJ Books** God gave her the actual visions of what actually happened during each mystery, followed by the actual words of the Most High Queen of Heaven, Mary, and what She did see and feel at moment. Also to St. Catherine Emmerich, St. Bridget of Sweden and accouple others. **Youtube: Life of the virgin Mary pt1 – 8**

Some people bury their head in their worldly activities, and never learn who God is, or how to befriend Him.
If you love someone you do whatever they ask of you, because you love them. And they will do anything for you, like letting you live with them in Their Kingdom in Heaven. (Study and read who is God. Lives of the Saints will tell you in a simple and best way. I used to read this to you every night after the Rosary. Now you have your own children.
Teach them the True Faith, that Saints have died for, and outside of which there is no salvation.)